Ireland for Food Lovers

Georgina Campbell

First published 2010

Georgina Campbell Guides

P.O. Box 6173, Dublin 13.

Text copyright Georgina Campbell Guides 2010

Main Text - Georgina Campbell

Regional Introductions - W.M. Nixon

ISBN 978-1-903164-29-7

ACKNOWLEDGEMENTS

Grateful thanks to the many individuals, organisations and public bodies who have contributed information and photography for use in this book, including the Irish Food Writers' Guild, Bord Bia, Bord Iascaigh Mhara, Fáilte Ireland, Waterways Ireland, Northern Ireland Tourist Board, the National Trust, Kilkenny Food Trail and many other producers and shops mentioned in the text. Thanks to Stephen Pennels, Paul Sherwood, James Connelly and Michael O'Meara for use of images. Particular thanks are due to W. M. Nixon for writing the regional introductions and supplying images, to Bob Nixon for photographs and undertaking the indexing – and to Brian Darling for his enthusiasm and patience.

Georgina Campbell.

Design: Brian Darling, The Design Station, Dublin.
Printed and bound in Spain.

FRONT COVER

Main image:	Lamb Stew Hotpot
Bottom, left to right:	Aran Islands Chickens; Pasture Grazing in the West;
	Galway Oysters & Irish Stout; Carrowholly Cheese.

BACK COVER   The English Market, Cork.

Contents

Introduction

Making our way around the country each year during the past three decades to research our hospitality guides, we at *Georgina Campbell Guides* have been very encouraged by the emerging artisan food culture in Ireland. Speciality local products were pretty thin on the ground when we started travelling regularly in the 1980s, but every year there have been ever more wonderful local foods to enjoy. They have become an increasingly important presence on menus, or to buy from speciality shops, markets and farm shops, to take home as a treat for another time. Many are now widely distributed, but there's something very special about enjoying them on their own home patch. These foods and their creators are the characters that have peopled and enhanced our travels, and could do the same for any visitor - especially if there is time to do a little homework before setting off.

So the aim of this book is to help anyone with an interest in good food who is travelling, eating out, shopping, cooking or simply having a day out in Ireland, to have a more rewarding experience. It's a delight to find the freshest, best, tastiest and most special foods and the people who make them, sell them, or serve them to guests, in whatever area they may be. This is not a scholarly history of Irish food, or even a comprehensive A to Z – comprehensive can be a dangerous word and, in any case, the world of good food is constantly evolving. But we have gathered together a wealth of information and hope that the regional organisation of this book ensures that the best local foods are never far away, and easy to find and enjoy.

Ireland is not yet seen internationally as a good food destination, in the way of countries like France with a long established culinary tradition. But

that is changing. There is a sense that this small country on the western edge of Europe is on the brink of becoming one of the most exciting places in the world for food. The foundation is in place, and many of the products and people who have laid that foundation feature in this book. And the time is right. Bord Bia's widely used slogan 'Ireland - the Food Island' may initially have seemed somewhat aspirational to those who have struggled at the coalface of small scale quality food production. But its time is emerging, as there is an obvious global need for change in attitudes to food, and this is seen by many here as an opportunity.

In his book *The Country Cooking of Ireland* (James Beard Foundation Book of the Year 2010), the acclaimed American food writer Colman Andrews described Ireland as "…simply one of the most exciting food stories in the world today", for reasons including "its superlative raw materials, its immensely satisfying home cooking, and its new wave of artisanal producers and imaginative but well-grounded chefs." (He also hinted diplomatically at variations in cooking standards, and was speaking for many Irish food lovers in doing so, but that is true of every country.) Other leading journalists are also drawing comparison between this country and others – New Zealand, for example, with which we have many similarities and from whom we could learn a lot. And there is always France, where the AC system for wine classification has inspired a call from the wine writer Tomás Clancy for a similar system to be adopted in Ireland for food and drink, in order to encourage a better understanding of the land and to help producers to strive for the best, rather than sanctioning standards at the lowest acceptable level.

Thanks to Ireland's recent economic problems, there are signs that political will to support quality practitioners in the food and hospitality sectors is growing. Hospitality comes naturally to the Irish, and discerning tourism is quite rightly seen as one of the ways in which we can properly realise our true economic potential. Recent surveys by Bord Bia (Irish Food Board) and Failte Ireland (the national tourism authority) confirm what many of us working at grass roots level have known for a long time. Visitors to Ireland like the people and the landscape (still beautiful, despite the recent spate of over development), and that they value the 'quirky'. This has obvious implications for individualistic operations that make for more interesting visitor experiences, and there are signs that these kinds of enterprise may be about to get an unprecedented level of support.

An impressive committee of interested parties ('stake holders') chaired by media personality and food specialist Derek Davis is developing the strategy for food in tourism which is central to making the future brighter for producers of all sizes, tourism service providers, visitors to Ireland – and, of course, Irish residents. Derek Davis is himself a pioneering food journalist, having toured Ireland in search of the best in this country's first major food documentaries, the phenomenally successful 1980s BBC series *A Taste of Ireland*. It ran to 36 episodes and, having made many other programmes since, on both television and radio, he is uniquely qualified for this key role.

As for the Irish small farm food producers who are responsible for so many of the good things which we now enjoy, they have come a long way in recent decades. In recent correspondence from Vermont, where she was giving a cheesemaking course at Vermont Institute of Artisan Cheesemaking, Giana Ferguson, of the wonderful Gubbeen Cheese in West Cork, noted: "We are seen here as a model for alternative value added agriculture and authentic food making." Such achievements are recognised by specialist food retailers and some of the smaller Irish-owned supermarket chains, which take particular pride in selling local produce. Yet the prevalence of international supermarkets who are more concerned about profit than provenance threatens local producers, no matter how good, and this has sparked calls by Bridgestone Guides authors, John and Sally McKenna, for the international principles of Fair Trade to be introduced in Ireland to protect local agriculture.

Seen in this context, the findings of a recent report by Professor David Bell and Mary Shelman of Harvard Business School, commissioned by Bord Bia, are useful. The Harvard team underlined the wisdom of valuing natural resources, and highlighted the need for Irish food companies to work together rather than in competition with each other, in order to create sufficient scale to compete in the global market. Pointing out that a number of Ireland's advantages - which include an international reputation as a trusted supplier – derive from being seen as 'green' and small ('not multinational'), they suggest that a confidence-building "Come See Us: We Are Open for Inspection" strategy would be appropriate for developing sales from Ireland. In fact, this would be building, on a national scale, what many of the producers featured in this book are already doing, by welcoming visitors to their farms and businesses.

On the upside, the pressure from unreasonably demanding supermarkets has had a positive effect, by driving small producers to seek alternative markets. The result? Direct sales – farmgate, at farmers' markets and online – which have empowered producers and offer consumers alternative shopping experiences, genuine value, and connection with those producers.

Whatever the challenges, the number of small and medium sized quality food producers in Ireland is increasing, and there is a feeling of change in the air. The respect for the environment, social contribution, and high standards achieved by these passionately committed people are increasingly widely recognised, both through awards schemes and by the general public – who, as consumers, ultimately have the power to make all the difference by choosing to buy their products.

A number of respected awards schemes are mentioned throughout this book, as they confer valuable recognition on quality foods and the people who produce them – and increase public awareness of the fantastic products which are there to be enjoyed. These include the annual Irish Food Writers Guild (IFWG) Good Food Awards (www.irishfoodwritersguild.ie); Euro-Toques Ireland Food Awards (www.euro-toques.ie); Blas na hEireann National Irish Food Awards

(www.irishfoodawards.com); Associated Craft Butchers of Ireland Awards (www.craftbutchers.ie); Bord Bia Horticulture Awards, and the National Organic Awards (www.bordbia.ie); and Listowel Food Fair Awards (www.listowelfoodfair.com). In addition, the respected Great Taste Awards (www.greattasteawards.co.uk), organised by the UK Guild of Fine Food, are also putting the international spotlight on hundreds of high calibre Irish entries and giving them valuable international publicity.

Awards aside, the general public has a growing interest in food and health – witness the huge success of the Grow-It-Yourself (www.giyireland.com) movement. Once people start to grow their own food and reconnect with the soil, it is much easier to appreciate the special contribution made by farmers and small producers, so this is a win-win situation for everyone who cares about the land, the food it produces and the legacy we will leave to our children.

All of which brings us back to the simple fact that a knowledge of quality local food – what to look for, where to buy it and eat it – can enrich anything from a tour around Ireland to a day out, or a simple foray to the shops. So all that remains is to wish you well on your way – and I hope this book will help you to get out there and enjoy all the good things that Ireland has in store.

Georgina Campbell.

Georgina Campbell, Editor.

Ireland for Food Lovers aims to help visitors to the country - and also Irish residents – to build the best possible food experience into a holiday, short break or simply a day out, and to make everyday shopping a more rewarding experience for both consumers and local producers.

CRITERIA: When making selections for this book, every effort has been made to reference as many special products/companies/producers as possible (both small and larger businesses), and to highlight the best places to shop for artisan foods; the selection excludes obvious 'non-Irish' elements, eg ethnic restaurants and specialists in coffee, wine and other drinks, unless relevant to local production or history.

Organised by geographical region for convenience when travelling; each of the seven regions includes:

GENERAL INTRODUCTION – Gives a sense of context and hints at the enjoyment to be had when travelling around this beautiful country.

FOOD OF THE REGION - Introduces the foods produced by famers, fishermen, food companies (artisan and some larger ones) that are special to a region, including reference to wild or foraged foods, and those that are most prevalent. The range and style varies, according to the demands of the region. 'Four of the Best' highlights selected people, products or organisations of special interest in each region.

WHERE TO BUY – A guide to each region's most exciting food shops, food markets, farm shops, local stores and internet suppliers.

EAT & STAY – A representative selection of just 20 places to eat and stay is given in each region. Chosen for their commitment to local produce and Irish hospitality, and also to offer a balance of style, cost, and geographical spread where possible, they take in both the very best restaurants and casual café/pubs/daytime meals; ♣ denotes those offering accommodation. See also **www.ireland-guide.com** for many more recommendations throughout the country.

RECIPES –Based on the foods of each region, these are selected for simplicity, with a bias towards the homely and traditional, although there are of course many excellent contemporary and international dishes to be enjoyed throughout Ireland.

Opening times may vary, especially off season, and the location of food markets may change. Please check details on websites, or phone before travelling.

Ireland: South-West
Cork & Kerry

The Lakes of Killarney

IN CORK AND KERRY,
they don't think of themselves as
"The Southwest". Local pride and
inter-county rivalry wouldn't allow it.
Cork may be Ireland's biggest
county – and it also prides itself on
being the Rebel County at that – but
Kerry folk aren't fazed by this. They
reckon it's no contest, as Kerry is the highest in the land,
and it's not really a county anyway - it's a kingdom which
has long since lifted itself above the triviality of such
minor regional rivalry. Unless, that is, Cork and Kerry
happen upon each other in the Munster Gaelic football
final. Should that occur, Kerry becomes the kingdom
county, and the match is the highlight of the summer, an
event beyond sport. But the idea that they would allow
themselves to be submerged in one bureaucratic area
simply won't do.

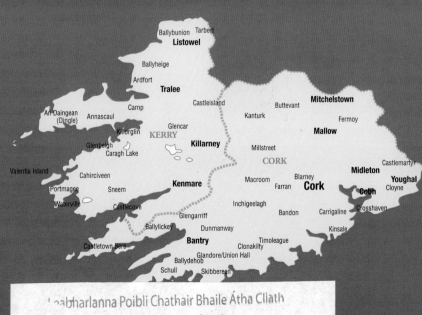

The Blasket Islands, Co Kerry

About the Region

However, combining the two counties provides the ideal setting for a leisurely touring and tasting holiday. But during it you'll soon find that they think of themselves as Corkmen or Kerrymen, never as people of the southwest. And even within each county, the divisions of distance, or mountains, or intervening sea, are so marked that North Kerry at its furthest limits beside the Shannon Estuary is a world apart from South Kerry, while the smoothly fertile farmlands of East Cork are another universe entirely from the rugged and rocky hillocks and headlands of West Cork.

In the highlands of each county, where life moves at its own pace, the sea is only a distant rumour. For sure, the Atlantic weather can be much in evidence when mist gathers on the purple hills above the narrow and vividly green valleys. But a descent to the coast brings us to another world. Even here, though, the abundance of natural harbours, with their communities clustered about the quiet water, suggests that the sea is something to be sheltered from, rather than faced openly.

It's said there are 148 recognised harbours on the long and intricate coastline which makes its winding way from Youghal in East Cork right round to Tarbert in the far north of Kerry. And that isn't including secret rock inlets or the hidden estuaries of small rivers, places where one or two little fishing boats may be moored. The sea is lived with and quietly used, but only confronted in the name of sport. On a dramatic coastline which, at its most rugged, faces the Atlantic and includes such features as the Fastnet Rock and the Blasket Islands, the seagoing sport which is readily available can be challenging in the extreme.

As for the high mountains, they're far from being lofty by international standards, but when set against the gentleness of the countryside they are impressive. Highest of all in Ireland is the range of the MacGillicuddy Reeks (try saying it "mackle-cuddy"), which soar to the peak of Carrantuohill above Killarney in Kerry, providing rambling, trekking, hill-climbing and mountaineering within easy reach of all comforts, yet in a climate which usually adds the spice of the unexpected.

So too does the terrain. Even in a seeming wilderness in the uplands, you will chance upon a hidden green valley which would make the perfect setting for *The Field*, that well-observed gem from playwright John B Keane who was of course a Kerryman, albeit from the far northern township of Listowel, a place of literary pilgrimage.

The many towns of the area have a varying awareness of nearby mountains. Even where the mountains are in another region - as in Youghal in East Cork, where those distant hills are in Waterford and Tipperary - there's the sense of a hinterland of remote heights. But Youghal is primarily an ancient river port, pronounced "yawl" as in the boat type, though it's from Eochaill, the yew wood. Its most noted association is with Walter Raleigh, who brought Europe the joys of tobacco and the potato. Though he spent little if any time there, in Raleigh's day Youghal's strategic location at the mouth of the magnificent salmon-rich River Blackwater meant it punched way above its weight as a port of access at a time when rivers provided the best means of transport to the farming wealth inland.

Beara, Co Cork

Ballydehob, Co Cork

Bantry Bay

In fact, so important was the Blackwater that it functioned as a regional highway rather than a territorial boundary. Above Youghal, it is wholly within Waterford county until it rediscovers Cork at Ballyduff, where it becomes a completely a Cork river as the prosperous valley ascends westward through Cork's key inland towns of Fermoy and Mallow, with the headwaters finally found in Kerry.

Although all the coast had been prey to the Vikings, through the Middle Ages it was only as the size and weatherliness of ships increased that the ports developed further west developed. Thus Youghal was to lose its primacy to Kinsale. But Kinsale's leading role was brief before Cork itself took over, though enough to leave behind a quaint town crowded about the winding estuary of the Bandon River, with all the style and vitality of a place seeing itself as Ireland's gourmet capital.

Through the 18th Century the bulk of the shipping trade and the naval presence moved to the majestic harbour of Cork with its expanding port on the River Lee. It is Cork, of all Ireland's cities, which most warmly gives the impression of being a place at comfort with itself, for it's the heart of a land flowing in milk and honey. Cork is all about the good things in life. While it may be stretching things a little to assert that the southern capital has a Mediterranean atmosphere, there's no doubting its Continental and cosmopolitan flavour, and the Cork people's relaxed enjoyment of it all in a small and friendly city of clear character.

Cork's unique qualities, and its people's appreciation of natural produce, make it a favoured destination for connoisseurs. Trading in life's more agreeable commodities has always been what Cork and its legendary merchant princes were all about, and at one time, the city was known as the butter capital of Europe. The way in which sea and land intertwine throughout the wonderfully sheltered natural harbour, and through the lively old city itself, has encouraged waterborne trade and a sea-minded outlook. Thus today Cork is at the heart of Ireland's most dynamically nautical area, a place world-renowned for its energetic interaction with the sea, whether for business or pleasure.

Westward from Cork city up the Lee valley, the inland route rises steadily as it progresses through Macroom and Ballyvourney and on to Killarney. Down along the coast, sinuous inlets shelter many little ports which bask in an increasingly balmy climate, places whose very names inspire fond memories such as Clonakilty, Rosscarbery, Glandore, Baltimore, Ballydehob, Schull and Skibbereen. The rest of Ireland has to accept that West Cork - and much of Kerry too - has milder weather. Life moves at a gentler pace, but there can be a buzz too - the main town down there still in Cork County is Bantry right at the head of its fine ria, the very epitome of a market town, and then its northward through lush Glengarriff and across the Beara peninsula until, in Kenmare, you're in Kerry.

The change is tangible. This is The Kingdom. There's nowhere else in Ireland quite like Kenmare, it's the perfect little township, and around it the scenery - having been attractive in West Cork - has become spectacular. It's big country, with many choices for the visitor, ringing the changes between remote focal points of hospitality and bustling Killarney, the visitor town par excellence, a tourism gluepot since 1750 and beyond.

Killarney is the lens through which Kerry is often seen, but away from the town it's remarkable how quickly the pace slackens. People live for ever in Kerry. The Blackwater Valley (it's yet another River Blackwater, there must be a dozen in Ireland) is along the road down the sea inlet of the Kenmare River towards Sneem, and in its hidden folds we find the place where people live longest in all Ireland, but they keep it quiet. However, in Sneem you'll find photos celebrating the late great Big Bertha, a cow of legendary repute - she lived for 36 productive years, a generous milker and ancestor of thousands of top-class progeny.

West of Sneem, it's O'Connell country up towards Cahirciveen beside Valentia Island at the outer limits of the Iveragh Peninsula, which faces north across Dingle Bay. But before savouring the delights of the Dingle Peninsula we find ourselves in characterful Killorglin beside fine farming country with great beaches nearby. And then down to Dingle with the Blasket Islands and the shimmering Atlantic beyond.

Dingle is Europe's most westerly port, and it ably fulfils this role, a miniature universe complete unto itself, a wonderful mix of fishing port and sailing haven and year-round hospitality. Over the mountains via the Conor Pass, the narrow road sweeps down to Brandon Bay and on east past more beaches to Tralee, another of those townships which is very much of itself. Beyond, we're out of the mountains, but the beaches become more spectacular than ever, and the sand dunes build up to one of the world's finest golf links at Ballybunion. To seaward, the outer reaches of the long Shannon Estuary are taking shape, and beyond Listowel there's only the pretty village of Tarbert before Cork and Kerry are becoming a fond memory.

Glencar, Co Kerry

Food of the Region

Dingle Peninsula, Co Kerry

Seafood Black Puddings

Smoked Fish

Cheeses Dingle Pies

Killarney Venison

Black Kerry Cow

Ice Cream

Cromane Mussels

Kerry Black-Faced Mountain Lamb

Sea Vegetables

Chocolates, Preserves, Relishes

Foods of Kerry

A large and varied county, but with no city to dominate it, Kerry's main centres of population are the county town of Tralee and Dingle/An Daingean in the North and West, and Killarney and the Heritage Town of Kenmare in the South. The foods of the area reflect the environment – clean Atlantic waters in Kerry's sheltered bays and inlets provide perfect conditions for environmentally friendly aquaculture (such as rope mussels in Kenmare Bay for example), while the perpendicular pastures in mountainous areas are ideal for sure-footed sheep. Kerry people are keenly aware of the importance of caring for the environment and, interestingly, at the time of going to press there are plans afoot to work towards making Kerry Ireland's first 'Green County', with an emphasis on sustainable tourism and food production.

Ireland may only be a small island, about 480km/300 miles long and 300km/185miles wide but, with a coastline extending for over 5,500km/3,500 miles, it should come as no surprise that **FISH and SEAFOOD** are among the most important and popular foods, especially catches from the cold Atlantic waters off the western seaboard. With its deeply indented coastline, Kerry has a disproportionately long coastline – The Ring of Kerry alone, for example, is a spectacular day's drive of about 176km/110 miles.

Dingle, Ireland's most westerly town, is a fishing port and Fenit (most westerly commercial port) is known especially for sea angling, while Caherciveen, on the Ring of Kerry, is home to successful fishing companies such as the highly regarded **Daly's Seafood** (+353 (0)66 947 2082), supplier to many top restaurants, and **Quinlans Kerry Fish**. Although, as elsewhere, commercial fishing is dominated by very large, sometimes foreign-registered boats, this family-run business distributes fish from its own trawlers and others in the region, and retails spanking fresh local fish and shellfish through its shops in the area and online. Lobster is the top favourite with visitors to the area, closely followed by crab, smoked salmon, and shellfish such as Dingle Bay Prawns (langoustines), Valentia Harbour scallops, Fenit oysters, Glenbeigh cockles and **Cromane mussels**.

Famed throughout the world for its beauty, many first-time visitors to Ireland head straight to the South-West - and they are unlikely to be disappointed by either the grandeur of its majestically rugged coastal landscape, or an exceptional hospitality culture which, around the romantic Lakes of Killarney and the dramatic Ring of Kerry (Iveragh Peninsula), dates back to Victorian times.

Despite man's best efforts at intervention, the foods of any region must always be the product of its landscape, and the specialities fashioned by the land, rivers, lakes and sea of the Cork and Kerry region are as diverse as the landscape itself, which range from the towering mountains and cliffs of Kerry's far south-west coast to the rich farmland and pastures of East Cork.

Kerry shepherd

Ted Browne is an especially interesting producer in Dingle, renowned for quality **organic smoked salmon, prawns and crab** – not only do they produce some of the best seafood in the south-west, but this enterprising company uses the waste from the crab and prawn processing to make an organic compost, which has the usual soil conditioning features plus a secret weapon – it's a natural bio-pesticide too, controlling many fungal plant diseases.

Leisure **fishing** of all kinds - trying your luck for salmon, sea trout and brown trout on the beautiful lakes and rivers, sea fishing, surf and shore angling - is one of the major attractions to Kerry, a fact reflected in the local foods offered in shops and restaurants, particularly **smoked salmon** which remains one of the area's most popular products.

The **MEATS** of the area are very much a product of the environment too, reflecting the rugged conditions and natural production methods. Traditional **Kerry black-faced mountain lamb** is a seasonal treat – the prized meat of these hardy, lean animals has the special flavours of the heather, wild herbs and grasses they feed on and is available late season (July-November). Another particular speciality is the **Blasket Island lamb**. The product of the salt-sprayed heathery pastures of this small group of uninhabited, but much-visited islands 3km/1.5m off Dingle peninsula

(www.blasketislands.ie), the meat is comparable to the famous pré-salé (salt marsh) lamb of Normandy and Brittany with yet an extra *je-ne-sais-quoi*; supplies are very limited, so catch it if you can when in the area.

Kerry beef is also a speciality, the sturdy little **black Kerry cow** being hardy and well-suited to the terrain; good all-rounders for both dairy and beef production. The Kerry breed is appreciated for its small, fine-textured joints of sweetly flavoured meat and milk with unusually small fat globules that make it easily digestible – local products using the milk include not only various cheeses, but **Murphy's Ice Cream**, which is made in Dingle. **GAME** is plentiful in season (winter) and a meat that is cherished in the area is **VENISON**, especially the meat of the native **Kerry Red Deer** from the Killarney National Park which is in season from November to February when the herd size is managed.

Speciality products to look out for in the area include **CHARCUTERIE** from the renowned German Butcher at Fossa (where you will also find local venison in season); **Kerry lamb pies** which are a speciality of Dingle and also known as Dingle Pies; and also rival styles of **black and white puddings**, championed variously by well known butchers in Annascaul, Sneem and Tralee. Also in Tralee, versatile products are made by well known local chef **Melanie Harty** (www.hartysfoods.com), notably her Harty's **PEPPER JELLY** range; and the family run company **Organic Harvest** (www.organicharvest.ie) produces a range of excellent handmade organic **SOUPS**.

The **CHEESES** of the area are full of character and include nationally recognised products like Eilish Broderick's **Kerry Farmhouse Cheese** from Listowel (a popular cheese in the range is flavoured with nettles);

Dingle Peninsula Cheese, made by Maja Binder near Castlegregory - where her husband collects **sea vegetables**, some of which are used in her award-winning, cheese **Dilliskus**; Wilma's **Killorglin Farmhouse Cheese**; and **Beal Organic Cheeses** (Listowel). Some lesser known cheeses such as **Bric Farm Cheese** (Dingle) and **Dereenaclaurig** farmhouse cheese (Sneem), are especially worth looking out for as they are

Four of the Best...

Cromane Mussels

The pure clean waters of Castlemaine Bay are the source of the area's famous - and very natural - product, Cromane mussels. The most abundant and versatile of Irish shellfish, the common or blue mussel (Mytilus edulis - or *an diúilicín* in Irish),

is a double-shelled mollusc with an inky blue-black curved shell; it is a native shellfish and has been eaten in Ireland since ancient times. They grow wild, using a filter system to feed on plankton; depending on the type of plankton, their flesh is white or orange in tone. Mussel farmers either grow them on ropes (as in Kenmare Bay), or dredge the wild mussel spat and move it to richer, shallower water to mature, as in Castlemaine Bay (hence the label 'wild mussels'); growth is a totally natural process, requiring only clean, plankton rich water. In addition to being on sale in fish shops and featuring on Irish menus, both live and processed Cromane mussels are a major export, mainly to continental Europe and the UK.

Cromane Pier Cromane Killorglin Co Kerry

Kerry Black-faced Mountain Lamb

Mountain lamb is a seasonal speciality – the earliest they reach the market is late July, high season is from late August to October, with some available as late as November. A diet of heather, wild grasses and herbs creates the very special

flavour of Kerry Mountain lamb, which graze the high mountains for 6-7 months by which time they weigh about 40kg and are ready for eating. It is a treat highly prized by gourmets and, farmer Patrick Moran – a champion sheep-shearer in his spare time – was recently singled out for an award by the Irish Food Writers' Guild. For four generations, the Moran family has farmed the mountain slopes on western edge of the Ring of Kerry. The mountain lamb Patrick and his wife Anne breed are directly descended from the Scottish Black Face breed, introduced into the mountainous areas of the South and West of Ireland in the mid-19th century; since then, they have evolved smaller and leaner, in response to local conditions. Mountain lambs are widely available from local Kerry butchers, and half or whole carcasses of Patrick's lamb on the bone can be bought from the farm for home-freezing.

Patrick & Anne Moran Maughernane
Waterville Co Kerry +353 (0)66 947 4589

only available locally. (Further information: Irish Farmhouse Cheese Assocation, Cáis, www.irishcheese.ie)

A speciality which many visitors find surprising – and has now taken hold in pockets throughout the country – is the artisan production of high quality **CHOCOLATE**, and it is worth allowing time for investigation when planning a trip around the Ring of Kerry as outstanding producers are to be found in unlikely places - **Cocoa Bean Artisan Chocolates** and **Skelligs Chocolate** (renowned for their beautiful hand-painted boxes as well as the contents), for example, share premises in remote Ballinskelligs – close to Noelle Campbell Sharp's internationally renowned Cill Rialaig Project, which has a gallery (with coffee shop) in the village. And, at the Kenmare end of the Ring, you'll find the superb **Benoit Lorge Chocolates**, which are made at Bonane (Glengarriff road).

Dingle Peninsula Cheese

Originally from Germany, Maja Binder makes artisan cheeses of real character, and her husband, Olivier 'On The Wild Side' Beaujouan, collects seaweeds and makes numerous products from  them, which are on sale at local markets. Using summer milk only from cows grazing the natural grasses and herbs on the south-west tip of the Dingle Peninsula, Maja makes several cheeses; her own favourite, and the one that has brought her numerous awards, is Dilliskus Cheese, made with seaweed. With a lovely handmade appearance, Dilliskus has great texture and a distinctive aroma and flavour; its many accolades include the 'Eugene Byrne Memorial Best in Ireland' at the British Cheese Awards, and also an award from the Irish Food Writers' Guild, who praised "a cheese that follows the ancient Irish tradition of flavouring foods with seaweed" and it was also the Supreme Champion in the inaugural Blas na hÉireann National Irish Food Awards, in 2008.

Kilcummin Beg Castlegregory Co Kerry
+363 (0)66 713 9028

Murphys Ice Cream & Café

Many would make the trek to Dingle solely for the pleasure of tucking into one of the treats on offer at the cheerful blue and white fronted Murphys Ice Cream Café down near the harbour. The larger-than-life  Murphy brothers, Kieran and Séan, are originally from America but visited Ireland often when growing up because their father is from Cork, and eventually opted to settle in Dingle, later to be joined by many of their extended family. Since 2000 they've been making ice cream here with fresh milk and cream from the black Kerry cow, and have earned a national reputation in the meantime. Now they supply a network of discerning restaurants and specialist outlets around the country, and have other cafés in Killarney and Dublin. A second speciality is Sean's wife Wiebke Murphy's superb German baking –her exquisite gateaux are utterly irresistible. The Murphy brothers cookbook, *The Book of Sweet Things* is available from bookshops, and from their own cafés.

Strand Street Dingle Co Kerry
+353 (0)66 915 2644 www.murphysicecream.ie

where to Buy

the special Foods of Kerry...

A guide to food shops, markets, farm shops, local stores and internet suppliers

Dingle Area

Ashes Butchers ANNASCAUL Dingle Peninsula *(+353 (0)66 915 7127 www.annascaulblackpudding.com)*. Renowned for its smooth, dense texture, Annascaul Black Pudding has been made here by hand since Ashe's shop was established in 1916, and is now joined by white pudding and homemade sausages, all using natural ingredients.

Dingle Indoor Market Dygate Lane. Crafts and artisan food, eg Phoenix Natural Food, Dingle Peninsula Cheeses, On the Wild Side (patés, smoked fish, seaweed products). Friday.

Jerry Kennedy Butchers Orchard Lane **DINGLE** *(+353 (0)66 915 2511)*. No ordinary butchers, this traditional shop run by Craft Butchers Association member Jerry Kennedy has been in the same family for generations, and it's where, among many other fine Irish meats, you get that special Blasket Islands lamb in late summer and autumn.

Ó Catháin Iasc Teo Fish Shop The Quay **DINGLE** *(+353 (0)66 915 1322 www.iascteo.com)*. A family run business established in 1975, this is one of Ireland's premier fish processors. A factory retail outlet stocks a wide variety of locally caught fish and shellfish. Closed Sun, also Mon in winter.

Piog Pies DINGLE *(+353 (0)87 794 4036 www.piogpies.com)*. Dingle has a long tradition of pie-making and, although these are not quite the traditional Dingle Pie (which is made with mutton and boiled in its own broth), there is a Kerry lamb & vegetable pie in Brid Ni Mhathuna's hand-made range. Sold at local Farmers' Markets and selected shops.

Murphys Ice Cream Strand Street **DINGLE** *(+353 (0)66 915 2644 www.murphysicecream.ie)*. Fans travel to Dingle especially to sample the ice cream with the cheery sky blue livery that's made here by brothers Sean & Kieran Murphy, with the milk of black Kerry cows; on sale in their own café-shops (Dingle, Killarney and Dublin) and distributed to specialist suppliers nationwide.

Tralee/Listowel Area

Kingdom Food & Wine Oakpark **TRALEE** *(+353 (0)66 711 8562 www.kingdomstore.ie)*. Maeve Duff's well-chosen range of Irish and international foods (and wines) includes local specialities not widely stocked, such as Piog Pies. Deli; catering service; hampers.

John R's Home Bakery & Delicatessen Church Street **LISTOWEL** *(+353 (0)68 21249 www.johnrs.com)*. Traditional home baking (soda bread, scones, fresh fruit pies), prepared meals, own label preserves, health foods & hampers (delivery anywhere in Britain & Ireland).

Killarney Area

The German Butcher Shop Fossa **KILLARNEY** *(+353 (0)64 33069)*. Supplies local venison as well as excellent charcuterie, German meat cuts and other specialities including tempting continental patisserie.

Ring of Kerry

Quinlans Kerry Fish *(+353 (0)66 947 2177 www.kerryfish.com)*. The Quinlan family operate four retail shops in **CAHERCIVEEN**, Killorglin, Tralee and Killarney. Fresh whitefish and shellfish is sourced from company trawlers and delivered daily to the shops from their processing plant just outside Cahirciveen at Renard Point. **Online shop**: fresh fish boxes delivered nationwide, smoked salmon internationally.

Valentia Island Farmhouse Ice Cream Kilbeg **VALENTIA ISLAND** *(+353 (0)66 947 6864 www.valentiaicecream.com)*. Made with full fat milk and cream from the Daly family's Friesian herd, with no artificial flavourings, colours or preservatives. The wide variety of flavours can be bought or sampled along with soft drinks, teas and coffees in a rustic little half-doored Ice Cream Parlour.

Skelligs Chocolate

Skelligs Chocolate Co and Cocoa Bean Artisan Chocolates BALLINSKELLIGS Iveragh Peninsula *(+353 (0)66 947 9119 www.skelligschocolate.com)*. Shared premises in this remote location on the Ring of Kerry for two high quality chocolate operations. Open Mon-Fri all year except Jan, weekends in Jul-Aug only. **Online shop**.

Westcove Farmhouse Shop Westcove Road **CASTLECOVE** Iveragh Peninsula *(+353 (0)66 947 5479 www.westcove.net)*. At this gem just off the Ring of Kerry,

Danish confectioner Jane Urquhart has a craft shop (with speciality foods on sale in summer), a small bakery and even a self-catering apartment to let.

PJ Burns Butchers SNEEM *(+353 (0)64 45139)*. The popular Sneem black pudding originated in this little butchers and is still made here, baked like a big cake and sliced as required.

Kenmare Area

Lorge Chocolates Bonane near **KENMARE** *(+353 (0)64 667 9994 www.lorge.ie)*. In a former post office between Kenmare and Glengarriff, French chocolatier Benoit Lorge makes exquisite chocolates; on sale here in the shop and widely distributed.

Jam 6 Henry Street **KENMARE** *(+353 (0)64 664 1591)*. James Mulchrone's delightful craft bakery and café in Kenmare is just the spot to stock up for a picnic; eat in or take away Also at: Old Market Lane, Killarney; Ballyseede Garden Centre, Tralee.

Truffle Pig Fine Foods The Square **KENMARE** *(+353 (0)64 668 9624)*. Good deli – gourmet salads, meats, cheeses, breads, pies, and other treats.

The Breadcrumb New Road **KENMARE** *(+353 (0)64 664 0645 www.thebreadcrumb.com)*. Manuela Goeb specialises in robust sourdough breads at her little bakery; Mon-Sat, 8.30-6.30 (7 days in high season) Also at markets: Dingle (Fri); Milltown (Sat).

Ireland South-West: Kerry Food Markets

For further information on Farmers Markets throughout Ireland
www.bordbia.ie • www.kerryfarmersmarkets.com

Caherdaniel Market Blind Pipers. Sun 12.30-6 May-Oct (weather permitting).

Caherciveen Market Community Centre. Thu 11-2 (high season).

Dingle Indoor Market Fri 10-3

Listowel Farmers Market Fri 10-1

Milltown Organic Market The Old Church, Milltown. Sat 10-2.

Eat & Stay

Packies, Kenmare

Caherciveen

QC's Seafood Bar & Restaurant

Local fish is the main draw at Kate and Andrew Cooke's atmospheric bar and restaurant - supplied by the family company, Quinlan's Kerry Fish at Renard's Point (one of their shops is just across the road). And there's a big Spanish influence, so expect delicious chargrills, with lots of olive oil and garlic: fresh crab claws and crabmeat are a speciality, also sizzling prawns, and pan-seared baby squid. Excellent local meats balance up evening menus: rack of Kerry lamb and char-grilled fillet steak (supplied by a local butcher). The most pleasing aspect of the food is its immediacy - everything is ultra-fresh, simply prepared and full of zest and, given the quality, it is also good value.

3 Main Street Cahirciveen Co Kerry
+353 (0)66 947 2244 www.qcbar.com

Dingle

The Chart House

Jim McCarthy's attractive stone-built restaurant has been one of Dingle's favourite dining destinations since 1997, and this is the place to come for the very best of local foods, especially mountain lamb in season, Annascaul black pudding, local cheeses, and seafood. One of head chef Noel Enright's favourite dishes is rack of Kerry mountain lamb, served simply with fondant potato and redcurrant & rosemary jus; seafood is excellent too but, unusually in this area, it tends to be the meat dishes that stay in the memory.

The Mall Dingle Co Kerry
+353 (0)66 915 2255 www.charthousedingle.com

Lord Baker's Restaurant & Bar

Believed to be the oldest pub in Dingle, this business was established in 1890 by a Tom Baker; a director of the Tralee-Dingle Railway, he was known locally as "Lord Baker". Cosy and full of charm, tables are set up in front of a welcoming turf fire in the front bar, where speciality dishes include a very good chowder with home-baked soda bread, and crab claws in garlic butter. And no detail escapes the notice of proprietor John Moriarty – what he doesn't know about Dingle isn't worth knowing.

Dingle Co Kerry +353 (0)66 915 1277 www.lordbakers.ie

Out of the Blue

Everything at Tim Mason's harbourside café depends on the fresh fish supply from the boats that day – if there's no fresh fish, they don't open. Discerning locals know how lucky they are to have such an exciting little restaurant on their doorstep and it's just the kind of place that visitors dream of finding – it is not unusual to hear a different language spoken at every table.

Waterside Dingle Co Kerry
+353 (0)66 915 0811 www.outoftheblue.ie

♣ Gorman's Clifftop House & Restaurant

Sile and Vincent Gorman's house is beautifully situated on the Slea Head scenic drive and Dingle Way walking route. Commanding superb sea views from the restaurant (sunsets can be spectacular), warm Dingle Bay prawn salad, potato cake & Annascaul black pudding, local fish and the ever-popular sirloin steak (Irish Hereford beef) taste even better in this setting, with salad and summer vegetables from their own organic garden.

Glaise Bheag Ballydavid Dingle Peninsula Co Kerry
+353 (0)66 915 5162 www.gormans-clifftophouse.com

Kenmare

Jam

James Mulchrone's delightful bakery and café has been a great success since the day it opened in March 2001 and, unlikely as this may seem in a town that has some of the best eating places in Ireland, it brought something new and very welcome. The stated aim is "to provide fresh, quality, imaginative food at affordable prices in nice surroundings"; this they are doing very well, both here and at their branches in Killarney *(Old Market Lane +353 (0)64 37716)* and Tralee *(Ballyseedy Home & Outdoor Living +353(0)66 719 2580).*

6 Henry St Kenmare Co Kerry
+353 (0)64 41591 www.jam.ie

Mulcahys Restaurant

In a town blessed with an exceptional number of good restaurants, Bruce Mulcahy is the most exciting chef. All produce used is local and certified organic, where possible but, when it comes to style, this original and friendly contemporary restaurant does not do 'traditional Irish'. Expect world cuisines, but with a special edge - Bruce has gone to the source to learn his skills. And upstairs, under separate management, Neil and Noreen Harrington's cosy guesthouse, ♣ Virginia's *(+353 (0)64 41021 www.virginias-kenmare.com)*, offers real hospitality and comfort, and their breakfasts are a point of honour.

36 Henry Street Kenmare Co Kerry +353 (0)64 42383

♣ Park Hotel Kenmare

The definitive place to stay in Kerry – perhaps in Ireland - brothers Francis and John Brennan are renowned for setting the benchmark by which all other Irish accommodation is judged at their perfectly located hotel on the edge of Kenmare Town. Excellent food, including an outstanding breakfast, is served in a classically beautiful dining room with views over gardens to the ever-changing mountains across the bay. Attention to detail is the hallmark of this national treasure – a secret now shared with viewers of the Brennan brothers' "At Your Service" TV programmes.

Kenmare Co Kerry
+353 (0)64 41200 www.parkkenmare.com

♣ Shelburne Lodge

Tom and Maura Foley's fine stone house is the oldest in Kenmare, and the feeling is of being a guest in a (very well run) private country house. Everything is lovely, but perhaps the best is saved until last, when superb breakfasts are served at tables prettily laid with linen napkins; juices, freshly-baked breads, home-made preserves, fresh fish, and Irish farmhouse cheeses are among the treats that begin a day here. For other meals in the town, Maura's sister Grainne O'Connell's daytime restaurant/bar **The Purple Heather** *(+353 (0)64 41016)* has been delighting visitors with its good home cooking since 1964; and, at the Foleys' warm and relaxed evening restaurant **Packies** *(+353 (0)64 41508)*, Martin Hallissey cooks the best of local produce with admirable simplicity, making this the town's favourite restaurant for many discerning visitors. What a hat trick.

Cork Road Kenmare Co Kerry
Tel: +353-64-41013 www.shelburnelodge.com

Killarney

Bricín

Upstairs, over a craft shop (which you will find especially interesting if you like Irish pottery), Paddy and Johnny McGuire's country-style first-floor restaurant has been delighting visitors with its warm atmosphere and down-to-earth food since 1990. Traditional dishes include the house speciality, boxty (potato pancakes); you can have them with various fillings - chicken, lamb vegetables - and salad.

26 High Street Killarney Co Kerry
+353 (0)64 34902 www.bricin.com

Gaby's Seafood Restaurant

One of Ireland's longest established seafood restaurants, Gaby's is priced in the 'treat' category, yet it has a pleasantly informal atmosphere and a cosy bar. Chef-proprietor Gert Maes offers seasonal à la carte menus in classic French style and in three languages. This is one of the great classic Irish kitchens and absolute freshness is the priority; although there are other choices, a note on the menu reminds guests that seafood availability depends on daily landings. Lovely desserts include "my mother's recipe" - an old-fashioned apple & raspberry crumble.

27 High Street Killarney Co Kerry   +353 (0)64 32519

Miss Courtney's Tea Rooms

Sandra Dunlea's premises has been in the family since 1909, albeit as a tea and confectionery shop until recently. With all the elegance and charm of a bygone age, it offers harrassed visitors the perfect antidote to the pushy modern world. Everything is served on proper china, delightfully mis-matched, and, despite the

unexpected presence of tiger prawns, there is a stated commitment to sourcing local and seasonal ingredients. Everything is very tasty - and gluten free sandwiches are available at all times.

8 College Street Killarney Co Kerry +353 (0)87 610 9500

The Garden Restaurant

Anyone interested in food should enjoy the traditional farm at Muckross House but, whatever the reason for your visit, the good food on offer at their appealing Garden Restaurant may come as a pleasant surprise at such a major tourist attraction. In-house baking is a particular strength.

Walled Garden Centre Muckross House Killarney Co Kerry
+353 (0)64 663 1440 www.muckross-house.ie

♣ Killarney Park Hotel

The Treacy family are Killarney's premier hoteliers, always raising the bar. In addition to this luxurious, well-run hotel - renowned for excellent cooking showcasing local produce, in both The Park Restaurant and bar - they have the town's cutting edge property **The Ross** (*+353 (0)64 31855 www.theross.ie*) across the road, which is known equally for its edgy design and theatrical fine dining restaurant, Cellar One. More recently these great hoteliers took over **The Malton** (*+353 (0)64 38000 www.themalton.com*) formerly Great Southern Hotel) and, although modernization of this gracious Victorian railway hotel has been controversial, its Peppers Steak & Seafood Grill remains a popular independent dining destination, with chef John O'Leary cooking local foods in contemporary style.

Kenmare Place Killarney Co Kerry
+353 (0)64 35555 www.killarneyparkhotel.ie

Killorglin Area

♣ Carrig House Country House & Restaurant

With lake and mountains providing a dramatic backdrop to Frank and Mary Slattery's romantic Victorian house, this is a gem of a hideaway. The clear waters of Caragh Lake originate in the MacGillycuddy Reeks, providing an ideal environment for healthy fish for game anglers, notably salmon and trout. The restaurant – a dining destination, not just for residents – showcases local products such as sea trout,

West Cork pork and Valentia ice cream, from nearby Valentia Island.

Caragh Lake Killorglin Co Kerry
+353 (0)66 976 9100 www.carrighouse.com

Jack's Coastguard Station Bar & Seafood Restaurant

Just a stone's throw from the sea at Cromane, where the mussels that the area is famous for are landed, this handsome, smartly maintained stone building is the place where classically trained chef Helen Vickers weaves her own special magic, with a superb range of seafood including, when available, hake, black sole, prawns, lobster, plaice on the bone, turbot, and scallops.

Water's Edge Cromane Killorglin Co Kerry
+353 (0)66 976 9102

Listowel

Allo's

Helen Mullane and Armel Whyte's characterful café-bar is the place to head for when hungry in Listowel, for great raw materials, careful cooking by a team well-led by Euro-Toques chef Armel, and smart service. Pub/bistro lunch dishes executed with flair include the most delightfully flavoursome fishy chowder, and evening menus highlight the day's fresh fish and seafood from Fenit, with some very good meat dishes too. Theme nights are often held.

41/43 Church Street Listowel Co Kerry
+353 (0)68 22880

Portmagee

❧ The Moorings

Overlooking the harbour in this attractive little fishing port, this is pretty much the one-stop shop in Portmagee these days, as Gerard and Patricia Kennedy work hard to provide everything the visitor could need in The Bridge Bar and The Moorings Guesthouse & Restaurant. A 'good home cooking' style suits the cosy atmosphere and maritime theme and, although there's a natural emphasis on fresh local seafood - Skellig crab cakes, Cromane mussels and oysters, Caherciveen smoked salmon and hot seafood platter are typical - Kerry lamb is another winner, and you may find unusual meat dishes that are not offered elsewhere.

Portmagee Co Kerry
+353 (0)66 947 7108 www.moorings.ie

Tralee

Val's Bar & Bistro

Noted local chef David Norris (who formerly operated the area's leading fine dining restaurant) is now cooking excellent informal meals at this well-known bar and bistro.

Bridge Street Tralee Co Kerry +353 (0)66 712 1559

Waterville

❧ The Smugglers Inn

In a scenic location, right beside the world famous championship Waterville Golf Links, talented chef Henry Hunt's cooking has a classical foundation, but includes modern dishes too, especially on the bar menu. Local ingredients star - seafood is the speciality and other choices include Kerry lamb and beef, also some good vegetarian dishes.

Cliff Road Waterville Co Kerry
+353(0)66 947 4330 www.the-smugglers-inn.com

WWW.IRELAND-GUIDE.COM FOR MORE OF THE BEST PLACES TO EAT, DRINK & STAY

Recipes

Black Sole on the Bone

In Ireland the fish known elsewhere as Dover sole is generally called black sole - and it is no relation to lemon sole, a much softer and less expensive fish. Black sole is a treat, by any standards, and it is the favourite fish for many people. Sole is superb grilled or pan-fried on the bone and served plain, with salad or vegetables as a separate course, or at least on a separate plate - the photograph shows how beautifully simply they do it at Jack's Coastguard Station Bar & Seafood Restaurant, Cromane. Unusually for fish, black sole is best when it is two or three days old, when the flavour has intensified. Get the fishmonger to remove the coarse black skin for you, but retain the white one as it adds flavour and keeps the cooked fish in shape. Cook the skin side first, if grilling, the reverse if pan-frying as it will be easier to serve.

Serves 4

4 medium-sized black sole

Juice of ¹/₂ lemon

Freshly ground black pepper

Melted butter

A little extra butter and oil (if frying)

Fresh finely chopped parsley

Lemon wedges.

Wash the fish and dry thoroughly with kitchen paper. Heat the grill or a heavy frying pan; oil the grill rack if using, or heat an equal quantity of butter and oil in the pan.

Season the fish on both sides with lemon juice and freshly ground pepper, then cook for 4 or 5 minutes on one side, depending on thickness; turn carefully with a fish slice and cook the second side until the flesh is opaque and comes away easily from the bone when tested with the tip of a knife. Carefully transfer the fish to warmed plates, pour over any pan juices, scatter with parsley (or include this in an accompanying lemon butter sauce), and garnish with lemon wedges.

New potatoes, served separately, are delicious with the sole, also a mixed leaf salad to follow.

Variations: Good, firm medium-sized plaice or lemon sole are also good cooked in the same way.

Kerry Lamb Pie

This very modern take on the traditional Kerry pie is light years away from the original that inspired it, but very tasty nonetheless - it is adapted from the cookbook *Roly's Bistro, The Restaurant and Its Food* (Gill & Macmillan), and has been a favourite dish at the perennially popular Dublin restaurant for many years. Kerry lamb pies – or, more particularly, Dingle Pies – were modest little mutton pies, not unlike Cornish pasties; the shortcrust pastry was made with mutton fat and the pies were often boiled in mutton stock, rather like dumplings. Today's modern versions are lighter (and probably more palatable); Piog Pies, of Dingle, include a Kerry lamb & vegetable pie in their handmade range.

The filling for these pies could be made ahead and cooled, leaving only the pastry and oven baking to finish before serving.

Serves 4

10 button mushrooms

2 onions

2 carrots

4 sticks celery

750 g / 1 lb 9oz diced leg of lamb

1 dessertspoon tomato purée

700 ml / 1¼pt good chicken stock

1 teaspoon gravy browning

200 ml / 7 fl oz white wine

bouquet garni

4 saucer-sized discs puff pastry, to cover four oven-proof soup bowls

15g / ½ oz butter

1 large or two small parsnips, diced and roasted in butter

1 egg, beaten

Salt and freshly-ground black pepper

Cut mushrooms in half and sauté in a little oil for about 10 minutes. Prepare the vegetables and chop into chunky pieces.

Seal the lamb in a hot saucepan with a little oil, and then season with salt and pepper and cook gently for 4-5 minutes. Add the onion, carrot and celery and cook with the lamb for a further 5 minutes. Add tomato purée and cook for a further 2-3 minutes, then pour in the chicken stock, gravy browning and white wine. Bring to the boil and simmer gently for about an hour until tender.

Towards the end of the cooking time, add the bouquet garni and the cooked button mushrooms.

Pre-heat the oven to 200°C/400°F/Gas 6.

Roll out the pastry discs, making them slightly bigger than serving bowl. Pan-fry the parsnips in some butter until tender. Ladle the lamb pie filling into the bowls, top with parsnips and cover with the pastry.

Brush with beaten egg and bake for 20 minutes, until pastry is golden brown. Serve immediately, with seasonal vegetables on the side.

Murphy's Earl Grey 'Tae' Ice Cream

Many of the Murphy's ice creams are seasonal – based on soft summer fruit such as strawberries or raspberries for example – but this unusual recipe, adapted from one in *The Book of Sweet Things* (Mercier Press), can be made at any time. Kieran Murphy says it was inspired by one he experienced (and didn't expect to like) at a famous little ice cream shop near Boston – and he found that the tannins in tea cut sweetness. Earl Grey tea generally has a mix of different black teas, including Darjeeling and China tea, but it is the bergamot that really makes it distinctive, so "If you want an adult ice cream that will surprise your guests, this is one to try." Solaris Botanicals, Galway, include an outstanding Earl Grey in their range of speciality teas.

Serves 8

130g/4 oz + 2 tablespoons caster sugar

5 egg yolks

250 ml / 9fl oz milk

6 Earl Grey tea bags, or the loose leaf equivalent

240 ml/ 81/2 fl oz cream.

Beat the sugar and egg yolks together until thick and pale yellow.

Bring the milk to a simmer. Add the tea and allow to sit for 10 minutes. Bring back to a low simmer, stir, and remove the tea/bags.

Beat the milk into the eggs and sugar in a slow stream.

Pour the mixture back into the rinsed pan, and place over low heat.

Stir continuously until the custard thickens slightly (around 65°-70°C) and just coats the back of a spoon. Don't over-heat, though, because at around 76°C you will scramble the eggs!

Immediately remove from the heat. Transfer the custard into a small container; cover, and refrigerate until cool (5°C).

Whip the cream until it has doubled in volume (you should have soft peaks - don't over-whip). Fold (gently stir) the cream into the custard.

Freeze using a domestic ice cream machine, or cover and place in the freezer, stirring every few hours to break up the ice crystals.

If using a domestic ice cream machine, transfer to a freezer-proof covered container when the ice cream has achieved a semi-solid consistency (around 15 minutes). Place it in the freezer, and continue to freeze until it is solid.

Muckross venison casserole

This recipe was given to me by George Graves (a nephew of the poet, Robert Gaves) when he and his wife Christiane ran Ballylickey Manor, near Bantry, as a guesthouse, and provided evening meals. (It is still open for guests, as a B&B, operated by their son Paco.) This wonderful wintry combination of gamey venison chunks from nearby Muckross Park and wedges of conference pears, is cooked in a rich red wine, thyme and juniper gravy. It makes a hearty dish for the colder months and the German influence is especially appropriate as there are many families of German descent living in the Killarney area - hence the popularity of the renowned German Butcher at Fossa.

Serves 4

60 ml /4 tbsp oil

1 onion, peeled & finely chopped

2 cloves garlic, peeled & crushed

2 lb/900g venison, in chunks

Seasoned flour

300 ml /1/2 pint red wine

150 ml /1/4 pint/ game or beef stock

10 juniper berries

3 sprigs fresh thyme, chopped

2 conference pears

Salt & freshly ground black pepper.

Heat 2 tablespoons/30ml of the oil in a pan and fry the onion and garlic gently until soft but not browned. Remove with a slotted spoon and transfer to a casserole. Dip the venison chunks in the seasoned flour and shake off the excess.

Add the remaining oil to the pan and fry the venison in batches to brown.

Transfer to the casserole, pour over the wine and stock and bring up to just below boiling point, when bubbles rise. (Do not boil). Add the juniper berries and thyme. Simmer gently for 1½ hours, or until the venison is tender. Add the pears, peeled, cored and cut into wedges, and cook for a further 10 minutes. Season with salt and freshly ground black pepper. Serve with spätzle or ribbon pasta, or potato purée.

Ireland: South-West, Cork
Food of the Region

Seafood Dexter Beef
Charcuterie
Ducks Smoked Fish
Free Range Pork
Tea
Clonakilty Black Pudding
Chocolates Breads/Mixes
Lullaby Milk *Apple Brandy*
Honey
Macroom Oats

Ireland's largest and most varied county, Cork is a favoured destination for the Irish taking home holidays – they come to West Cork, especially, for its beautiful coastline and away-from-it-all atmosphere and, increasingly, for the county's outstanding food.

cork city

Cork may be the second city but it has long been known as Ireland's food capital, and that is no boastful claim. Not only is the county brimming with good things from land and sea but, in **Cork City**'s **English Market** (www.corkenglishmarket.ie), it has a culinary gem beyond price. No Irish food lover goes to Cork for even the briefest of visits without at least walking through this wonderfully vibrant market, to breathe in the sights, the sounds and the smells that make it so special. Dating back to 1788 – just a few years after the **Cork Butter Exchange** (www.corkbutter.museum) was established nearby at Shandon, bringing world fame for graded Irish butter - this permanent covered market is right in the centre and, with its variety of traditional and more contemporary stalls (likely to offer foods from afar), it remains the living heart of the city to this day. This is the place to come to see **SPECIALITIES** including O'Reilly's famous stall selling the **tripe and drisheen** that's become synonymous with The English Market (drisheen is a local speciality blood pudding, traditionally served with tripe & onions), **buttered eggs** (once widely available, before refrigeration; the eggs are rubbed with butter to seal the porous shells, they then keep fresh for months) and pork products like **cruibíns** (pig's trotters). Many stall holders, including fishmongers, butchers and poulterers, have been here for generations and there's great banter as well as pride; more recent arrivals include plenty specialising in organic foods, and some with a cosmopolitan tone – the range and quality of **olives** offered by the Real Olive Company is exceptional, for example (and you may also find something really unusual, like genuine **Irish buffalo mozzarella**), and the renowned **sourdough loaves** made by former Cork hotelier turned master baker Declan Ryan, of **Arbutus Breads** (www.arbutusbread.com), are sold by On the Pig's

The English Market, Cork

The English Market, Cork

Back (www.onthepigsback.ie) at the English Market, where Isabel Sheridan's excellent range of foods includes **cured meats** and **farmhouse cheeses**, and delectable homemade continental patés and terrines. All of which makes the market just the spot for putting a picnic together, or for self-catering visitors to stock up the larder.

Foods produced nearby that are worth looking out for – and may well be on sale in The English Market - include Anne Bradfield's evocatively named 'Taste A Memory' pies (www.tasteamemory.ie) which are made in the Kinsale Road Commercial Centre on the western edge of the city and have earned a huge fan club, thanks to the fresh local ingredients used and real homemade flavours - and, if you're looking for gluten- and wheat-free baking, you won't find better than the goodies from **Delicious** (www.delicious.ie; **online shop**) of Ballincollig, a short distance west of Cork. Also produced west of the city is Ann and Pat O'Farrell's versatile semi-soft **Carrigaline Farmhouse Cheese** (www.carrigalinecheese.com), which is made in three flavours (natural, garlic & herbs and smoked) and widely available. There are several outstanding **CHOCOLATE** makers in the area - the sought-after

O'Conaill Chocolates are handmade in Carrigaline, although their main outlet is in Cork city centre at the cute O'Conaill Chocolate Shop on French Church Street Sweet (also a popular destination for their gorgeous hot chocolate), and another unmissable destination for chocolate lovers is **Eve Chocolates** (www.evechocolates.ie) which is made near Dennehy's Cross and the on sale there. Sweet-toothed visitors should also head for Petits Fours (www.petitsfours.ie), on Washington Street, where top quality **CONFECTIONERY** and patisserie is to be found. An unusual treat to keep an eye open for in speciality shops is the iconic **Hadji Bey's Turkish Delight** (www.hadjibey.ie), which was a Cork speciality for many years until production ceased in the 1970s; recently revived by L.C. Confectionery of Newbridge, Co Kildare, this delicious and beautifully packaged product in re-usable boxes has been welcomed back to Cork as one of their own and is available from selected stockists, chocolate shops and several stalls at the English Market including Paradise Garden.

Luckily, Cork city is also blessed with special drinks to wash these good foods down. Guinness (Dublin's pride and joy) may be the big name among Irish **STOUTS**, but Corkonians have the luxury of choosing between two traditional local **BREWS** – **Beamish** (similar to Guinness in character and, until very recently, made in the Beamish & Crawford factory in Cork city) and **Murphy's**, which is a lighter, sweeter brew; both are now made at the Heineken factory in Cork. (A tasting of the three stouts, together with what many feel to be their natural partner – various kinds of oysters – can be entertaining and instructive.) **The Francisan Well Brew Pub** (www.franciscanwellbrewery.com) on North Mall keeps up the tradition of independent brewing today – and, not far away at Ladysbridge, in East Cork, **Rupert's Farm** (www.rupertsfarm.com) is not only setting up a new brewery but also growing the hops, along with other crops. But a more famous brew than any beer by far is TEA: **Barry's Tea** (www.barrystea.ie) has been close to the nation's hearts since 1901, and is shipped all over the world to soothe, comfort and refresh an Irish diaspora who find they cannot live without it… Gold, Classic, and Original Blend (Breakfast Green) all have their dedicated followers, and there are many more to choose from too.

North Cork

Heading west from Cork City, the main route takes the traveller towards Killarney through rolling, fertile countryside and some north Cork towns of note, including Macroom, which is famous for a simple yet outstanding product: traditional stone-ground **OATMEAL**, made by Donal Creedon at **Macroom Oat Mills** (+353 (0)26 41800), Massytown; although unfortunately not open to visitors, it appears on some distinguished breakfast menus, including Ballymaloe House, and can be bought in selective outlets, along with their wholemeal flour. Not far along, at Ballynakeera, **Follain PRESERVES** (www.follain.ie) reflect the abundance of the area; renowned for their purity and flavour, they have won numerous awards and are widely available.

North-west Cork is not only highly productive, but fascinating where innovation is concerned so, rather than yield to the magnetic attractions of Kerry or West Cork for now, the curious foodlover may feel drawn

north, to the unspoilt town of **Kanturk**, where people come from far and wide to find an exceptional range of **MEATS** – including **local free range pork,** Aberdeen Angus **beef,** Duhallow **milk lamb** and **free range chicken,** speciality products including **North Cork pancetta** and **Ardrahan cheese & smoky bacon sausages** (and exceptional service) from Jack McCarthy butchers (www.jackmccarthy.ie); McCarthy's - that's Jack, his son Tim who is the fifth generation McCarthy, and their staff) are unique for many reasons, a recent one being the Gold Medal being awarded for their **black pudding** at the annual awards organised by La Confrérie des Chevaliers du Goûte Boudin (the 'Brotherhood of the Knights of the Black Pudding'), the highest award ever received by an Irish entrant to the competition – an achievement which could have something to do with McCarthy's special ingredients of cream and whiskey… all leading to much excitement, including a civic reception in Cork city for visiting members of the ancient brotherhood. Kanturk is also famed for the wonderful **Ardrahan** (www.ardrahancheese.ie), a pungent semi-soft cows' milk **CHEESE**, made nearby by the Burns family, who also produce a milder cheese, **Duhallow,** and the magical **Lullaby Milk,** milked before first light to retain the maximum amount of melatonin which helps the body to regulate sleep-wake patterns naturally; the premier Irish cheese prize at the British Cheese Awards is the Eugene Burns Memorial Trophy, given in honour of Mary Burns' late husband. Another excellent cheese made in the area is **Coolea** (www.cooleacheese.com), a distinctive, slow-maturing Gouda style cheese made to an old Dutch recipe by the Willems family since 1979. Further north in the Charleville area, Tom and Lena Biggane make a hard goats cheese, **Clonmore** – it is mainly available locally and well worth looking out for.

Not far from Kanturk, near Newmarket, John and Olive Forde have effected an agricultural somersault that many would argue is impossible at Knocktullera Farm (+353 (0)29 60079), which they have converted from dairy and now successfully operate as a traditional mixed farm, using working horses, and produce **organic meats** for sale on the farm and at local markets. Nearby, at Mallow, the O'Callaghans of **Longueville House** (www.longuevillehouse.ie) always

Fishing, Longueville House, Co Cork

who relish the wonderful raw materials and rich food culture of the area. The abundance of fresh **FISH & SEAFOOD** is of course a major treat for visitors, with small boats in Baltimore, Schull and Kinsale supplying the markets and restaurants of the area with a wide range including lobster, crab, prawns (langoustines), haddock and cod, monkfish, plaice and black (Dover) sole – plus many other lesser known species which are increasingly being offered by innovative chefs. But the fruits of the sea are far from being the only treats in a region that specialises in high quality small production across a wide range of foods. Helped by the arrival of talented and dedicated small farmers and producers from Britain and Europe who wanted a less commercial life – and, spotting the potential for quality food production, chose to settle here a generation ago - this area was quick to embrace the food revolution that has been taking place in Ireland over the last forty years. It was also one of the first to brand its special qualities – anything sporting the quality **Fuchsia** brand ('a place apart'), whether it be food, craft or hospitality, is now instantly recognisable for its West Cork association.

have something new to offer at their beautiful property, complete with in-house **PRODUCTS OF LAND AND RIVER**: salmon from Ireland's most famous fishing river, the Blackwater, **lamb** from the farm and **Eden apple brandy** from the orchard; William O'Callaghan has a smokehouse for their fish and other foods, he makes seasonal **preserves, patés** and other artisan treats for sale, and he hosts **mushroom** hunts at Longueville each autumn. And there is another highly regarded smokery not far away, the **Old Millbank Smokehouse** (www.goodfoodireland.ie) at Buttevant, where Geraldine Bass produces organic **oak-smoked salmon**.

West Cork

With its spectacularly beautiful coastline, and waters warmed by the Gulf Stream contributing to a uniquely benign climate, West Cork has great appeal as a holiday destination – especially for food lovers,

Ireland's love affair with the **Slow Food** movement began here too, as artisan producers shared its values and lost no time in spreading the word. Many of Ireland's most famous, multi-award-winning **CHEESES** are from the area, and West Cork is at the heart of the renaissance of Irish farmhouse cheese-making. The daddy of them all, Norman and Veronica Steele's washed rind pasteurised whole milk cheese **Milleens** (www.milleenscheese.com) has been made in Eyeries on the mountainous Beara Peninsula since 1976 (and produced commercially since 1978); at Coomkeen, on the Sheep's Head Peninsula, Jeffa Gill has produced her beautiful raw cows' milk semi-soft cheese **Durrus** (www.durruscheese.com) since 1979. Near Schull, at around the same time, Bill Hogan and Sean Ferry of the West Cork Natural Cheese Company (http://www.wcnc.ie) established production of their extraordinary Swiss style thermophilic cheeses, **Gabriel** and **Desmond**, both of which are matured for at least 10 months although they are very different cheeses - Desmond is hard and piquant while the extra hard Gabriel is aromatic. But not all of the 'new traditionalist' cheesemakers were new arrivals however - Tom and Giana Ferguson who produce **Gubbeen** (www.gubbeen.com) are the latest in a long line of dairy farmers near Schull - they started production of their pasteurised cows' milk cheese (which is also available smoked) in 1979 and, like many of the other cheese pioneers, a new generation is now bringing new energy to their enterprises.

The Schull area has also earned a name for **CHARCUTERIE,** with Frank Krawczyk's **West Cork Charcuterie** (notably his delicious salami) appreciated nationally, and Fingal Ferguson's **Gubbeen Smokehouse (**www.gubbeen.com/smokehouse) distinctive products – dry cured bacon, ham, sausages, burgers and salami - now almost as famous as his parents' wonderful cheeses. Some distinguished West Cork **SMOKED FISH** products have attracted unprecedented international praise in recent years: produce from Sally Barnes' renowned **Woodcock Smokery** (www.woodcocksmokery.com) at Castletownshend deals exclusively with wild fish, including very limited amounts of wild salmon – and, in competition with over 4,500 other products, has been a Supreme Award at the Great Taste Awards. The Cresswell family of **Ummera Smokehouse** (www.ummera.com; +353 (0)23 884 6644), near Timoleague, have also garnered awards a-plenty for

their quality smoked foods, notably salmon and eel – and also chicken, bacon and Silver Hill duck; since the ban on drift netting salmon, they use only organic farmed salmon from Clare Island and Bantry Bay.

Away from the coast, between Skibbereen and Macroom, Dunmanway is at the heart of West Cork, especially in sporting terms – it was the birthplace of Sam Maguire (see his statue in the town square). Food-wise it offers something different – at Keenrath, for example, having reintroduced the native rare breed **Dexter cattle** to the area, Paul and Yvonne Johnson of **The Traditional Meat Company** (+353 (0)23 55710/ (0)86 328 9631) now produce **organic BEEF** here. And, high quality **BAKING** is a feature throughout this area – Seymour's (www.seymours.ie) superb handmade **shortbread,** made with local butter in Bandon is an excellent example - and Dunmanway can boast not one but two unusual small bakeries. At **Pâtisserie Régale** (+353 (0)23 885 5344; www.regale.ie), patissier Richard Graham-Leigh makes an exceptional range of confectionery using local, preferably organic, ingredients, and markets his 'Cookies of Character' nationwide; and **The Baking Emporium** (+353 (0)23 884 5260; www.bakingemporiumltd.com), a Fuchsia brand company producing a wide range of quality baking, including bespoke orders.

Gubbeen Cheese

Jeffa Gill, Durrus Cheese

Tradition plays a major role in almost all West Cork food enterprises, even the ones that have a more contemporary or sophisticated face, such as French chocolatier Gwendall Lasserre's **Gwen's Chocolates** (www.gwenschocolate.co) in Schull, perhaps, or Valerie and Alan Kingston's **Glenilen Dairy Products** (www.glenilenfarm.com) which are made at Glenilen Farm, Drimoleague and, although only in full commercial production since 2002, their innovative range of natural dairy products has been a runaway success. An old-fashioned treat hand-made for the sweet-toothed, is **Mella's Fudge** (www.mellasfudge.com); made to the very highest traditional standards at Clonakilty, its fame has spread throughout the land – and Sheridan's Cheesemongers even sell it in London. And then there are the traditional icons without which it would be impossible to imagine eating in West Cork - food such as delicious **Skeaghanore Duck** (+353 (0)28 37428), produced by Eugene and Helena Hickey on their farm near Ballydehob, and the famously grainy **Clonakilty Black Pudding** (www.clonakiltyblackpudding.ie) made by Edward Twomey butchers and now synonymous with the town. Not quite as well known in Ireland, perhaps, but a force to be reckoned with, is **Stauntons** (+353 (0)23 46128) of Timoleague; pork butchers who gave up the shop to concentrate on production of their most popular foods,

brown, black and white puddings, their brown pudding is now one of only a few Irish foods to have gained EU protected status – in this case PGI (Protected Geographical Indication).

And, lest it be forgotten that West Cork is great growing country, with all that that implies, remember that the farmers' markets and shops will be laden with wonderful fresh **FRUIT AND VEGETABLES,** throughout the summer months especially – and, thanks to the distinctly warmer climate and longer growing season down here, there will be some produce not easily available elsewhere in Ireland, such as globe artichokes and less usual herbs. Look out for organic foods from **Devoys Organic Farm** (www.devoysorganicfarm.com), Rosscarbery, who produce a wide range of vegetables, apples, and also free range organic eggs, for sale in local shops, markets and through box delivery; and also organic meat, vegetables, chicken and eggs from **Maughanasilly Organic Farm** (+353 (0)276 6111), at Kealkil, near Bantry, where Martin and Yvonne O'Flynn operate a box delivery scheme. **Peppermint Farm** (www.peppermintfarm.com), near Bantry, produces a wide range of **organic herbs and herbal teas**, available locally and online, and just outside Skibbereen, at Church Cross, the **West Cork Herb Farm** (+353 (0)283 8428) produces both fresh herbs and a range of excellent herbal products, available from the farm and locally; nearby, **Brown Envelope Seeds** (www.brownenvelopeseeds.com) sell their own organic seeds online. Excellent garden centres include **Hosford's** (www.hosfordsgardencentre.ie) at Enniskeane, where there's a restaurant and market (Sunday, monthly), and **Fruit Hill Farm** (www.fruithillfarm.com) near Bantry, which offers all the gear that organic gardeners need online. And, with all that luscious growing going on, there's plenty of nectar for Tim Rowe's bees at **Rose Hives** (www.beekeepinginireland.com/honey), Ballylickey; the honey is available locally and Tim also sells beeswax and beehives – and looks after both the bees and poultry at Bantry House, where he gives beekeeping and poultry keeping classes as part of the **Bantry House Country Courses** (bantryhousecountrycourses.com), which include vegetable growing, willow basketry and unusual skills such as seed saving and learning how to use the working horses, Winnie and Henry. The courses are the first step in a plan to re-build the working farm at Bantry House - fascinating stuff.

East Cork

East Cork shares many of the specialities found elsewhere in the county – notably wonderful **FISH** coming in to Ballycotton and Youghal harbours, and excellent **seafood products** from companies like **William Carr & Sons Ltd** (www.wmcarr.com; +353 (0)58 56216) at Curraglass and **Yawl Bay Seafoods** (www.yawlbayseafood.ie) in Youghal, as well as superb smoked fish from craft smokers like Frank Hederman at **Belvelly Smokehouse** (www.frankhederman.com) Cobh, and **Bill Casey** (+353 (0)21 464 6955) at **Casey's Smokehouse** in Shanagarry.

The rich pastures of East Cork produce wonderful vegetables (Ballycotton potatoes are held in especially high esteem) and excellent **MEATS** and **POULTRY** – beef and lamb, and also free range pork at Noreen and Martin Conroy's **Woodside Farm**, Ballincurrig (www.woodsidefarm.ie) and Ballymaloe Cookery School, and wonderful organic poultry from **JJ and Dan Aherne** (+353 (0)21 463 1058), Midleton. Where fruit and vegetables thrive, the bees will follow and, among the best of this local produce, you will find Leslie Kingston's **Lislanley Honey** (+353 (0)21 465 2627) from Cloyne, and **HONEY** produced near Midleton by Michael Woulfe of **Glenamore Apiaries** (+353 (0)21 463 1011), who also teaches the art of beekeeping.

The area also has its fair share of very good **CHEESE** – notable examples, both near Cork city, are the excellent, long-established **Ardsallagh Goats Cheese** www.ardsallaghgoats.co) at Carrigtwohill, and the aged **Hegarty Farmhouse Cheddar** made by Dan Hegarty of Whitechurch Foods Watergrasshill. At Cobh, Kevin & Deirdre Hilliard of **The Just Food Company** (www.jusstfood.ie) supply their delicious handmade organic dishes, notably **SOUPS**, to selected shops and restaurants.

In North-East Cork the Green family is doing interesting things at the lovely Ballyvolane House (www.ballyvolanehouse.ie) near Fermoy; renowned for its fishing, beautiful gardens and arboretum, they now also make a range of natural products – notably **preserves and cordials** based on fruit from their walled gardens – which are for sale at the house and from their restaurant, O'Brien Chop House, in Lismore, West Waterford. And, in a dynamic combination of cultural traditions, Justin Green and Arun Kapil of **Green Saffron Spices** (www.greensaffron.com) in Midleton regularly work together to bring special culinary (and perhaps theatrical) events to Ballyvolane House and O'Brien Chop House - sometimes with Cormac O'Dwyer and Tom Dalton's Dungarvan Brewing Company involved too, which makes for a heady mix. Also of note in the Fermoy area is Frank and Gudrun Shinnick's **Fermoy Natural Cheese Company** (+353 (0)25 31310; www.irishcheese.ie) range of five cows' milk cheeses, from varying from soft to mature hard cheeses; and, on a bigger scale, the **Silver Pail Dairy** (+353 (0)25 31466; www.silverpail.com) which includes some excellent premium ice creams in their product range.

But the food enterprise that has become synonymous with East Cork, and indeed with Ireland, is based at Shanagarry. While West Cork may be the glamorous front runner in Ireland's artisan food stakes – and the new wave of idealistic small holding settlers in the 1970s was undoubtedly a catalyst for major change - the deeper roots of the current culinary revolution are in the rich farmland of East Cork, where the doyenne of Irish food, Myrtle Allen, began it all when she and her husband, the late Ivan Allen, opened The Yeats Room restaurant at **Ballymaloe House** in 1964. Since then, the achievements of Myrtle herself, her daughter-in-law Darina Allen at Ballymaloe Cookery School, and numerous other members of the family have had far-reaching effects on attitudes to food and food production throughout the country (and beyond). Enterprises broadly under the Ballymaloe umbrella range from the **farming** which remains central to the family ethos, and **Ballymaloe Cookery School** (www.cookingisfun.ie) which is at the centre

of an organic farm, to the shops at both house and school, the café, the **Cully & Sully** (www.cullyandsully.com) ready meals and soups, the products made under the brand **Ballymaloe Country Relish** (www.ballymaloecountryrelish.ie), and of course Rachel Allen's popular TV shows. Although not directly connected to Ballymaloe, Ireland's first farmers' market was in nearby Midleton, and Darina Allen's involvement from the outset is no doubt one of the reasons for its outstanding success (it is now used as a model for aspiring marketeers); she has also supported key farmers' markets in other areas, including Temple Bar Market, in Dublin, and St George's Market in Belfast. The wonder of Ballymaloe is that, despite the numerous related businesses and the extended family now involved, they have managed to stay true to their philosophy and retain a genuine simplicity, which is both inspiring and relaxing for visitors – and totally in tune with the local environment. Some achievement.

Mrs. Myrtle Allen

The Gate House, Ballymaloe, Co. Cork

Four of the Best...

CÁIS - The Association Of Irish Farmhouse Cheesemakers

Cheesemaking was once an important part of everyday life in Ireland but fell into decline due to historical factors, including the 19th century demand for butter, and original recipes were lost. Then, after over a quarter of a century when a cheddar-style factory product was virtually the only cheese made in Ireland, a renaissance began in the 1970s and it was the beginning of a new era, not only for cheese, but for all Irish artisan food production. The story begins in West Cork, with an influx of creative people who settled here seeking a different life, and is well documented. It starts with Milleens, the powerfully territorial cheese that Veronica and Norman Steele first made on their small farm at Eyeries on the Beara Peninsula in 1976. Others soon followed, leading to the formation of the Irish Farmhouse Cheesemakers Association (Cáis) in 1983. Founding members included giants of the farmhouse cheese movement like the Maher family who produce the classic camembert style Cooleeney in Tipperary, and the Berridge family of Co Wexford who make the iconic hexagonal camembert style Carrigbyrne. Of the original Cáis members, no less than five are in West Cork and, having introduced new cheese traditions to replace forgotten Irish recipes, still produce some of the very best artisan cheeses made in Ireland today. They include the Steele family, of course, who still make Milleens; the Willems family (Coolea); Jeffa Gill (Durrus); Bill Hogan and Sean Ferry (Gabriel and Desmond) and Tom and Giana Ferguson (Gubbeen). Today Cáis has over thirty members and represents one of the most vibrant aspects of the new Irish food culture - and, with outstanding results in international competition, the focus has progressed from its initial educational purpose to mutual support and the successful marketing of these wonderful, passionately personal, and territorial cheeses.

(www.irishcheese.ie)

Glenilen Farm Dairy Products

Scenically situated on the River Ilen (after which the farm takes its name), Alan and Valerie Kingston's small West Cork dairy farm has been in Alan's family for generations. In 1997 Valerie started using the creamy milk to make cheesecakes to sell at Bantry Country Market, and they were so popular that her hobby quickly grew into a business - and the Kingstons have since earned national recognition for their range of Glenilen Farm Dairy Products. It's a family affair, with Alan in charge of milk production and Valerie overseeing production of a growing range of excellent handmade products which includes clotted cream, double cream, low fat cream cheese (crème fraîche and quark) and yoghurts - including a lovely variety layered with fresh fruit compôte, in classy glass jars. There are also fresh desserts in the range (including a cream and fruit mousse and four varieties of cheesecake) and - most interestingly given this region's proud history of quality butter - farmhouse butter, which is made in the traditional manner, using ripened raw milk. These fresh artisan products are made without preservatives, and delivered directly to shops and restaurants for faster distribution - well worth looking out for, in the area and beyond.

Gurteeniher Drimoleague Co Cork
(+353 (0)28 3117 www.glenilen.com)

Arbutus Breads

Gubbeen Farmhouse Products

When Declan Ryan sold the legendary Arbutus Lodge Hotel in Cork city in 1999, it was obvious that retirement would not suit him. So, inspired by breads he had enjoyed in America and France, Declan set about learning the art of sourdough baking from some of the best bakers in France, then he set up a little artisan bakery in his two car garage. Delivery was from the back of his jeep in the early days, and his first customers were Isabel Sheridan (On the Pig's Back, English Market) and his brother Michael, of Isaacs Restaurant, both still customers today. Now - still using only the finest ingredients and traditional, slow methods - he operates from new premises where, together with his son Darragh and an international crew of five full time bakers, he produces a range of over two dozen speciality breads. They come in varying shapes and sizes, using different flours and flavourings (if any), but all are made to the same exacting standard. Most - including a crusty Cork Beer Bread - are sourdough, but you'll also find Irish specialities among them: a white West Cork soda bread, for example, and a nutty brown version including Macroom pinhead oatmeal - the recipe is on their website and it's available as Granny Ryan's Soda Bread Mix too, to buy from O'Keeffe's and Nash 19 in Cork, and farmers' markets (or order it by email through the site). Arbutus Breads are now distributed to selected outlets nationwide, and they run baking courses too.

Unit 2B Mayfield Industrial Estate Mayfield Cork.
E: info@arbutusbread.com www.arbutusbread.com

Tom and Giana Ferguson are the fifth generation to care for this beautifully located family dairy farm and, inspired by Giana's experience of continental cheeses when growing up in Spain and France, they wasted no time before experimenting with making fresh cheeses. Then, in 1979, this pioneering couple began production of one of Ireland's best-loved cheese, the beautiful semi-soft Gubbeen - which they still make, and is now available both plain and smoked. Today, Gubbeen is a more complex family affair and, while not organic, every aspect of their lives is informed by a philosophy that reflects a sense of stewardship and care for the land, their animals and the growing range of products that they make. Their son, Fingal, now operates another successful business on the premises, producing a much-admired range of smoked meats, hams, rashers, sausages and salamis, while their daughter Clovisse produces organic vegetables and herbs for supply to local restaurants and shops - and Fingal also uses her herbs in his traditional cures. Their mainly pasture-fed cows are a 'cheesemakers' herd' of several breeds - including the black Kerry Cow - which bring different qualities to the milk, and the dairy and pork businesses are interdependent, the pigs enjoying a fine sea view from their large straw-filled pens, where their wholesome diet includes whey remaining from the cheese-making process. It is a satisfying combination and the products made by this dedicated family are consistently outstanding - a taste of Ireland's best.

Gubbeen House Schull Co Cork (www.gubbeen.com)
Gubbeen Cheese: +353 (0)28 28231
Gubbeen Smoke House: +353 (0)28 27824

The English Market, Cork

Where to Buy

the Special Foods of Cork...

A guide to food shops, markets, farm shops, local stores and internet suppliers

Cork City

THE ENGLISH MARKET

(+353 (0)21 427 4407 www.corkenglishmarket.ie). Ireland's most famous speciality food market, this municipal covered market occupies a large site between GRAND PARADE and PATRICK STREET. Renowned for the diversity of its produce, it supplies the city's leading restaurants and is a favourite shopping destination for both local residents and visitors. Today the mixture of stalls may be becoming much more cosmopolitan (full details of current stallholders are given on their excellent website), but for a flavour of this magnificent shopping destination, consider just a few:

K O'Connell Fishmongers 13-20 Grand Parade Market Grand Parade Cork *(+353 (0)21 4276380 www.koconnellsfish.com).* O'Connell's renowned fish stall began life over 40 years ago, started by the late Kay O'Connell, mother of Paul and Pat, who run it today. O'Connell's stall stretches to an impressive eighty feet in length offering a vast range of fresh whitefish and shellfish with live lobster, crab and oysters available from a tank in-store. They have recently added a seafood delicatessen, which brings a contemporary dimension to the business.

On The Pigs Back Stall 11 The English Market Patricks Street Cork *(+353 (0) 21 4270232; www.onthepigsback.ie).* French born Isabel Sheridan has been a key figure at the English Market for many years – and she has earned a national reputation, both for the quality of her own charcuterie – notably her patés and terrines - and for the range of Irish and French artisan foods that she has collected to sell alongside them, including Declan Ryan's Arbutus breads, the best farmhouse cheeses, Caherbeg free range pork products, Rosscarbery sausages, Krawczyk's products, Gubbeen Smokehouse products and many more. [Now also at: Unit 26 St Patrick's Mill Douglas Co Cork; +353 (0)21 4617832 (with café)].

K. Noonan Pork & Bacon 21 Grand Parade Market Cork *(+353 (0)87 2971895).* Kathleen Noonan first took a stall in the Market in 1955 and is now semi-retired, so her daughter Pauline has taken up the baton, selling traditional pork

products. It is the only stall dealing exclusively in pig meat – crubeens (trotters or pigs feet), pig's tails, bodice, skirts, kidneys, loin bones, knuckles, hocks as well as more familiar cuts like rashers and collar bacon.

The Meat Centre Stall 16 Aisle 1 The English Market Cork One of the great characters of the Market, Ken Barrett has held a stall since 1980 and he farms the cattle, sheep and pigs that are butchered here, so the food chain is as short as it gets. As well as all the regular cuts, you'll find the old traditional ones such as bodice, sheeps' tongue and pickled pigs head – maybe also mutton, which is hard to find these days.

The Real Olive Company The English Market *(www.therealoliveco.com)* Toby Simmonds is a legend at The English Market and his Real Olive Company – which he started in 1994 to provide best in olives, oils, and Mediterranean fare at a time when choice in Ireland was limited - has become a popular fixture at famers' markets around the country too. The range has grown a lot, but the underlying principles of choice and quality remain in place.

The Chocolate Shop The English Market *(+353 (0)21 425 4448 www.chocolate.ie)* Nowhere is the new Irish passion for quality chocolate better provided for than in Cork. This specialist shop is not affiliated to any manufacturer and sells an exceptional range of the best artisan Irish chocolates and famous brands from abroad, including organic, diabetic and gluten-free chocolate, cooking and drinking chocolates and other speciality confectionery such as the Pandora Bell lollipops - and the famous Hadji Bey's Turkish Delight (www.hadjibey.ie).

Cinnamon Cottage Monastery Road Rochestown CORK *(+353 (0)21 489 4922).* Carol and Kieran Murphy make delicious things to go for their deli – try the peppered beef in Murphy's stout – and offer a catering service too.

Eve's Chocolate Shop Dennehy's Cross CORK *(+353 (0)21 434 7781 www.evechocolates.ie).* Singled out for an Irish Food Writers' Guild Chocolate Lovers' award, Eve St

Simon & Patrick O'Flynn

Leger's very special shop near University College Cork may be a little out of the way, but her wide range of exquisite artisan treats makes it 'worth a detour' for chocoholics. The distinctive black and white boxes are also easy to spot in other shops.

O'Conaill's Chocolates French Church Street CORK. This is the main retail outlet for these well known hand made chocolates, which are made by third generation chocolatiers in Carrigaline (+353 (0)21 437 3407), just south of Cork city. Only the highest quality ingredients are used, and it shows. Products include diabetic chocolate and (many people's favourite) premium hot chocolates, which is also on hand to warm shoppers at the English Market and local farmers' markets.

O'Flynn's Butchers Marlborough Street CORK (+353 (0)21 427 5685). Brothers Simon and Patrick O'Flynn run this legendary butchers shop a block away from the English Market; a very traditional outfit, known for quality meats and skilled butchering, their spiced beef is a speciality.

O'Keeffe's Shop St Lukes Cross Montenotte CORK (+353 (0)21 450 2010 www.okeeffes-shop.ie). Cork food-lovers head to this long-established store just a short distance from

the city centre for its treasure trove of local artisan foods - including Arbutus breads (and Granny Ryan's Soda Bread Mix), Belvelly Smokehouse fish, Caherbeg free range pork, Glenilen dairy products and cheeses (supplied by On The Pig's Back); excellent deli, and wines too. Take a moment to browse their product range **online** – then build a visit into your itinerary when visiting Cork.

Quay Co-op Sullivan's Quay CORK (+353 (0)21 431 7660 www.quaycoop.com). Founded as a radical alternative community project in 1982, Cork's original organic food store, in-house bakery and vegetarian restaurant is more rounded now but has retained its character.

Petits Fours at Sugar Café Washington Street CORK (+353 (0)21 480 6530 www.petitsfours.ie). Delectable classic French patisserie is sold at this traditional French café, including products such as beautiful designer macaroons by up and coming young French-trained patissière, Iseult Janssens, from her Co Dublin company, The Cake Stand. Patisserie classes also offered.

CORK CITY AREA

The Pavilion Garden Centre & Earthly Delights Café
BALLYGARVAN *(+353 (0)21 488 8134 www.atthepavilion.ie)*.
Attractive well run garden centre, with good home bakes (eat
in or take home), homewares and cookbooks.

Delicious BALLINCOLLIG *(+353 (0)21 487 5780*
www.delicious.ie). This well-named enterprise produces hand
made gluten - and wheat-free breads and cakes. **Online shop**.

Healy's Honey Maglin BALLINCOLLIG *(+353 (0)21 487 1258*
www.healyshoney.ie). A keen beekeeper, Patrick Healy,
developed a business from his hobby when he established this
company in the 1970s, and it is now a successful family-run
enterprise producing, purchasing and distributing honey,
which is widely available from independent stores and
supermarkets.

Ó Crualaoí Butchers BALLINCOLLIG *(www.ocrualaoi.com)*.
Family butchers in business since 1957 and now with
branches at Fermoy and Wilton Shopping Centre, Cork.
Selling 'real food' is the mission, including aged beef,
sourced directly from local farmers.

The Good Fish Company CARRIGALINE
(+353 (0)21 437 3917 www.goodfish.ie) Denis Good has been
processing and wholesaling seafood in Carrigaline for many
years. This recently constructed outlet offers a wide range of
fresh whitefish and shellfish products with live lobster and
crab available from a tank in-store. Also at: Ballincollig.

Coolea Cheese

North Cork

Jack McCarthy Butchers KANTURK *(+353 (0)29 50178*
www.jackmccarthy.ie). One of Ireland's most famous butchers;
not only do Jack and Tim McCarthy stock an exceptional
range of fantastic meats, including local free range pork,
Aberdeen Angus beef, Duhallow milk lamb and free range
chicken, but you'll also find speciality products including
spiced beef, air-dried beef and Ardrahan cheese & smoky
bacon sausages here – plus their amazingly successful black
pudding, which has earned Gold Medal approval from like-
minded butchers in Normandy, no less. And, bang on the
money commercially too, they have an excellent **online shop**;
delivery anywhere in Ireland, free on orders over a fixed limit.

Coolea Farmhouse Cheese Coolea MACROOM
(+353(0)2645204 www.cooleacheese.com). The Willems family's
great mature gouda-style cheese is widely distributed. Visitors
welcome weekdays 8-5.30, except bank hols.

Knocktullera Farm Produce NEWMARKET
(+353 (0)29 60079). John and Olive Forde's organic meats are
produced on a mixed farm, using working horses, and sold
either directly from the farm or from Killavullen Farmers'
Market at the Nano Nagle Centre.

The Secret Garden Centre Aghaneenagh NEWMARKET
(+353 (0)29 60084 www.thesecretgardener.com). Unusual small
plant-focused eco-friendly garden centre, with local foods
(their own honey, jams, preserves) on sale and local baking
served in the little café.

West Cork

Hudsons BALLYDEHOB *(+353 (0)28 37565)*. Long
established store offering a good range of organic wholefoods,
home baking, local produce; also a small vegetarian café.

West Cork Gourmet Store BALLYDEHOB
(+353 (0)28 27613). Joanne Cassidy stocks an eclectic range
of food and food/wine related items, and tempting daytime
food, including cream teas.

Mannings Emporium BALLYLICKEY near Bantry
(www.goodfoodireland.ie). Whether to pick up the morning
newspaper or drop in for something much tastier, Val
Manning's roadside aladdin's cave of good things is not a

place to pass by. A supporter of local West Cork artisan producer for many years, Val Manning is rightly credited with playing an important part in making the food revolution happen - any food lover visiting the area should allow time for a browse here.

Rory Conner Knives BALLYLICKEY near Bantry *(+353 (0)27 50032 www.roryconnerknives.com)*. Bespoke knives and associated services from a master craftsman.

URRU McSwiney Quay BANDON *(+353 (0)23 885 4731 www.urru.ie)*. A culinary icon of West Cork, nobody passes Bandon without a visit to this smartly irresistible artisan food, wine, book and kitchenware shop; small in-store café too.

Sea Urchins

Central Fish Market New Street BANTRY *(+353 (0)27 53714 www.seafoodcircle.ie)*. Colman Keohane's well stocked shop offers a large range of whitefish and shellfish both fresh and frozen with live lobster available from a tank in-store; above it, The Fish Kitchen restaurant puts the produce to good use for hungry customers.

Fruit Hill Farm BANTRY *(www.fruithillfarm.com)*. **Online** organic garden supply shop. Visits by appointment only (+353 (0)27 50710, Mon-Fri 9-4).

Organico Glengarriff Road BANTRY *(+353 (0)27 51391 www.organico.ie)*. Sisters Hannah and Rachel Dare run this artisan bakery and health food shop; Rachel is a Ballymaloe-trained cook and they have a lovely café upstairs.

Bantry Market The Square BANTRY. This is one of the best in the county and draws shoppers from a wide area every Friday, beginning early; all the area's best produce is to be found here, and much more besides.

The Stuffed Olive New Street BANTRY *(+353 (0)27 55883)*. Excellent specialist foodstore and café.

Taste CASTLETOWNBERE *(+353 (0)27 71842)*. In a scenic area without many places to stop for a bite, this good shop selling artisan deli and picnic food meets the need perfectly.

Scallys SuperValu Bridge Cork Road CLONAKILTY *(+353 (0)23 883 3088 www.supervaluclon.ie)*. One of five Cork SuperValu stores to be awarded Seafood Counter membership in the BIM Seafood Circle (www.bim.ie), Scallys has a strong focus on regional speciality foods, including a great range of fresh fish and shellfish landed by West Cork fishermen.

Edward Twomey Pearse Street CLONAKILTY *(+353 (0)23 883 3365 www.clonakiltyblackpudding.ie)*. Renowned for making their deliciously dark and grainy Clonakilty Black Pudding famous worldwide, this fine traditional butchers shop does everything else well too.

Durrus Farmhouse Cheese Coomkeen DURRUS near Bantry *(+353 (0)27 61100 www.durruscheese.com)*. Jeffa Gill welcomes visitors to her dairy in the quiet Coomkeen Valley on the Sheeps Head Peninsula (open 'nearly every day', 9am to 3pm; please call ahead on Sundays). Durrus Farmhouse Cheese tastings are available and, if you'd like to buy some, it is best to drop by between 9am and 11am - or after 1.30pm. Also freshly laid free range eggs for sale.

Milleens EYERIES Beara *(+353 (0)27 74079 www.milleenscheese.com)*. Here on their farm in a remote and beautiful location, Norman, Veronica and Quinlan Steele produce the iconic Milleens cheese – the first of the new wave of Irish farmhouse cheeses, which they first introduced to the market in 1978.

Fishy Fishy Café @ The Gourmet Store Guardwell KINSALE *(+353 (0)21 477 4453 www.fishyfishy.ie)*. There are two sides to Martin and Marie Shanahan's remarkable seafood operation: the smart new restaurant and the original Fishy Fishy premises nearby. This shop still sells the freshest and best of locally caught seafood prepared for cooking, seafood deli - and excellent traditional fish & chips in the more recently opened **Fishy Fishy Chippie**.

Quay Food Company Market Quay KINSALE *(+353 (0)21 477 4000 www.quayfood.com)*. Since 1996, David and Laura Peare's wholefood shop and deli near the Tourist Office has long been the perfect place to pick up an artisan picnic (made to order), or for self-catering visitors to stock up with local goodies.

Tom's Artisan Bakery Main Street KINSALE *(+353 (0)21 477 3561)*. Irresistible artisan breads and pasteries. Also sells at Ballincollig market.

Devoys Organic Farm ROSSCARBERY *(+353 (0)23 8848763 www.devoysorganicfarm.com)*. Look out for John and Sara Devoy's organic vegetables, fruit and eggs at farmers' markets and local shops; box delivery available.

Gubbeen Farmhouse Products Gubbeen House SCHULL *(Cheese:+353 (0)28 28231 Smoke House: +353 (0)28 27824 www.gubbeen.com)*. Although not generally open to visitors, it is sometimes possible to make appointments, and both the cheeses and Fingal Ferguson's smoked products are widely distributed and can always be found at Schull, Skibbereen, Bantry and Mahon Point farmers' markets. They also offer beautiful hampers – including, for example, Gubbeen cheeses, smoked salami, their own oatcakes and chutney – all packed in lovely hand painted wooden trays, for delivery by courier or collection from selected farmers' markets; order by phone or email cheese@gubbeen.com.

Gwen's Chocolates SCHULL *(+353 (0)28 27853 www.gwenschocolate.com)*. French chocolatier Gwendall Lasserre sells exquisite chocolates and patisserie at his gorgeous shop on the main street; also **online sales**.

Brown Envelope Seed Co Ardagh Church Cross SKIBBEREEN *(+353 (0)28 38184 www.brownenvelopeseeds.com)*. Madeline McKeever, who is also involved in Irish Seed Savers, grows her own organic vegetable, herb and edible flower seeds on her West Cork farm. Events are occasionally held on the farm, where they sometimes have their own Ardagh beef for sale. Good **online shop** for seeds.

Fields SuperValu Main Street SKIBBEREEN *(+353 (0)28 21400)*. No ordinary supermarket - central to the community and supportive of local suppliers, Fields is a must-visit shop when in West Cork.

Ummera Smokehouse Inchybridge TIMOLEAGUE *(+353 (0)23 884 6644 www.ummera.com)*. Superb smoked speciality foods, notably eel (when available) and organic salmon. Visitors welcome, also **online sales**.

The Fish Shop Main Street UNION HALL *(+353 (0)28 33818 www.irishprawns.com)*. At this factory outlet overlooking the beautiful fishing harbour of Union Hall - one of Ireland's main fishing ports - Peter Deasy stocks a vast range of fish and shellfish straight from the boats. Live shellfish available from a tank in-store.

East Cork

Midleton Distillery

Belvelly Smokehouse COBH *(+353 (0)21 481 1089 www.frankhederman.com)*. Frank Hederman is well known at farmers' markets, notably Midleton and Cobh, and his internationally renowned produce from Ireland's oldest smokery is also available by mail order and from their shop, which is well signed on the main Cobh road (phone for opening hours).

Rupert's Farm LADYSBRIDGE *(+353 (0)86 168 5312 www.rupertsfarm.com)*. Kitchen produce and hops grown for their own brewery in the making are special features at this organic farm – watch their website for news of brewery developments… visitors welcome by arrangement. Sells at Midleton (Thu) and Mahon Point markets.

Dan Ahern Organic Chickens Ballysimon Organic Farm MIDLETON *(+353 (0)21 4631058 / (0)86 1659258)* Dan and Anne Ahern are old hands at Midleton Market, where they sell their renowned organic chickens, and also tender young grass-fed beef, which is hung for three weeks.

Ballycotton Seafood Main Street MIDLETON *(+353 (0)21 461 3122 www.ballycottonseafood.ie)*. Second generation husband and wife team, Adrian and Diane Walsh, manage this famous company. Many products are made with fresh fish caught by their own boats landing into Ballycotton and processed in the company facility in Garryvoe near Ballycotton. Also at: The English Market, Cork.

Green Saffron Spices Unit 16 Knockgriffin MIDLETON *(+353 (0)21 463 7960 www.greensaffron.com)*. Family connections in India source top quality, ultra-fresh spices for Arun Kapil and his Green Saffron team, who then distribute them nationally, use them for their in-house curry nights (see website) and do things which make them peculiarly Irish – eg creating a Christmas mixed spice blend for their Christmas puddings, (soaked for 60 hours in Beamish stout, Jameson whiskey etc etc…) to make puddings that are accurately described as having "funky twist". For stockists of spices and puddings, see greensaffron.com; also by mail order (an **online shop** is planned).

The Farmgate Coolbawn Court MIDLETON *(+353 (0)21 463 2771)*. Sisters Maróg O'Brien and Kay Harte run, respectively, The Farmgate and The Farmgate Café (English Market, Cork). Maróg's quirky country store and restaurant has been bringing single-minded foodies to Midleton for many years; the shop – which you have to pass through to reach the restaurant at the back – is laden down with good things, both freshly made on the premises and from the locality (and beyond). Unique and not to be missed.

The Jameson Experience Midleton MIDLETON *(www.jamesonwhiskey.com)*. Dating back to 1780, a tour of the old distillery is worthwhile; you can, among many other interesting things, see the world's biggest pot still, take part in a whiskey tasting - and, perhaps, buy a bottle of the unique Midleton Very Rare to take home. (You can have a bite to eat here too.)

Midleton Farmers' Market MIDLETON *(www.midletonfarmersmarket.com)*. This market merits special mention. Over the last decade or so many dozens of farmers' markets have sprung up all over Ireland; the standard varies, but the Midleton market (which was among the first) has set a benchmark, genuinely bringing together the produce and people of the area with benefits to the East Cork community. Its success can be judged by the fact that there was demand for a second day, so Midleton recently became the first Irish town to host a farmers' market twice weekly.

The Ballymaloe Shop SHANAGARRY *(www.ballymaloe.ie)* Ballymaloe is known for a variety of enterprises, and many visitors come especially to browse the always-tempting selection of kitchenware, cookbooks, clothing, crafts and even hand-made furniture in Wendy Whelan's delightful shop. No **online sales**, but a worldwide mailing service is available. And there's good food to be had too (of course), in the 'Café at the end of the shop'. Well worth a journey – and, refreshed, you can proceed to **Ballymaloe Cookery School & Gardens** Kinoith (www.cookingisfun.ie), where the **Farm Shop** sells organic treats including their own free range pork (fresh and frozen); a small selection of gift items is also available **online**.

Yawl Bay Seafoods Ltd Foxhole Industrial Estate YOUGHAL *(+353 (0)24 92290 www.yawlbayseafood.ie)*. The Browne family sells home-smoked salmon and a wide selection of other fish and shell fist from around the Irish coast.

The Farmgate

Ballymaloe Cookery School

Ireland South-West: Cork Food Markets

For further information on Farmers Markets throughout Ireland
www.bordbia.ie • www.irishfarmersmarkets.ie

CORK CITY MARKETS:

English Market *(www.corkenglishmarket.ie)* Princes Street & Grand Parade. Mon-Sat 8-6.

Bishopstown Farmers Market Dunnes Stores Bishopstown Court Thu 10-2.

Coal Quay Farmer's Market Cornmarket Street. Sat 9-3.

Mahon Point Farmers' Market *(www.mahonpointsc.ie)* West Entrance Mahon Point Shopping Centre. Thur 10-2. The location of Cork's largest, best attended and smartly organised farmers'market is not central, but worth the effort to see the best the area has to offer.

Douglas Farmers' Market *(www.douglasfarmersmarket.com)* Grounds of Douglas Community Centre. Sat 9.30-2.

Douglas Food Market Douglas Court Shopping Centre. Sat 9.30-2

East Douglas Village Market Fri 10-2.

CORK CITY AREA MARKETS:

Ballincollig Farmers' Market Ballincollig Shopping Centre. Wed 10-2.30.

Blackrock Village Farmers' Market Car park, Sun 10-2.

Carrigaline Country Market Crosshaven Road. Fri from 9.30.

Crosshaven Farmers' Market Village Square. Sat 10-2.

NORTH CORK

Duhallow Farmers Market Thu & Sat 10.30-1.30.

Kanturk Food Market behind Supervalu Kanturk. Thu & Sat, 10.30-1.

Mallow Farmers' Market Home Car Park Mallow. Fri 10-2.

Kilavullen Farmers Market Nano Nagle Centre. Every 2nd Sat 10.30-1.

WEST CORK

Ballygarvan Farmers' Market Paddos Bar Ballygarvan. Sat 10-3.

Bandon Farmers' Market Old Market Yard behind Spar. Sat 9-2

Hosfords Garden Centre Market Bandon Area (Clonakilty Rd (N71), 8 km west of Bandon). Apr-Sep, 1st Sun 12-5.

Bantry Market every Friday (extended market last Fri of month). From early morning.

EAST CORK

Cobh Farmers' Market seafront. Fri 10-1

Midleton Farmers' Market Hospital Road. Sat 10-1.30

Midleton Tuesday Farmers' Market outside 4Home superstores. Tue 10-2

Longueville House, Co Cork

Eat & Stay

Cork City

Café Paradiso

Paradise indeed for vegetarians, but even the most committed carnivores relish every mouthful of Denis Cotter's exciting mainstream vegetarian cooking at this acclaimed restaurant. Try it at home with his books, "Café Paradiso Cookbook" among them.

16 Lancaster Quay Western Road Cork Co Cork
+353 (0)21 427 7939; www.cafeparadiso.ie

Farmgate Café

Sister to the **Farmgate Country Store and Restaurant** in Midleton (+353 (0)21 427 8134), Kay Harte's lively daytime restaurant located in the gallery above the English Market shares the same commitment to serving fresh, local food – and it doesn't come fresher or more local than this. They offer regional dishes based on market produce, and lesser known foods such as corned mutton alongside famous old Cork ones with a special market connection, like tripe & drisheen and corned beef & champ with green cabbage. Great value for money too.

English Market Cork +353 (0)21 427 8134

Isaacs Restaurant

Run by Michael and Catherine Ryan, together with partner/head chef Canice Sharkey, since 1992 - when the only choice was between fine dining and fast food. In a quiet, low-key way, this large, atmospheric and informal modern restaurant has played a leading role in Ireland's culinary revolution, offering an original blend of Irish and international themes, quality food and good value. And, whether for lunch or dinner, a visit here is always fun.

48 MacCurtain Street Cork +353 (0)21 450 3805

Jacques Restaurant

An integral part of Cork life since 1982, many would cite sisters Eithne and Jacqueline Barry's restaurant as their favourite in the city. Together with Eileen Carey, who has been in the kitchen with Jacque Barry since 1986, they've always valued the provenance and quality of ingredients above all. Long before it was fashionable to do so, their menus were based on carefully sourced ingredients from a network of local suppliers built up over many years, and Jacque is now closely involved with the Cork Slow Food Convivium. Freshness, simplicity, value – happy customers.

Phoenix Street Cork Co Cork
+353 (0)21 427 7387 www.jacquesrestaurant.ie

North Cork

❧ Longueville House

Overlooking the River Blackwater, the location of the O'Callaghan family's estate is truly lovely. Home- and locally-produced food is at the heart of all of owner William O'Callaghan's cooking, including an artisan product range made for sale. The river, farm and garden supply fresh salmon in season, the famous Longueville lamb, all the fruit and vegetables; in autumn, mushroom hunts yield an abundance of fungi. Extensive orchards supply fresh apple juice – and they even make their own apple brandy, aptly named 'Eden'.

MALLOW Co Cork +353 (0)22 47156;
www.longuevillehouse.ie

O'Callaghan's Delicatessen, Bakery & Café

The ideal place to break a journey, O'Callaghans offers tasty fare for a snack or full meal in the café. And stock up here with delicious home-baked breads and cakes, home-made jams and chutneys from their impressive deli and bakery – includes a home-made gluten free range.

19/20 Lower Cork Street MITCHELSTOWN Co Cork
+353(0)25 24657 www.ocallaghans.ie

West Cork

Glebe House Gardens

The café at Jean and Peter Perry's wonderful gardens just outside Baltimore is destination in its own right, with a growing fan base. Unpretentious, sensibly short, menus use organically grown ingredients from the garden and from named local craft suppliers, and everything is cooked (to order) to a very high standard indeed. Prices are very fair - and they generously allow you to bring your own picnic too, if preferred. Magic.

Glebe Gardens BALTIMORE Co Cork
+353 (0)28 20232 www.glebegardens.com

The Poachers Inn

Barry and Catherine McLaughlin's roadside bar and restaurant just outside Bandon may look unremarkable, but Barry brought to his own kitchen valuable experience gained at two of the finest restaurants in an area well known for great food - Fishy Fishy Café and Casino House. Here he turns out wonderfully flavourful dishes, based on fresh local seafood (from Castletownbere), and this dedicated couple have earned a great reputation well beyond locality, for their fine food and hospitality.

Clonakilty Road BANDON Co Cork
+353 (0)23 41159 www.poachersinnbandon.com

Mary Ann's Bar & Restaurant

If they never served a bite at Fergus and Patricia O'Mahony's much-loved old pub, the faithful would still flock to soak up the atmosphere – but they do serve food, local seafood to be precise, and it is superb. The wide choice offered in the bar as well as the

restaurant includes daily blackboard specials, which may offer real treats like lobster thermidor or lobster mayonnaise. Modern gastro-pubs eat your heart out!

CASTLETOWNSHEND Skibbereen Co Cork
+353 (0)28 36146 www.maryannsbarrestaurant.com

Deasy's Harbour Bar & Seafood Restaurant

Just across the road from the water in the pretty village of Ring, this traditional bar overlooking Clonakilty Bay enjoys a sea view and has plenty of local and nautical memorabilia to make an atmospheric setting for fine seafood. Menus may give few clues to house or local specialities, but you'll find a wide range of seafood, including less usual varieties such as shark as well as fairly classic prime fish dishes - and good cooking is also seen in tasty vegetables and delicious desserts, and details like lovely breads and thoughtful presentation.

Ring Village CLONAKILTY Co Cork +353 (0)23 35741

❧ Blairscove House

In a stunning waterside location at the head of Dunmanus Bay, Philippe and Sabine de Mey's beautiful Georgian property is a wonderful place to stay. In the atmospheric high-beamed restaurant (with wood burning grill), Richard Milnes showcases the best of local foods with a style and his partner Anthea backs up his excellent cooking with warm hospitality and smart service – all combining to ensure a memorable experience.

DURRUS Bantry Co Cork
+353 (0)27 61127 www.blairscove.ie

Good Things Café

Great ingredients-led contemporary cooking is the magnet that draws those in the know to Carmel Somers' little café-restaurant just outside Durrus village. Well-placed to make the most of fine local produce - West Cork fish soup, or West Cork Ploughmans make the perfect lunch; she also sells some specialist foods from Ireland and abroad, runs a cookery school – and has published an excellent cookbook. This little place sure packs a mighty punch.

Ahakista Road DURRUS Co Cork
+353 (0)27 61426 www.thegoodthingscafe.com

Island Cottage

Just a short ferry ride from the mainland yet light years away from the "real" world, John Desmond and Ellmary Fenton's restaurant is unique. The no-choice 5-course menu depends on the availability of the fresh local, organic (where possible) and wild island ingredients of that day. Cooking is exceptional and off-season cookery courses offered.

HEIR ISLAND near Skibbereeen Co Cork
+353 (0)28 38102 www.islandcottage.com

Casino House

Achieving special recognition in an area which takes such pride in the excellence of its food is no mean feat,

but it is well worth the effort of getting to Kerrin and Michael Relja's delightful restaurant west of Kinsale. The setting is beautifully understated and the simple sophistication of Michael's food is a great tribute to fine local ingredients: Ballydehob duck is a speciality – and don't miss his wonderful lobster risotto.

🍀 Accommodation is offered nearby at Guy and Diana Scott's Glen Country House (www.glencountryhouse.com) is nearby.

Coolmain Bay Kilbrittain near KINSALE Co Cork
+353 (0)23 49944 www.casinohouse.ie

Fishy Fishy Café

Kinsale lays claim to the title 'gourmet capital of Ireland' and, while that is rightly challenged by several other contenders, Martin and Marie Shanahan's superb restaurant is indisputably 'vaut le détour'. The widest possible range and freshest of fish is served here, much of it supplied by third generation Kinsale fisherman and local food hero, Christy Turley. Nearby, the original **Fishy Fishy Gourmet Store** offers seafood prepared for cooking, a seafood deli - and excellent traditional fish & chips in **Fishy Fishy Chippie**.

Crowley's Quay KINSALE Co Cork
+353 (0)21 470 0415 www.fishyfishy.ie

O'Callaghan-Walshe

Steaks theoretically share the billing at larger-than-life proprietor-host Sean Kearney's unique restaurant in the old village of Rosscarbery, but Martina O'Donovan's cooking of West Cork seafood 'bought off the boats at auction' steals the scene.

The Square ROSSCARBERY Co Cork +353 (0)23 48125

East Cork

♣ Ballyvolane House

Garden lovers will find a stay at Justin and Jenny Green's gracious mansion especially rewarding; surrounded by its own farmland, magnificent wooded grounds, a trout lake and formal terraced gardens, it also has productive walled gardens beautifully maintained by Justin's green-fingered father, Jeremy – which supply the kitchen here and at their restaurant, O'Brien Chop House, nearby in Lismore Co Waterford. Beautiful and relaxed, this hospitable house is a gem.

Castlelyons FERMOY Co Cork
+353 (0)25 36349 www.ballyvolanehouse.ie

♣ Ballymaloe House

Ireland's most famous country house, Ballymaloe has earned a unique place in the hearts of food lovers, and everyone who values the combination of quality and simplicity. A food philosophy focused on using only the highest quality ingredients is central to everything done at Ballymaloe. Much of the produce comes from their own farm and gardens, and the rest comes from leading local producers - including smoked seafood from Frank Hederman in Cobh, Bill Casey's Shanagarry smoked salmon, Tadgh O'Riordan's fish and Willie Scannell's spuds from Ballycotton. There are few greater pleasures than a fine Ballymaloe dinner followed by a good night's sleep in one of their thoughtfully furnished country bedrooms - including, incidentally, Ireland's most ancient hotel room which is in the Gate House.

SHANAGARRY near Midleton Co Cork
+353 (0)21 465 2531 www.ballymaloe.com

♣ Aherne's Seafood Restaurant
& Accommodation

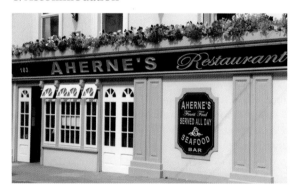

Run by third-generation owners, brothers John and David FitzGibbon and their wives, this is one of Ireland's great classic seafood restaurants – and, equally, a classic bar serving great informal food. It's for the ultra-fresh seafood straight off the fishing boats in Youghal harbour that people come, and David reigns over a busy kitchen. Even a quick bowl of chowder and their excellent brown bread can be memorable – but, if time permits, enjoy a relaxed evening meal and stay overnight.

163 North Main Street YOUGHAL Co Cork
+353 (0)24 92424 www.ahernes.com

WWW.IRELAND-GUIDE.COM FOR MORE OF THE BEST PLACES TO EAT, DRINK & STAY

Ireland: South-West, Cork
Recipes

Ballymaloe House, Co Cork

Ballymaloe Irish Stew

The approach to Ballymaloe House is charming, through lush green fields with sheep grazing all around - and it should come as no surprise that the lovely, simple dishes served at this legendary house usually favour the traditional version, as this Irish Stew from Myrtle Allen does. Regarding the great debate as to whether or not an Irish Stew should have carrots in it, Mrs Allen explains that 'it is common practice to include them in the south'. Although there are signs of a comeback, mutton is not widely available nowadays, so ask your butcher for hogget (one year old lamb), which can be used instead; adjust the cooking time according to the choice of meat - which may be taken off the bones before serving if preferred. This simple country dish is open to adaptation - modern versions are sometimes made with boneless meats, but the flavour is diminished.

Serves 4

For the mutton or lamb stock (optional, see note):

1.3kg/2lb mutton or lamb bones

Peelings from carrots and trimmings from other vegetables, such as onion tops

Sprigs of fresh herbs, such as thyme and marjoram

To make the optional drippings:

100g/4oz mutton or lamb fat (OR 3 tbsp unsalted butter, lard or bacon fat, melted)

For the stew:

1.3kg/3lb mutton neck chops or shoulder lamb chops, bone in

4 carrots (about 225g/8oz total), peeled and quartered

4 onions (about 350g/12 oz total), peeled and quartered

$^1/_2$ tsp salt

$^1/_4$ tsp freshly ground black pepper

4-6 small potatoes (about 450g/1lb total)

15g/$^1/_2$ oz butter

1 tbsp chopped parsley leaves

1 tbsp snipped fresh chives

600ml/1 pint reserved stock (or water and a stock concentrate).

To make the fresh lamb stock: Put the bones, vegetable peelings and trimmings, and herbs into a saucepan, and add enough cold water to cover them by 5cm/2". Bring to the boil, then lower the heat and gently simmer the mixture, partially covered, for about 2 hours. Strain and skim the fat. Reserve 600ml/1 pint of the stock for the stew.

To make the optional drippings: Chop the fat into small pieces and fry it over fairly low heat in a heavy pan until it is rendered. Reserve 45ml/3 tablespoons for the stew.

To make the stew: Heat the reserved drippings in a heavy saucepan and brown the chops in it, in batches. Do not crowd the meat. Add the carrots, onions, salt (see note), pepper and the 600ml/1 pint reserved stock.

Peel the potatoes and put them on top.

Simmer the stew gently for 1$^1/_2$ to 2 hours, or until the meat is tender. Using a slotted spoon, transfer the meat (boned, if you wish) and vegetables to individual bowls. Skim the fat from the cooking liquor, then taste and correct seasonings as necessary. Swirl in the butter, parsley and chives and ladle the sauce over the meat and vegetables.

[Note: If commercial stock is used to replace the lamb stock, the $^1/_2$ teaspoon salt should be omitted.]

Lobster with Lemon & Dill Mayonnaise

Fergus and Trish O'Mahony own the delightful Mary Ann's Bar & Restaurant in the pretty village of Castletownshend in West Cork, which is equally loved for its atmosphere and Trish's delicious seafood. Lobster is a great favourite and this tempting salad is often offered on the bar menu, to be served with their famous brown bread. The salad could also be made with fresh crabmeat.

Serves 4

2 live lobsters, each about 500g/1lb 2oz

1 small onion, sliced

1 slice lemon

1 bay leaf

2 fresh dill sprigs

handful of fresh parsley stalks

a few black peppercorns

120ml/4fl oz white wine

100g/4oz mixed salad leaves, such as chicory, rocket and lollo rosso

2 tbsp French vinaigrette (homemade or quality commercial, eg Ballymaloe)

salt and freshly ground black pepper

For the lemon and dill mayonnaise:

4 tablespoons homemade mayonnaise, or best available commercial alternative

finely grated rind of 1/2 lemon

1-2 tablespoons chopped fresh dill, to taste.

Freshly baked brown soda bread to serve

To prepare the lobsters, place each one on a board and cover it with foil and a cloth. Hold firmly down with one hand and, with the point of a large knife, pierce down to the board through the cross on the centre of the head.

Put enough salted water to cover the lobsters into a large deep pan, and bring to the boil. As a guide allow at least 1 litre/13/4 pints to 1 teaspoon of salt per 500g/1lb 2oz lobster. Add the onion, lemon, bay leaf, dill sprigs, parsley, peppercorns and white wine and simmer for 5 minutes to allow the flavours to combine.

Increase the heat and when the flavoured water is boiling, add the lobsters and boil for 5 minutes for the first 500g/1lb 2oz, adding an extra 3 minutes for each extra 500g/1lb 2oz. When the lobsters are cooked, the colour changes to bright red. Transfer to a large sink or basin of iced water to cool down immediately.

When the lobsters are cool enough to handle, pull the claws from the bodies. Crack the claws and remove the meat. With a large chef's knife, cut each lobster in half from the back, along the length of its body, and remove its intestinal tract, then discard. Remove the tail meat and slice it up neatly.

Blend the mayonnaise with the grated lemon rind and chopped dill.

To serve, toss the salad leaves in the French vinaigrette, then season to taste and pile in the centre of each serving plate. Arrange the lobster meat on top and spoon a dollop of mayonnaise onto each plate. The remainder can be served in a small dish on the table along with a basket of freshly baked brown soda bread, allowing guests to help themselves.

Hints: If preparing ahead, do not serve the lobster over-chilled. Freeze the leftover shells and use them to make stock for soups and sauces.

warm salad of Gubbeen cheese and Bacon

This delicious salad is a favourite of one of Ireland's most highly esteemed chefs, Rory O'Connell (www.rgoconnell.com; +353 (0)86 851 6917), who is known for a pure, simple style that highlights the quality of seasonal and artisan ingredients. He gives intensive one-day classes at his home at Ballycotton in East Cork.

Serves 6

15ml/1tbsp olive oil

350g/12oz streaky Gubbeen bacon or other streaky bacon

6 handfuls of mixed green leaves, washed and dried

65g/2oz Gubbeen cheese, or similar cheese, cubed

Dressing:

45ml/3tbsp sunflower oil

45ml/3tbsp olive oil

5m/1tsp of Lakeshore Whole Grain Mustard or other wholegrain mustard

30ml/2 tbsp David Llewellyn's Fruit and Vine Cider Vinegar, or other natural cider vinegar

Salt, freshly ground pepper and sugar to season.

Heat a frying pan and add a little olive oil. Cut the bacon into lardons.

When the oil is smoking, add the lardons of bacon and fry until crisp. While the bacon is cooking, put all the ingredients for the dressing in a bowl and whisk with a fork.

Toss the leaves in the dressing and divide between six hot plates. The leaves should be just glistening with the dressing.

Sprinkle the cubes of cheese around the leaves and finally the bacon straight from the pan.

Serve immediately.

Summer Berries in Lemon Scented Geranium Syrup

There is nothing more refreshing than a seasonal fruit salad to round off a meal, and this pretty dessert is easy to prepare. It makes a change from plain fresh soft fruit (delicious though that is) and any single fruit or combination of fruits can be used, depending on availability. When the soft fruit season is over, top fruits can be prepared in the same way, but use the syrup hot, or poach them in it for a few minutes, depending on the amount of softening they need; in winter, pour the hot syrup over frozen berries such as raspberries, which freeze very well. The flavourings can be varied - you could, for example, replace the lemon-scented geranium leaves with a chopped stalk of lemongrass, and use lime instead of the lemon. Serve with a bowl of good natural yoghurt or crème fraîche, such as Glenilen.

Serves 4

200g/7oz sugar

225ml/8fl oz water

4 large lemon scented geranium leaves

zest and juice of 1/2 lemon

175g/6oz raspberries

175g/6oz strawberries, hulled and quartered

150g/5oz blueberries or blackberries

Natural yoghurt to serve

Put the sugar, water and scented geranium leaves into a saucepan and stir over moderate heat until the sugar dissolves, then bring gently to the boil. Reduce the heat and simmer for 2 minutes. Cool for 5 or 10 minutes, the pour the warm syrup over the fruit. Chill for several hours, or overnight, to allow the flavours to infuse.

To serve, divide the fruit between four bowls, pour over some syrup and scatter with a little extra lemon zest. Any leftover syrup will keep in the fridge for up to three weeks. Serve with a bowl of natural yoghurt, or crème fraiche

Ireland: South-East
Carlow, Kilkenny, Tipperary, Waterford & Wexford

Clashganny Lock, Co Carlow

This is a region of rivers, a land of sublime valleys winding their way gently through a rich landscape flanked by elegant mountains. But despite the more obvious attractions of its better-known features, there are large and often lovely tracts of this area which remain off the busier tourist trails, quiet places of enchantment to be savoured by the connoisseur.

It's usually thought of as "The Sunny South-East". And it is, too - at its southeastern outpost of Carnsore Point, they get upwards of 1700 hours of the elusive orb on annual display, whereas Ireland's least sunny part, in the midst of the Sperrin region of County Tyrone in the north, has to make do with glimpsing the sun for less than 1200 hours.

The Nore Valley, near Inistioge, Co Kilkenny

About the Region

Don't think, though, that so much sunshine - relatively speaking - means less rain. It's the Greater Dublin area which is drier than anywhere else in Ireland. The rainfall in the far southeast matches that of damper spots like Limerick and Fermanagh. So some of the secret of the sunshine is in its breeziness. The average wind down towards the southeast corner matches Belmullet in far Mayo, and Carnsore Point itself records less days of calm than any other weather station. Thus the patch of flat land down at the point is a concentrated wind farm.

But although Carnsore Point is breezy, sunny and showery, if you move inland from it, the sunshine holds on quite well, but the breeziness soon eases, and profound rural peace reigns. The southeast doesn't do the spectacular in-your-face scenery of the more renowned tourist areas. It's the quiet beauty of many river valleys of an enduring loveliness, while the coast is remarkable for the sheer length of its unspoilt beaches. Most of Wexford's east coast is of

Ballina, Co Tipperary

flawless sand that seems to go on beyond the horizon - there's so much beach that they were able to select parts of it to be Normandy for the filming of the award-winning epic *Saving Private Ryan*.

Along the area's southern shore, the coast becomes more rugged as it trends westward, with Hook Head's ancient lighthouse - the oldest in Ireland, it was originally lit by monks - rich in history. When Oliver Cromwell was sending an invasion force to this area, as the Normans had done centuries earlier, he was informed that the best route was in past Hook Head and on up Waterford Estuary past the village of Crooke on the west shore. So he told the general (his son-in-law): "We'll take Ireland by Hook and by Crooke". And they did.

Before Cromwell and the Tudors before that, there were Normans and Vikings. However, way before that, the Ardmore area of West Waterford - known as The Decies - had a neighbourhood holy man, St Declan, who was doing his good works down there before St Patrick arrived on his missions. More recently, it was the Normans, coming across from their strongholds in southwest Wales, who made the more lasting impression, taking to the place so well that they became more Irish than the Irish themselves. In an area like this, it was the natural thing to do, for it had the attractions of their most recent homeland in Pembrokeshire, but on a much larger scale.

The river valleys flow luxuriantly among some truly beautiful mountains ranges and fine forests and farmland. In west Waterford, the Blackwater comes eastward along the southern slopes of the Knockmealdowns past the dreaming castellations of Lismore before making a sudden turn southward at Cappoquin to be joined by the Bride for a stately meeting with the sea at Youghal.

Above Dungarvan, which is Waterford's county town to offset any undue concentration of administrative power in Waterford city, the Colligan River is a modest stream, but it descends from the hidden beauties of the Monavullagh and Comeragh Mountain. There, the River Nire emerges in its

Lismore Castle, Co Waterford

remote valley to set a high standard of upland beauty within easy reach of the rich countryside of Tipperary to the north, where it joins the mighty River Suir.

Tipperary may not be Ireland's biggest county, but there are times when this agriculturally affluent region seems bigger than anywhere else. It stretches from Clonmel in the southeast to Lough Derg - one of the Shannon's great lakes - in the northwest. Centuries ago, early attempts to impose rule on it proved so difficult that the authorities in Dublin divided it in two, with Tipperary North Riding having its county town at Nenagh up towards the Shannon, while the South Riding is focused on Clonmel.

Once upon a time, Cashel in mid-Tipperary, with its famous rock topped by ancient ecclesiastic buildings, was the capital of the Kingdom of Munster. But for now, there are two Tipperaries, despite suggestions that they might become one again with an agreed capital at Cashel. Through all this, the stately River Suir (it's pronounced "Shure") makes its growing progress. Rising in the Devil's Bit mountain up towards Nenagh, it is already of substantial size as it passes near Cashel at the village of Golden. The word is derived from "little fork in the river", but the prosperous farmland through Cashel and beyond

Tipperary town into East Limerick has become known as the Golden Vale, and with fine valleys between its graceful mountains, we can think of Tipperary as being the land of half a dozen Golden Vales. The Suir meanwhile, having headed south through Cahir, trends north once it has been joined by the Nire, By now marking the border between Tipperary and Waterford, it then curves east through Clonmel - the "Honey Meadow" - and the ancient river port of Carrick-on-Suir in a handsome valley, the Comeragh mountains to the south, and the gentle peak of Silevenamon - the mountain of the women - to the north.

The land to the northeastward of Carrick is County Kilkenny, but Waterford county holds sway along the south shore of what is now a substantial tidal waterway as it passes the historic port city of Waterford itself. The freight section of the port may have been moved across the river and downstream, but Waterford's picturesque old quays provide a

Kilkenny Castle Yard, Kilkenny City

colourful setting for maritime gatherings such as the Tall Ships, while the estuary provides a natural stadium when fleets head seaward.

And it becomes even bigger just east of Waterford, as the Suir is joined by another large river, the Barrow, coming in from the north. In its turn, the "goodly Barrow" has been joined upstream by the Nore coming through Kilkenny city. Together, the Suir, Barrow and Nore are the Three Sisters, dominating the geography of the southeast, with the Barrow and Nore in particular having sweet valleys in harmony with a landscape which, to the east, rises handsomely to the Blackstairs Mountains and their peak of Mount Leinster over towards Wexford.

While the Nore rises to the northwest near the source of the Suir in the Devil's Bit Mountain, it is known primarily as the fine river which flows through the Mediaeval city of Kilkenny, an ancient strategic route. But today it is the Barrow which is the primary waterway, with its saltwater port at New Ross on the east bank in County Wexford. It was a major Norman town, and above it the valley descends gently through superb country with lovely little river ports such as Graiguemanagh, coming in from the north through Carlow county. As the saying goes, the Creator was in fine form when he created Carlow, it's a gem. While all of the Three Sisters were much used as thoroughfares by early travellers and invaders, it is only the Barrow which links northward to the all-Ireland inland waterways system via a line of the Grand Canal.

Eastward of the Blackstairs mountains, there's yet another major river valley, the Slaney. It rises way north in the Wicklow hills, and is a substantial stream by the time it is in County Wexford, coming through the charming hill town of Bunclody and on through Enniscorthy until it meets the sea in the broad expanses of Wexford Harbour, where the old town with its long quay has experienced much history to become its own unique self, famed for its theatrical links and a popular annual Opera Festival in the Autumn "when we feature operas nobody has ever heard of before, and have ourselves a fine old time".

The Barrow Valley, Co Carlow

Rapeseed and Bee Hives, Urlingford, Co Kilkenny

Food of the Region

Craft Beer

Baking

Apples

Whiskey

Oatmeal

Boozeberries

Whiskey Downes No 9

Rapeseed Oil

Honey

Country Butter

Christmas Puddings

Flour

Organic Chickens

Waterford Blaa

Pork, Sausages

Beef

Dry Cure Bacon

If ever there was a land flowing with milk and honey, it has to be the south-east of Ireland. Blessed with a benign climate - the moniker 'sunny south-east' is well-earned - this is an area of lush river valleys, beautiful trees and wonderfully fertile farmland. There is a healthy rivalry between the counties of this highly productive region, each keen to demonstrate the supremacy of its foods through a growing number of markets, competitions, food festivals and other events - successful examples include the autumn Savour Kilkenny Food Festival (www.savourkilkenny.com), the spring and autumn festivals in Co Waterford (www.waterfordfestivaloffood.com) - and the annual Long Table Dinner (www.tipperaryfoodproducers.com), an intriguing event that is held simultaneously in several locations in Co Tipperary in late summer, with each venue serving only food from Tipperary at a sumptuous traditional feast.

Many of the products that Ireland is known for throughout the world are produced in this region - great grass makes for excellent **DAIRY PRODUCE** and pasture-fed meats, especially **BEEF** - and, although it is Wicklow that claimed the 'Garden of Ireland' title, the kitchen garden (and, particularly, the fruit garden) is perhaps seen at its best in Co Wexford. **ORCHARD FRUITS**, notably apples, are grown throughout Ireland and there are several outstanding producers in the south-east, but Wexford is renowned for its **SOFT FRUIT** production - in summer, roadside stalls all over the country tempt passers-by with 'Wexford Strawberries'. Many other fruits are grown as well of course, although - with the exception of blackcurrants, which are an important crop, but almost exclusively destined for an international soft drinks company - quantities of other fruits tend to be smaller. And where there is fruit, bees cannot be far away so it should be no surprise to find excellent **HONEY** here, notably the award winning **Mileeven** brand (www.mileeven.com); produced at Piltown, Co Kilkenny by Eilis Gough and her daughter, Sarah, who supply organic and manuka honey throughout Ireland, and also organic preserves, fruit cakes and Christmas specialities including plum puddings.

Many varieties of **APPLES** are grown, with production well distributed through the region, and including some of Ireland's most highly regarded producers. Perhaps best known of these is **The Apple Farm** (www.theapplefarm.com) at Cahir Co Tipperary, where Con Traas grows 60 varieties of apples and produces a range of juices, including a unique cloudy sparkling juice, and cider vinegar. Pears, plums, sweet cherries, strawberries and raspberries are also grown here, and there is even a Camping and Caravan Park on the farm. Of several fruit farms in Co Waterford, the well known **Crinnaughtaun Juice Company** (www.irishapplejuice.com) at Cappoquin, is a small family-run company producing award winning cloudy juices, which are widely distributed. Also in Co Waterford, **Vogelaar's Apple Farm** at Mullinabro, Ferrybank, welcomes visitors and has a farm shop in season. And although Co Wexford is famed mainly for its soft fruit, the von Engelbrechten family's **Ballycross Apple Farm** (www.ballycross.com) at Bridgetown

offers an idyllic rural family day out during the season, and a range of single variety and mixed pressed juices, whole fruit and other products. But many of the region's apple farms are in counties Kilkenny and Carlow; Alan Gilbert's **Apple Barrel** (+353 (0)59 914 2014) apple juice and apples, for example, are sourced from the home farm at Quinagh, Co Carlow; Lennons@Visual, Carlow is among the discerning businesses he supplies. Philip and Oren Little's **Little Irish Apple Co** at Piltown (+353 (0)51 387109) produces both pasteurised pressed juice and apples; some of the Littles' production is now organic, and demand is increasing. Nearby at Cuffesgrange, the apple orchards are all organic at **Highbank Farm** (+353 (0)56 772 9918). Contact Rod Calder-Potts for details of farm shop; also at English Market, Cork.

When it comes to the **SOFT FRUITS** for which the Sunny South-East - especially Wexford - is so famous, the most significant producer is **Green's Fruit Farms** (www.greensberryfarm.ie) at two locations near Gorey, both with excellent farm shops. Near Ballon, in Co Carlow, **Malone's Fruit Farm** (+353 (0)59 9159477)

grows a very wide variety of fruit including strawberries, raspberries, blackberries, gooseberries, loganberries, tayberries, redcurrants, blackcurrants, whitecurrants and rhubarb; as well as selling their fresh fruit in season and frozen at other times, the Malones make a range of homemade products that are available all year round. And the abundant supplies of quality produce have inspired many entrepreneurs in the region to specialise in fruit products too - brands to be enjoyed include **Wexford Home Preserves** (www.wexfordpreserves.ie) of New Ross, who have been making traditional preserves by hand since 1988, with the core products based on local fruit, and **Crossogue Preserves** (www.crossoguepreserves.com) of Thurles, Co Tipperary, who offer an extensive range of excellent handmade products including diabetic jams and marmalades. In Nenagh, Co Tipperary, Mary Ward of **Country Choice** (www.countrychoice.ie) has become something of a national heroine for the vast amounts of excellent preserves she makes by hand every year - and for her renowned Christmas puddings too; nearby, on a more industrial scale, Florrie Purcell of **The Scullery** (+353 (0)86 174 4402) is well known for the gluten, preservative and additive free products (notably relishes, pickles, glazes and Christmas puddings), made at Springfort Industrial Park in Nenagh and widely distributed.

A new product which looks set to play an important role in Ireland's agriculture and cuisine is **RAPESEED OIL** and, while the changes this crop brings to the landscape are not universally welcome, the product itself is proving to be a very acceptable alternative to imported olive oil. An early success story is Kitty Colchester's **Happy Heart** extra virgin rapeseed oil (+353 (0)87 926 5423; www.secondnatureoils.com), which is also rather confusingly branded Second Nature. It is grown on Drumeen Farm, near Urlingford, Co Kilkenny, which was established by her parents Ben and Charlotte in 1976 and is the longest-established organic farm in Ireland; the ethos continues - no potentially hazardous synthetic chemicals, fertilisers or GM seeds are used - and the culinary quality of the oil is ensured by pressing the seed weekly, to retain the maximum nutritional value and taste. And taste good it certainly does - although the official launch was delayed until autumn 2010 (with national distribution in place at that stage), Euro-Toques Ireland had already selected it for one of their highly valued Food Awards the previous year, following successful trials. Also with healthy eating in mind, look out for the impressively tasty 'free from' **SOUPS** made by **M&S Browne** (www.msbrowne.com) in Tipperary Town; available from selected supermarkets and independent stores, they make best use of locally produced ingredients.

Michael Kelly & Darina Allen

Quite aside from commercial production, a quiet revolution is going on in the back gardens and (increasingly popular) allotments of Ireland, and it was given a kick start in Waterford when journalist and author, Michael Kelly, went in search of a local growers' group in order to share information and meet like-minded people. Finding that no such group existed, the idea for **Grow it Yourself Ireland** (+353 (0)51 302191; www.giyireland.com) was born. It came at a time when the quality of mass produced food was a source of growing concern among consumers - and touched a nerve in a population suddenly faced with economic insecurity and also yearning to pursue a more meaningful way of life, where 'shopping' was not the automatic leisure activity of choice. All this plus the drive of an energetic and media-savvy founder, and the

support of sponsors including Darina Allen of Ballymaloe Cookery School (who started the farmers' market movement in Ireland) and Joy Larkcom, acclaimed author of the productive gardener's bible, 'Grow Your Own Vegetables', helped the GIY movement to take off and - although only established in 2009 - it quickly found a niche. The timely arrival of Darina Allen's wonderful book 'Forgotten Skills of Cooking' helped younger gardeners to re-learn many of the methods their grandparents used for dealing with large quantities of the seasonal produce grown, and preserving it for use throughout the year.

'Forgotten Skills of Cooking' also touches another growing area of interest - our countryside and coastline, and the **wild foods** that are there for the taking, if we only knew what they are and what to do with them; it makes a good home reference to partner Roger Phillips' classic 'Wild Food' and a pocket guide like the compact Collins Gem edition of Richard Mabey's Food For Free. **Foraging** was a way of life for many Irish people until recently - and, while it is worrying to see how quickly the old knowledge can be lost, it's also very encouraging to see renewed interest above and beyond the token cheffy inclusion of, for example, trendy wild garlic in cooking. Foraging days are offered by Ballymaloe Cookery School and others, including Roger and Olivia Goodwillie at **Lavistown House** (www.lavistownhouse.ie), Kilkenny. Some of the most familiar wild foods easily available in this region and throughout Ireland include sorrel, horseradish, watercress, elderflower, blackberries, bilberries (fraughans), crab apples, damsons, elderberries, rose hips, sloes, hazelnuts and many varieties of mushroom. There are of course many more that are less easily recognised, and that's not even touching on the coastal plants - and then there are the catches to be had from (licensed) **game hunting** (www.nargc.ie), and **fishing** (www.irishfisheries.com) on the region's many productive rivers, and much more…

As elsewhere in Ireland, **SEAFOOD** is extremely popular and, with fishing ports like Dunmore East, Helvick, Kilmore Quay and Duncannon supplying fresh fish and shellfish daily, it is a speciality at many of the pubs and restaurants along the coasts of Waterford and Wexford. But the region's extensive

Ben & Charlotte Colchester, Drumeen Farm, Co Kilkenny

fertile farmland ensures that **MEATS** get their fair share of the limelight in the South-East - at Borrisokane, Co Tipperary, for example, the renowned **organic lamb** and **Galloway beef** farmer, Michael Seymour, produces superb meat which he sells at Nenagh market and supplies to Country Choice in Nenagh. At the other end of the scale, and of the county, **Good Herdsmen Ltd** (www.goodherdsmen.com) at Cahir is the largest organic meat processor in Ireland and the UK, and co-ordinates the supply, processing and marketing of around 200 certified organic farmers; director Josef Finke's nearby **Ballybrado House & Farm** (www.ballybrado.com) has been known for its stoneground organic flour since 1983 and, more recently, also for baked products and mixes. And there are those who can show that, where the will exists, even the less fertile land on hill farms makes a real contribution to sustainable productivity, as proved by the **'Organics with Altitude'** initiative and Ballymacarbry farmers Joe and Eileen Condon's organic production of traditional breeds on uplands farms - of which the first project is **Omega Beef Direct** (www.omegabeefdirect.ie), recently selected by the Irish Food Writers' Guild (www.irishfoodwritersguild.ie) for their **Environmental Award**. Other environmentally friendly meat producers in the region include several farms raising **free range pork** and bacon - at Dundrum in Co Tipperary, for example, free range pork produced at **Crowe's Farm** (www.crowefarm.ie) is then processed at their on-farm butchery to make natural handmade bacon products, puddings and sausages, which are available from good food stores throughout Ireland. Other excellent pork products from the South-East to look out for include dry cure rashers and bacon joints from both **Oakpark Foods** (www.bordbia.ie/marketplace) of Cahir, Co Tipperary, and **O'Neill Foods** (www.goodfoodireland.ie) near Ferns, Co Wexford. In Co Kilkenny, **Knockdrinna Farm** (www.knockdrinna.com) is mainly famed for superb cheeses, but a more recent complementary business is **whey-fed pork**; and, at **Lavistown House** (www.lavistownhouse.ie), Kilkenny, the original producers of Lavistown Cheese, Roger and Olivia Goodwillie are mainly known nowadays for rural courses at their Study Centre - but they also produce superb sausages, which will be seen on many a menu in the area.

If finding a supply of good quality pork has become an issue in Ireland - with Euro-Toques chefs stating recently that they would willingly pay a premium for quality - the question of quality **POULTRY** is, as elsewhere, even more pressing. So the South-East is fortunate to have local supplies of free range chicken from Bertram and Celine Salter's **Carlow Foods Ltd.** (www.carlowfoods.com), near Fenagh in Co. Carlow; unusually, the Salters have complete control of the whole process right through to delivery - and they also supply turkey at Christmas. Down in Co Waterford, Paul Crotty's **Born Free Organic Chickens** (+353 (0)51 383565) at Dunmore East are the local poultry heroes, fed on homegrown organic grain feed, reared outdoors and sold through markets and selected outlets such as Ardkeen Quality Food Store, Waterford.

While West Cork is home to Ireland's vintage cheesemakers and undoubtedly the heartland of this culinary revival, the large areas of exceptionally rich pastureland in the South-East (which take in part of the lush Golden Vale, covering sections of counties Limerick, Tipperary and Cork) produce an abundance of top quality milk and, consequently, an exceptional range of artisan dairy products. These include some of Ireland's finest **FARMHOUSE CHEESES**: in Co Tipperary, for example, the Grubb family have produced Ireland's original artisanal blue cheese, the world famous **Cashel Blue** (www.cashelblue.com) at Fethard since 1984, and its younger sheeps' cheese cousin, **Crozier Blue**, is made nearby. Near Thurles, Breda and Pat Maher's magnificent camembert style **Cooleeney Farmhouse Cheese** (www.cooleeney.com)

Juliet & Paddy Berridge

is one of a range of cheeses made at their farm, and available both pasteurised and raw. At Mount Anglesby, Clogheen, Dick and Anne Keating make the raw cows' milk cheese **Baylough** (+353 (0)52 65275) and visitors are welcome. Famous cheeses made nearby in West Waterford include Agnes and Wolfgang Schliebitz's **Knockalara** range of cows', sheep's and goats' farmhouse cheese, made at Cappoquin; and Eamonn and Patricia Lonergan's range of **Knockanore Cheese** (www.knockanorecheese.com), made near Villierstown from the raw cows' milk of their pedigree Friesian herd. At **Carrigbyrne Farmhouse Cheese** (www.carrigbyrne.ie) near Enniscorthy, Co Wexford, Paddy and Juliet Berridge make another of Ireland's best-loved cheeses the mulit-award winning brie style **St Killian** (pasteurised milk from their own herd, vegetarian rennet) sold in the trademark hexagonal box, and also the larger **St Brendan Brie**; and the astonishing range of environmentally-friendly initiatives undertaken at Carrigbyrne has attracted due recognition, including the inaugural Irish Food Writers' Guild (www.irishfoodwritersguild.ie) Environmental Award. Also made in Co Wexford are Anne and Luc Van Kampen's lesser known but exceptionally fine (and multi award-winning) goat's

Co Kilkenny Cheeses

milk cheeses, including the silky little Mine Gabhar, and hard gouda style Blackwater, named after their nearest village. Co Kilkenny's most famous cheeses **Knockdrinna** and **Lavistown** (www.knockdrinna.com) are now both made by Helen Finnegan at Knockdrinna; and, in Co Carlow, the one to look out for is the unusual (for Ireland) edam style **Carlow Cheese** (www.irishcheese.ie), made in several flavours by Elizabeth Bradley at Fenagh.

Specialist cheese production has proved an excellent way for many an Irish farmer to diversify, and **OTHER DAIRY PRODUCTS** are now becoming equally successful. At **Tinnock Farm** near New Ross, for example, John Murphy (+353 (0)87 220 3300) produces an impressive range of foods including not only lamb and beef but also free range eggs (duck as well as hen), **homemade butter** (known as 'country butter') and its by-product, **buttermilk** - the real thing, and very different from commercially produced buttermilks; Tinnock Farm produce is sold at local markets (Kilkenny, Campile, Wexford, New Ross and Enniscorthy) and also the Sunday market in Dun Laoghaire, Co Dublin. Over near Enniscorthy, Nicholas and Judith Dunne have been making their well known sharply-flavoured bio-live **Killowen**

Yogurt (www.killowenyogurt.com) for over 25 years. Made from the full-fat milk of a single herd, and available in fruit flavours, it is sold at selected markets, retail outlets and also under the Superquinn Superior Quality own-label. Quality dairy products are made on a larger scale too, of course - one example in Co Tipperary is **Compsey Creamery**, a subsidiary of Mullinahone Co-Operative which dates back to 1893 and is Ireland's oldest working co-operative; they make an excellent range of fresh dairy products (soft cheeses, soured cream and crème fraîche, mascarpone, yoghurts) whose accolades include one of the earliest IFWG awards, in 1995.

Then there is **ICE CREAM** and, judging by the success of premium handmade ranges in recent years, the Irish palate must now be educated to expect nothing but the best. In this region alone, you'll find several: the Brennan family's **Gathabawn Farmhouse Ice Cream** (E:gathabawnicecream@eircom.net) is not widely retailed but you'll notice this quality product credited on restaurant menus both in the area and beyond; Nigel and Carol Harper's **Cramers Grove Ice Cream** (+353 (0)56 772 2160 www.cramersgrove.com) cones are sold at Kilkenny Castle Park and The People's Park in Waterford; tubs are available at selected stores including Ardkeen Quality Food Store, Waterford, and Knockdrinna Farm Shop; sorbets and frozen yogurt are made as well as ice cream. At Boulabán Farm (www.boulabanefarms.ie) near Roscrea in Co Tipperarary, Michael and Kate Cantwell use milk and cream from their pedigree Holstein/Friesian herd to make **Boulabane Ice Cream** - an adventurous range offering lots of flavours includes fruit sorbets, diabetic ices and soya ices, and they're picking up awards a-plenty. Near Tullow in Co Carlow, **The Chocolate Garden** (www.chocolategarden.ie) offers two of the nation's favourite treats under one roof - quality handmade chocolates and handmade **Tipperary Organic Ice Cream** (www.tipperaryorganic.ie), which is widely available. And while on the subject of chocolate, one of the best of Ireland's many excellent artisan chocolate producers is in this region - so, if you see the name **Gallweys** (www.gallweys.ie) on a box, snap it up, especially if it's full of their Irish Whiskey Truffles: although now in new ownership, the history of the company goes back to 1835, when the family was in whiskey…

Along the great river valleys of this beautiful region there are many signs of a relatively recent milling past, a reminder that the grains grown here once brought prosperity to whole communities - not that this proud rural tradition has been lost entirely, as can be seen at **Mosses Mill** (www.kellswholemeal.ie) at Bennettsbridge, where seven generations of the Mosse family have stoneground local **wheat** to make their wholemeal Kells Flour; and also **Flahavans** (www.flahavans.ie), who have milled **oats** at Kilmacthomas since the late 18th century. So it should come as no surprise to find that good **BAKING** is a feature of the area, with outstanding examples to look out for including **Seerys** (+353 (0)59 9142461 www.seerys.ie) of Tinryland, Co Carlow, who have earned an international reputation for their traditional **Irish fruit cakes and puddings**, notably Christmas specialities - as indeed have **Country Choice** (+353 (0)67 32596; www.countrychoice.ie) of Nenagh, Co Tipperary, who are especially renowned for the quality of ingredients (also available in their shop). Florrie Purcell's **The Scullery** (+353 (0)86 174 4402), also of Nenagh, frequently include individual Christmas puddings in their praised traditional range. A very different kind of traditional food is the **Waterford Blaa**, a floury square yeast roll unique to Waterford City and surrounds and produced there since the 1600s; it is still made in the traditional way by four bakeries in the area - M&D Bakery and Hickey's in Waterford City, Harney's of Kilmacow and Barron's of Cappoquinn - jointly honoured by Euro-Toques recently. But, while tradition plays a part in most of Ireland's best bakeries, in Clonmel, American-born Cate McCarthy of **The Cookie Jar** (www.tipperaryfoodproducers.com) uses locally-sourced ingredients to make her authentic American cookies for distribution to local restaurants and selected outlets nationwide. And, also proving that you don't have to be a multi-generational business to do well, or even to be very small to maintain an artisanal ethos, Katherine Carroll and Vincent Power's very successful **Stable Diet Food** (+353 (0)53-913 1287; www.stablediet.com) at

Yoletown, Co Wexford, began with Katherine making a few carrot cakes for a local shop. Although they now employ over two dozen people, the philosophy is unchanged and their range of cakes, breakfast cereals and flapjacks is widely acclaimed, with accolades including an Irish Food Writers' Guild Award. An interesting newcomer to keep an eye open for is Rebecca Smyth's gluten-free range of baked treats, made by **Rebecca's Nutritious Cuisine** (+353 (0)85 118 0690; www.rebeccasmyth.com) at Bilboa, near Carlow; her products are flying off her stall at Carlow Farmers' Market

- and no less than three of them (hazelnut digestives, white chocolate and macadamia cookies, and cinnamon and raisin cookies) were singled out for stars at the 2010 Great Taste Awards.

DRINKS associated with the region are many and varied, and the purest example is **natural mineral water**. Irish water has been bottled for sale since the early 1980s and **Tipperary Water** (www.gleesongroup.ie) is an outstanding example, consistently winning international awards at blind tastings.

O'Brien Chop House, Lismore, Co Waterford

Also based on natural products is the brilliantly named **Boozeberries** (www.boozeberries.com; +353 (0)59 9156312), made at Tullow Co Carlow. The brainchild of Michelle Power who developed a family recipe to preserve summer fruits, this artisan berry liqueur is made in small batches and three flavours (blackcurrant, blueberry and wild cranberry), then stylishly bottled and packed at a former Bailey's plant. This attractively simple idea has been predictably well received - and it may even be healthy. More traditionally, the O'Hara family's **Carlow Brewing Company** (+353 (0)59 972 0509; www.carlowbrewing.com), situated at Bagenalstown in the malt growing Barrow Valley, was established in 1998 to revive the once thriving brewing culture; this **CRAFT BREWERY** uses only natural ingredients to produce a unique range of brews that have found a ready niche, and recognition - especially for the **O'Hara's Irish Stout**, which offers a real alternative to the mass-produced internationally known brands. More recently, in Templemore, Co Tipperary, **White Gypsy** (+353 (0)86 172 4520; www.whitegypsy.ie) has been founded by Cuilan Loughnane, brewer in Messrs Maguire brew pub on Dublin's quays, using equipment that became available when another craft brewery closed. Although in the early stages of production, they are making a number of beers including two stouts, a lager and several ales and, although mainly sold at festivals to date, have started to win awards.

Meanwhile, down in Dungarvan, Co Waterford, young artisan brewer Cormac O'Dwyer has opened Ireland's most recent micro-brewery, **Dungarvan Brewing Company** (dungarvanbrewingcompany.com; +353 (0)58 24000), and is producing a range of bottle-conditioned craft beers with local names - Black Rock Irish Stout, Copper Coast Red Ale and Helvick Gold Blonde Ale - all brewed and bottled on site. Their arrival in an area that is keen to promote local artisan products is well-timed, and interesting partnerships are developing - with Slow Food members O'Briens Chop House in Lismore, for example, who host frequent special nights, sometimes with the innovative fresh spice importer, **Green Saffron** (+353 (0)21 463 7960; www.greensaffron.com) which is based just a few miles away in East Cork. And finally, while spirits in the region also come mainly from neighbouring East Cork, a unique **whiskey** blend is always a possibility - when visiting Waterford City, make a point of seeking out the unique **Henry Downes** pub, on Thomas Street (+353 (0)51 874 118); established in 1759, and in the same (eccentric) family for six generations, John de Bromhead's unusual, atmospheric and very friendly pub in Waterford is one of the few remaining houses to bottle its own whiskey, **Downes No 9**. Sláinte!

Four of the Best...

Knockdrinna Farm House Cheese

If you want to buy some seriously good artisan produce and see an outstanding example of rural diversifation, a visit to Robert and Helen Finnegan's farm in the village of Stoneyford is highly recommended. What began for Helen as an experiment in the back kitchen soon became a full time cheesemaking operation, and has developed into an impressive and fascinating business. First there was goats' cheese, with a neighbour, Hugh Daniels, supplying top quality milk from his certified herd. Next came Knockdrinna Meadow, a ewes' milk cheese using milk sourced from Henry Clifton Brown (who makes the magnificent Crozier Blue cheese, in Co Tipperary); although very pure - just milk, rennet, culture and salt - the golden rind of this distinctively earthy cheese results from washing it three times weekly with organic white wine… accolades include an IFWG (Irish Food Writers' Guild) award. Not one to rest on her laurels, Helen took over production of Olivia Goodwillie's famous Caerphilly style cheese, Lavistown, the following year, using cows' milk from nearby farmers PJ Byrne and his brother Seamus - and, very logically, this was soon followed by diversifation into whey fed pigs. Converted stone farm buildings have proved ideal for both the production unit and a farm shop - and they have now introduced Knockdrinna Cheese Tours (daily) and Cheese Courses (Fri). Their excellent website gives full details on all aspects of the business, including availability.

Stoneyford Co Kilkenny
+353 (0)56 772 8446 www.knockdrinna.com

Ballycross Apple Farm

With its beautiful stone courtyard and the family friendly activities that make it a perfect weekend destination, the rural idyll that is the Von Englebrechtan family's farm, belies the dedication and hard work that go into producing a superb range of single variety apple juices, speciality mixed fruit juices, and weekly production of fresh-pressed juice. West of Rosslare, on the R376 (Wellington Bridge road). The farm is open to coincide with the ripening of different apple varieties from late summer until the spring blossom, and it makes a great day out where children can meet farm animals (and other children), and see the apple trees. Visitors are encouraged to bring wellies and warm clothes for the trail through the woodland and orchards, where varieties including Elstar, Discovery, Cevaal and Jonagold are all grown for flavour and availability over a long season, and there's other fruit too, including pears and blackcurrants. Back at the courtyard, apples and juices take pride of place in the shop but you'll also find homemade preserves, other speciality foods and hampers - and you can sit in the courtyard to enjoy a coffee and freshly made waffles from their waffle bar. Upstairs, meanwhile, visiting the extensive interiors and gift shop may take some time…

Bridgetown Co Wexford
+353 (0)53 913 5160 www.ballycross.com

Flahavan's Oats

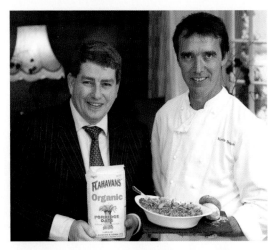

One of the unsung heroes of the Irish food scene, oats are widely grown, inexpensive, nutritious and extremely versatile. There's much more to oats than breakfast but, whether in porridge or other oat-based dishes like granola, their slow-release energy means they're pretty much the perfect start to the day. Growing conditions in Ireland suit oats well and this sixth generation family firm has been milling oats at Kilmacthomas for over 200 years, making it one of Ireland's longest-running family businesses. All of their standard oats are produced in Ireland, and they're actively encouraging more Irish organic oat production to meet demand. Over a million servings of Flahavan's porridge are consumed nationwide each week, so we're told, and the taste of the nation was confirmed in recent Great Taste Awards when two of their products - Flahavan's Organic Porridge Oats and Flahavan's Organic Jumbo Oats - were awarded a gold star for their texture and taste. Rightly keen to emphasise their versatility, Flahavans commission recipes from celebrity chefs such as Kevin Dundon (above, of nearby Dunbrody House Hotel) and - very useful for everyday ideas - there's a handy booklet of Mary Flahavan's own Simple Oat Recipes too.

E. Flahavan & Sons Limited Kilnagrange Mills Kilmacthomas Co Waterford
+353 (0)51 294107 www.flahavans.com

Omega Direct Irish Organic Beef - Farming with Altitude

Joe and Eileen Condon's organic hill farm on the edge of the Knockmealdown mountains, in Co Tipperary, is a model farm for "Farming with Altitude", a state initiative to encourage sustainable use of commonage in Ireland. Wishing to produce entirely grass-fed beef, the Condons selected Galloway cattle which, thanks to a double coat of hair and thick skin, thrive outside all year - and they fertilise the land, eliminating the need for artificial fertilisers. The stocking level discourages scrub and encourages plant diversity: a recent ecological survey revealed 64 different plant species per hectare - an ideal diet for producing well-flavoured beef, it is also thought to increase levels of omega 3 and reduce methane emissions, as well as helping to build up the soil and prevent flooding. Nearby, in Lismore, a respected craft butcher undertakes slaughtering, and the carcass (including all the less popular cuts, which are now often dumped) is returned to a new unit on the farm for packing. Their company, Omega Beef, employs a modern traceback system, also an open farm gate policy - meaning that customers are welcome to visit by arrangement and see this unique low-impact organic beef farm first-hand. Joe and Eileen Condon's achievements in sustainable farming have been recognised by the Irish Food Writers' Guild's Environmental Award.

Clashavaugha, Ballymacarbry, Clonmel, Co. Tippperary
+353 (0)87 273 5447 www.omegabeefdirect.ie

William Keogh, Keogh's Model Bakery, Callan, Co Kilkenny

Where to Buy

the Special Foods of the South East...

A guide to food shops, markets, farm shops, local stores and internet suppliers in counties Carlow, Kilkenny, Tipperary, Waterford & Wexford

Co Carlow

Malone's Fruit Farm Closh, **BALLON**, Co Carlow (+353 (0)59 9159477 / +353 (0)87 8472765). The Malone family grows a wide variety of fruit - strawberries, raspberries, blackberries, gooseberries, loganberries, tayberries, redcurrants, blackcurrants, whitecurrants and rhubarb - on their 12 acre farm near Altamont Gardens. Fresh fruit is sold at the farm shop in season, and frozen fruit and a full range of homemade products are available all year round. Many of the products are also on sale in retail outlets and markets, including Carlow Farmers' Market. May-Oct open daily, 8am-8pm; Nov-Apr, Mon-Sat 9am-5pm.

Hennessy Fine Food Store Dublin Street, **CARLOW** (+353(0)59 913 2849). Trisha Hennessy's great deli and café has earned a following for the carefully selected artisan foods stocked and wholesome meals served.

Tasteworks The Cottage Rathellin, **LEIGHLINBRIDGE** (+353 (0)59 972 2786 www.tasteworks.ie). Christine Jordan has a small farm shop at her Tasteworks Cookery School: stock includes home baked bread, biscuits and cakes, seasonal vegetables and fruit, artisan cheeses, eggs, free range pork, farmhouse icecream and sorbet, smoked trout - and her excellent all butter frozen pastry. Open from 12noon, Thu-Sat.

The Chocolate Garden Rath, near **TULLOW** Tel: +353 59 648 1999; www.chocolategarden.ie). Aka Wicklow Fine Foods, Jim and Mary Healy's innovative family-run business recently re-located to customised new premises alongside Rathwood Home and Garden World (www.rathwood.com) and Rath woodlands (where there are recreational walks). Offers a quality range of handmade chocolates, biscuits, fudge, chocolate spreads, and their own Tipperary Organic Organic Ice Cream, which is made in Clonmel; also chocolate workshops, a café and **online sales**.

Co Kilkenny

Keoghs Model Bakery Bridge Street **CALLAN** (+353 (0)56 7725254). In the family for over a century, William Keogh (opposite), his father and wife, Ann, use the best ingredients in tried and tested recipes to produce everything from sliced pan bread to wedding cakes, novelty cakes, and handmade chocolates; they supply outlets within a 20 mile radius. Open Mon-Sat, 7-5.

Highbank Organic Orchards **CUFFESGRANGE** (+353 (0)56 772 9918 www.highbankorchards.com). Since 1969 the Calder-Potts family have grown apple varieties specifically selected for their juicing properties, used to make delicious single vintage apple juice with only ascorbic acid added for preservation; new 'Mulled Apple' juice comes with a spice pack to make your own healthy hot brew. On sale at their Organic Farm Shop (Mon-Fri, 8-5, Sat by appointment, closed bank hols) also at selected farmers' markets, and from Iago's at the English Market, Cork.

Vogelaars Apple Farm Mullinabro, **FERRYBANK** via Waterford. (+353 (0)51 872544 / (0)87 252 7829); apples and fresh juices available at the farm shop, when in season.

Blueberry Larder Market Yard **KILKENNY** (+353 (0) 56 776 1456 www.blueberrykilkenny.com). Will & Kerry Fitzgerald's smart and highly professional city centre deli and takeaway offers seasonal, hand prepared 'classics with a twist', and carefully selected local products including Cramers Grove Ice cream and Truffle Fairy chocolates.

Cillín Hill Dublin Road **KILKENNY** (+353 (0)56 772 1407 / +353 (0)56 778 9778 www.cillinhill.com). For a very different kind of outing, why not visit Ireland's flagship livestock sales centre, Kilkenny Mart. Everyone is welcome to go and see cattle and sheep being bought and sold in the fine new sales rings - it's great fun watching the auctioneers at work, and then you can queue up with the farmers for a bite at Langtons @ Cillín Hill (Mon-Sat 7.30-4, Sun 9.30-4).

The Gourmet Store Main Street **KILKENNY** *(+353 (0)56 777 1727 www.thegourmetstorekilkenny.com)* Padraig and Irene Lawlor offer a well chosen range of Irish and continental deli fare, plus a wide range of freshly prepared food to go and good coffee.

Harneys Bakery KILMACOW. This popular bakery is now run by Nickie Grace, baker for two decades under the Harney ownership, and his brother Paul. Although in Co Kilkenny, Kilmacow is only 8km/5 miles from Waterford City and Harneys and was one of four bakeries jointly selected for a Euro-Toques Award, in celebration of the traditional local speciality made by them all, a square white yeast roll dusted with flour known as the Waterford blaa. Soft and crusty versions have their followers - Harneys favour the crusty blaa.

A Slice of Heaven Ballygowan **PILTOWN** *(+353 (0)87 9533870 www.asliceofheaven.ie).* Not content with making fantastic special occasion cakes and cupcakes, Mary McEvoy makes sure that they are exquisitely presented in decorative boxes too. Visit her lovely website and you will be won over in a flash.

Little Irish Apple Co Clonmore House **PILTOWN** *(+353 (0)51 387109).* Philip and Oren Little have delicious pasteurised pressed juice and apples for sale at their farm shop all year round; also supplied to markets and independent retailers.

Knockdrinna Farm Shop STONEYFORD *(+353 (0)56 772 8446 www.knockdrinna.com).* In addition to the Knockdrinna and Lavistown cheeses made here, the Finnegan family produce their own whey fed free range pork, which is on sale (frozen), along with a wide range of farmhouse cheeses and a deli counter offering home made pies and quiches, home cooked ham and turkey, salads, seasonal ready meals, home made preserves and local bread, confectionery and farmhouse icecream. Tue-Sat 11-6 (also Sun in summer).

Goatsbridge Premium Irish Trout Goatsbridge Trout Farm, **THOMASTOWN** *(+353 (0)86 818 8340 www.goatsbridgetrout.ie).* Previous generations of husband and wife team Margaret and Gerard Kirwan's family business took over where the Cistercian monks of old left off in this area, ensuring there's trout a-plenty in the Little Arrigle River in the Nore Valley - enough, in fact, for the restocking of lakes, rivers and fisheries all around the country. They supply hotels, restaurants, wholesalers and fish counters and welcome visitors to see their eco-friendly working environment and try their Premium Fresh and Smoked Trout. Open all year, with direct sales available to all - just call ahead.

Truffle Fairy THOMASTOWN *(+353 (0)87 286 2634 www.trufflefairy.com).* Chef Mary Teehan - who also offers speciality baking, savoury preserves and

Margaret & Gerard Kirwan,
Goatsbridge Trout Farm, Co Kilkenny

Christmas hampers - makes gorgeous handmade truffles, using the best Belgian chocolate; can purchase through website by email, or phone to order.

Oldtown Hill Bakehouse TULLAROAN *(+353 (0)56 776 9263)*. Joy Moore's craft bakery is on the family's dairy farm; they produce a range of breads and cakes based on high quality ingredients - perhaps it's using their own full cream milk that gives that special flavour. Open by appointment, and they sell to wholesale and retail.

Co Tipperary

Seymour Organic Farm "Sheepwalk" Finnoe Road **BORRISOKANE** *(+353 (0)86 400 0680 www.tipperaryfoodproducers.com)*. Organic since 1999, the animals on Michael Syemour's farm near Borrisokane are allowed to mature naturally on old pastures, producing wonderfully flavoursome meat - Texel cross lamb and Aberdeen Angus beef - all year round. It is available from the farm, or may be ordered by phone or email (delivery can be arranged). Also sold at Ennis and Nenagh Farmers' Market.

The Apple Farm Moorstown **CAHIR** *(+353 (0)52 744 1459 www.theapplefarm.com)*. At one of Ireland's best known fruit farms, Con Traas grows not only about 60 varieties of apples, but also pears, plums, cherries, strawberries and raspberries. Situated on the main Cahir - Clonmel road (N24) 6km from Cahir, there's an all year farm shop, open daily and offering fresh fruit in season, fruit juices (including a unique sparkling apple juice) and preserves. Visitors are welcome to walk around and see the fruit growing - and there is even a spacious caravan/camping site on the farm, with good facilities. The bottled products are also available **online**.

O'Brien's Farm Shop Outrath New Inn near **CAHIR** *(+353 (0)52 746 2282; www.tipperaryfoodproducers.com)*. Pat O'Brien and family grow a range of floury potatoes, and apples for their O'Briens Apple Juice. These are sold in the farm shop, along with limited amounts of home produced pork and bacon and other local food products including vegetables, free range eggs, Baylough cheese, and William's honey. Also at Cahir Farmers' Market.

The Spearman CASHEL *(+353 (0)62 61143)*. This bakery and café is a charming old-style place to take a break and buy some home-bakes to take home.

Hickey's Bakery & Café West Gate **CLONMEL** *(+353 (0)52 21587 www.tipperaryfoodproducers.com)*. This charming fourth generation craft bakery and café has been pleasing customers (including the author, William Trevor) since 1901; Nuala Hickey now continues the family tradition baking her unique traditional crusty bread, artisan bread, and cakes including the famous Hickey's barm brack, available **online**. Also excellent coffee.

James Whelan Butchers Oakville SC **CLONMEL** *(+353 (0)52 612 2927; www.jameswhelanbutchers.com)*. Specialising in dry-aged grass-fed Hereford and Aberdeen Angus beef from their own family farm, this innovative butcher was one of the first to go online; they are now Certified Organic Meat Retailers and offer organic chicken. Also lamb, pork and bacon, and some smoked fish. **Online sales**.

Omega Beef Direct Clashavaugha Ballymacarbry near **CLONMEL** *(+353 (0)87 273 5447 www.omegabeefdirect.ie)*. Joe and Eileen Condon welcome visitors by arrangement to their organic farm in the foothills of the Knockmealdown Mountains. Delivery nationwide; sold at Ardkeane Stores Waterford.

Cashel Blue and Crozier Blue Cheese J & L Grubb Ltd Beechmount **FETHARD** *(+353 (0)52 31151; www.cashelblue.com)*. Ireland's most famous blue cows' milk cheese (Cashel Blue) has been made by Jane and Louis Grubb and family on their farm near Fethard since 1984. Their nephews, Henry and Louis Clifton Brown, have been making Crozier Blue (one of very few blue Irish sheeps' milk cheeses) from the milk of their sheep grazed on pasturelands near Cashel, since 1999. Both cheeses are consistent award winners in Irish and international competition.

Country Choice Kenyon Street **NENAGH** *(+353 (0)67 32596; www.countrychoice.ie).* Peter and Mary Ward's iconic food business is much more than the sum of this delightful shop and café, Peter being one of the most energetic and dedicated movers and shakers in the wonderful world of artisan foods, and Mary one of Ireland's most prolific cooks - she famously makes around 1,000 Christmas puddings by hand each year, plus countless jars of marmalade and other preserves. They are committed Good Food Ireland members and often to be seen at GFI events at home and internationally, busily demonstrating the quality and diversity of artisan foods produced in Ireland. Their shop is a treasure trove of the very best foods from Ireland and abroad, so food lovers in the know plan their itineraries with care to take in a light meal and a little serious shopping here.

Quigleys NENAGH *(+353 (0)67 31188 www.quigleys.ie)* Established in 1890, this family-run bakery now has shops and cafés in 11 locations including Athlone, Tullamore and Roscrea.

Cooleeney Cheese Cooleeney Moyne near **THURLES** *(353 (0)504 45112 www.cooleeney.com).* The Maher family make an astonishing range of cow and goats milk cheeses including the trademark Cooleeney (camembert style), which has become a benchmark for the very best of Irish farmhouse cheeses - and their Tipperary brie is making waves, with a 3 star Gold at the Great Taste Awards (at which other cheeses frequently play starring roles). Other products include the Dunbarra range (semi-soft, flavoured), Gortnamona (goat), Maighean (pungent, raw cows' milk); they also export other farmhouse cheeses in addition to their own range. The better known cheeses are widely available from speciality stores; hampers, including their own chutneys and preserves along with cheeses and wines by David Dennison Fine Wines, are available to order (For further information, email Breda Maher: breda@cooleeney.com)

Crossogue Preserves THURLES *(www.crossoguepreserves.com).* An extensive range of products including diabetic jams and marmalades is widely available; stocked by all the Avoca outlets, Butler's Pantry and the Kilkenny Group. **Online shop**.

Co Waterford

Barron's Bakery & Coffee Shop CAPPOQUIN *(+353 (0)58 54045; www.barronsbakery.ie).* Esther and Joe Barron's business dates back to 1887, and this wonderfully traditional bakery still uses the original Scottish brick ovens to make breads with real flavour and an old-fashioned crust; the range is wide (and well worth investigating), but the Waterford 'blaas' are unique. Barron's is one of four bakeries recently awarded by Euro-Toques for their production of this traditional square white yeasted roll.

La Touche Organics Aglish **CAPPOQUIN** *(+353 (0)86 394 0564).* Siobhán La Touche produces organic fruit and vegetables, apples, juice and flowers. Sells at Dungarvan and Clonmel markets.

The Country Store Shopping Arcade Mitchell Street **DUNGARVAN** *(+353 (0)58 43061 www.thecountrystore.ie).* With local suppliers including The Tannery (www.tannery.ie) Eunice Power (www.eunicepower.com) of Powersfield House and Baldwin's Ice Cream (www.baldwinsicecream.com) from Knockanore, you'll find plenty of local speciality foods alongside everyday items here.

Nude Food DUNGARVAN *(+353 (0)58 24594 www.nudefood.ie).* Already well known in the area from her Naked Lunch market stall, Louise Clark was certain to succeed when she opened this charming café, bakery and deli in Dungarvan town. To reach the café you have to pass a great range of freshly made and artisan products on sale at the front, so why not give in gracefully and have a coffee here while you browse.

John David Power Butchers Main Street **DUNGARVAN** *(+353 (0)58 42339).* Renowned for his dry-cured bacon and sausages, the fine products sold by this traditional butchers have a strong local following - and have graced the menu of the town's leading restaurant, The Tannery, since it opened.

Michael McGrath Butcher Main Street **LISMORE** *(+353 (0)58 54350).* A rare treasure in this age of supermarket meat counters, this highly-prized fourth generation butcher is of the old school, where traditional methods decree that meats will hang in the shop awaiting the customer's order. With on-premises abattoir, not only do they slaughter their own cattle, but also offer the facility to other local farmers. You'll find McGrath's meat on many a fine table, including

The Tannery, in Dungarvan, Ballyvolane House near Fermoy and O'Brien Chop House, just across the road.

Ardkeen Quality Food Store Dunmore Road **WATERFORD** *(+353 (0)51 874620 www.ardkeen.com)*. Ireland's premier cheesemongers, Sheridans, have partnered with Ardkeen - which says a lot about the special nature of this extraordinary store, with its absolute commitment to quality and community, and its foundation of very local artisan stocks. And not only is the shop definitely worth a detour, but the website also merits a special visit; their Food Heroes menu alone will blow you away - and how many shops can boast a Fresh Food Advisor like former Euro-Toques commissioner Martin Dwyer (www.martindwyer.com)? Small **online shop** too, for hampers, wines and gift vouchers.

Henry Downes 8-10 Thomas Street **WATERFORD** *(+353 (0)51 874118)*. Established in 1759, this unusual pub is one of the few remaining houses to bottle its own whiskey. Friendly, humorous bar staff enjoy filling customers in on the pub's proud history and will gladly sell you a bottle of their unique Henry Downes No.9 to take away.

Hickeys Bakery Barrack Street **WATERFORD** *(+353 (0)51 375388)*. The Hickey family has been running this bakery in Waterford city centre for over half a century, and it was one of four bakeries honoured by Euro-Toques for maintaining the tradition of making the 'Waterford blaa' the floury yeast roll that is peculiar to the area.

Gallweys Irish Handmade Chocolates Unit 5B Six Cross Roads Business Park **WATERFORD** *(+353 (0)51 334970 www.gallweys.ie)*. The Gallweys company has a long history in Waterford and the business is run by the O'Brien family - Ger and Yvonne O'Brien, their daughter Sarah Jane and her husband Bernard Deegan. Their handmade chocolates are a justifiable source of pride, and they chocolates are now available **online**, as well as from their cafes in Waterford and Tramore, and selected outlets nationwide. Chocolate classes are held too - see website or call for details.

M&D Bakery 4 Mount Sion Avenue **WATERFORD** *(+353 (0)51 378080)* named after two brothers and third generation bakers, Michael and Dermot Walsh, this highly regarded bakery is one of the four bakeries recognised by Euro-Toques for continuing to include

Michael McGrath Butcher, Lismore, Co Waterford

the traditional Waterford blaa in their range. They supply many catering and retail businesses in the area.

Tom Kearney's Butchers John Street **WATERFORD** *(+353 (0)51 874434)*. Waterford has more than its fair share of good butchers; and Tom Kearney's stands out especially for their beef; they raise their own animals for supply to some of the city's most discerning customers.

Co Wexford

Ballycross Apple Farm BRIDGETOWN *(+353 (0)53 913 5160 www.ballycross.com)*. Single variety and mixed fruit juices, homemade jams and preserves, gift hampers. Farm Shop open weekends in apple season (dates vary, late summer to spring); juices can be ordered **online**. Family friendly; orchard trail; refreshments; also quality interiors items and gifts.

Sugar & Spice Main Street **BUNCLODY** *(+353 (0)53 937 6388)*. Charming old world home bakery and 'foodhall'.

Tinnock Farm Produce Tinnock **CAMPILE** *(+353 (0)87 220 3300)*. You will see Peggy Gaffney and John Murphy's lamb, beef, free range hen and duck eggs, buttermilk and homemade butter at local farmers' markets & Dun Laoghaire (Sun).

O'Neill Foods Bolinadrum **FERNS** *(+353 (0)87 677 9803)*. Pat O'Neill's dry cured bacon is widely sought after in the South-East and available from the factory at Enniscorthy (phone for details), Sugar & Spice in Bunclody, specialist shops such as Ardkeen Quality Food Store in Waterford, Nolan's of Clontarf and Donnybrook Fair in Dublin and from Farmers' Markets.

Noirins Bakehouse McDermott Street **GOREY** *(+353 (0)53 936 7335 www.noirins.ie)*. Dedicated husband and wife team Vincent and Nóirín Kearney produce an impressive range of handmade sweet and savoury bakes and preserves at their Ferns bakery, all based on quality ingredients. On sale at their coffee shop on in Gorey, and at specialist outlets; also at farmers' markets (including Dublin area). Well worth looking out for.

Greens Berry Farm Shops near **GOREY** & **COURTOWN** *(www.greensberryfarm.ie)*. At Tinnock (N11, 2 miles north of Gorey) and Tomsilla, near Courtown, these are the major fruit producers in the

area; over 50% of the total production is sold through the two farm shops. From early May to September, the Tinnock Farm Shop is open 8.30-6 daily, selling a wide range of fruits, fruit products and (in season) new potatoes; the Courtown Road Farm Shop opens for July & August, 10-6 daily, and also offers a small selection of locally produced cheese, honey, yogurt, bacon etc., and some wines (ideal when self-catering in the area). Bistro (evenings) +353 (0)53 942 5666.

In a Nutshell 8 South Street **NEW ROSS** *(353 (0)51 422 777)*. Philip and Patsy Rogers' emporium is a rewarding find for lovers of good food: traditional country methods, handed down recipes and a respect for fresh produce are at the heart of this delightful shop and café, where everything is freshly made every day - and 'chemically treated or pre-prepared foods are not welcome'.

Wexford Home Preserves **NEW ROSS** *(+353 (0)51 426646 www.wexfordpreserves.ie)*. Producers of traditional preserves here since 1988; available from independent shops, small multiples (SuperValu, Centra etc) and tourist attractions in the area; supplies Ferrycarrig Hotel, Wexford.

Kate's Farm Shop McQuillans Cross Clonard **WEXFORD** *(+353 (0)53 913 9848 www.goodfoodireland.com)*. Situated in a former garage forecourt just outside Wexford Town (off N25), Kate and Ollie O'Mahony's large food shop is well stocked with an outstanding selection of local and artisan foods.

Pettitts SuperValu St. Aidans Shopping Centre **WEXFORD** *(+353 (0)53 912 4055 www.pettitts.ie)*. Part of the SuperValu franchise this foodstore has a strong food management team who are particularly dedicated to improving the consumers experience with seafood. Good range of fresh fish on offer throughout the week. Open 7 days.

Stable Diet **YOLETOWN** *(+353 (0)53 913 1287 www.stablediet.com)*. It all began with carrot cake and flapjacks and, although Katherine Carroll's bakery range has expanded considerably, "nature knows best" remains the mantra. Production is at Yoletown, Broadway, Co Wexford and there's a smart little café & patisserie on Main Street, Wexford Town, where a changing menu is offered through the day and the full range of their delicious additive-free cakes, flapjacks, breakfast cereals is on sale, together with a newer range of dips, sauces and chutneys.

Ireland South-East: Food Markets

For further information on Farmers Markets throughout Ireland
www.bordbia.ie • www.irishfarmersmarkets.ie

CARLOW

Carlow Farmers' Market Potato Market. Sat 9-2.

KILKENNY *(www.kilkennyfarmersmarket.com)*

Kilkenny Farmers' Market Market Yard
(beside Dunnes Stores). Thu 9.30-2.30.

Callan Farmers' Market Main Street. Sat 10-12.

TIPPERARY

Cahir Farmers' Market Craft Granary. Sat 9-1.

Carrick-on-Suir Farmers' Market Heritage Centre.
Fri 10-2.

Clonmel Farmers' Market beside Oakville Shopping
Centre, Sat 10-2.

Premier Organic Farmers' Market Clonmel
Showgrounds. Fri 11-6.

Nenagh Farmers' Market Kenyon Street. Sat 10-2.

Thurles Farmers' Market Greyhound Track. Sat 9.30-1.

WATERFORD

Dungarvan Farmers' Market Gratton Square. Thu 9-2.

Dunhill Farmers Market Parish Hall, Last Sun of
month. 11.30-2.

Kilmacthomas Market Fri 9.30-2.

Lismore Farmers' Market Blackwater Valley
(Call +353 (0)26 621 5916 for details).

Stradbally Community Market Carrigahilla, Stradbally.
1st Sat of month 10-12.30 (Easter-Christmas).

Ardkeen Producers' Market Ardkeen, Waterford.
Quality Food Store; 2nd Sun of the month.

Waterford Farmers Market Jenkins Lane, Waterford.
Sat 10-4.

WEXFORD

Dunbrody Farmers' Market Dunbrody Abbey Centre.
Some days in Jul-Aug *(see www.bordbia.ie for details)*.

Enniscorthy Farmers' Market Abbey Square Carpark.
Sat 9-2.

Gorey Farmers' Market Gorey Community School Car
Park Esmonde Street. Sat 9-2.

New Ross Farmers' Market The Quay. Sat 9-2.

Wexford Farmers' Market, Supervalu car park
(Key West) Wexford Town. Fri 9-2.

O'BRIEN CHOP HOUSE

TRADITIONAL SUNDAY
LUNCH ROASTS
FROM 12 NOON - 4 PM

PURPLE SPROUTING BROCCOLI
+ WILD GARLIC NOW ON

ROASTS, CHOPS, PIES, WHOLE
FISH, SOUPS, CHOWDER,
ILLY COFFEE + LOOSE LEAF
TEAS + HOMEMADE SCONES

WINEMAKERS DINNER WITH
CHARLES SIMPSON OF DOMAINE
SAINTE ROSE ON APRIL 14.

O'Brien Chop House, Lismore, Co Waterford

COUNTY CARLOW
Bagenalstown

♣ Lorum Old Rectory

Bobbie Smith's very comfortable mid-Victorian cut stone granite rectory makes an ideal base for exploring the lush South-East; everybody loves staying here and her easy hospitality keeps bringing guests back - also very good food. Bobbie, a Euro-Toques member, is committed to using local produce and suppliers whenever possible and is renowned for delicious home cooking using mainly organic and home-grown ingredients; rack of local lamb is a speciality, and residents dine at a long communal table, where wonderful breakfasts are also served.

Kilgraney Bagenalstown Co Carlow
+353 (0)59 977 5282 www.lorum.com

Ballickmoyler

♣ Coolanowle Country House

Organic farm, produce on sale, lovely B&B accommodation, self-catering, holistic treatments - is there nothing they don't offer at Bernadine and Jimmy Mulhall's family farm? Close to the Carlow-Kildare-Laois-Kilkenny borders, it's handy to much of the South-East (and Dublin) but, with a real country living experience (natural woodland, lakes, the farm) on site, you may prefer to stay put. Home-produced organic food is the USP, along with traditional home cooking - tea with home bakes on arrival, great breakfasts, dinner by arrangement - even a traditional Sunday lunch featuring joints of their own organic meats.

Ballickmoyler Co Carlow
+353 (0)59 862 5176 www.coolanowle.com

Carlow Town

Lennons @ Visual

Well known restaurateur Sinead Byrne and her son Ross run the restaurant at this new gallery and theatre in the heart of Carlow Town, and it benefits from the stylish contemporary setting - and a view of Carlow Cathedral. But even if it had none of that, fans would still beat a path to the door for the wholesome, informal dishes that Lennons built their reputation on. Head chef Gail Johnson continues the long established Lennons philosophy of using the best local and regional artisan produce, and her appealingly simple, cooked to order, food just hits the spot.

Visual Centre for Contemporary Art Old Dublin Rd Carlow
+353 (0)59 917 9245 www.lennons.ie

Clonegal

Sha-Roe Bistro

In a pretty village 'on the road to nowhere', Henry and Stephanie Stone's beautifully appointed small restaurant has earned renown for Henry's excellent food and their unique combination of professionalism and charm. Deceptively simple menus based on seasonal foods include Dublin Bay prawns (langoustines), an Irish charcuterie plate, local beef - matured for seven weeks - and Wexford lamb; there's always an appealing vegetarian dish too, also local cheeses. Faultless cooking and good value make Sha-Roe well worth a detour - and nearby historic Huntington Castle merits a visit too.

Main Street Clonegal Co Carlow +353 (0)53 937 5636

COUNTY KILKENNY

Kilkenny City

Campagne

Kilkenny's leading restaurant is run by Garrett Byrne, former head chef at Dublin's celebrated Chapter One, and his partner and restaurant manager, Brid Hannon. A set of striking abstract landscape paintings dominate the room and, in tune with a passionately held food philosophy that involves local food producers in the cooking, this well-named French-inspired restaurant reflects rural values in a contemporary style. Menus balance the luxurious with the rustic, with Irish traditions seen in many dishes. Extremely professional, and good value too.
The Arches, Gashouse Lane, Kilkenny
+353 (0)56 777 2858 www.campagne.ie

Kilkenny Design Centre

Situated in the former stables and dairy of Kilkenny Castle - and overlooking the craft courtyard - this deservedly popular self-service restaurant offers wholesome and consistently delicious fare. The appetising food on display is all freshly prepared every day: home baking is a strong point, also simple hot food - seafood chowder with home-made soda bread, for example, or a speciality chicken & broccoli crumble with local Lavistown cheese. Very reasonably priced and well worth a visit. [Also serves breakfast for guests at ♣ Butler House (www.butler.ie), across the garden.]
Castle Yard Kilkenny
+353 (0)56 772 2118 www.kilkennydesign.com

♣ Zuni Restaurant & Boutique Hotel

Although Zuni is an hotel (youthful 'boutique' style), the atmosphere is more restaurant with rooms: an in-place for discerning Kilkenny diners, who enjoy chef Maria Raftery's wide-ranging menus and consistently good cooking. Seasonal use of local ingredients lends a distinctive Irish tone - Lavistown cheese gives relevance to a Waldorf salad with green apple sorbet, for example, the antipasti slate offers cured meats from Gubbeen Smokehouse in West Cork, and local cheeses Knockdrinna, Cashel Blue and Cooleeney are likely stars on the cheeseboard. An all day café offers casual fare.
Patrick Street Kilkenny
+353 (0)56 772 3999 www.zuni.ie

COUNTY TIPPERARY

Cashel

Chez Hans & Café Hans

The Matthia family runs these perfectly complementary businesses: a long-established fine dining restaurant in an atmospheric converted church, and the contemporary lunchtime café alongside; each excels in its way, both are favourite destinations for a wide-ranging clientèle. Expect excellent cooking, with colourful, sassy dishes including lots of salads in the café, and seriously fine food in the evening restaurant, where specialities include a magnificent cassoulet of seafood (half a dozen varieties of fish and shellfish with a delicate chive velouté sauce), and, of course, the great lamb and beef for which the area is renowned.
Moor Lane Cashel Co Tipperary
+353 (0)62 61177 & (0)62 63660

Clogheen

♣ The Old Convent Gourmet Hideaway

A stunning destination, in one of the most beautiful and unspoilt parts of Ireland. Dermot and Christine Gannon offer adults 'a short getaway from it all experience' and the restaurant - still complete with stained glass windows - makes an unusual setting for an exceptional meal: Dermot, a gifted chef, offers only a nightly 9-course Tasting Menu, plus an optional cheese platter of seven Irish cheeses served with Traas Farm fruit and plum jam. Ingredients are home grown or sourced locally (and organic) when possible and the cooking is knockout good. Gorgeous rooms too.
Mount Anglesby Clogheen Co Tipperary
+353(0)52 65565 www.theoldconvent.ie

Nenagh

Country Choice Delicatessen & Coffee Bar

Peter Ward is a leading light on the Irish food scene, so food-lovers plot and plan journeys around a visit to this unique shop where he and his wife Mary offer an extensive range of the finest Irish artisan produce, plus some from further afield. Specialities include a great terrine, made from the family's saddleback pigs, also Mary's legendary home-made jams, marmalade - and Christmas puddings! Old hands fortify themselves in the little café first, with simple home-cooked food that reflects the seasons - if the range is small at a particular time of year, so be it. Well worth a detour.
Kenyon Street Nenagh Co Tipperary
+353 (0)67 32596 www.countrychoice.ie

COUNTY WATERFORD

Ardmore

♣ The Cliff House Hotel

Since opening in 2008, this beautifully located boutique hotel has become one of Ireland's key dining destinations, thanks to Dutch Head Chef Martijn Kajuiter's ambition and dedication: simply-worded menus speak volumes for his philosophy - organic Clare Island salmon, Irish free-range pork, local Suffolk lamb, Helvick turbot, hake and monkfish, Skeaghanore duck (from nearby County Cork) and homegrown seasonal produce all feature - yet they appear in a highly sophisticated international cuisine, featuring many original touches. A new focus for an unspoilt area which has somehow remained a well-kept secret until now.
Ardmore Co Waterford
+353 (0)24 87800 www.thecliffhousehotel.com

Ballymacarbry

♣ Hanora's Cottage

The Wall family's gloriously remote guesthouse and restaurant is a very special place, offering country air, comfort, genuine hospitality and great food - notably their legendary breakfast buffet, a gargantuan feast designed to see you many miles along the hills before you stop for a little packed lunch (prepared that morning), and ultimately return for dinner... Keen supporters of small suppliers, Euro-Toques chefs Eoin and Judith Wall offer imaginative menus using local produce - fresh fish from Dunmore East, free-range chickens from Stradbally and local cheeses, for example.
Nire Valley Co Waterford
+353 (0)52 36134 www.hanorascottage.com

Cappoquin

♣ Richmond House & Restaurant

Good food is at the heart of the Deevy family's fine 18th century country house and restaurant just outside Cappoquin. An ardent supporter of local produce, Paul Deevy sources everything with tremendous care: meats come from his trusted local butcher, fresh seafood is from Dunmore East and Dungarvan, while seasonal fresh produce is their own, or grown organically nearby. Hard to resist specialities include roast rack of delicious West Waterford lamb - presented on braised puy lentils and buttered green beans - and a separate vegetarian menu is offered. Great breakfasts too.

Cappoquin Co Waterford

+353 (0)58 54278 www.richmondhouse.net

Dungarvan

The Tannery

In 1997 Paul Flynn forsook a high-flying career in top kitchens to open this stylish contemporary restaurant in his home town, with his wife Maire - ultimately making Dungarvan a food lovers' destination. Deceptive simplicity is the key to Paul's skilful cooking; menus with a strongly Irish feeling are based mainly on local ingredients, which Paul supports avidly and sources with care - local seafood of course, meats including pork and bacon supplied by renowned local butcher JD Power, also their own home grown seasonal produce. The Tannery Cookery School and Organic Garden are nearby.

Quay Street Dungarvan Co Waterford

+353 (0)58 45420 www.tannery.ie

Lismore

O'Brien Chop House

Justin and Jenny Green (of Ballyvolane House, East Cork) now run this former bar and, with its mainly contemporary yet atmospheric interior, the spirit of the original pub is alive and well. Homemade and local food is at the heart of this enterprise - shelves behind the bar are laden with homemade treats such as Ballyvolane relishes, preserves and elderflower cordial to purchase, and all ingredients are impeccably sourced. Great meats are the backbone of the menu - the beef, lamb, mutton and pork come from the renowned McGrath's butchers shop along the street - and one-off events with other likeminded folk, eg Green Saffron and Dungarvan Brewing Company, are often held.

Main Street Lismore Co Waterford

+353 (0)58 53810; www.obrienchophouse.ie

Waterford City

♣ Waterford Castle Hotel & Golf Club

Idyllically situated on its own wooded island (complete with 18-hole golf course) and reached by a private ferry, this atmospheric hotel dates back to the 15th century and meals are served in an impressive, richly panelled dining room. Menus are not long but outstanding food is intelligently sourced and spankingly fresh and local, displaying chef Michael Quinn's Euro-Toques and Slow Food background. Each concisely-worded dish tells the story of its origins: O'Flynn's beef tongue and cheek salad; seared Kilmore Quay scallops; tian of Mrs Bate's crab; Paul Crotty's organic chicken breast; local cheeses, including Knockalara Sheep's and Crozier Blue. Magic.

The Island Ballinakill Waterford

+353 (0)51 878 203 www.waterfordcastle.com

COUNTY WEXFORD

Arthurstown

♣ Dunbrody Country House Hotel & Cookery School

Set in parkland and gardens on the Hook Peninsula, Catherine and TV chef Kevin Dundon's elegant Georgian manor is known especially for its food. The Harvest Room restaurant looks over lawns to a productive organic vegetable and fruit garden, and local suppliers are given full credit: fresh fish is delivered daily from nearby Duncannon harbour, shellfish from Kilmore Quay, and meats com from Wallace's butchers of Wellington Bridge. Kevin Dundon's 'eat local' philosophy comes through on all his menus, with local meats like rack of Wexford lamb often topping the bill - and outstanding breakfasts too.
Arthurstown Co Wexford
+353 (0)51 389 600 www.dunbrodyhouse.com

Carne

The Lobster Pot

Ciaran and Anne Hearne's handsome country pub is handy to Rosslare ferry port and renowned for seafood. Daily deliveries ensure fresh fish supplies and, the catch dictates daily specials. Simple but carefully prepared meals are served all day in the bar, typically including an outstanding seafood chowder (salmon, crab, prawns, cod, cockles & mussels in a rich fish base), while an extensive evening menu listing 21 fish in eight different languages offers treats like River Rush oysters and lobsters from the sea tank.
Ballyfane Carne Co Wexford +353 (0)53 913 1110

Rosslare

♣ Kelly's Resort Hotel & Spa

With its special brand of relaxed professionalism, the Kelly family's renowned beachside hotel sums up all that is best about the sunny South-East for its many regular visitors. Among its outstanding features (exceptional hospitality; great facilities; a stunning art collection…) the hotel's two restaurants and meticulously sourced wine list score highly (a family connection with a French winery helps) and, although offering contrasting styles, both restaurants reflect the value placed on fresh local produce, with ingredients like Wexford beef, Rosslare mackerel, Slaney salmon and locally sourced vegetables used in daily-changing menus.
Rosslare Co Wexford
+353 (0)53 913 2114 www.kellys.ie

Wexford Area

♣ Killiane Castle

The past and present mix effortlessly in the Mernagh family's friendly farm B&B: the farmhouse and towerhouse are 17th century and some of the 13th century Norman Castle still stands - they hope to restore it in the future. The working farm allows visitors to see a modern dairy in action and their own hens supply the eggs for the delicious breakfasts that Kathleen Mernagh serves here buffet-style, in a warm, cosy dining-room. No dinners are offered, but the restaurants of Wexford are very close, or Kathleen will advise guests on the best local choices.
Drinagh Wexford Co Wexford
+353 (0)53 915 8885 www.killianecastle.com

Recipes

Gortnamona Goats' Cheese Baskets

This simple starter is easy to prepare and full of flavour. One of the many outstanding cheeses made in the South-East, Gortnamona is a soft mould ripened Irish goats cheese, one of a range produced by the Maher family at Cooleeney Cheese near Thurles in Co Tipperary. Goat cheeses are not only delicious, but also useful for meeting special dietary requirements - Gortnamona is non-dairy, made with vegetarian rennet and low in cholesterol. Select large, naturally ripened, evenly-sized tomatoes; vine tomatoes usually have the best flavour.

Serves 2

2 or 4 tomatoes, depending on size

75g/3 oz Gortnamona cheese, or other soft goats' cheese

40g/1 1/2 oz crème fraîche

15ml/1 tbsp chopped chives

2.5ml/1/2 tsp chopped basil

extra chopped chives, whole chives and mixed salad leaves to serve

Wash and dry the tomatoes. Slice off the top of each tomato and scoop out the pulp; lightly salt the inside of each tomato and turn over to drain.

Mix the cheese, crème fraîche, chives and basil in a bowl and fill the tomatoes with the mixture.

Sprinkle with chopped chives and replace the caps over the cheese if you wish. Serve immediately on a bed of tossed leaves, with fresh crusty bread to accompany.

Fish Pie with Oat Topping

Everybody loves a good fish pie, and it is a versatile dish. Oats are an important crop in this region and the oat crumble topping used here makes a nice variation on the usual potato or pastry. Fresh fish from ports like Helvick, Kilmore Quay and Duncannon is easily available, and the combination can be varied - the special mixtures sold in chunks by fishmongers may also be used instead of fillets in this recipe, but be careful not to overcook them. And don't use more than half the quantity of smoked fish at the most, as the strong flavour will overpower other ingredients. This pie can be assembled and grilled to serve immediately, or prepared ahead then reheated and browned in the oven.

Serves 4-6

600ml/1 pint milk

225ml/8 fl oz cream

1 bay leaf

900g/2lb mixed firm-fleshed fish fillets

225g/8oz mussels, well scrubbed (optional)

salt and freshly ground black pepper

50g/2oz butter, preferably unsalted, plus extra for greasing

1 onion, finely chopped

75g/3oz plain flour

175ml/6fl oz dry white wine or cider

2 leeks, trimmed and thinly sliced

6 tbsp freshly chopped mixed herbs

Topping:

75g/3oz butter

100g/4oz fresh breadcrumbs

100g/4oz flaked oats

Grated zest of one lemon

50g/2oz hard cheese, grated (optional)

3 dessertspoons freshly chopped herbs

2oz/50g flaked almonds (optional)

First, prepare the topping: Melt the butter and add the breadcrumbs, oats, grated lemon zest, grated cheese (if using), chopped herbs and flaked almonds (if using). Mix well and set aside.

To cook the fish: Place the milk in a saucepan with the cream and the bay leaf. Add the fish fillets, bring just up to boiling point and poach gently for 3-5 minutes or until just tender, depending on their thickness. Transfer to a plate with a fish slice and set aside until they are cool enough to handle. Strain the poaching liquid into a jug.

Meanwhile, cook the mussels, if using: cook well-scrubbed mussels briefly in a dry lidded pan until they open. Discard any which don't snap closed when scrubbing them, or which don't open when cooked. Remove the cooked mussels from their shells and strain any juices.

Flake the cooled fish into bite-sized chunks; discarding the skin and any bones.

To make the sauce: Melt the butter in a large non-stick pan. Add the onion and cook gently for 4-5 minutes until softened but not coloured, stirring occasionally. Stir in the flour and cook for 2 minutes, stirring continuously. Pour in the wine or cider and allow to reduce, then add the reserved poaching liquids, a little at a time, whisking continuously after each addition. Reduce the heat and stir in the leeks. Simmer gently for 6-8 minutes until the leeks are softened and tender and the sauce has slightly reduced and thickened, stirring occasionally. Stir in the herbs and season to taste.

Suggested fish:

salmon, haddock or cod (fresh or undyed smoked) and/or monkfish

Suggested herbs:

flat leaf parsley, chives and dill - avoid very strongly flavoured herbs, which will overpower the delicate fish

To assemble: Lightly butter a large baking dish and add a couple of tablespoons of the sauce. Scatter over the poached fish flakes, and the mussels if using, then spoon the remaining sauce on top to cover completely. Spread the prepared oat crumble topping over the fish mixture and even it out lightly with a fork.

To serve immediately: Finish under a medium grill; when the pie is thoroughly heated through and the topping is crisp and golden brown, serve from the dish at the table straight onto warmed plates. Offer potatoes and fresh seasonal vegetables or salad to accompany.

To serve if made in advance: Preheat the oven to 180°C/350°F/Gas 4. Bake for 15-20 minutes or until heated through and the top is golden brown. (If using a fan-assisted oven, bake from cold at 160°C/325°F.)

Roast Rib Of Hereford Beef With Béarnaise Sauce

Providing the best beef is used, this is the perfect traditional roast, and it is served regularly by Justin and Jenny Green's at both O'Brien Chop House in the Heritage Town of Lismore, Co Waterford, and Ballyvolane (www.ballyvolanehouse.ie), their country house in East Cork. Their beef is supplied by the renowned butcher Michael McGrath, whose magnificent meat is prepared as it always has been in his traditional shop on the main street in Lismore. Ask your own butcher to saw through the chine bone of the joint for easier carving. Roast potatoes and buttered leeks make perfect partners for the beef.

Serves 6-8

olive oil, for cooking

8 lb/3.6kg rib of beef on the bone (preferably well hung Hereford or a similar breed)

12 large potatoes (such as rooster)

2 large leeks, trimmed & washed well

4 oz/115g butter

For the Béarnaise:

2 small shallots, finely chopped

2 tsp tarragon vinegar or white wine vinegar

1 fresh tarragon sprig

12 oz/350g butter cut into cubes

4 egg yolks (free range if possible)

salt and freshly ground black pepper

Preheat the oven to 220C/425F/Gas 7. Rub olive oil lightly into the beef and season to taste. Place in a roasting tin and cook for 30 minutes. Reduce the oven temperature to 170C/325F/Gas 3 and roast the beef for another 1 hour and 30 minutes for rare. (Cook longer to your taste if you prefer your beef medium or well done.)

Meanwhile, chop the potatoes into even-sized pieces and place in a roasting tin. Toss in a little olive oil and season to taste. Roast on the top shelf of the oven for 1 hour until crispy and golden brown, turning them occasionally to ensure they cook evenly.

Cut the leeks on the diagonal and place in a pan with a lid. Add the butter and four tablespoons of water. Cover and cook for 5 minutes, then strain and season to taste. Keep warm, or leave to cool and reheat as necessary. Strain, then season with salt and pepper.

To make the béarnaise sauce: place the shallots in a small pan with the vinegar. Strip the leaves from the tarragon sprig and chop finely, then set aside. Add the tarragon stalk to the pan and reduce over low heat until there is almost nothing left. Allow to cool for 5 minutes, then remove the tarragon sprig. To finish the béarnaise sauce, place the reduced shallot mixture back on a very low heat and whisk in the egg yolks, then very slowly add the butter piece by piece until the sauce thickens. If the sauce curdles, whisk in one teaspoon of cold water. Add the reserved chopped tarragon and season to taste. Use immediately, or keep the sauce warm in thermos flask.

When the beef is cooked, remove from the oven and wrap in foil, then leave to rest for 20 minutes. Carve the beef into slices and arrange on warmed plates with the roasted potatoes, buttered leeks and a dollop of the béarnaise sauce.

Marlfield Rhubarb Chutney

Marlfield House (www.marlfieldhouse.com) is a fine Regency period mansion just outside Gorey in Co Wexford and, in the hospitable hands of the Bowe family, it makes an exceptional small hotel. Carefully tended kitchen gardens supply much of the fresh fruit, vegetables and herbs required by the house, and guests enjoy going to see for themselves the good things which will later feature at dinner - which is served in an elegant dining room with period-style conservatory overlooking the beautiful gardens. This chutney is a versatile accompaniment for many foods. One suggestion is to serve it with cheese fritters which could be either a first course or an end of meal savoury, in this case using smoked Abbey Brie cheese made by Pat Hyland at Ballacolla, Co Laois.

1lb/450g rhubarb, trimmed and sliced

12oz/350g onions, peeled and sliced

6oz/175g raisins

13oz/375g brown sugar

3/4 pint/450ml cider vinegar

3 tsp salt

1 tsp ground cinnamon

1 tsp ground ginger

1/2 tsp ground cloves

a pinch of cayenne pepper

Put all the listed ingredients into a stainless steel preserving pan and set over a low heat. Stir with a wooden spoon until the sugar has completely dissolved, then bring to the boil.

Stirring frequently, simmer over gentle heat for two hours, or until the chutney has reduced and thickened.

Spoon the chutney into warmed sterilised jars.

Best kept in a cool dark place for 1 month before using.

Smoked Abbey Brie fritters:

2 x 200g/7oz wheels of smoked
Abbey Brie

a little plain white flour

2 eggs, beaten

about 4 oz/110g white breadcrumbs

Divide the cheeses into 16 wedges. Dust with the flour, then dip first into the beaten egg, and then into the bread crumbs.

Heat some fresh oil to 170°C / 325°F and deep fry the fritters for 30 seconds. Drain and serve hot, with a small salad and the chutney.

Ireland: East
Dublin, Louth, Meath, Kildare & Wicklow

River Liffey, Dublin

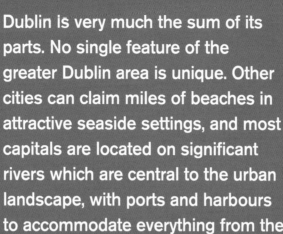

Dublin is very much the sum of its parts. No single feature of the greater Dublin area is unique. Other cities can claim miles of beaches in attractive seaside settings, and most capitals are located on significant rivers which are central to the urban landscape, with ports and harbours to accommodate everything from the largest cruise liners to small craft. Other capitals have mountains within easy reach, and most are near prosperous farmland, and dotted with extensive public parks. Dozens of cities have a vibrant cultural life with an intriguing history and handsome architecture with a thriving hospitality industry. Many have a lively interaction with sport of all kinds, served by stadiums of international standard, major horse-racing venues in convenient locations, the sea on the doorstep, and a selection of globally renowned golf courses. You can find some and often most of these amenities in any city. But perhaps it is only Dublin which has them all.

Glendalough, Co Wicklow

About the Region

And compared to the world's largest cities, Dublin manages it in a relatively compact area. The River Liffey, for instance, which so defines the city, is by no means the largest in Ireland. Even within this region, its near neighbour the River Boyne to the north, reaching the Irish Sea at Drogheda, is longer and larger. And these east coast rivers are mere streams by comparison with the majestic waterways of the south, west and north coasts.

But the way that the Dublin region has so much within a relatively small area is epitomised by the Liffey. It rises in seeming remoteness high in the Wicklow Mountains, yet its source is just 22 kilometres south of its seamouth in Dublin Bay. But by the time the river blends into salt water it has descended and meandered through Wicklow and the elegantly lakelike Blessington reservoir, then on through Kildare to glimpse Meath before becoming the heart of the city on the Liffey, celebrated as Anna Livia Plurabelle, integral to Dublin's history, folklore and culture.

Dublin city is half a circle, the other half being the sea. The landward semi-circle is neatly outlined by the M50. Road travel in Ireland has been much improved in recent decades with a network of motorways which have taken gridlock out of many smaller towns, and reduced rat runs through otherwise gentle countryside. But there aren't fifty motorways, or anything like it. So how come we've the M50? Well, there may be official explanations, but Dubliners assume that because other cities have ring-roads with fancy names, and especially because London has the M25, then the Dubs have the M50, and that's all there is to it.

Beyond the semi-circle of the M50, the people of the greater Dublin area are as locally patriotic as anyone else in Ireland. Although new roads have brought much of this region within an hour's easy reach, even those who commute to the city from the area's most remotely rural corners will have twin affiliations. They enjoy and feel pride in Dublin in working hours, but are fiercely loyal to their own neighbourhood down the country when at home.

This division between city and country is well rooted in time and tradition. The development of Dublin as a commercial and administrative centre saw recruits to the workforce being drawn in from all over the country. This was particularly the case with the growth of the public service from the mid-19th Century onwards.

The origins of the notion of the Dublin Jackeens versus the Culchies from the country are lost in the mist of times. But it has long been the case that the sure way to tell who was which lay in what happened at the weekend. Only the Culchies went home. The Dubliner was already there, and always there, incapable of leaving the city even when physically elsewhere, as James Joyce so memorably demonstrated.

Within Dublin, the river has long defined a divide in the city which goes back at least to the final years of Viking dominance, and probably further. As the new Norman invaders (Norse Vikings with French manners) began working their way northward in 1170 from their beachheads on the south coast, the settled mainly Danish Vikings in Dublin retreated north of the river to base themselves around what is now Oxmantown, originally Ostmanstown, the settlement of the Eastmen, otherwise the Danes.

The resulting northside/southside divide became so embedded that centuries later when the introduction of postal districts reflected the schism with odd number generally north of the river, the powers that be somehow arranged that one of the northside's more agreeable features, the Phoenix Park which is entirely north of the river, has its address in Dublin 8. Way before all this, the fortified Norman city was entirely south of the river around Dublin castle, its crowded streets filled with tradesmen and craftsmen who catered for the needs of the ruling and administrative classes.

The glovemakers, lacemakers glassblowers and silversmiths of mediaeval Dublin were renowned throughout Europe. Even as the city, expanded its industries were geared towards personal consumption, and the industrial revolution largely passed it by. Dublin didn't do heavy industry. The biggest employer emerged as the Guinness brewery - you cannot get more personalised than that. Even as employment in other industries rocketed in the 1990s, it was computer manufacture which was the engine. The fact that computers need a pleasant air-conditioned atmosphere for their successful manufacture is worthy of further study in the Irish context. Far from being dark Satanic mills, a modern computer plant with its controlled environment provides a pleasant haven from the Irish weather at its worst. It could be argued that the Irish climate played a key role in the growth of the Celtic tiger, and certainly the world of computers accords well with the Dubliner's way of life.

It may be trite to suggest that central to the Dublin character is the notion that they work to enjoy life, rather than live to work. But their city and its region reinforce this attitude. It's a very pleasant place to live, and the good things of life are expected and enjoyed. And if they tire of urban bustle, Dubliners and those around them have ample choice of ready alternatives.

Within the city, there are many distinctive urban villages. And circled around Dublin are convenient counties of intriguing variety, and clearcut character. It may be an over-simplification, but Wicklow is mountainy men and seafarers and gardeners, Kildare is horse country, Meath - Royal Meath of the pastures - is farmers and ranchers and more horse people, and little Louth - Ireland's smallest county - is a bit of everything: farming, fishing, mountain country, border territory, and trading.

It is an ample region of sea and hills. Only Kildare lacks any sea coast, but it is well served by rivers and canals. The Greater Dublin area always responds to genuine interest, and at its heart is this intriguing city, this sea-facing, river-embracing hill-girt town for our times, a place on a very human scale where streets of fine architecture provide views to mountains which are on a gentle scale to embrace the city rather than hem it in. Those hills invite exploration, yet always there is the lively city within easy reach.

River Boyne at Slane, Co Meath

Ireland: East
Food of the Region

Paul Cathcart over a decade ago; and one of the country's best known quality chocolate manufacturers, **Butlers Chocolate** (+353 (0)1 671 0599; www.butlerschocolates.com) who also have cafés around the city. The increasingly cosmopolitan population is reflected in businesses like Natasha Czopor's health-conscious vegetarian speciality foods, **Natasha's Living Foods** (www.natashaslivingfood.ie) which are made in Stoneybatter Dublin 7, and sold through farmers' markets and speciality stores, and there are many other quality products which are traditionally 'un-Irish' such as the smartly presented jars of **Olvi oils** and vinaigrettes - hand-made by Miriam Griffith in Beaumont, these find their way into classy delis such as nearby Andersons - and **Laragh Stuart Foods** (+353 (0)1 6174827), which supplies sauces and soups made in the north of the city to speciality food stores and delis around Ireland.

Dublin is frequently hailed as a 'vibrant young multi-cultural city' - as, in many ways, it is and its recently settled multi-cultural population has brought unprecedented change (and variety) to its food - yet many visitors, and indeed residents, still wish to seek out the great **traditional foods and drinks**. While street vendors hawking 'cockles and mussels' may be a thing of the past (or, at any rate, they have moved into the markets these days) unique dishes like **Dublin Coddle** (a simple stew of sausages, bacon, onion and potato) and **Gur Cake** (a spicy fruit 'cake' made up daily by Dublin bakers, using leftovers from the previous day's unsold stock; the modern 'fruit slice' is similar) tell their own social history. Although they have been out of favour in recent years, these specialities are still made and are now enjoying a revival of interest. Few of the specialist **pork butchers** that supplied the ingredients for Dublin Coddle and were so much a part of the city's everyday life remain, alas, although many that do, such as **J. Hick & Sons** of Dun Laoghaire, are outstanding – and, of course, the ingredients are widely available from other butchers.

Should there be any doubt about interest in the great **DRINKS** that are synonymous with Dublin – notably whiskeys such as **Jameson,** also **Baileys Irish Cream** (a whiskey based product) and, of course, **Guinness** -

Dublin City

As the eastern area in and around the capital is by far the most heavily populated part of Ireland, the emphasis in the Dublin region would be expected to shift to buying and eating the foods of Ireland as a whole, rather than food production. In fact, however, although it's certainly Ireland's biggest marketplace, the Dublin area is surprisingly well supplied with excellent **FOOD PRODUCERS**, both artisan and larger scale. Surrounded by the sea and a hinterland of rich farmland, Dublin is blessed with easy access to fresh natural produce, and the city itself there are artisan producers, including craft bakeries and niche producers of specialised or luxury items. Diverse examples include the **Irish Flapjack & Muffin Co**, Tallaght (+353 (0)1 4610001; www.ifmc.ie), a quality snack company set up by well known Dublin chef massive visitor attendance at the **The Old Jameson Distillery** (www.jamesonwhiskey.com), at Smithfield, and the **Guinness Storehouse** (www.guinness-storehouse.com) at the St James's Gate Brewery confirms enduring public fascination with these icons of the city. Meanwhile, those who prefer things to be on a smaller scale will find that brewing is far from being a thing of the past, judging by the success of latter day **brew pubs** such as the **Bull & Castle** (www.bullandcastle.ie), **Messrs Maguire** (www.messrsmaguire.ie) and **The Porterhouse** (www.porterhousebrewco.com), all in Dublin 2, near the banks of the River Liffey; The Porterhouse was the pioneer although, as it has several branches - including one at London's Covent Garden, and **Porterhouse North** (+353 (0)1 830 9884) on the Royal Canal at Cross Guns Bridge, Dublin 9 - its beers are now brewed in the Dublin suburb of Blanchardstown.

Despite the fact that most of the population now lives in urban areas, Ireland remains a rural country at heart. **Airfield** (+353(0)1 298 4301; www.airfield.ie), Dublin's unique **farm in the city**, is a reminder of those rural roots - which are also to be seen in some areas of the inner city, where fading signage on old buildings bears poignant witness to the dairies and other food-related businesses that still had relevance until about half a century ago. Many of these

reminders are near the Victorian redbrick **Dublin Corporation Fruit, Vegetable & Flower Market,** north of the Liffey at Smithfield, which has so far escaped the fate of the nearby Fish Market (recently demolished); some renovation has been undertaken in recent years and it is very much in business, and open to the public from 5am to 1pm, six days a week. It has been feared that that the massive redevelopment planned for this area would spell the end for the market but, in the more thoughtful atmosphere that has followed the Celtic Tiger years, there is hope that it may be saved. Ideally many would like to see it developed along the lines of the English Market in Cork, as Dublin has no comparable daily food market. Although it remains to be seen whether many of the schemes planned in the boom will ever be completed - this may not be an impossible dream, as a plan envisaged for the area between Smithfield and O'Connell Street would see the Victorian market as the centrepiece of a new square, renovated and with additional retail space for new business. Some thirty independent fruit, vegetable, flower and fish traders operate out of the market, and there is certainly potential for more; many of the current traders have been here for generations - **Jackie Leonard & Sons Ltd** (www.jackieleonards.com) for example, are in the fourth generation and go back to 1892, when the building was first opened. **Smithfield Outdoor Food Market** is also held at Smithfield every Friday (10-3) – and this is also the site of the controversial Traditional Horse Fair (www.visitdublin.com); this is an inner city tradition held on the 1st Sunday of the month and, despite calls for its closure on welfare grounds, traders claim an ancient market right to hold their sales on the land.

Markets have had a key role to play in Dublin for many centuries, and while they have evolved to meet the demands of the time, they are going through a period of regeneration that is bringing new life to the city's streets and squares. The growth in **Farmers' Markets** (www.bordbia.ie/aboutfood/farmersmarkets) has been a major Irish food story since the late 1990s, with the greatest concentration to be found in the Dublin region – all following on the success of the

Temple Bar Market, Dublin

North County Dublin

With the twin advantages of fertile farmland and a relatively sunny climate, north county Dublin (also known as Fingal) is **'Ireland's Market Garden'**, renowned for its production of fruit and vegetables, notably potatoes – in high summer delicious second early 'Rush Queens' and 'Skerries Queens' are sold along the roadsides - carrots, cabbages and Brussels sprouts, often grown on farms that have been in the same family for several generations. Small family farms, such as the **McNally Family Farm** at Balrickard near Naul, are the backbone of the area's farming community; Jenny and Pat McNally farm organically, growing heritage varieties of potatoes, carrots, tomatoes, saladings and herbs, which are in great demand at their market stalls - look out for them at the Saturday Temple Bar Food Market. Also in the Naul area, Denise Dunne's organic nursery, **The Herb Garden** at Forde-de-Fyne (+353 (0)1 841 3907; www.theherbgarden.ie) offers culinary, medicinal and special use herbs (seeds and plants), also herb garden design and consultancy services; an interesting place to visit, but by appointment only.

The many glasshouses seen on farms along the coastal roads of north Dublin are a reminder of the delicious

Temple Bar Food Market in the Dublin 2 'Cultural Quarter' (established in 1997), there are now over two dozen farmers' markets held regularly in Dublin city and county alone. Regulations have recently been tightened up to ensure that stallholders genuinely represent Irish farmers and small producers and, as a result, you can be certain of meeting specialist producers from all over Ireland at these markets, including many from the surrounding area. Other markets are thriving too, including the **Dublin Food Co-op** (www.dublinfoodcoop.com; near St Patrick's Cathedral Dublin 8), which is renowned for its 'local, organic and sustainable' shopping and events. **Country Markets** (www.countrymarkets.ie) also have never been more popular, and you will find them in towns and villages all over the south; they have a broader base than farmers' markets, offering not only food (especially garden produce, home baking and preserves) but also local handcrafts.

James and the Giant Onion...

Keelings Peppers

traditionally grown **tomatoes** they are famous for, although the number of **market gardeners** has been in decline recently, mainly due to a combination of small profit margins and the high value of land during the Celtic Tiger years. A renewed appreciation of locally-produced food by Irish consumers may now help to turn this around, however; one interesting recent development has seen farmland turned over to **allotments** to meet public demand - and, by contrast, there has been investment in the sector by forward-looking producers, including major players like the **Keelings Group** (+353 (0)1 813 5600; www.keelings.com), at St. Margaret's, who have greatly increased their protected crop production. Still a family-run company after over six decades, albeit a very large one now, Keelings are both growers and distributors; in recent years the company has brought large-scale commercial **sweet pepper** growing to the area (Keelings won an Irish Food Writers' Guild Award for this initiative) and, through further investment in glass houses, they have now succeeded in extending

the Irish **strawberry** harvesting season right through to December - both initiatives have reduced dependency on imports and brought employment to the area.

Apples are also grown in north Dublin, and a key producer is David Llwellyn of **Llewellyn's Orchard Produce** (+353 (0)1 843 1650) at Lusk. He grows a range of apple varieties and tops up with additional apples purchased from other Irish growers as demand for his products, especially the signature cloudy apple juice, now outstrips supply; the juice, which is pressed and unfiltered, is made with different apples to produce tangy, medium and sweet juices. In smaller quantities he also makes real (pressed) cider, cider vinegar and a speciality balsamic cider vinegar – and, to the amazement of many who said it couldn't be done (and the exact opposite of the late Michael O'Callaghan of Longueville House in Co Cork, who turned from wine to apple brandy production because apples are a more reliable crop) he has also been growing grapes recently, to produce both red and white wines, branded Lusca. You'll find Llewellyn products at markets (Temple Bar, Dun Laoghaire, Macreddin) and you can also buy from the farm; the juices are also available from some good stores, including Superquinn.

But, important as it is, produce in the Dublin area is not restricted to the land: **FISH AND SEAFOOD** are key products, and visiting the interesting small ports strung along the east coast between Carlingford Lough and Dublin (and eating the delicious fresh seafood) is always a particularly enjoyable experience. **Skerries** has great charm and there is much to interest food lovers, including the restored windmills and nearby **Ardgillan House** (www.fingalcoco.ie), which has lovely grounds and productive walled gardens. Clogherhead in Co Louth, and Skerries and Howth in Co Dublin all supply the fish markets and, in some cases, local restaurants. In general, the larger boats fish mainly for white fish while, as elsewhere around the Irish coast, small-boat fishermen using traditional skills fish for shellfish and crustaceans on a seasonal basis. In **Howth**, for example, although a quieter fishing port these days than it once was, walkers on the pier or around the cliff path will see lobster pots a-plenty, their floating markers bobbing on the waves - and the famous range of fish shops and restaurants lining the West Pier continues to expand. **Dublin Bay prawns** (langoustine), landed mainly at Clogherhead and Skerries, are plentiful in the north Irish Sea and highly prized; many would cite them as their favourite seafood, even when competing with the coveted lobster, crab, and scallops, which are also abundant in season. A more unusual speciality of Howth however, is **BAILY BEEF** from the Bellingham family farm at "The Cliffs" on Howth Head, where they have been finishing beef cattle since the 1830's; the cattle graze free-range for the final summer of their lives, and thanks to the complex mix of grasses and plants, achieve wonderful condition and weight. Numbers are small and the season is short, making this a special treat when visiting the area in autumn - and a similar product is now available that has been finished on nearby **Lambay Island**.

And, lest you think north County Dublin is impossibly wholesome, there are some exquisite sweet treats to be found here too, as the superb **Chez Emily** (www.chezemily.ie;) **handmade chocolates** are crafted by Ferdinand Vandaele & Helena Hemeryck at The Ward, near Mabestown.

Hick's Sausages

South County Dublin

With a large residential population, the emphasis in South Dublin is mainly on retail rather than production, although there are some honourable exceptions. **PORK BUTCHERS**, once such a familiar feature of the Dublin streetscape, are less common nowadays but those remaining, such as esteemed Dun Laogahire pork butchers **J Hick & Sons** (+353 (0)1 284 2700; www.hicks.ie) make up in quality anything the city may have lost in quantity. In contrasting style but demanding equal skill, a young French-trained patissier, Iseult Janssens, who grew up on a farm in Co Wicklow, has recently set up her own business **The Cake Stand**, at Newcastle, Co Dublin (+353 (0)86 040 7676; www.thecakestand.ie), making exquisite special occasion cakes, pastries and other treats; you'll find her pretty Cake Stand

macaroons at branches of Avoca, where she also does occasional demonstrations, and at a growing number of speciality stores.

Dublin's wonderful **URBAN FARM**, **Airfield House** (+353 (0)1 298 4301; www.airfield.ie), is also in south County Dublin, at Upper Kilmacud Road, Stillorgan; former owners, sisters Letitia and Naomi Overend, set up the Airfield Trust, leaving their much-loved estate for educational and recreational purposes. It includes a 20 acre working farm which is run on sustainable lines as a traditional mixed farm, focused on livestock. Calves and lambs are the main production animals raised, but the animals stocked range from cattle, sheep, goats, pigs, donkeys, miniature horses and ponies to geese, chickens, and ducks – and a recently acquired herd of Jersey cows, the breed favoured by the Overend sisters. There is always something going on, and both the farm and the beautiful gardens make for a wonderful family day out.

Co Kildare

Just south-west of Dublin, Kildare is famous above all for its equestrian activities and it's a great farming county with **BEEF, ORGANIC CHICKENS, HANDCRAFTED HAMS, ORGANIC PIES** and superb **SAUSAGES** among the special foods that say 'Kildare'. The county is also blessed with some exceptionally dedicated and inspirational people, who have put the county very firmly on the map as far as quality produce is concerned - and some outstanding places to eat it, too.

CHICKEN may be the nation's favourite protein but imports are high and the quality and provenance can give cause for concern, so the Bord Bia Quality Assured mark is important – and it's wonderful to see established producers of free range and/or organic poultry thriving, with strong demand encouraging new producers to come on stream. This part of the country is exceptionally well supplied with quality chickens, notably from the renowned organic producer Margaret McDonnell of **Ballysax Organic Chicken** (+353(0)45 442473; Martinstown Road, Ballysax, Curragh), who has been supplying restaurants with her wonderful chickens for many years, and offering farmgate sales too. More recently, Sandra Higgins - wife of Finbar Higgins, Executive Head Chef at the exclusive K Club at Straffan – and her father Eddie McKeon have started **Carbury Free Range Chicken** (+353 (0)46 9552958) at Rathmore, near Carbury; they farm on traditional lines, mainly for supply to restaurants. Nearby, **Deirdre & Norman O'Sullivan** (+353 (0)46 955 3337; www.organicguide.ie) are long-established organic mixed farmers, with laying hens among their range of products.

SAUSAGES have a new image these days, and that's in no small way thanks to producers such as Jane Russell, whose commitment to quality has earned a national reputation (and many an award) for her **Jane Russell's Original Irish Handmade Sausages** (+353 (0)45 480100; ww.straightsausage.com), made at Kilcullen, Co Kildare; her motto is "No off cuts. No short cuts. Just prime cuts." No wonder the humble sausage has gone from poor relation to gourmet category in so many kitchens. From sausages to **PIES**, and the **Morrin O'Rourke organic pies** (+353 (0)1 628 4411; www.morrinorourkefarmfoods.com) which are made at Kilcock, Co Kildare, with the best of ingredients including using **beef and lamb** from the family's organic farm; well known in the area and worth looking out for, they're sold at Temple Bar Food Market and also popping up in selective retail outlets, including Dublin's Fallon & Byrne and Ardkeen Quality Stores in Waterford. The **organic vegetables** used in the pies are also grown locally – a well known supplier is Liam Ryan and Yuki Kobayashi's **Moyleabbey Organic Farm** (+353 (0)59 862 3800; www.moyleabbey.ie; www.organicguide.ie) near Athy. But if proof is needed that larger scale operations can also be quality led, **Brady Family Ham** (+353 (0)45 863650; www.traditionalham.com), produced at Timahoe, near Naas, is a good example. An IFWG award winner, all-Irish pork is used for the hams, which are still handcrafted by traditional methods and available in various guises; at Christmas

Carlingford Oyster & Mussel Fishery

this includes an understandably popular part-boned ham which is easily carved. A recent high end addition to the range is the result of collaboration with the renowned butcher James McGeough, of Oughterard, Co Galway, whose Connemara range of **air-dried lamb, pork and ham** is marketed under the Brady Family brand, and has won accolades from Euro-Toques and the Great Taste Awards.

Brady Family Ham

And Co Kildare is home to some indulgences too, including one of Ireland's best-selling CHOCOLATE brands, **Lily O'Briens** (+353 (0)45 486800; www.lilyobriens.ie); named founder Mary Ann O'Brien's daughter Lily (now working in the company with her mother) it has been made in Newbridge since 1992.

Co Louth

Known variously as 'the Wee County' and 'Land of Legends', Louth may be Ireland's smallest county but it is remarkably diverse and this is reflected in foods that come from contrasting sources, ranging from the Cooley Mountains, the Irish Sea and Carlingford Lough to the east, and the fertile river plains of the western areas. **BEEF** is not just a great food around here, it's the stuff of myth and legend – it's here in Louth that the legendary tale, The Táin ('The Cattle Raid of Cooley') was acted out, and where Cuchulainn, Queen Maebh and the Brown Bull of Cooley met their fate. With **SEAFOOD** however the emphasis is firmly on the present – even in the Cooley area, where **Carlingford Oysters** are a special attraction for visitors to this stunningly beautiful area. Nestled into the foothills of the Cooley Mountains and with views across the lough to the Mountains of Mourne, the little mediaeval village of Carlingford is uniquely situated – and a charming setting for the annual **Oyster Festival**. Further south, **Clogherhead Prawns** take centre stage – these delectable crustaceans are the same as Dublin Bay prawns (langoustine) – and between the two, at Annagassan, Terry Butterly's **Coastguard Seafoods** (+353 (0)42 9372527) supplies top restaurants along the east coast; in 2007 Terry won a Euro-Toques Award, in recognition of his special interest in conservation and the service he provides in informing chefs about the seasonality and availability of fish.

Although not a big **CHEESE** producing area, Co Louth is home to two of the country's more recently introduced and very successful cheeses. At Dunleer, the extraordinary **Glebe Brethan** (+353 (0)41 6851157; www.**glebebrethan**.com) thermophilic gruyère-style cheese is made on the Tiernan family farm, using unpasteurised milk from Montbeliarde cows which originate from the Jura region of eastern France; made in great 45-kilo wheels and matured for up to18 months, this multi-award winning cheese is supplied to a number of restaurants around Ireland, including nearby Ghan House, in Carlingford, and available from specialist outlets nationwide and some local markets (including Sonairte at Laytown). By contrast, at Glyde Farm Produce, Castlebellingham, Peter and Anita Thomas (+353 (0)42 937 2343) make the much smaller but also exceptional **Bellingham Blue Farmhouse Cheese,** a semi-hard raw milk, natural rind cheese which is much in demand. Also in the

Castlebellingham area, there are interesting things going on at **Derrycamma Farm Foods** (+353 (0)87 822 3875; www.rapeseed-oil.ie), where they produce **free range chickens and eggs**, and traditional crops of **wheat, barley and oats** – but, recently, Derrycamma has joined the growing band of innovative farmers who grow oilseed rape for culinary use. Not only is **RAPESEED OIL** a healthy alternative to other oils (having, for example, lower saturated fat and higher levels of Omega 3 than olive oil) but, most importantly, it does very well in taste tests too – and consumers just love the beautifully short food miles. Look out for it in local shops.

Co Meath

Meath may be just medium-sized in relation to other Irish counties, but The Royal County lives up to its name in many ways, with its ancient historical sites and the big, prosperous farms bounded by magnificent trees that make it an important **equestrian** county and Ireland's leading producer of **POTATOES**; Meath is also a significant producer of **BEEF, BARLEY, MILK, WHEAT, ROOT VEGETABLES - and SOFT FRUIT.** The Clarke family's 56 acre soft fruit farm is one of the largest in Ireland producing strawberries and also some raspberries and blackberries (look out for **Clarkes Soft Fruit** at Stillorgan Farmers Market); Pat Clarke takes pride in producing top quality, flavoursome fruit - and his high standards were endorsed by a recent Bord Bia title of Best Grower of the Year; blueberries are the latest addition to the range, and a farm shop is planned. What better county then, for **Sonairte National Ecology Centre** (+353 (0)41 982 7572; www.sonairte.ie; open Wed-Sun) at Laytown, where there is plenty of interest for visitors, including an organic garden, nature trail and river walk, alternative energy courtyard and a beekeeping museum, as well as an eco farm shop, Mustard Seed Café and fortnightly farmers' market. Run as a registered charity, it offers unusual trees for sale in various sizes, interesting gardening courses (both commercial and individual), and it's a great place for a family outing.

With all its lush farmland, it should come as no surprise that Co Meath produces great **DAIRY PRODUCTS**, and an outstanding example to look out for is **Kilbeg Dairy Delights** (+353 46 924 4687; www.kilbegdairydelights.ie) made at Carlanstown in the Kells area by Kieran and Jane Cassidy, who use the milk of their pedigree Holsteins to make a sophisticated range of products; renowned Slane patissier George Heise uses their cream cheese ('like German quark') in his cheesecakes. Other treats to keep an eye open for include their crème fraîche and sour cream, mascarpone cheese, buttermilk and smoothies; and – proving that simple is often best – their distinctive single cream (pasteurised but not homogenised) is a Great Taste Awards gold medal winning product, adjudged 'thicker, creamier and tastier' than comparable products.

Over at Corbalton in the Tara area, meanwhile, the famously creamy milk from the Burke family's herd of Jersey cows goes into **Burke Farm Jersey Ice Cream**

(+353 (0)46 902 5232); Bernie Burke makes it in a lot of flavours, including classics like vanilla and chocolate but also unusual ones such as rhubarb & custard, and apple crumble (very popular); at Christmas you may find novelty flavours, such as plum pudding ice cream; look for it in local shops, also at Ilia in Mullingar.

Meath could also be said to be the **cheese capital of Ireland**, as Ireland's most important purveyors of cheese **Sheridans Cheesemongers Ltd** (+353 (0)46 924 5110; www.sheridanscheesemongers.com) are based here, at Virginia Road Station, Carnaross; visitors are welcome at the warehouse Thu-Sat, when manager Franck Le Moenner is available to answer queries.

And some small temptations for the sweet-toothed connoisseur also emanate from Co Meath – when Mary White and Connie Doody established **Lir Chocolates** (www.lircafe.com) to provide employment in the East Wall area of Dublin in 1989, they were pioneers of the luxury Irish handmade chocolate revolution and received one of the earliest IFWG Awards, in 1994; although bought by Kinnerton Confectionery in 2008 and now made in Navan, the handmade quality has been retained and the brand is thriving. Not far away, in Summerhill, **Celtic Chocolates** (+353 (0)46 955 7077) is a small

Sheridans Cheese

family-run company producing some excellent after dinner chocolates – and their unusual speciality is **chocolate products for people with food allergies and sensitivities**; their gluten free, wheat free, dairy free, egg free and no added sugar chocolate products are widely available in Ireland (and increasingly in the UK too). And at Ballivor, Co Meath, Tomás Póil - who is originally from the Aran island of Inishere - makes his **Man of Aran Fudge** (+353 (0)86 256 6542; www.manofaranfudge.ie) a product that is relatively unusual in Ireland, it is handmade and available in many flavours.

Co Wicklow

South of Dublin city, **'The Garden of Ireland'** is aptly named, as this exceptionally beautiful county takes in not only the famous mountainous areas - the Dublin Mountains and the Wicklow Hills, which are mainly National Park and a wonderful amenity for Dubliners - but, with the mountains surrounded by fertile land in the foothills, and sloping down to the sea on the eastern flank, this largely unspoilt county is also the source of many good things to eat.

County Wicklow is a major **ORGANIC STRONGHOLD**, with Ireland's only certified organic restaurant, The Strawberry Tree, to be found here, at the delightful BrookLodge Hotel Macreddin (+353 (0)402 36444; www.brooklodge.com) – where there is a monthly organic food market and there are many other good things going on, including beer production at their own **micro-brewery.**

Wicklow is known for its excellent vegetables and farm produce, with growers including a clutch of the country's most famous organic suppliers. The daddy of them all, Marc Michel's **Organic Life** (+353 (0)1 201 1882; www.organic-trust.org) at Kilpedder, which became Ireland's first certified organic farm in 1983; Hilda Crampton and Dominic Quinn's **Castleruddery Organic Farm** (+353 (0)45 404925; www.organic-trust.org), is another of the longest established organically certified Irish farms (1989) at Donard. **Gold River Farm** (+353 (0)404 36426 / (0)86 858 7080; Alan Pierce) near Aughrim, where the Pierce and Winterbotham

Hens at BrookLodge Hotel, Co Wicklow

family's organic vegetables, fresh fruit and herbs are grown - they're in great demand from hotels and restaurants; and Denis Healy's **Organic Delights** (www.organicdelights.ie) is at Kiltegan - and in the same area Penny and Udo Lange grow their renowned **bio-dynamic produce**. Over in east Wicklow, at Glenealy, a mixed farm known for its organic lamb, poultry and eggs is Martha and Gary **Crocker's Organic Farm** (+353 (0)404 44854). These are names which will quickly become familiar to visitors, as they are proudly acknowledged on menus, both locally and in the best Dublin restaurants, and their produce may also be found at markets and some selective stores.

DAIRY PRODUCTS are also well represented in County Wicklow, with some especially good ones to keep an eye open for including The McDonnell family's much-lauded **Old MacDonnell's Farm** (+353 (0)1 282 8992; www.oldmacdonnellsfarm.ie) yogurts and fresh cheeses from Glen o'the Downs; and the Heppenstall family's **Wicklow Farmhouse Cheese** (+353 (0)402 91713; www.wicklowfarmhousecheeseltd.ie), which is made near Arklow – accolades for their Wicklow Blue include an IFWG Award in 2008, and they have since gone on to produce a brie style cheese (Wicklow Baun) and a pasteurised cheddar type, Wicklow Gold, which is available in several flavours including nettle & chive.

And, as elsewhere in dairying areas, **artisan ice creams** are proving a winner – some special ones to look out for when visiting Wicklow are **Baron von Kuul's** "flavours of the world" ice cream, made by Christian and Ruth von Teichmann, Ashford, **Golden Hill Farmhouse Ice Cream** (+353 (0)1 458 2058; www.goldenhill.ie) of Manor Kilbride, and **Three Wells Farmhouse Ice Cream** (+353 (0)402 36570; www.visitwicklow.ie) which is made in a wide range of flavours at Aughrim, along with some classic sorbets.

If you're hoping to find good **HOME BAKING AND PRESERVES** when visiting this proudly rural area, look out for the cakes, tarts and scones that Olive Finlay makes at Stratford-on-Slaney under her brand **Ballyhubbock Home Foods** (+353 (0)45 404706); and **Kilmurry Jams** (+353 (0)1 286 3790), who make a range of jams, marmalades and preserves by traditional methods at Kilmacanogue – you'll see them in local supermarkets and they're also distributed nationally. For something more savoury, **Janet's Country Fayre** (+353 (0)1 204 1957; www.janetscountryfayre.com) is the brand to seek out and it will be easy to spot, once you know the smart packaging with its arty handwritten labels - and Fresh, The Good Food Market, is among the Dublin area stockists; a Good Food Ireland member,

Janet Drew is known for her integrity, promising 'pure taste and additive free goodness' in her ever-growing range of chutneys, relishes sauces, pestos, salsas, and dressings; several – including an unusual 'chutney for cheese & wine' – have taken Gold in the Great Taste Awards. And, not far away in Wicklow Town, John Paul Pritchard and Michael Martin's **Organic Herb Company** (+353 (0)404 69651; www.organicherbco.com) produce the beautifully presented **Garden of Ireland** range of organic herbs, spices, snacks and herb blends – also a popular savoury seed mixture which is perfect for salads.

The **MEAT** the area is best known for is **Wicklow lamb** and very delicious it is too - as many walkers have found when dropping in to The Roundwood Inn (+353 (0)1 2818107; www.visitwicklow.ie) for example, for a bowl of their excellent house-style Irish Stew - but, more surprisingly perhaps, as the atmosphere is so rural, **FISH AND SEAFOOD** are also a strong point, with fresh supplies – notably crab – normally coming from Greystones harbour as well as other east coast ports. A speciality to look out for is **Fish Out Of Water** (www.fishoutofwater.ie) smoked seafood and patés, made in Arklow.

But perhaps the best food of all to find in an area like County Wicklow is **wild and free** – well, initially

Wicklow Blue Cheese

anyway; when processed and brought to market the **WILD GAME** of the area naturally commands a healthy price. The specialists are Michael Healy's **Wild Irish Game** (+353 (0)404 46773; www.visitwicklow.ie) of Glenmalure, near Rathdrum, who source wild game including venison, pheasant, partridge, pigeon, wild duck, woodcock, grouse and rabbit, both for retail sale and use in hotels and restaurants. But one of the joys of having access to a large area of unspoilt countryside is the opportunity for **foraging,** and there are many wild foods there for the taking, including bilberries (the blueberry's smaller wild cousin, also known as *fraughan*), blackberries, rowanberries, damsons, sloes, and mushrooms, which are all plentiful at various times of year. If you have a yen for some serious foraging, Bill O'Dea (www.mushroomstuff.com) from Glenageary Co Dublin organises mushroom hunts in County Wicklow locations such as Avondale Forest Park and Druids Glen. For those who prefer to go it alone on a small scale, the blackberries and rowanberries are easy picking (the latter make a wonderfully astringent jelly to accompany your game), and the bilberry is a tiny treasure; in summer the hills are covered with them, although the little blue-black berries hide in the foliage and make for slow picking – and you have to get to them before the birds do, which is more easily said than done.

Four of the Best...

Temple Bar Food Market

The Saturday Temple Bar Food Market in Dublin's 'Cultural Quarter' was established, in 1997, by a group of half a dozen like-minded folk - some of whom are still stall-holders today - with the support of pioneering teacher and chef Darina Allen, of Ballymaloe Cookery School (www.cookingisfun.ie). There are now over two dozen farmers' markets held regularly in Dublin city and county alone, and the Temple Bar market is one of the best in the country. People love it for the buzz as well as the satisfaction of buying the very best fresh seasonal and artisan produce at a good price, and meeting the producers themselves - David Llewellyn of Llewellyn's apple juice and cider vinegar, perhaps, Ed Hick of the famous pork and sausage dynasty and Noirin Kearney up from Wexford with temptations from Noirin's Bakehouse. Tastings are often offered, and there's plenty of food to go - west coast oysters with lemon wedges and soda bread, (perhaps even with a complimentary glass of white wine), or delicious pancakes from Tina Cropp and Oisin Healy's Crêpes In The City - children, respectively, of original stallholders Silke Cropp, producer of the wonderful Corleggy Cheeses (Belturbet, Co Cavan), and Denis Healy of Organic Delights (Wicklow), this pair certainly have market trading in their blood. And, as always with markets, there's a strong social aspect to the activities here, so lots of people just think it's a great way to spend Saturdays.

Meeting House Square Dublin 2
(+353 (0)1 677 2255 www.templebar.ie)

J. Hick & Sons Gourmet Foods Ltd

The pig is central to Irish culinary history and with it the pork butcher, once a feature of every main street. There are less now but those remaining can be outstanding, especially where there is a German connection, as there is with fourth generation pork butchers J Hick & Sons - now synonymous with pork in Dublin - whose skills date back to predecessors in 19th century Germany. More recently, Jack and Betty Hick's dedication to traditional pork butchery and craft manufacturing skills has been widely recognised and, having passed these skills and values on to the next generation, their sons, Ed and Brendan Hick (who are also German trained), continue the Irish/German tradition. They make a wide range of traditional and innovative pork products on the premises, notably superb speciality sausages, traditional puddings, dry cured bacon and hams - and the wonderful Kassler that Jack Hick was responsible for introducing to Ireland. Their magnificent sausage range includes numerous speciality continental varieties, and a venison sausage - and, most recently, a premium organic pork range was introduced. The company now also trains Culinary Arts graduates in the art of pork butchery.

Rear 15A, Georges St Upper, Dún Laoghaire, Co Dublin
(+353 (0)1 284 2700; www.hicks.ie)

The BrookLodge Hotel

Looking at it now, it's hard to credit that this visionary enterprise began as recently as 1999, as nothing more than a huddle of ruined cottages on a remote hillside. Today, thanks to the determination of brothers Evan, Eoin and Bernard Doyle, to pursue their dream, The BrookLodge is much more than an hotel; creepers now soften the main building and their imaginative 'village street' of complementary businesses - including a micro-brewery - has matured and gained authenticity. The driving force is Evan, a pioneer of the organic movement with his Killarney restaurant, The Strawberry Tree, which relocated here when the hotel opened and remains Ireland's only certified organic restaurant. The hotel is a very focused business, with excellent wedding and conference facilities, a spa, and an equestrian centre. But the USP is their stance on wild, seasonal and organic food. Dining at the Strawberry Tree is a unique experience, and organic food markets, held on the first Sunday of the month (first and third in summer) have proved a great success. Known for the barbecues and a relaxed atmosphere as well as a wide range of foods, they make a great family day out. BrookLodge also makes a natural venue for meetings of like-minded groups such as Euro-Toques and Slow Food, especially on market days.

Macreddin Village Co Wicklow
(+353 (0)402 36444 www.brooklodge.com)

Castlefarm

In a country where a true Dubliner may still be defined as 'someone who doesn't go home for the weekend', the urban-rural divide is clearly not as embedded as in many other societies. Yet the Irish population is increasingly urbanised, and the boom years brought growing signs of disconnection with our rural roots. But issues like food security, food miles and provenance, have stimulated a fresh appreciation of seasonal, local produce - and inspired thousands to grow their own food, often on allotments. Energetic, passionate and multi-talented people like Peter and Jenny Young, fourth generation custodians of this 170-acre organic farm, are making a valuable contribution to this changing scene with their farm shop, open farm policy (tours arranged), and communications skills. Although mainly dairy (Jersey cross and British Friesian cows) plus organic tillage, poultry and beef, Castlefarm is rapidly diversifying. Certified organic in 2008, they grow organic vegetables and fruit, produce honey - and their milk is now used by local cheesemaker Elizabeth Bradley of Carlow Cheese (www.carlowfarmersmarket.ie) to make Castlefarm Natural (gouda style) and Shamrock (with fenugreek) cheeses. Kildare's first farmhouse cheese, it's easily recognised by its distinctive green wax coating. At Castlefarm Farm Shop, Jenny says "Visitors will not only receive a warm country welcome, but will leave having learnt something new about farming and experience a real food and taste sensation." Jenny also has a stall at Athy Farmers' Market and Craft Fair every Sunday, and both she and Peter are influential journalists. A powerhouse package if ever there was one.

Narraghmore near Athy Co Kildare
(+353 (0)59 8636948 www.castlefarmshop.ie)

A Dublin Market

where to Buy

the Special Foods of the East...

A guide to food shops, markets, farm shops, local stores and internet suppliers in counties Dublin, Louth, Meath, Kildare & Wicklow

Dublin city

Epicurean Food Hall corner of Lr Liffey Street and Middle Abbey Street **DUBLIN 1.** This buzzy place brings together a collection of independent food units with a common seating area; open during the day every day (opens later on Sunday, remains open for late shoppers on Thursday evening) and offers a wide range of gourmet foods, cooked and uncooked - and the wines to go with them. Tenants quite often change but it's always an enjoyable place to browse, with lots of little shops and cafés, including ethnic ones.

Mitchell & Son CHQ building IFSC **DUBLIN 1** *(www.mitchellandson.com).* One of this famous wine retailer's three Dublin outlets (the others are in Sandycove and Rathfarnham). They are responsible for the survival of the unique Green Spot whiskey, which was formerly matured in sherry casks by Irish Distillers. Today, Mitchells are proud to say that "Green Spot is made entirely from seven and eight year old Midleton pot still, a healthy 25% coming from sherry cask, which is quite evident in its aroma and taste."

Avoca 11-13 Suffolk Street **DUBLIN 2** *(+353 (0)1 672 6019 www.avoca.ie).* City sister to the famous lifestyle shop, foodhall and café with its flagship store in Kilmacanogue, Co Wicklow, this centrally located shop is a favourite lunch spot for discerning Dubliners; meticulously sourced ingredients like Hederman mussels, Gubbeen bacon and Hicks sausages sit happily alongside the home baking for which they are famous - much of which can be bought downstairs in the extensive delicatessen.

Bewley's 78-79 Grafton Street **DUBLIN 2** *(+353 (0)1 672 7720 www.bewleys.com).* A Dublin icon, this unique (carbon-neutral) café and bakery is famed for its Harry Clarke windows, own-brand coffee, art exhibitions and theatre.

Blazing Salads 42 Drury Street **DUBLIN 2** *(+353 (0)1 671 9552 www.blazingsalads.com).* The energetic and focused Fitzmaurice family are behind one of Dublin's greatest food success stories – what began as one of the city's first wholefood restaurants, in 1982, has developed into a thriving deli business, and also a certified organic bakery which supplies speciality food shops with beautiful hand rolled sourdough breads every day. Favourite dishes feature in The Blazing Salads Cookbook; available **online** from their website, or from bookshops.

Celtic Whiskey Shop 27 Dawson Street **DUBLIN 2** *(+353 (0)1 675 9744 www.winesonthegreen.com).* The shop for serious whiskey lovers. Offers Ireland's most comprehensive range of Irish whiskey and international whiskies and spirits, served by helpful, knowledgeable staff; exclusive whiskeys (including special releases from Ireland's only independently owned distilleries, Cooley Distillery and Old Kilbeggan Distillery), whiskey launches, tasting evenings and distillery trips are often arranged. Also wines (many imported directly) in the connected shop, Wines on the Green.

Fallon & Byrne Exchequer Street **DUBLIN 2** *(+353 (0)1 472 1000; www.fallonandbyrne.com).* Restaurant, wine bar and a proper Food Hall - Fallon & Byrne has it all. As they say themselves: "Just-caught fish, well-hung meat, mighty coffee, sinful cakes, fine artisan foods of every kind, the freshest of fruit and vegetables." Well worth a visit.

Kilkenny 6 Nassau Street **DUBLIN 2**
(+353 (0)1 67770; www.kilkennyshop.com). Renowned for a wide, design-led selection of mainly Irish home and giftware – also good food, including an excellent own brand range of products, based on fresh and additive-free ingredients; home cooked flavours feature at the café & restaurant on the first floor overlooking Trinity College.

Kitchen Complements Chatham Street **DUBLIN 2**
(+353(0)1 677 0734 www.kitchencomplements.ie). Off Grafton Street at the St Stephen's Green end, this is the first (and probably only) port of call for keen cooks looking for the right gear for the job. Demonstrations are frequently held here. **Online shop**.

Listons Camden Street **DUBLIN 2**
(+353 (0)1 405 4779; www.listonsfoodstore.ie). Boasting "a product range of over 4,000 lines with many organic products in all categories", this highly regarded food store believes in choice and offers carefully sourced deli and grocery ranges; also wines, and a great seasonal fresh food menu to download from their website.

Murphy's Ice Cream 27 Wicklow Street & Temple Bar Square **DUBLIN 2** *(www.murphysicecream.ie)* The well known Dingle ice cream brand now has two Dublin shops.

Queen of Tarts Dame Street **DUBLIN 2**
(+353 (01) 633 4681 www.queenoftarts.ie); also Cow's Lane, Temple Bar (with terrace). Sisters Yvonne and Regina Fallon run these bakery-cafés in the heart of 'old Dublin'; renowned for their homely atmosphere and home cooked fare, everything on the menus is also available to go.

Sheridans Cheesemongers

Sheridan's Cheesemongers Sth Anne Street **DUBLIN 2**
(+353 (0)1 679 3143; www.sheridanscheesemongers.com). Just as the pioneering West Cork cheesemakers revived artisan cheesemaking in Ireland, the Sheridan brothers transformed attitudes to maturing it, buying it and caring for it. Stocks reflect the seasons and are mainly Irish, but other equally carefully sourced European foods are also stocked. Also at: Galway, Waterford (Ardkeen Quality Food Store) & Carnaross, Co Meath.

Kennedy's Food Store & Bistro Fairview Strand **DUBLIN 3** *(+353 (0)1 833 1400 www.kennedysfoodstore.com)*. Deli, bakery, takeaway, daytime café and evening bistro, this attractive place has many faces; the common denominator is their home cooked food for sale, and to eat in.

Nolans Supermarket Clontarf **DUBLIN 3**
(+353 (0)1 833 8361). A supermarket with a difference, this excellent well-stocked independent grocers and speciality food store is the place northsiders head for when they want a good range of artisan foods from all around Ireland.

The Food Room Clontarf Road **DUBLIN 3**
(+353 (0)1 833 2259 www.thefoodroom.ie). Putting a former car showroom to good use, Alison and Barry Stephens' deli, grocers and café always hits the spot; open 7 days.

Wrights of Marino Marino Mart **DUBLIN 3**
(+353(0)1 833 3636 www.wrightsofmarino.com). "If it swims we have it!" is the motto – especially if it's oak smoked salmon you're looking for. Closed Sun.

Brownes Sandymount Green **DUBLIN 4**
(+353 (0)1 269 7316). Popular high quality deli/café by day, and evening restaurant.

Clynes Bros Fitzwilliam Street **DUBLIN 4**
(+353 (0)1 660 2091 www.otoolesbutchers.com). Ringsend. Branch of O'Toole Master Butchers, Terenure, Dublin 6W. Organic specialists.

Donnybrook Fair Morehampton Road Donnybrook **DUBLIN 4** *(+353 (0)1 668 3556 www.donnybrookfair.ie)*. Joe Doyle's chic foodhall in Donnybrook has a restaurant & cookery classes upstairs; breakfast & lunch office deliveries can be ordered **online**. Also at: Donnybrook Fair, Upper Baggot Street, Dublin 4 *(+353 (0)1 668 3556)*, and Greystones, Co Wicklow *(+353 (0)1 287 6346)*.

Matthews Cheese Cellar 17 Upper Baggot Street **DUBLIN 4** *(+353 (0)1 668 5275 www.matthewscheesecellar.com)*. As well as selling an enthusiastically collected range of cheeses from Ireland and Europe, this atmospheric custom-designed cellar is home to cheese & wine tasting evenings.

The French Paradox Shelbourne Road **DUBLIN 4** *(+353 (0)1 660 4068 www.thefrenchparadox.com)*. This wine emporium with food is mainly a francophile's dream – with the noble exception of the Bill Hogan salad featuring West Cork cheeses Desmond and Gabriel… lovely deli fare.

Roly's Cafe & Bakery 7 Ballsbridge Terrace Ballsbridge **DUBLIN 4** *(+353 (0)1 668 2611 www.rolysbistro.ie)*. A relatively recent addition to the original (1992) bistro, the café is ideal for a casual bite; also sells breads from their own bakery and dishes (a range of about 15) to take home.

Roy Fox 49a Main Street Donnybrook **DUBLIN 4** *(+353 (0)1 2692892)*. Joanne Donnelly, daughter of the late Roy Fox, runs this renowned grocery, gourmet foods vegetable and health food store just off the main road through Donnybrook. Everything stocked is super fresh and/ or organic and the staff are exceptionally helpful.

Terroirs Donnybrook **DUBLIN 4** *(www.terroirs.ie)* Seán and Françoise Gilley's wine and food shop in Donnybrook, first port of call for covetable gifts for foodies. Feast for the eyes as well as the palate, and fun too - Best seller is 'les champignons' caramel mushroom. All French but ooh la la…

Craft Bakery Upper Rathmines Road **DUBLIN 6** *(+353 (0)1 4126154 www.craftbakery.ie)*. Eugene Davis runs his bakery on traditional lines, with rye and sourdough topping the polls.

Fothergills Deli Upper Rathmines Road **DUBLIN 6** *(+353 (0) 496 2159 www.fothergillsdeli.com)*. Quality catering company/deli with branches at Castleknock, Dublin 15 *(+353 (0)1 820 9686)* and Foxrock Dublin 18 *(+353 (0)1 289 0016)*. Great salads, sandwiches, freshly baked cakes, pastries crumbles…

Lawlors Butchers Upper Rathmines Road **DUBLIN 6** *(+353 (0)1 497 3313)*. Highly regarded butchers specialising in well aged steaks and good service. Also in Ranelagh, at: Mortons@Beechwood *(www.mortons.ie/beechwood)*.

The Gourmet Shop Highfield Road **DUBLIN 6** *(+353 (0)1 497 0365 www.gourmetshop.ie)*. Speciality foods, quality baking ingredients, hampers.

Morton's Dunville Ave **DUBLIN 6** *(+353 (0)1 497 1254 www.mortons.ie)*. Since 1934 Mortons has been supplying provisions to discerning Dubliners, and this third generation store continues to hold its place as one of the great Dublin food stores. Fresh fruit, veg, meat and fish; Irish organic produce; farmhouses cheeses, deli products and wines: "With a wealth of products both everyday and luxury, you're sure to find exactly what you want - and if by chance you don't, Mortons will do everything we can to source it for you …" That's the promise – and you can be sure they will deliver. Branches at Hatch Street (near St Stephen's Green) and Beechwood, Ranelagh.

Kiernans SuperValu The Rise Mount Merrion **DUBLIN 6** *(+353 (0)1 288 1014 www.supervalu.ie)* SuperValu supermarkets are renowned for their individuality, hands-on service and commitment to supporting local producers and Irish artisan products. 'Real Food, Real People' is the slogan and it is especially apt at Kiernans, who stock an exemplary range of artisan foods.

O'Toole Master Butchers 138 Terenure Road North **DUBLIN 6W** *(+353 (0)1 490 5457 www.otoolesbutchers.com)*. Renowned for their commitment to organic meats since the early 1990's, O'Toole's also introduced the world famous Wagyu Kobe Beef into Ireland. Also at: Sandycove (Glasthule), Co. Dublin.

John Downey & Son Terenure Road **DUBLIN 6W** *(+353 (0)1 490 9239 www.organicfoods ireland.com)*. Suppliers of organic meat, poultry, eggs etc; also game and exotics (incl Irish wild boar, Irish buffalo, Irish ostrich). Awards include traditional spiced beef - normally a Christmas speciality, now sold all year. Can order & collect.

The Corner Bakery Terenure Road North **DUBLIN 6W** *(+353 (0)1 490 6210)*. Family run craft bakery, strong on pastry and cakes (will make to order). Also good sandwiches and coffee to go.

Fresh – The Good Food Market Smithfield Village **DUBLIN 7** *(www.freshthegoodfoodmarket.com)*. Irish owned independent Dublin supermarkets, with emphasis on fresh and speciality produce; premium brands stocked include Blazing Salads organic breads and Janet's Country Fayre chutneys and relishes. Also at: Grand Canal Square, Dublin 2; Camden St, Dublin 2; Eurospar Northern Cross, Dublin 17.

Kish Fish, Dublin

Kish Fish Bow Street Smithfield **DUBLIN 7** *(+353 (0)1 872 8211 www.kishfish.ie)*. Established in 1966 by Tadgh O'Meara, Kish Fish is currently under the stewardship of his three sons Bill, Tadgh and Damien, ably assisted by their mother Fedelma, who looks after the shop with Jimmy Smith - attached to the processing plant, it offers a wide range of fresh

fish and shellfish. Closed Sun & Mon (1/2 day Sat). Also at: Malahide Industrial Park, Coolock, Dublin 17 *(+353 (0)1 8543900)*.

Lilliput Stores Rosemount Terrace Stoneybatter **DUBLIN 7**. Small but perfectly formed, this tiny shop just off Arbour Hill brings many a treat to a recently gentrified area; run by Brendan O'Mahony (the Dublin face of the Real Olive Co - well known at markets), it stocks artisan products (the gorgeous Chez Emily chocolates list them as suppliers) and quality everyday foods. Closed Sun.

Bretzel Bakery Lennox Street **DUBLIN 8** *(+353 (0)1 475 2724; www.bretzel.ie)*. This famous Jewish bakery was established in 1870 and, although no longer strictly kosher since the 1990s, it's still reckoned to sell the best bagels in Dublin.

Ennis Butchers 464 South Circular Road **DUBLIN 8** *(+353 (0)1 454 9282)*. Craft butchers in Rialto village; also stocks other quality fare, including organic vegetables.

Liberty Bakery Meath Street **DUBLIN 8** *(+353 (0)1 454 7725)*. A traditional bakery in a very old area of the city, where you may still expect to find proper Dublin bakes like soda bread, gur cake, apple puffs.

Lovin Catering Francis Street **DUBLIN 8** *(+353 (0)1 4544 912 www.gallickitchen.com)*. Kevin Doyle, former manager of The Gallic Kitchen (relocated to Abbeyleix, Co Laois) now owns this business renowned for baked goods with his wife Natasha, and renamed it Lovin Catering. Buy from the shop, also Dun Laoghaire and Stillorgan farmers' markets.

The Cake Café The Daintree Building Pleasants Place **DUBLIN 8** *(+353 (0)1 478 9394 www.thecakecafe.ie)*. Pleasant by name and pleasant by nature, this highly popular spot offers baking classes, private cookery classes, and even wine classes as well as charming everyone with their quirky home baking, to eat in the café or take home. Personalised cakes to order – even 'breakfast in bed' (complete with newspapers) delivered to your door, if you live nearby…

The Cheese Pantry Upper Drumcondra Road **DUBLIN 9** *(+353 (0)1 797 8936 www.thecheesepantry.com)*. With its custom-built temperature-controlled cheese room, shelves of 'foodie' pantry items and an impressive selection of wines, this former pork butchers shop looks like a deli and wine shop, but Aidan and Karen McNeice's popular deli (north Dublin's only dedicated cheese supplier) is also a café/restaurant, serving breakfast, lunch and dinner. Well worth a visit, to shop and eat.

Andersons Food Hall & Café The Rise Glasnevin **DUBLIN 9** *(+353 (0)1 837 8394 www.andersons.ie)*. Handy to the Botanic Gardens, Noel Delaney and Patricia van der Velde's delightful delicatessen, wine shop and continental style café is just the place for a casual bite, or to pick up a picnic from their wonderful selection of charcuterie and cheese from Ireland and the continent, accompanied by carefully selected chutneys - from the award-winning Crossogue preserves *(www.crossoguepreserves.com)* range, perhaps - vinaigrettes by Olvi Oils *(+353 (0)1 490 6728)*, or maybe one of the Laragh Stuart Foods *(353 (0)1 617 4827)* relishes, which are made nearby in North King Street…

J.L. Fitzsimons Fresh Fish Shop Kimmage Road West Crumlin Cross **DUBLIN 12** *(+353 (0)1 455 4832 www.seafoodcircle.ie)*. This second generation family-run shop began life in the old Fish Market (Smithfield); it offers a wide range of fresh whitefish and shellfish with live lobster, crab and oysters available from a tank in-store. Closed Sun & Mon.

Al's Fish Shop Lakelands Road Kilmacud **DUBLIN 14** *(+353 (0)1 207 3055 www.seafoodcircle.ie)*. A BIM Seafood Circle member, Al's sources a wide range of species from the market each morning. Closed Sun & Mon.

Butlers Chocolate Clonshaugh Business Park **DUBLIN 17** *(+353 (0)1 671 0599 www.butlerschocolates.com)*. These chocolates have become a favourite Irish indulgence and both chocs and the more recently introduced ice creams are widely available, from the Butlers Chocolate Cafés in Dublin and elsewhere, plus other selected retail outlets, eg Donnybrook Fair, Dublin 4; Thomas's Dublin 18; Mortons of Ranelagh, Dublin 6; and various SuperValu stores. See website for café locations and opening times, also retail outlets. **Online shop**.

Thomas's Brighton Road Foxrock **DUBLIN 18** *(+353 (0)1 289 4101 www.thomasoffoxrock.ie)*. A hard shop to pass by, with its appealing balance of artisan, organic and other quality foods from Ireland and abroad, and well-chosen wines too. Slow Food members.

McConnells Fish Whitestown Ind Est. **DUBLIN 24** *(+353 (0)1 4524 100 www.mcconnellsgsf.ie)* Established in 1928, McConnells was once a fond fixture on Grafton Street; known especially for salmon, including smoked organic and speciality long-sliced salmon, also gravadlax and barbecue salmon; other products include smoked mackerel and smoked trout. Also available are duck & chicken, including whole smoked chicken. **Online shop**.

County Dublin

NORTH CO DUBLIN

Gourmet Food Parlour **BALLYBOUGHAL** – see DUN LAOGHAIRE.

Ray Collier 3 Main Street **HOWTH** *(+353 (0)1 832 2002)*. Highly regarded Associated Craft Butchers of Ireland member known for quality meats and customer care. This is the place to find the local Baily beef (finished on Howth peninsula), and Lambay Island beef; it is available for only a short season in autumn.

The Country Market Main Street **HOWTH** *(+353 (0)1 832 2033)*. Visitors to Howth tend to stay around the harbour area but there are some nice little restaurants and shops 'up in the village'. Just above the church, past the flower shop, The Country Market is where locals go for the less usual foods that wouldn't be in Centra (the main shop); an upstairs café is a pleasant meeting place. Speciality foods include a good range of Irish artisan produce alongside similar items from, say, Wales and Scotland, and there are some ready meals.

HOWTH: FISH SHOPS ON THE WEST PIER
Howth offers an exceptional choice of shops for fish lovers and, although very few now eat fish on Fridays as penance, Dubliners continue the tradition of Thursday night shopping for fish and browsing the fishmongers that sit cheek by jowl along the West Pier, overlooking the fish dock. Afterwards a walk along the East Pier, perhaps, or a meal in one of the many seafood restaurants that line the harbour, before heading back into town.

Beshoff's the Market 17-18 West Pier **HOWTH** *(+353 (0)1 839 7555 www.beshoffs.ie)*. The first fish shop on Howth pier was founded in 1914 by Ivan Beshoff, a survivor of the Russian Imperial Navy battleship Potemkin mutiny; various Beshoff's enterprises are still run by his descendants and the name is synonymous with seafood in Ireland. Here, Alan Beshoff offers a wide range of whitefish and shellfish with live crab, lobster and crayfish available from tanks in-store; there is also a deli, oyster bar and restaurant.

Dorans on the Pier West Pier **HOWTH** *(+353 (0)1 8392419 www.dorans.ie)*. Sean Doran recently added this retail dimension to the family's long-established seafood wholesaling and processing business, and soon afterwards opened 'The Oar House' restaurant next door (atmospheric and very popular, it is run by highly regarded local chef, John Aungier). Expect a wide selection of fresh whitefish and shellfish with live lobster and oysters available from a tank in-store.

Howth Harbour, Co Dublin

Mulloys West Pier **HOWTH** *(+353 (0)1 661 1222 www.mulloys.ie)*. Established in 1938 at Lower Baggot Street, Dublin, T. Mulloy Ltd., have moved to Howth, where the family business grows into its third generation with a new processing factory, smokery and retail shop. They specialise in prime fish and their own premium smoked salmon.

Nicky's Plaice West Pier **HOWTH** *(+353 (0)1 832 3557 www.nickysplaice.ie)*. This is the last fish shop on the pier, and many regulars make a beeline for it. A family run concern with a long tradition in the fish business in Howth, it was founded by Nicky McLoughlin (recipient of the IFWG Lifetime Achievement Award 2010) and is now run by his son Martin; the shop offers a wide range of fresh whitefish and shellfish and all smoked fish is processed on the premises in their smokery – one of the last of its kind. A very traditional process (involving some secret ingredients) ensures an outstanding product and Nicky's Plaice has many loyal customers, including The King Sitric Restaurant who will serve no other smoked salmon.

Oceanpath Seafood West Pier **HOWTH** *(+353 (0)1 864 3100 www.dunns.ie)*. Dating back to 1822, Dunns of Dublin is Ireland's oldest fish company and remained in the family until it was sold to another family-run company, Oceanpath, in 2006. Their factory is now in Finglas, Dublin 11 *(www.oceanpath.ie)*, and they have a shop on West Pier. Smoked seafood products are their speciality - smoked salmon (wild when available, Irish Organic, and farmed salmon), of course, but also other smoked and ready to eat seafood products such as Irish trout (including organic), mackerel, gravad lax and a unique blackened salmon which is marinated using an Irish stout.

FoodWare Store Old Street **MALAHIDE** *(+353 (0)1 845 1830 www.foodwarestore.com)*. Aisling Boyle and Jill Sloan are both Ballymaloe trained, and it shows in both the homecooked foods that they prepare for customers, and in the carefully selected items they offer for sale, whether it be dry goods, artisan cheeses or wines.

The Herb Garden **NAUL** *(+353 (0)1 841 3907 www.theherbgarden.ie)*. Denise Dunne grows herbs of many kinds, and specialises in herb garden design. Visitors by appointment only.

Egan's Ocean Fresh Strand Street **SKERRIES** *(+353 (0)1 489 5224 www.tasteofskerries.com/egans)*. With over 80 years in business this is a fourth generation family fishmongers, trading since 1926 in Dublin and 1932 in the Midlands. The friendly and helpful Skerries shop opened in 2008 and stocks a wide variety of fresh, locally caught fish, including Loughshinny Crab and Dublin Bay Prawns (landed in Skerries and Balbriggan).

Olive Delicatessen & Café SKERRIES
(+353 (0)1 849 0310 www.olive.ie). Delightful spot
with pavement tables for warm weather and delicious
food backed up by an impressive list of Irish artisan
suppliers; excellent bakery products (including frozen
pizza balls, ready to roll), great cheeses from Ireland
and abroad, chocolates made locally by Chez Emily
(and Skelligs Chocolates, Co Kerry), wines by Red
Island Wines.

Gourmet Food Parlour SWORDS
(see Dun Laoghaire, South Co Dublin)

Chez Emily Cool Quay **THE WARD**
(+353 1 835 2252 www.chezemily.ie). Exquisite
handmade chocolates are crafted here at The Ward,
near Mabestown, by Ferdinand Vandaele & Helena
Hemeryck. Shop: Mon-Fri, 8-4. Also shops at: Sweet
Mocha, Swords & Chocolate Boutique, Ashbourne, Co
Meath (Mon-Sat).

SOUTH COUNTY DUBLIN

The Butler's Pantry Temple Hill **BLACKROCK**
(+353 (0)1 276 1094 www.thebutlerspantry.ie). Founded
in 1987 by Eileen Bergin, this was soon known as the
place to go for really tasty 'home style' food - great
tasting breads, ready meals, desserts – a reputation
built on fresh, quality-led, additive-free ingredients,
seasonality and a special 'homeliness' that they have
successfully retained in today's much larger volume
production, a philosophy reflected in the *Butler's Pantry
Cookbook*. Also at: Mount Merrion Avenue;
Donnybrook; Monkstown; Sandymount; Clontarf;
Rathgar; Greystones; Sandycove.

Cakes & Co Jane Cottage Newtownpark Avenue
BLACKROCK *(+353 (0)1 283 6544
www.cakesandco.com)*. Known for innovative cakes,
specially designed for specific occasions and
celebration; also gluten free cakes. Suppliers of
sugarcraft equipment.

The Organic Supermarket Main Street **BLACKROCK**
(+353 (0)1 278 1111 www.organicsupermarket.ie). The
brainchild of proprietor Darren Grant, this is Ireland's
first dedicated organic supermarket. Weekly vegetable
box scheme offered. Open 7 days; also **online shop**,
with next day delivery.

Hicks of Dalkey Castle Street **DALKEY**
(+353 (0)1 285 9568). A brother of Ed and Brendan
Hick, of J. Hick & Sons Gourmet Foods, Donal Hick is
equally gifted and, like his brothers, also trained in
Germany. He produces a similar range of pork
products of the same high quality - Irish breakfast
sausage, speciality sausages, salami, Kassler, dry cured
bacon etc, which he sells from this family shop.

Select Stores Railway Road **DALKEY**
(+353 (0)1 295 9611 www.selectstores.ie). This
landmark corner building has been a store since being
opened in 1959 by Margaret and the late Paddy
McCabe. Today it seems superficially unchanged but,
in 2004, their younger son Oliver transformed Select
Stores – they still do fruit and veg, but the emphasis
is on organic, and it's now also a natural health food
store and juice bar.

Thyme Out Castle Street **DALKEY** *(+353 (0)1 285 1999
www.thymeout.ie)* "Fresh, wholesome, tasty and always
gone at the end of the day", that's the philosophy at
Thyme Out shop and deli, where evening meals are
ready in the fridge and everything is made on site.
Ingredients are top notch: Glenilen dairy products;
Roscarberry bacon pieces, rashers, free range sausages,
puddings; Crocker's organic eggs; Helen Gee jams;
Chez Emily handmade Chocolates… enough said.

George's Fish Shop Monkstown Court Monkstown
Farm **DUN LAOGHAIRE** *(+353 (0)1 230 3011
www.georgesfishshop.com)*. The Rogerson family have
been selling seafood in Monkstown Farm for over 30
years. Branching out from processing and wholesaling
business they recently opened George's Fish Shop
which offers a wide range fresh fish and shellfish.
Closed Sun & Mon.

Peter Caviston
Cavistons Food Emporium Co Dublin

Gourmet Food Parlour Cumberland Street
DUN LAOGHAIRE *(+353 (0)1 280 5670*
www.gourmetfoodparlour.com). Appealing modern deli
and café with an emphasis on quality at an affordable
price; mainly daytime but open for tapas with music
on Fri & Sat evenings. Also at: Swords and The Grange
at Ballyboughal (with art gallery).

J. Hick & Sons Rear 15A Georges Street Upper
DUN LAOGHAIRE *(+353 (0)1 284 2700 www.hicks.ie)*.
Fourth generation pork butchers. Ed & Brendan Hick
make a wide range of pork products on the premises
which are then distributed, mainly within the Dublin
and Wicklow areas. They are especially renowned for
their sausage range and an unusual service offered is to
butcher 'backyard pigs' that have been reared by
inexperienced new farmers. They've also been avid
supporters of farmers' markets since they started, so
you'll meet them at both Temple Bar Food Market and
Farmleigh House in the Phoenix Park; their products
are also sold here, in their factory shop (at wholesale
prices), and available at premium retail outlets eg
Avoca Handweavers, Cavistons and BrookLodge, Co
Wicklow. Factory shop: Wed-Fri 10-2.

Cavistons Food Emporium Glasthule Road
Sandycove area **GLASTHULE** *(+353 (0)1 2809120*
www.cavistons.com). Dublin is fortunate to have a half
dozen or so outstanding food stores and the number
one, for many regular shoppers, would be this
treasure of a fish shop, deli and speciality food store.
The Caviston family have been here since 1947 and
this characterful shop now offers en extensive choice
of speciality food products, a wide range of whitefish
and shellfish with live crab, lobster and oysters
available from a tank in-store, and a seafood
restaurant next door. Home smoked salmon is a
speciality – and so is old-fashioned service. Open
Mon-Sat. (Rest since 1996, L Tue-Sat, D Fri & Sat).

O'Toole Master Organic Butcher Glasthule Road
GLASTHULE *(+353 (0)1 284 1125*
www.otoolesbutchers.com). Branch of the famous
Terenure organic butchers, see Dublin 6.

Superquinn Newcastle Road **LUCAN** & branches *(+353
(0)1 6240277 www.superquinn.ie)*. Dating back to
1960, when Senator Feargal Quinn first started the
supermarket era in Ireland, Superquinn may no longer

be family owned, but this chain of 23 stores specialises in fresh food and – unlike most other supermarket chains currently operating in Ireland - it demonstrates a commitment to local producers: "4 out of every 5 euro we spend is on fresh produce from local suppliers". And, while competitively priced, products offered are not exclusively price-led; the SQ Superior Quality range, for example, is just that – endorsed, among other accolades, by an IFWG Award in 2008, for their Superior Quality Irish rib-eye dry-aged Hereford beef.

Michael's Food & Wine Deerpark Road **MOUNT MERRION** *(+353 (0)1 278 0377)*. Michael and Mary Lowe's wine shop, Italian deli and little trattoria style restaurant is mainly known for its simplicity and for excellent Italian food and wine, imported directly; but you'll also find some special Irish artisan products at the deli – Mossfield cheeses are stocked here, for example, among the treats to take home.

Lett's Craft Butchers NEWCASTLE *(+353 (0)1 458 0156 www.lettscraftbutchers.com)*. A member of the Irish Craft Butchers Association, meats at this interesting shop include beef from a single farm, Fitzpatrick's of Castledermot, Co Kildare and, among other good things, they also stock game in season, fresh vegetables supplied by Leonard's of the Dublin Corporation Market and fish from Kish Fish in Coolock, Dublin 17.

Avoca Rathcoole Naas Road **RATHCOOLE** *(+353 (0)1 257 1800 www.avoca.ie)*. This purpose-built branch of Avoca may be less pretty than the others, but its convenience on one of Dublin's main arterial roads has made it a popular meeting place, and it is handy for picking up good deli products/food to go - for a functional but tasty self-service meal, or something more relaxed in their Egg Café.

county Kildare

Castlefarm Shop Narraghmore, near **ATHY** *(+353 (0)59 8636948 / (0)87-6785269 www.castlefarmshop.ie)*. Thanks to Jenny and Peter Young's dedication, drive and determination to spread the word about the farming experience that they value so highly, their organic farm on the western edges of the Wicklow Mountains is one of the most significant (and increasingly recognised) farming enterprises in Ireland. The Farm Shop sells homemade and home-grown food,

Castlefarm Shop, Co Kildare

much of it (including Castlefarm Cheese) from their own farm; however, the wide range offered includes conventional as well as organic produce including other local Irish produce: "honest to goodness homemade and home grown food". A new orchard area is a haven for wildlife and feeds the growing number of Castlefarm bee hives. Farm tours offered. Farm Shop Fri & Sat 10am-6pm, Sun 12-5pm; Jenny also sells at Athy Farmers' Market and Craft Fair (Sun).

Moyleabbey Organic Farm Ballitore **ATHY** *(+353 (0)87 215 3332 www.moyleabbey.ie & www.organicguide.ie)* Liam Ryan and Yuki Kobayashi grow organic fuit and vegetables here on 13.5 acres; they supply good local restaurants, eg Gargoyle's Café in Athy, and you'll find their produce at Newbridge and Athy Farmers' Markets (Sat & Sun respectively). Farmgate stall Fri (12-8).

Carbury Free Range Chicken Rathmore **CARBURY** *(+353 (0)46 955 2958)*. Good Food Ireland member Sandra Higgins - wife of Finbar Higgins, Executive Head Chef of the K Club at Straffan – and her father Eddie McKeon farm their 'Hubbard' chickens on traditional lines, mainly for supply to restaurants. On sale at the farm gate.

Deirdre O'Sullivan & Norman Kenny Nurney House CARBURY *(+353 (0)46 955 3337 www.organicguide.ie)*. Long established mixed organic farm supplying a wide range of products including fruit, vegetables and cereals, honey and eggs. Sold at

*Herbs at Mount Usher Gardens,
Co Wicklow*

and you'll find a wide range on sale at the delicatessen (and at a newer deli branch in Drogheda); he also attends the farmers' markets at Sonairte and Dublin Food Co-Op.

county wicklow

Mount Usher Gardens ASHFORD

(+353 (0)404 40205 www.mount-usher-gardens.com) Not only are there magnificent Robinsonian gardens to enjoy here beside the River Vartry but, with the Pratt family of Avoca having taken on their stewardship, the Garden Café @ Avoca offers good food throughout the day, and there is a shop.

Avoca Handweavers AVOCA VILLAGE

(+353 (0)402 35105 www.avoca.ie). The Original premises of the known family-owned craft design company (see Kilmcanaogue); here you can watch the hand-weavers who produce the lovely woven woollen rugs and fabrics which became the hallmark of the company in its early days. Also wide range of gifts; speciality foods.

Grangecon Café Kilbride Road BLESSINGTON

(+353 (0)45 857892). The café is Richard and Jenny Street's main business here, but they also produce freshly-cooked meals that are a boon to take home on a busy day.

Harvest Fare BLESSINGTON *(+353 (0)45 891636*

www.harvestfarehealthshop.com). A surprisingly comprehensively stocked shop to find in a rural town – and they offer vegetarian cookery classes and therapies too. Closed Sun.

Killruddery Farm near BRAY *(+353 (0)1 286 3405 /*

(0)87 772 9882 www.killruddery.com). Situated between Bray and Greystones, the Brabazon family's extensively operated farm offers quality produce (lamb, beef and apple juice) for delivery or collection. Also firewood and mulch. Kilruddery Gardens are open in season; the Garden Café serves light meals and afternoon tea (garden entrance ticket required).

Castleruddery Organic Farm DONARD

(+353 (0)45 404925 / (0)87 807 7254 www.organic-trust.org). Donard, West Wicklow. Organically certified since 1989, Hilda Crampton and Dominic Quinn run one of the longest established organic farms in Ireland; they produce a wide range of vegetables and herbs, and also import carefully selected organic fruit and vegetables to provide all year supply. Farm Shop (Thu & Fri); also at Naas Farmers' Market (Sat).

Avoca Powerscourt ENNISKERRY

(+353 (0)1 204 6000 www.avoca.ie). Not the biggest of the Avoca stores (see Kilmacanogue), but the most beautifully located and well worth a special visit;

small but well stocked foodhall and pleasant self-service restaurant, the Terrace Café (try to get a window or terrace table, the view is spectacular). Garden lovers should allow time to browse the Garden Pavilion garden centre, which stocks some less usual plants.

Crocker's Organic Farm GLENEALY *(+353 (0)404 44854 www.crockerorganics.com)*. At 100 acres, Martha and Gary Crocker's mixed farm near Ashford is one of the larger farms in organic production, and you will find their produce named on menus and in specialist shops (Avoca, Butler's Pantry, Thomas's of Foxrock for example). No farm shop, but you can order their lamb, beef, turkeys, chicken and eggs by phone, or email through their website.

Organic Delights Talbotstown Kiltegan KILTEGAN *(+353 (0)59 647 3193 / (0)87 248 5826 www.organicdelights.ie)*. Denis Healy is one of Ireland's most prominent suppliers of organic fruit and vegetables, both grown on the family farm in Wicklow and imported. A great supporter of farmers' markets, and one of the founding stallholders at Dublin's Temple Bar Food Market. Orders can be arranged for collection at the large number of markets attended. You can also buy direct, and delivery is possible in some areas.

A. Caviston Church Road GREYSTONES *(+353 (0)1 2877 637 www.acaviston.ie)*. Related to, but not a branch of, the renowned Caviston family emporium (See Dun Laoghaire), Amy Caviston and her partner Shane Willis run an informal restaurant here as well an excellent deli and fish shop; they stock a wide variety of fresh seasonal seafood and sell live crab and lobster from a tank in-store.

Donnybrook Fair Grattan Court GREYSTONES *(+353 (0)1 287 6346 www.donnybrookfair.ie)*. Branch of the chic D4 food hall.

The Happy Pear Church Road GREYSTONES *(+353 (0)1 287 3655 www.thehappypear.ie)*. Twins David and Stephen Flynn run this cheerfully ethical vegetable shop and food market, with smoothie bar, café and an evening tapas bar. If that all sounds a lot for a vegetable shop, it is, but the (vegetarian) food is simple and tasty, and this place has real heart. A telling detail about this pair – they run their van on local rapeseed oil. Now that is walking the walk.

Nature's Gold Killincarrig Road GREYSTONES *(+353 (0)1 287 6301)*. In business since 1977, this is one of the oldest shops in Greystones - and one of Ireland's oldest health stores; a USP for foodies is the extra virgin olive oil, produced on their own olive farm near Barcelona.

The Steak Shop Trafalgar Road GREYSTONES *(+353 (0)1 255 7737)*. A jaunty striped awning announces this traditional butchers; known especially for their steaks - "Reared from our own farm and meats matured for at least 21 days" says proprietor Barry King - they also sell other meats and quality poultry. Meat like it used to be.

The Butler's Pantry Church Road GREYSTONES *(+353 (0)1 201 0022 www.thebutlerspantry.ie)*. A branch of Eileen Bergin's classy convenience foodstore (see Co Dublin); open 7 days, times vary.

Avoca Handweavers KILMACANOGUE *(+353 (0)1 286 7466 www.avoca.ie)*. This large shop and restaurant, off the N11 south of Dublin, is the flagship premises of Ireland's most famous group of craft shops (now 'lifestyle') As well as good food in both Fernhouse Café and the self-service area, there is a wide range of excellent delicatessen fare and artisan produce for sale in the shop. *Avoca also at: Avoca village; Powerscourt, Enniskerry; Mount Usher Gardens, Ashford; Rathcoole Dublin 17; Suffolk Street, Dublin 2; Arthur Street, Belfast.

The BrookLodge Hotel Macreddin Village MACREDDIN *(+353 (0)402 36444 www.brooklodge.com)*. Among the little 'village' of complementary businesses at this unusual hotel, The Store Rooms offers treats for sale including wild and organic preserves, jams, chutneys and a speciality wild garlic pesto; also home smoked fish, meats and vegetables, and a range of organic breads baked on-site, at Wicklow's only organic bakery. Purchases complete, you can slip next door to the atmospheric Actons Country Pub for an organic lager or stout from their microbrewery. Farmers' markets some Sundays.

Sweetbank Farm Tiglin near NEWCASTLE *(+353 (0)86 173 0497 / (0)1 818 4162 www.sweetbankfarm.ie)*. Debbie and David Johnston sell their beautiful hand-picked seasonal fruit through outlets such as Avoca, and their lamb can be ordered in half or whole boxes, for collection from the farm.

Ireland East:
Sample the Region's Food Markets

For further information on Farmers Markets throughout Ireland
www.bordbia.ie • www.irishfarmersmarkets.ie

DUBLIN CITY MARKETS

Dublin Docklands Farmers' Market Mayor Square IFSC Dublin 1 Wed 12-2

The Point Village Market Dublin 1 Sat & Sun 8-4.30 *www.dublindocklands.ie/index.jsp*

Temple Bar Market Meeting House Square Dublin 2 Saturdays

Red Stables Food Market Dublin 5 *www.redstables.ie*

Irish Village Markets Dublin 6 (& others) *www.irishvillagemarkets.com*

Smithfield Outdoor Food Market Dublin 7 Fri 10-3

Dublin Food Co-Op Dublin 8 Sat 9.30-4

Marlay Park Dublin 14 Sat 10-4

Farmleigh Farmers' Market Dublin 15 *www.farmleigh.ie*

Dundrum Farmers Market Dublin 16

Tallaght Irish Village Markets Dublin 24 *www.irishvillagemarkets.com*

CO DUBLIN MARKETS

Blackrock Market (mixed) Sat & Sun (& bank hol Mon) 11am-5.30, *www.blackrockmarket.com*

Dalkey Farmers' Market Heritage Ctre Fri 10-4 www.dlrcoco.ie/martkets

Dun Laogahire Farmers' Market People's Park Sun 11-2

Howth Gourmet Market Sun

Leopardstown Organic Market Racetrack Fri 11-7 Sean McArdle Markets *www.irishfarmersmarkets.ie*

Malahide Farmers' Market GAA club Church Street Sat 10-4 *www.irishfarmersmarkets.ie*

CO KILDARE MARKETS

Athy Farmers' Market (with crafts) Emily Square Sun 10-3

Naas Farmers' Market Sat 10-3

CO LOUTH MARKETS

Castlebellingam Farmers' Market Bellingham Castle 1st Sun of month, 11-5

Dundalk Farmers Market The Square Fri 10-2 & County Museme Sat 10-2

West Street Farmers' Market Drogheda Fri 10-5

CO MEATH MARKETS

Kells Farmers' Market Sat 10-2

Laytown Farmers Market Sonairte 2nd Sundays

CO WICKLOW MARKETS

Arklow Farmers' Market Fri 10-1

Aughrim Farmers' Market The Pavilion Sat 11-2

Bray Farmers' Market Heritage Centre Sat 11-3

BrookLodge Organic Market Macreddin 1st Sun month Mar-Oct

Kilternan Country Market Golden Ball Sat am

Newcastle North Wicklow Country Market Community Centre Sat 10.30-12.30

Eat & Stay

The Winding Stair, Dublin

COUNTY DUBLIN

Dublin City

Chapter One Restaurant

In the former home of the great John Jameson of whiskey fame, a stylish and atmospheric arched basement beneath the Irish Writers' Museum houses one of Ireland's finest restaurants. Together with an outstanding team, the proprietors - chef-patron Ross Lewis and front of house manager Martin Corbett - have earned an enviable reputation for exceptional modern Irish cooking, superb service and good value. Ross, a former Euro-Toques Ireland Commissioner-General, showcases speciality Irish produce at every opportunity; special treats include a magnificent charcuterie trolley, farmhouse cheeses in peak condition – and a Chef's Table.

18/19 Parnell Square Dublin 1
+353 (0)1 873 2266 www.chapteronerestaurant.com

The Winding Stair

This much-loved café and bookshop overlooking the Ha'penny Bridge is one of the most atmospheric eating places in town – and proprietor-manager Elaine Murphy's strong vision ensures plenty of 'the organic and real' on menus that include a signature Irish charcuterie plate (Connemara dry cured lamb and beef, salami from the Gubbeen smokehouse in County Cork), and outstanding renditions of classics such as bacon and cabbage with parsley sauce. Known for simple, high quality food (and an interesting wine list), it also has a lovely ambience - book a window table for a view of the river.

40, Lower Ormond Quay Dublin 1
+353 (0)1 872 7320 www.winding-stair.com

Ely Winebar & Café

Since 1999, when Erik and Michelle Robson opened this imaginatively renovated Georgian townhouse just off St Stephen's Green, they've revolutionised stylish informal dining in Dublin and earned an unrivalled reputation for their wines. But they also offer premium beers, and wholesome food includes organic pork, beef and lamb from the family farm in County Clare - and not just premium cuts, but also products like home-made sausages and mince, which

can transform simple dishes such as sausages and mash. Sister establishments are **'ely bar & brasserie'** IFSC and **'ely gastro pub'** Grand Canal Square.
22 Ely Place Dublin 2 & branches
+353 (0)1 676 8986 www.elywinebar.ie

L'Ecrivain

The cooking style at Derry and Sallyanne Clarke's stylish and highly acclaimed city centre restaurant may be classic French, but Derry is a leading figure in Euro-Toques Ireland and a longtime champion of Irish artisan foods, so specialities change with the seasons, often offering a fine modern interpretation of traditional Irish themes. Neglected ingredients like rabbit, or not-so-humble bacon and cabbage take their place alongside prime seafood, lamb, beef and game, in season, and vegetarian dishes are handled with trademark style. The attention to detail is legendary – as is the value (service charge is not added to the price of their excellent wines).
109a Lower Baggot Street Dublin 2
+353 (0)1 661 1919 www.lecrivain.com

One Pico Restaurant

Quietly located in a laneway near St. Stephen's Green and regarded as a 'best-kept secret' until not so long ago, Eamonn O'Reilly's stylish One Pico is now deservedly one of Dublin's most popular fine dining restaurants, known for sophisticated, technically demanding dishes that are invariably executed with confidence and flair. Stellar standards matched with outstanding value (especially on certain set menus) are the twin magnets that discerning Dublin diners find irresistible – and Eamonn O'Reilly allows an occasional (modern)

nod to Irish traditions in his classical French cooking, based on tiptop local ingredients.
5-6 Molesworth Place Schoolhouse Lane Dublin 2
+353 (0)1 676 0300 www.onepico.com

❧ Thornton's Restaurant

Above the Fitzwilliam Hotel, overlooking St Stephen's Green, Kevin and Muriel Thornton's renowned restaurant features arresting photography - shot by Kevin, who is as adept with a camera as a sautée pan. Otherwise, the understated linen-clad tables leave no doubt that the food is to be the star here, so – as many would cite this uncompromising chef as Ireland's greatest - diners come to be wooed by his passion for transforming the most meticulously sourced seasonal ingredients into a feast for the eye and the palate. Gold leaf may well feature (available all year, luckily) yet, paradoxically, good value too.
128 St Stephen's Green Dublin 2
+353 (0)1 478 7008 www.thorntonsrestaurant.com

O'Connells in Donnybrook

Tom O'Connell's iconic Ballsbridge restaurant relocated to the former Madigan's Pub in Donnybrook in 2010, with respected Euro-Toques Chef Lorcan Cribbin in the kitchen. It's an appealing package, with a cosy 'Around the Corner' bar, an upper floor available for private dining - and a characterful ground floor dining room where the many fans of this dedicated team can enjoy what they have always done best: serving great, simple ingredients-led food, guided by the Irish seasons. Producers and suppliers (some of 11 years standing) continue to be the stars of the show, along with house specialities including O'Connells Smoked Fish &

Shellfish Plate – and Hereford Prime Rib-Eye Steak, cooked on the specially imported charcoal Josper grill. Great food – and great value for money too.
135 Morehampton Road Donnybrook Dublin 4
+353 (0)1 665 5940 www.oconnellsdonnybrook.com

Roly's Bistro

Just across from the US Embassy, this bustling bistro hit the ground running when it opened in 1992, today it's a Dublin institution. Founding chef-patron Colin O'Daly's paintings adorn both walls and menu card in the bistro – where head chef Paul Cartwright's imaginative, fairly priced seasonal menus offer what might be called informal fine dining; specialities that have evolved over the years include an upbeat version of traditional Kerry lamb pie and luscious Dublin Bay Prawns are always in demand. A ground floor café offers casual meals, and breads from in-house bakery also on sale.
7 Ballsbridge Terrace Ballsbridge Dublin 4
+353 (0)1 668 2611 www.rolysbistro.ie

The Chop House

Although the exterior of this gastro-pub may not be very impressive, it belies the attention to detail shown in every plate of food served inside. With not just one, but two of Dublin's best younger chefs –Kevin Arundel (a Euro-Toques Ireland Commissioner) and Conor Dempsey - sharing the driving seat here, it should be no surprise to find that ingredients are carefully and thoughtfully sourced, and the short menus are seasonal, varied and interesting. Carlingford oysters perhaps, to start, then slow roast belly of spotted pig (with gorgeous crispy crackling); excellent cooking does justice to the fine ingredients.
2 Shelbourne Road Dublin 4
+353 (0)1 660 2390 / (0)87 299 4176

County Dublin

Cavistons Seafood Restaurant

Caviston's of Sandycove has long been a mecca for lovers of good food - here you will find everything that is wonderful, from organic vegetables to farmhouse cheeses, cooked meats to more exotic items. But fish and shellfish were always a focus at

Cavistons - even down to providing a collection of well-thumbed recipe books for on-the-spot reference. And, at their little restaurant next door, they serve an imaginative range of simple, colourful, perfectly cooked seafood dishes influenced by various traditions. It's a class act - and there's a younger cousin, A Caviston, at Greystones too.

59 Glasthule Road Dun Laoghaire Co Dublin
+353 (0)1 280 9245 www.cavistons.com

❧ King Sitric Fish Restaurant & Accommodation

Aidan and Joan MacManus's harbourside restaurant with rooms is one of Dublin's longest established fine dining restaurants, and a prime destination for those who seek tiptop foods, especially seafood, along with choice, value, and service. The fishing boats and lobster pots supplying the kitchen can be seen from the first floor restaurant – and specialities worth travelling for include a luscious red velvet crab bisque, classics like sole meunière - and lobster 'Dublin Lawyer.' An avid supporter of local produce for many years, Aidan's menus name valued suppliers and list Irish fish in six languages - other seasonal specialities include game and Baily beef, finished on Howth peninsula.

East Pier Howth Co Dublin
+353 (0)1 832 5235 www.kingsitric.ie

❧ Red Bank House & Restaurant

Terry McCoy is one of the great characters of Irish food and a champion of local and artisan foods, so you'll find that fresh seafood from Skerries harbour provides the backbone of the menus at his restaurant with accommodation in this characterful little town. And

this is also just the place to find the great produce of the land like Rush potatoes, vegetables and tomatoes. Pride of place is evident throughout the menu, with dishes named for their local relevance - grilled goat's cheese St. Patrick, for example, is a reminder that the saint once lived on Church Island off Skerries.

5-7 Church Street Skerries Co Dublin
+353 (0)1 849 1005 www.redbank.ie

county Kildare

Ballymore Inn

The secret ingredients at the O'Sullivan family's bar are simple: fantastic food and genuine hospitality. Nobody understands the importance of careful sourcing better than Georgina O'Sullivan, who has long been a trailblazer for artisan foods. Fans beat a path to the door to enjoy stylish cooking of handpicked ingredients like Margaret McDonnell's chickens, Penny Lange's biodynamic salads from Co Wicklow, best Slaney beef, and fresh fish from Duncannon in Co Wexford. In both the smart Café Bar area, and the big, buzzy 'Back Bar', every item offered is special of its type – try the speciality pizza, based on Irish artisan products.

Ballymore Eustace Co Kildare
+353 (0)45 864 585 www.ballymoreinn.com

Fallons of Kilcullen

Proprietor Brian Fallon (of Fallon & Byrne in Dublin) is well known in Ireland for doing things right, and Chef Rose Brannock - a longstanding member of this team – is key to Fallons' reputation for consistently excellent food. Her style of really good, simple bistro cooking is well-established: there's a sense of place and personality, with producer names sprinkled through the menu and a real feeling of commitment - and real people - behind each dish. And real they certainly are: smiling out at you on their unique 'Supplier Family' page, which profiles suppliers.

Main Street Kilcullen Co Kildare

+353 (0)45 481 063   www.fallonb.ie

county Louth

♣ Ghan House

The Carroll family's 18th century house on the edge of Carlingford village enjoys views across the lough to the Mountains of Mourne and is a one stop shop for foodies, offering accommodation, a restaurant and a cookery school. The focus is on home-grown (vegetable, fruit and herbs), home-made (breads, ice creams, everything that can be made on the premises) and local produce, notably Cooley lamb and beef. And, of course, seafood: oysters are synonymous with Carlingford – and there are also mussels from the lough and lobster from Ballagan, while smoked salmon and crab come from nearby Annagassan.

6 Carlingford Co Louth

+353 (0)42 937 3682   www.ghanhouse.com

county Meath

♣ Tankardstown House

Owners Trish and Brian Conroy have restored and renovated this appealing period property near Slane with consideration – and have also acquired the 80 acres of land that belonged to the original estate. The overall impression is one of immaculate taste and, in addition to offering luxurious comfort to residential guests, there is now a choice of two restaurants – The Bistro and Brabazon – both offering excellent, carefully sourced food in stylish surroundings. A farmers' market is held on some weekends (check website for dates).

Rathkenny Slane Co Meath

+353 (0)41 982 4621   www.tankardstown.ie

county Wicklow

♣ Ballyknocken House & Cookery School

Catherine Fulvio is a household name in Ireland these days, thanks to her successful TV cookery programmes, but her charming Victorian farmhouse and cookery school in the foothills of the Wicklow Hills still come first. Her cookery school is in a renovated milking parlour in the grounds, and Catherine also cooks four-course dinners for guests, based on local produce, including vegetables and herbs from the Ballyknocken farm and gardens, which are planted with fruit tree, roses and herbs. All this, plus extensive breakfasts and great picnics - a relaxing base for exploring the Garden County.

Gleanealy Ashford Co Wicklow

+353 (0)404 44627   www.ballyknocken.com

Grangecon Café

The name of Jenny and Richard Street's smashing café harks back to an earlier version in a nearby village, but their stated aim, "to provide you with a really good food stop", is unchanged. Wholesome aromas will draw you in and everything is made on the premises, including the breads, pastries and ice cream; the ham hocks for the quiche lorraine are cooked here, the pork meat in the sausage rolls is organic, fruit and vegetables come from Castleruddery organic farm, and other ingredients are mainly organic and/or free rang. Ready meals to buy, too. Not cheap, but great value.

Kilbride Road Blessington Co Wicklow
+353 (0)45 857 892

❀ Rathsallagh House

Breakfast could well be the most important meal at the O'Flynn family's gorgeous, rambling country house as they've won a superfluity of awards for a magnificent Edwardian breakfast buffet offering every conceivable good thing, including reminders of yesteryear like smoked salmon kedgeree, and devilled kidneys in silver chafing dishes. But brilliant as breakfasts are, dinner is the main meal and a real treat it is too, with interesting daily-changing menus based on local and seasonal produce, much of it from Rathsallagh's own farm and their beautiful walled gardens – which garden lovers will adore.

Dunlavin Co Wicklow
+353 (0)45 403 112 www.rathsallagh.com

Avoca Handweavers

The Pratt family's company dates from the 18th century and has only sold food since 1990, yet it's now universally recognised as the pioneer of modern Irish café cooking – a quality model that brings people from all over to shop, and to tuck into wholesome home-cooked food, which is mainly based on local and artisan produce. The style is eclectic – there's great baking and traditional dishes like beef and Guinness casserole, but their salads and vegetables are also legendary; the common denominator is quality. Restaurants/self-service cafés & delis at: Avoca Suffolk Street, Dublin (www.avoca.ie); Avoca Rathcoole, Saggart, Co Dublin (www.avoca.ie); Avoca Powerscourt, Enniskerrry, Co Wicklow (www.powerscourt.ie); Mount Usher Gardens (www.mountushergardens.ie), Avoca Belfast, Arthur Street, Belfast (www.avoca.ie).

Kilmacanogue Bray Co Wicklow
+353 (0)1 286 7466 www.avoca.ie

Grilled Scallops with Black & White Pudding

Aidan MacManus, of The King Sitric Seafood Restaurant in Howth, Co Dublin, sources the freshest and best scallops and traditional puddings for this dish, which features a classic combination of ingredients. Locally produced culinary rapeseed oil now offers a comparable alternative to olive oil, if preferred. The black and white puddings are already pre-cooked when purchased, so the cooking time is short. As the ingredients are filling, this quantity would be adequate for a main course when served with side vegetables, or it could be adapted slightly to serve two as a starter.

Ingredients (per portion)

2 or 3 scallops, depending on size

1 slice each of good quality black and white pudding

olive or rapeseed oil

To serve (per portion):1 tbsp red onion marmalade & 1 tsp pesto (see below)

Red Onion Marmalade:

2 red onions

a little olive oil or rapeseed oil

cracked or coarsely ground black pepper

2 tablespoons caster sugar

glass each of water and red wine

Pesto: (see below)

First make the red onion marmalade: Slice the onions and sauté in oil over a low heat for several minutes. Season with the pepper, add the sugar, water and wine and bring to the boil. Simmer gently for about 20 minutes until it reaches a shiny, jammy consistency. (Any left over can be kept in a screw-top jar in the fridge.)

Meanwhile, make the pesto: Blend together 100g/4oz basil leaves, 1 tsp pine kernels, 100g/4oz olive or rapeseed oil, and 100g/4oz grated parmesan-style cheese, to make a paste. If it is too thick, add a teaspoon of cold water.

To cook the scallops & black pudding: Preheat a ridged grill pan and, unless it is non-stick, brush lightly with oil; cook the slices of pudding hot through and attractively browned. On the same pan, sear the scallops for 1 minute on each side. Do not overcook.

To serve: Place a tablespoon of the red onion marmalade on the centre of the plate, arrange the pudding and the scallops neatly on top and drizzle with the pesto.

Pan-Fried Chicken with Walnut & Lemon Dressing

A growing number of Irish farmers are now producing top quality poultry, with several excellent suppliers in the Dublin region. Buy the best quality chicken you can find for this easily prepared dish, and it will reward you with excellent flavour and succulence. Also take care to use fresh walnuts, as a high oil content gives them a short shelf life; they keep fresh longer if stored in the fridge.

Serves 4

4 part-boned chicken breasts, preferably free range and organic if possible, skin on

Salt, freshly ground black pepper and lemon juice

Dressing:

100g/4oz walnuts

2-3 cloves garlic

Juice of 1 lemon

1 tsp ground cumin

2 tbsp coriander leaves, chopped

125ml/5fl oz olive oil

Salt freshly ground black pepper and sugar to taste

4 scallions, chopped

Season the chicken with salt, pepper and lemon juice. Set aside. Preheat the oven at 180°C, 350°F Gas Mark 4.

Toast the walnuts in a dry pan, then tip them into the processor with the other dressing ingredients. Blend for a few seconds. Taste for seasoning, then leave in the fridge until ready to serve.

Heat an ovenproof frying pan or black grill pan, brushing lightly with oil if not non-stick.

Cook the chicken, skin side down, for 4-5 minutes to get a crisp skin, then turn over and cook for another 2-3 minutes.

Put the pan and its contents into the hot oven and cook for another 10-15 minutes until thoroughly cooked through.

Very good served with spinach, a few boiled potatoes and a spoonful of the dressing on top. Any leftover dressing will last for a week in the refrigerator.

Dublín coddle

Said to be Dean Swift's favourite meal, this traditional dish is every bit as comforting as it sounds; made on pay day or on Saturday nights, it is a very forgiving dish and always welcoming, whatever the time. It combines two foods known since the earliest Irish literature - bacon and sausages - and, like all very simple dishes, success depends on the quality of the ingredients, so use the very best sausages you can find, and good dry-cured bacon. The traditional version is a simple stew; this modern variation ("Campbell's Coddle") is made with the same ingredients but has a crispy topping.

Serves 6-8

450g /l lb good quality pork sausages

325g/12 oz streaky rashers, preferably dry-cured

6 large potatoes, peeled and thickly sliced

2 medium onions, peeled and sliced

4-6 carrots (about l lb/450g), scraped and sliced

$^1/_2$ pint/300 ml stock or water, or as required

4-6 tbsp freshly chopped parsley

l rounded tablespoon mild wholegrain mustard (optional)

Sea salt and freshly ground black pepper

Preheat a moderate oven, 350°F, 180°C, Gas mark 4.

Lay the sausages in a single layer in a large, shallow ovenproof dish. Put them into the oven to brown a little and release some of their fat. Put the thickly sliced potatoes into a saucepan, barely cover with cold water, bring up to the boil and par-boil for 5-10 minutes; drain well. (This stage can be omitted if time in the oven is not at a premium.) Trim any bits of bone or gristle out of the rashers, but don't bother to remove rinds; set aside.

Remove the sausages from the oven, lift out with a slotted spoon and drain off all accumulated fat.

Arrange the sliced onions and carrots in the base of the baking dish, scatter with chopped parsley and seasoning then add the stock or water. Arrange the sausages on top of the vegetables, then the potatoes, and scatter with more parsley and seasoning. Finally, add the rashers, spread out to cover the layer of potatoes as neatly as possible. Cook in the preheated oven for 40-50 minutes or until the vegetables are tender and the rashers and potatoes crispy and brown. Alternatively, cook at a lower temperature, adding extra liquid as required, for as much longer as is convenient. Serve with a green vegetable such as spring cabbage, lightly cooked in as little water as possible.

steak with Grilled vegetables

'A good steak' has long been the nation's favourite meal, and this easy recipe makes a handy dish for two; as preferred, it can be cooked in a grill pan as below, or over the barbecue and the vegetables can be varied depending on what's in season. There is now more choice in the breed of beef when buying steak, many swear by Angus but other breeds have their advocates too, including the hardy little black Dexter; dry ageing is preferred, hung for a minimum of 21 days - longer hanging times are becoming popular and produce more tender beef.

Serves 2

2 well aged steaks of your preferred breed, sirloin, striploin, ribeye, or fillet

1 or 2 courgettes, cut into thick slices

1 or 2 peppers, deseeded and cut into thick slices

1 small red onion, peeled and cut into thick slices

1-2 tablespoons olive oil or rapeseed oil

Salt and plenty of freshly ground black pepper

1 tablespoons balsamic or wine vinegar

4-6 small to medium potatoes, scrubbed

Unless cooking over the barbecue, heat a large dry grill pan (or two medium pans) over high heat for about 10 minutes until very hot - cast iron ridged pans give excellent results.

Meanwhile put the steaks into a shallow dish, and the prepared vegetables into a bowl. Mix together the oil, salt, black pepper and balsamic vinegar. Pour half of the mixture over the steaks and the remainder over the vegetables, mixing well.

When ready to cook, place the vegetables on the grill pan, toss around quickly to sear and then push to the edges, allowing the steaks enough space to make full contact with the hot pan. Add the steaks and then reduce the heat to moderate; do not overcrowd - use two pans or cook in two batches if necessary.

Cook the vegetables and steaks for about 5-8 minutes, to your liking. Turn the steaks once and stir the vegetables around a little occasionally to cook them evenly. Meanwhile boil the scrubbed potatoes in their jackets.

When the steaks are cooked to your liking and the potatoes are tender, arrange everything on heated plates and serve hot. Add a dash of wine and knob of butter to any tasty bits left in the hot pan, swirl around and pour onto the plates.

Ireland: Midlands

Cavan, Laois, Longford, Monaghan, Offaly & Westmeath,

Clonmacnoise, Co Offaly

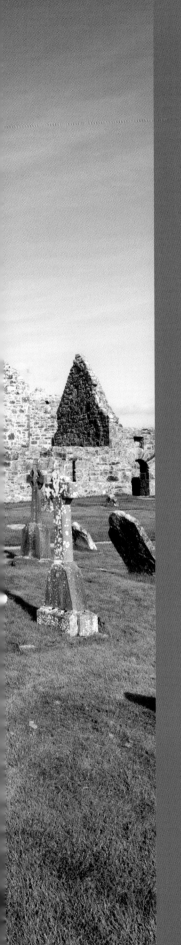

In times past in the quest for schoolroom simplicity, junior geographers would be told that Ireland was like a dish, with all the mountains around the edge, and in the middle a vast plain with the River Shannon flowing slowly southwards across it, murmuring through its majestic lakes and dropping gently towards the sea.

A notion of engaging clarity, and true up to a point. Yet, think Irish scenery, and you'll think purple mountains with some farmland to offset the dramatic wilderness, or a lively sea. And certainly for an island of its size, the variety and beauty of Ireland's mountain ranges is remarkable, though it has to be admitted that in comparison with the world's more elevated countries, Ireland's highlands would scarcely rate as hills, let alone mountains.

Shannonside grazing

About theRegion

But even then, a large tract of the middle of Ireland is low-lying. There is no high road from Dublin to Galway - the main road west scarcely takes you above 150 metres. In fact, it is possible to get from Dublin to Sligo, Westport, Limerick, Waterford or Wexford without topping the two hundred metre mark. But Galway is the most clearcut case. There's a great swathe of low lying country running right across Ireland from Dublin Bay to Galway Bay, and much of it spreads north and south in this midland region.

So with handsome mountains setting the scenic standards in Ireland, this part of the country doesn't rate high on the must-see rankings. Yet in the northern part of the midlands, through Westmeath, northeast Longford, Cavan and Mongahan, the rising ground provides lines of hills which undoubtedly rates as areas of beauty, particularly where they are augmented by attractive lakes. And there are many lakes, some quite large, others hidden among the rolling hills, and most of them well-known to anglers who have no wish to see their favourite fishing places becoming popular with non-piscatorial visitors.

In the south of the region, on the border between Laois and Offaly, is Slieve Bloom, the region's only designated "mountain". They certainly get their value from it. The highest peak, Arderin, is a modest 528 metres. But as there are two other peaks nearby of 517 and 511 metres, enthusiasts talk of the Slieve Bloom Mountains, and it's an area of such charm that both Offaly and Laois lay claim to exclusive ownership, while Tipperary close by to the southwest has been known to include Slieve Bloom among its attractions, which is pushing it a bit.

That there is such strong area pride indicates that the Midlands region deserves attention. There is of course some great farming country, and the rivalry of neighbourhood agricultural shows is matched only by the intensely competitive sporting spirit. But any regional pride is balanced by strong local civic loyalty. In theory, the three towns of the south midlands - Tullamore, Athlone and Mullingar - are inter-connected in various regional development projects. But it's an idea which, while it may have looked good on a planner's desk up above in Dublin,

simply doesn't make sense on the ground. Mullingar and Tullamore are busy places with their own clearly defined hinterlands, while Athlone is the largest town on the middle section of the Shannon, a river port which is also a road and rail junction. It's in a world complete unto itself with the river and adjacent Lough Ree - an inland sea - defining the individual nature of the place.

Away to the north, Cavan and Monaghan are seen as sister towns - they are, after all, the southern outposts of the ancient province of Ulster. But the third town in the north midlands - Longford - seems a place apart, out on its own over to the west. Its name suggests that it became a fort of the Vikings as they thrust their longships northward up the Shannon, and it has long been of significance as the convenient midpoint on the route from north Mayo and Sligo towards Dublin. Longford is a place betwixt and between - it's of the midlands, but hinting of the west, and the east coast seems further away than it really is.

Belturbert, Co Cavan

Along the west of the Midlands, everything relates to the Shannon. There are few spectacular views of the great river, for only in its head waters and as it cascades toward the sea above Limerick, does the Shannon have anything approaching a valley. Instead, it is a presence, always there yet sometimes a surprise when you come upon it.

In Athlone, the river has gone through several perceptions over the ages. It was both a highway and a barrier - the Shannon crossing at Athlone, the first one south of the inland sea of Lough Ree, was always of strategic importance, yet those who controlled the waterway and readily used the river as a line of communication held sway for many centuries. Then in the 19th Century the railways rapidly eclipsed Ireland's island-wide inland waterways system. But the railways in turn were pushed into the background by the growing viability of road transport.

Modern Athlone reflects all these realities. For a while, it was almost as though the town had forgotten the Shannon's existence. Certainly there were always significant numbers who used the river and its lakes for recreation, but recreation wasn't seen as big business, and their basic economic significance was long in decline. It is only relatively recently that Athlone has looked again towards the river in a positive way; the railway too, after decades of decline, has been revamped; and the main road from Dublin to Galway has been re-routed as a motorway north of the town such that it is less than a morning's drive from the east coast to the west. So now Athlone rediscovers itself as a river town in a very pleasant part of the country, a town which seeks to affirm its own character.

Along the river to the south, the land becomes ever flatter as the the Shannon winds through the callows, the water meadows whose occasional flooding, however inconvenient for those living locally, is supportive of the broader ecology. In such country, any higher land is of historic significance and at the gentle riverside slopes of Clonmacnoise the remains of a large monastic university are eloquent testimony of past greatness.

Southward still with Galway to the west and Offaly to the east, the evidence of the strategic importance of the river crossings at Shannonbridge and Banagher is obvious. South of Banagher, the Shannon slides into a watery land of huge skies and flat horizons, where the remote river crossing at Meelick was known only to fugitives and missionaries, an extraordinary place with a little chapel where time stands still and the great river moves silently on.

Lough Ree

Food of the Region

Silke Cropp, Corleggy Cheese, Co Cavan

The midlands of Ireland – sometimes referred to as the 'heartlands'– cover a large and diverse area, some of which is now part of the recently launched 'Lakelands & Inland Waterways' midland corridor, stretching from Limerick right up to Belleek in north Fermanagh. With its many lakes, rivers and canals, it is heaven on earth for fisherfolk and everyone who enjoys messing about in boats, and this very productive area has many interesting – and some unusual – foods to be enjoyed.

Midlands **BEEF** is legendary, notably in Westmeath, and, of the many excellent beef farmers in the area; a mention of just three examples gives an idea of the quality and scope to be found here: at Gigginstown House near Mullingar, for example, Ryanair chief executive Michael O'Leary's **Angus** herd has earned its place as a benchmark for the breed since it was established in 1997; **Herefords** are well-represented by members of Hereford Prime (www.irishhereford.com)

and you will find rare breeds too – such as the dual-purpose (dairy and beef) **Irish Moiled Cattle** at Lough Bishop House & Organic Farm (www.derrynagarra.com). Quality **LAMB** is widely produced, and some parts of the region – notably Cavan and Offaly – are renowned for their **PORK & BACON (**and related products, including **cured meats**), whilst Cavan and Monaghan are indisputably the national headquarters for **DUCK** and **MUSHROOMS.**

The north-midlands area, is also home to a particular Irish speciality made with potatoes, **BOXTY**; it is made in a number of variations including 'boxty on the pan' which can be a potato cake or thinner pancake (which may be used as a wrap), 'boxty in the oven' (like potato scones, or more like bread - baked in a casserole and then sliced) and 'boxty dumplings' (a boiled version). It appears on menus in the area (including breakfast menus) and may be seen on sale in traditional bakeries.

Large areas of the midlands are covered by bogland, where the acid soil conditions are ideal for growing **BLUEBERRIES** - and also **CRANBERRIES**, on Ireland's only cranberry farm. Many other more prolific **FRUITS** are widely grown, including soft fruits and rhubarb destined to become **JAMS and PRESERVES.** **ORGANIC PRODUCTION** is strongly supported in the region, often on mixed farms producing a variety of foods including **ORGANIC MILK** and **CHEESES** – as is the case throughout Ireland at the moment, the sheer diversity and quality of farmhouse cheeses produced in the midlands region is astonishing.

County Cavan

At **Belturbet**, on the southern bank of the River Erne which divides counties Cavan and Fermanagh, one of Ireland's longest-practising and highly-regarded cheesemakers, Silke Cropp, makes the renowned **CORLEGGY FARMHOUSE CHEESE** (www.corleggy.com; +353 (0)49 952 2930) which has earned many accolades, including an IFWG Award.

is the oldest traditional pig slaughtering and pig curing company in Ireland. The McCarren family has been involved in the bacon curing business since 1860 and they source all pigs locally to produce a wide range of Quality Assured fresh, cured, and cooked products; a factory outlet is planned.

RELISHES & CHUTNEYS are the natural accompaniment to the protein-rich foods of the area, so Jane and Dion Govender – who are South Africans of Indian descent – chose well when they decided to produce their highly regarded **Govender's** (www.govenders.com) at Virginia, Co Cavan; their success inspired a new range of savoury dishes including onion bhajis and vegetable samosas, and they also make fresh fruit jams. And, on that sweet note, Meath's loss has been Cavan's gain where top quality **CHOCOLATE** is concerned: Master Chocolatier Ann Rudden's **AINE HAND-MADE CHOCOLATES** (www.chocolates.ie) originally earned their reputation in Co Meath, but Ann now makes these at **Stradone**, Co Cavan.

county Laois

The **Abbeyleix** area is the source of a great many good things these days - beginning with **G's Gourmet Jams** (www.gsgourmetjams.ie); making a good old-fashioned product with natural flavour is the main selling point for Helen Gee's traditional handmade jams, chutneys and relishes, a business that started as an alternative farm enterprise in 1998. Local fruits are used, with no additives, and Helen's husband Cyril, a tillage farmer, now also grows rhubarb and raspberries; their family - Roy, Clive and Sandra - are all involved with the business – you'll meet them at Food Fairs, and they do hampers too.

Near Abbeyleix, at **Ballacolla**, Pat 'Paddy Jack' Hyland and his wife Joan have a mixed organic farm and their Abo Cheese Co Ltd (+353 (0)57 873 8599), at Cuffsborough, makes **Abbey Organic Cheese**. Best

Now operating out of a state-of-the-art facility in **Blacklion**, Kenneth Moffit's **THORNHILL FARM DUCKS** (+353 (0)71 98 53044; www.thornhillduck.com) have been 'rearing, nurturing and supplying duck and goose to the hospitality and retail sector all over Ireland' for two decades – celebrated chef, Neven Maguire, of MacNean House & Restaurant in Blacklion, is a great ambassador for the quality of Thornhill duck and you will always find it on his menus.

Cavan has been synonymous with **PORK** for many generations and, although most pork production is now intensive there are some honourable exceptions, notably **Alpha Organics** at Farren-Connell Estate, Mountnugent (+353 (0)87 912 0001; www.organic-trust.org) where Richard Moeran produces a range of highly regarded range of foods – including beef, lamb, cereals and, most recently, chicken - but he is best known for his rare breed pigs. His produce is mainly sold through Irish Organic Meats and, as an officially designated organic demonstration farm, he takes part in the Demonstration Farm Open Days – details of the year's events are on the Organic Trust website (+353 (0)1 853 0271 www.organic-trust.org).

On a much larger scale and at the other end of the production chain, **McCarren & Co. Ltd** (+353 (0)49 4331066; www.mccarrenmeats.com), of Cavan Town, known is Abbey Blue, a mild lightly-blued brie style cheese which is made with pasteurised cows milk and vegetarian rennet and gains flavour with age - plain Abbey Brie and a smoked version are available, and a feta-style cheese, St Canice. They also raise lambs, chickens, ducks and geese - and you'll meet Paddy Jack selling all this produce (and that of other producers, eg homemade jams from Malone's Fruit Farm) at markets, including Temple Bar.

Not far away, at **Cullahill**, near Portlaoise, Patrick O'Connell's toasted breakfast cereal "**Paddy's O'Granola**" (+353 (0)86 3976215; www.goodfoodireland.ie) has been a runaway success, as a cooking ingredient as well as a breakfast cereal; Patrick sources ingredients from health food suppliers in Kerry and Kilkenny, and honey from Helen Gee of G's Gourmet Jams. You'll find it on the best breakfast menus and in good shops, including The Kitchen & Food Hall in Portlaoise. And baking enthusiasts are certainly in the right place around here, as production of the well known **Sowan's Organic Bread Mix** (www.sowansorganic.ie) has moved from Cork to Stradbally; the range – which now offers pancakes and cakes as well as breads - has earned a following and includes spelt and gluten-free products (can also be dairy free, if soya milk is used). 'Simple, satisfying, nourishing' is the mantra and these quality mixes taste delicious and offer a quality-led convenience option for time-strapped bakers, especially those restricted by special diets – their very successful organic gluten-free brownie mix was a first in Ireland. Look out for them locally and in independent stores throughout Ireland, or request retail details through the website.

county Longford

Chocoholics should plan journeys in this area with care, as Co Longford excels in **quality chocolate production**: In Longford Town the delightful Torc Café & Foodhall specialises in handmade chocolate (now also in Athlone, Co Westmeath) and, at Aughnacliffe,

there is **ChocO'Neill** (www.choconeill.ie) where Jimmy and Beatrice O'Neill make **chocolate** for connoisseurs, focusing on single origin chocolate beans from particular places; visit by appointment only.

county Monaghan

MUSHROOMS are widely grown in marginal farming areas, as they are not weather or soil dependent; anyone travelling through Monaghan will notice a lot of mushroom farms and, with one of the world's most advanced and largest mushroom producing companies, **Monaghan Mushrooms** (+353 (0)47 38200; www.**monaghan-mushrooms**.com), based partly at **Tyholland**, this area is undoubtedly the mushroom capital of Ireland (at least). Established by local entrepreneur Ronnie Wilson in 1981, the company is now owned jointly by the Wilson family and Donegal Creameries plc, and it owns the largest mushroom farms in the UK and Canada as well as Ireland. A new facility recently opened in Co Monaghan, confirming the company's unique position in the market. Much in demand in Ireland and abroad, this 'superfood' boasts three times the anti oxidant power of tomatoes, low GI, high fibre, B6, low in calories, fat and sodium… and they like to grow in the dark!

Another food closely associated with Co Monaghan is **MEAT**, especially **PORK AND BACON** products – pig production has been a feature of the border counties for generations and there is a good sprinkling of interesting businesses here today, some of them making unique products. At Lough Egish, near Castleblayney, for example, **Malone's Speciality Meats** (+353 42 97 45102; www.malonefoods.ie) is a 5th generation family business (currently run by two brothers and two sisters); specialising in cured meats, using local rare breed middle white pigs and grass fed Irish beef according to product, their range includes Monaghan **dry-cured ham;** Irish whiskey salami (made with Cooley whiskey) and outstanding beef products – **pastrami**, which invariably attracts particular praise, and delicious **Irish stout-cured beef** (made with O'Hara's Celtic Stout; see www.carlowbrewing.com). They also make excellent traditional spiced products, such as **spiced beef** and **black and white puddings** and have earned many accolades, including Great Taste Awards - and some continental ones too. Retailed pre-sliced in handy packs, they are available in good stores.

And then there is **DUCK** – although a relatively recent arrival in the area, the Steele family's environmentally-friendly duck business, **Silver Hill Foods** (+353 (0)47 87124; www.silverhillfoods.com) is now synonymous with Emyvale, Co Monaghan and, as well as distributing both in Ireland and abroad, they have a Farm Shop, which sells not only food but also other quality products.

county offaly

Pretty much in the centre of Ireland, Offaly is a county of contrasts with a landscape ranging from the lovely, unspoilt Slieve Bloom Mountains in the south-east to the bogland, which is most typical of the area and has the Grand Canal running through it. A unique and interesting area for food production – perfect for **HONEY** as demonstrated by third generation apiarist Andrew McGuinness, at **Meadowsweet Apiaries** Ballinahown (+353 (0)86 884 4938). Now recognised nationally for the beautiful **honey and beeswax products** the McGuinnesses have been producing since 1956, their honeys are natural (no heat filtration) and regional, reflecting the varying flowers and herbs available to the bees in different areas within a 32km/20 mile radius of the farm as they change through the summer. It will be found at farmers' markets (Athlone, Ballinalsoe, Farmleigh) and speciality food shops.

Co Offaly is also home to some outstanding **DAIRY PRODUCERS** – one of the best known is the Cleary family's **Glenisk Organic Dairy** (www.glenisk.com; +353 (0)57 934 4000) at Killeigh. Totally committed to the organic philosophy ("we have a vision of an

Royal Canal, Ballymahon, Co Longford

Organic Ireland, where the future health and wellbeing of all our children is assured"), the Cleary products include cows' milk and yogurt, a children's range – yogurt and fromage frais – and goats' milk and yogurt. Glenisk works with about 50 organic farmers and uses 90% of all Irish organic milk production; sufficiently well known and on a scale to compete efficiently with mainstream products, they say: "Yesterday, we were seen as an alternative business, but today it seems that more and more people are choosing organic food…" And their delicious products, which are readily available from supermarkets and independent food stores, have attracted well-earned acclaim, including an IFWG Award.

West Cork tends to get the credit for reviving artisan **CHEESE MAKING** in Ireland (and with good reason, on the whole) but one of the longest-established farmhouse cheeses is **Mont Bellair**, made since 1983 by Pat Stones at Bellair Farm, Ballycumber (Ballyard Foods Ltd; +353 (0)506 36113). A semi-hard pasteurised cows' milk cheese made using vegetarian rennet, it is made in

Ralph Haslam, Mossfield Organic Farm

big 3kg waxed rounds and gains a mature flavour quite early; **Cais na Ri** is similar in style but has a milder flavour. They're not well known outside the area, so worth seeking out. By contrast, Ralph Haslam of **Mossfield Organic Farm** (+353 (0)57 9131002 / +353 (0)86 8928375; www.mossfield.ie) at Clareen, near Birr, has been farming at Mossfield since 1970, converting to organic in 1999. Although only producing their organic gouda style cheeses since 2005, they were soon winning many awards including both gold and silver at the World Cheese Awards, and also an IFWG Award. Like many of the best cheeses, the Mossfield range is made with milk produced on limestone soil, and organic production allows a wider range of grasses and herbs to flourish and add flavour; five gouda style cheeses are currently produced, the most admired being a deeply-flavoured mature plain cheese which is at least eight months old when released to their own shop in Birr town and good speciality stores.

It is always a treat to find a good sheeps' cheese as they are more unusual, and it is certainly a surprise to find hard cheeses made to a Swiss mountaineers' recipe in this flat bogland area – yet that's exactly what Beni and Elfie Gerber are doing with their **Mill House Sheep's Cheese** (+353 (0)57 934 4334; www.millhouseireland.com) at **Killeenmore**, near Tullamore. Made using only the raw milk of their flock of happy East Fresian sheep ("we treat them like babies"), the 2kg wheels are ripened for at least 3 months before release, and in the case of Hobelkäse (an extra hard cheese with even fuller flavour, used shaved or grated, like parmesan) for 12 months; they also make a soft seasonal cheese, Pastorello, which is available both plain and flavoured. They are available through Cheese Etc (www.cheesesofireland.com) but not widely known, so it will be rewarding to find these unusual cheeses when visiting the area.

The Birr area is known for **PORK & BACON**, notably products made by the Rudd family who have been involved with high quality foods here for over twenty years. Mother and son, Prue and Simon Rudd, currently run the speciality food company **Prue & Simon's** (+353 (0)505 45206; www.prueandsimons.com) at

Busherstown, Moneygall, near Birr; they produce traditional dry-cured bacon, sausages, and black and white puddings of exceptional quality, all made to their own original recipes, and also homemade preserves and handmade Christmas puddings. Their products, which have achieved recognition at the Great Taste Awards, feature on menus in the region and beyond. Available at selected independent retailers, mainly in the South-East/Dublin areas; also perhaps to order directly through the website. And nearby, in Birr town, the company formerly owned by the Rudd family, **Rudd's Fine Foods** (www.rudds.ie) is now in common ownership with Brady Family Ham (see Co Kildare) and continues to produce pork and bacon products; they use their own recipes and, although producing on a larger scale, have won both ACBI and Great Taste Awards since the change of ownership.

If you enjoy your five a day, this is a good place to be with oodles of well grown organic **FRUIT and VEGETABLES**. Near Tullamore, Tony Garahy of **Lough Boora Farm** (+353 (0)59 345005; www.organicguide.ie) grows over 40 varieties of vegetables organically, mainly for sale through a very successful box scheme; At **Coolnagrower Organic Produce Ltd** (+353 (0)57 912 1562; www.coolnagrower.ie / www.organic-trust.org), Fortal, near Birr, one of the country's biggest organic growers, Philip Dreaper, has been producing a range of vegetables since 1992 - renowned for his expertise, he grows mainly carrots, potatoes, swede, leeks, onions and beetroot, which he brings to the mainstream market by selling through supermarkets as well as organic stores and farmers' markets; he is also one of the organic farmers around the country selected to host open days (www.teagasc.ie), when anyone interested is welcome to visit.

Not far away, Orla and Sean Clancy farm on a smaller scale at Clanwood Farm (+353 (0)87 649 4477; www.clanwoodfarm.com), Cloghan, where they have their own organically reared beef, pork and eggs - and are known especially for the excellent **Clanwood Farm Organic Soups** that Orla has been making since 2007, earning her an Artisan Food Award in the County Enterprise Awards. And, for an accompaniment with real flavour and texture, you won't do better than some

of Layla O'Brien and Swiss baker Jonas Hein's crusty rustic **organic bread** from **Coolfin Gardens Bakery**, Coolfin House, Banagher (+353 (0)87 204 5593), which is distributed with the Lough Boora vegetable boxes (see above), and sold at markets by Layla – including the impressive new farmers' market at The Point in Dublin 1. On a larger scale, a business that merits mention is fifth generation **O'Donohue's Bakery** of Tullamore (Kilcruttin Centre, + 353 (0)57 932 1411), a craft baker currently run by Cathal O'Donohue and family, whose products have recently been winning gold at the Great Taste Awards on an annual basis; their success is down to a combination of traditional and innovative products – all of which have a genuine home-baked flavour. Buttermilk soda, batch bread, spelt & honey bread and low GI multiseed bread are among the most popular – and the more recently introduced wholewheat soda is going down a treat too.

Just as the limestone pastures produce outstanding milk and, ultimately, very special dairy products, the acid conditons of the boglands in this area make it possible to grow some crops that are not seen anywhere else in Ireland, notably **CRANBERRIES and BLUEBERRIES**. **Slievebloom Farmhouse Foods** (+353 (0)57 913 1372; www.slievebloomfarmhousefoods.com) has been run

by Ciara Morris in her home village of Clareen, near Birr, since 1997, making a range of preserves, chutneys and sauces, several of which – including a mulled wine & cranberry sauce – have achieved success at The Great Taste Awards. A committed supporter of organically grown Irish produce, she promotes the health benefits of using natural products - especially locally produced cranberries and blueberries. In 2006 she took this a stage further when she and her business partner, local farmer/fitter, Michael Camon acquired **Ireland's only cranberry farm**, which was first started by Bord Na Mona as a pilot project - and now successfully produces fresh fruit for supply to some of Ireland's top restaurants. They also have three traditional thatched cottages available for visitors, nearby in Belmont (www.osierbrookcottages.ie). Imported **blueberries** are available all year but fresh Irish blueberries are very much a seasonal fruit, produced near Portarlington at **Derryvilla Blueberry Farm** (+353 (0)57 864 2882 / (0)87 2466643; www.derryvillablueberries.com. Pick-Your-Own visitors are welcome during August and September, which makes a great family day out.

county Westmeath

The world's oldest licensed **WHISKEY** distillery is on the Brosna River, in the village of Kilbeggan - better known in recent years for its convivial horse racing events, as the distillery was closed for half a century. Until the completion of the Dublin-Galway motorway in 2009, Kilbeggan was mainly a through village where travellers might consider a journey break at the distillery restaurant The Pantry (+353 (0)57 9332795) and ponder on this sleeping giant's past and future - and the great thing is that there was a future, because it is now in the active ownership of Ireland's only independent whiskey distillery, Cooley Distillery, Co Louth, which is owned by John Teeling and his son Jack. Having first opened in 1757, **Old Kilbeggan Distillery** (www.kilbegganwhiskey.com) is credited with producing some of the world's finest whiskeys for two centuries, but closed in 1957. Just 50 years later, in 2007, the new owners began distilling once more in the oldest pot still in the world, with the first release (June 2010) of Kilbeggan Distillery Reserve Malt now available from the distillery and in shops. The distillery is open to the public once again, and the aim is "to bring the Old Kilbeggan Distillery and its brands back to their former glory", with a visitor centre, shops and restaurants all part of the plan.

ORGANIC PRODUCTION is well represented in Westmeath, with well known producers including Jens Krumpe at **Terryglass Organics** Ballykeeran, near Athlone (+353 (0)90 974 7341); specialising in Angus beef (hung, in the traditional way, on-the-bone for 21 days), he also produces pork, chicken and eggs for sale at farmers' markets (and can deliver countrywide). And, while Angus is the beef of choice for many consumers (partly, perhaps, because it is best known) it is always a joy to find farmers rearing rare breeds – as, for example, **Lough Bishop House** (www.derrynagarra.com), Collinstown, where Irish Moiled Cattle are bred on an organic farm; you will also find Irish draught horses here – and a comfortable bed for the night.

There is wonderful farming land in this region and particular pride in beef production – but the rivers, lakes and canals have an equally important role. Not

Moiled Cattle, Lough Bishop House, Co Westmeath

only do they shape the landscape and contribute movement and mystery, but they are also of great interest to visitors for relaxation and sport – and, of course, a source of food. So, although most of Ireland's fish smokers are near the coast and specialise in sea fish, especially salmon, it is appropriate that one of the country's best **TRADITIONAL SMOKERS**, John Rogan, is to be found here, in a beautiful spot on the banks of the River Inny. A dozen or so miles west of Mullingar, at **Rogan's Real Smoked Fish**, Corry Lane, Rathowen (+353 (0)43 762 64; www.rogansfish.com), he smokes a number of fish - organic salmon and sea trout from the west coast and mackerel from Donegal – but the reason for the location is that John Rogan specialised in wild Irish eel, caught in the river just behind his house. A total ban on eel fishing was recently introduced in the Republic of Ireland, for conservation purposes, so the smokery now concentrates on other products - and very successfully too, winning a Great Taste Awards gold star for their Beechwood Smoked Bacon.

Whatever their product, it is smoked over a hot beech wood fire, and no artificial colours, preservatives or flavourings are added: a totally natural product, flavoured only by woodsmoke. The Rogan's products are sold in Tesco stores nationwide, independent shops in the area, at farmers' markets and from the smokery.

By contrast in terms of style but sharing qualities with other artisan producers in the pride they take in their business, Liz Gilhooley and her husband Bob run the Westmeath speciality **BAKERY**, **Kitchen of Liz**, at Sli-an-Afrinn, Athlone (+353 (0)90 647 5463; www.kitchenofliz.ie). Liz, a winner of the 'Best Woman in Business' in the County Enterprise Board Awards, is committed to using only the best natural ingredients and traditional methods in her baking, and it shows in a thriving business that services a 95km/60-mile radius around Athlone, covering eight counties; although probably best known for special occasion cakes, they make excellent everyday foods too – including homemade preserves and breads as well as a range of cakes and pastries.

Four of the Best...

Corleggy Farmhouse Cheese

In rich pasture land beside the River Erne, Silke Cropp makes her wonderful range of goat, sheep and cows' milk cheeses. Silke is one of Ireland's longest-practising cheesemakers, and the original, Corleggy, is a natural rind hard goats' cheese with complex flavours. In addition, this dedicated artisan now makes Quivvy, a soft goats' cheese preserved in oil; Drumlin, a hard raw cows' milk cheese, named after the prettily undulating small hills that characterise the area and made in several flavours; and Creeny, a semi hard raw milk sheep's cheese. Handmade daily in small batches, the flavours vary according to season and maturity, but the quality is consistently superb and they're much sought after by leading restaurants. The hard cheeses, Corleggy and Drumlin, are delicious cooked as well as for the table and keep in rind for months, improving with age. There is always a ready market for the limited production available - through Trevor Irvine's speciality company Cheese Etc (www.cheesesofireland.com), from carefully selected retailers, online, and from the markets that Silke attends (where you will also find her daughter Tina and her partner Oisin Healy, of Crêpes in the City). And Silke sometimes offers cheesemaking lessons, so you could even learn how - with time and patience - to make something similar yourself.

Belturbet, Co Cavan
+353 (0)49 9522930 www.corleggy.com

Moon Shine Dairy Farm

The 'organic-plus' concept behind Mary and Gerry Kelly's unusual dairy farm near Mullingar is unfamiliar to many people, as it is farmed not only organically but biodynamically. To simplify the philosophy, they plan work on their organic farm according to the most favourable phases of the moon. Whether or not this is understood, the quality of the produce speaks a universal language - and, surprisingly perhaps, they can sell their foods at competitive prices. The farm was certified organic in 2002 and is all in grass, with natural herbage for their small hardy cows - a cross between the traditional but rare Irish moiled cattle and their mainly Ayrshire herd that, as Mary explains, "go easy on themselves, rarely get ill, and are ideally suited to organic farming". Having made soft cheese and yoghurt for the family, Mary developed herb flavoured soft cheeses, yoghurts and yoghurt drinks for sale at Mullingar Farmers' Market, and then - as a result of their passion for milk that is not de-natured and tastes real - they started producing their delicious, creamy non-homogenised Moonshine Organic Milk, which was an IFWG Award winner in 2010 and is something special to look out for in the area and from the farm.

Lough Ennell Ladestown Co Westmeath
+353 (0)44 934 4631 www.kellysorganic.com

Silver Hills Foods

Ronnie and Lyla Steele started Silver Hill Foods in 1973, originally intending to breed ducks and sell the day-old ducklings to Irish producers. Since then, they have indeed bred ducks - but for the table. And their good husbandry has produced a unique breed of Pekin duck, with more breast meat, less fat and, most importantly, great flavour - good enough, in fact, to attract special praise from super-chef Heston Blumenthal; other accolades include an inaugural IFWG award in 1993, and another in 2005 (for their environmental contribution), while some fans - including London's Chinatown - vote via their order books. The ducks are fed on a special all-natural formula with no GMO products, and the entire operation is owned and controlled by Silver Hill Foods, allowing complete traceability. Ronnie and Lyla's son, Stuart Steele, currently runs the business and has recently opened a farm shop, selling the full duck range and also the by-products for which this exceptionally green company is also known - luxurious feather and down products, for example, and manure pellets for gardeners - and other local artisan products. Very much part of the community, Silver Hill is also involved with an allotment scheme just across the road - well worth a look.

Emyvale, Co Monaghan
+353 (0)47 87124 www.silverhillfoods.com

Derryvilla Blueberries

The cutaway peat bogs on the Irish midlands may look barren to the untrained eye but the acidic growing conditions favour certain crops, such as blueberries - a relative of the smaller native Irish *fraughan* or bilberry. Widely recognised as a 'superfood', blueberries have more antioxidants than most other fruits and vegetables; these delicious and versatile fruits are very familiar to Irish consumers and (thanks to imports) seen as an all year product. So the high bush American blueberries produced on John Seager's Derryvilla Blueberry Farm near Portarlington are very much a seasonal treat, and all the more precious for that. No pesticides are used at Derryvilla and the farm, which is managed by Nuala O'Donoghue, is labour intensive: each year begins with hand pruning the bushes and cutting the grasses; they then flower in May and by mid-July, weather permitting, handpicking begins, with pick-your-own visitors joining regular pickers in July and August. Most of their delicious, naturally grown berries and the products made with them - a tangy blueberry tonic and preserves (both of which are out-sourced to other artisan food producers) - are supplied directly to fruit traders and selected retailers, or sold at Farmleigh Food Market and the farm shop.

Derryvilla Blueberry Farm Portarlington Co Offaly
+353 (0)57 8642882 www.derryvillablueberries.com

where to Buy

the Special Foods of the Midlands...

A guide to food shops, markets, farm shops, local stores and internet suppliers in counties Cavan, Laois, Longford, Monaghan Offaly, Westmeath

County Cavan

Corleggy Farmhouse Cheese Corleggy **BELTURBET** *(+353 (0)49 952 2930 www.corleggy.com)*. Silke Cropp's renowned cheeses can be ordered **online**, also through Cheese Etc (www.cheesesofireland.com), from carefully selected retailers, and markets.

PJ Crowe Connolly Street CAVAN. Award winning butchers, member of Associated Craft Butchers of Ireland (ACBI).

O'Leary's Bridge Street **COOTEHILL** *(+353 (0)49 555 2142)*. A gem worth seeking out in this charming little planned town – a small and friendly grocery-deli, jam-packed with good things including local foods (eg Govender's and Aines chocolates, Mossfield cheeses) and with a tiny café serving Illy coffee.

Irish Organic Meats Burren Doogarry near **NEWTOWNGORE** *(+353 (0)49 433 3915 Declan: +353(0)87 981 8420 Deirdre: +353 (0)86 126 0875 www.irishorganicmeats.com)*. Declan and Deirdre McCarthy's mobile butchery is a familiar sight at farmers' markets in Leitrim and Roscommon, but they also operate a delivery scheme for organic beef, pork, lamb and chicken, covering counties, Cavan, Leitrim and Longford – and deliver to Dublin once a month. You can order (including special needs, eg rusk-free sausages) through the website, or call to the house.

Aine Hand-Made Chocolates STRADONE VILLAGE *(+353 (0)49 432 3744 www.chocolates.ie)*. Master Chocolatier Ann Rudden's handmade Irish chocolate company was originally in Co Meath, and - to the great delight of the locals - these high quality (multi-award winning) chocolate products are now made at Stradone Village in Co Cavan. Based entirely on natural ingredients, the range is wide, covering sugar free chocolates and hot chocolate, bars and truffles, gift bags and hampers, wedding favours and special occasions. Widely distributed within Ireland and internationally. **Online shop**.

County Laois

The Gallic Kitchen ABBEYLEIX *(+353 (0)86 605 8208 www.gallickitchen.com)*. Sarah Webb started her acclaimed business The Gallic Kitchen in Dublin around twenty years ago, producing and selling superb handmade pies, tarts, quiches, relishes, chutneys, jams and marmalade among many other items. The Dublin business has now been taken over by the former manager, Kevin Doyle (and renamed Lovin Catering), while Sarah set up a commercial kitchen in Durrow, Co Laois, supplying the shop in Abbeyleix - which also offers other premium delicatessen foods. Also at farmers' markets (Temple Bar and Marley Park Courtyard, Dublin) and at festival events; catering offered for both large and small events.

The Kitchen and Foodhall Hynds Square **PORTLAOISE** *(+353 (0)57 866 2061 www.kitchenfoodhall.com)*. Jim Tynan's commitment to quality at this long-established informal restaurant and shop attracts loyal customers from all round Ireland, both for the wholesome, no-nonsense fare served in The Kitchen, and the carefully selected range of Irish and European products sold in the Foodhall. Hand baked cakes and desserts are a particular

Derryvilla Farm Blueberries PORTARLINGTON
(+353 (0)57 8642882 +353 (0)87 2466643
www.derryvillablueberries.com). Fresh blueberries and
products on sale at the farmshop, and Pick Your Own
in August and September.

Delicious Caffé Harbour Street **TULLAMORE** *(+353*
(0)57 932 5943 www.deliciouscaffe.ie). Anne Williams
(of the family who previously made Tullamore Dew)
has run this appealing smart casual café and deli near
the Grand Canal since 2006 and it's a popular place
for a stylish daytime bite, or to buy some nice bits
and pieces or a bottle of wine to take home.

Farm Factory Direct Kilcruttin Business Park
Spollenstown Road **TULLAMORE**
(+353 (0)57 934 3238 www.farmfactorydirect.ie).
Margaret and Ivor Deverell's business is a direct sales
outlet for top quality locally produced meat - grass-fed
Irish Hereford beef is supplied by Hereford Prime, a
breeders' group that promote the raising and
management of the breed, which is known for the well-
marbled meat that give it tenderness and flavour, and
also lamb from the Offaly Lamb Producers Group.

C.R. Tormeys Butchers Bridge Street **TULLAMORE**
(+353 (0)57 932 1426 www.crtormeys.ie). ACBI
(Associated Craft Butchers of Ireland) members, these
third generation farmers and family butchers are well
known in the west and midlands, with shops in
Mullingar, Tullamore and Galway. Recognised for
high standards, combining tradition with innovation,
they have achieved numerous awards for excellence –
notably for their beef.

County Westmeath

Torc Café & Food Hall Dublingate Street **ATHLONE**
(+353 (0)90 647 0529 www.torccafe.com). An outpost
of the Longford original, fans can expect great baking
– many of the cakes, slices, muffins and cookies are
chocolate-based, using Torc's own brand of quality
chocolate, but there's also a tempting array of savoury
foods and other gateaux including lemon drizzle,
Baileys coffee and carrot. Torc offers a take out service
and the shelves are stocked with homemade
condiments, unusual confectionary and gourmet
treats from Irish and overseas artisans. Hampers are
available to order too.

Old Kilbeggan Distillery KILBEGGAN
(+ 353 (0)1 833 2833 www.kilbegganwhiskey.com).
After a 50 year closure, whiskey production began here
once more in 2007, and the first release (June 2010) of
Kilbeggan Distillery Reserve Malt is now available from
the distillery.

Gallery 29 Oliver Plunkett Street **MULLINGAR**
(+353 (0)44 49449). Ann and Emily Gray's black-
painted traditional shopfront is smart and welcoming
and, although only open three days a week (Thu-Sat),
they're great bakers, and the buzz of an open kitchen
and freshly cooked food on display draws people in.
You'll find good soups, salads, savoury tart of the day,
and "tailor-made" sandwiches, and also hot main
courses on offer. Outside catering, picnics and freshly
made dishes for home freezing are also offered.

Moon Shine Dairy Farm Lough Ennell Ladestown
MULLINGAR *(+353 (0)44 934 4631 /*
+353 (0)87 993 4108/ +353 (0)87 417 8122
www.kellysorganic.com). Gerry and Mary Kelly's
biodynamically produced dairy products are sold at
the Dublin Co-op from several outets in Dublin and
from The Cheese Barn, on the farm (phone for times).

Ilia Gourmet Oliver Plunkett Street **MULLINGAR**
(+353 (0)44 471825 www.ilia.ie). Retail arm of
Mullingar's leading coffee shop, "Ilia - a coffee
experience", just cross the road. The shelves are
laden with carefully selected good things from
Ireland - including outstanding speciality Irish
products such as the Janet's Country Fayre range,
made nearby in Co Wicklow – and abroad. Also
excellent freshly prepared meals and salads,
sandwiches, snacks and drinks to take away, and
freshly baked breads and cakes.

CR Tormey & Sons Harbour Place **MULLINGAR**
(+353 (0)44 934 5433 www.crtormeys.ie). Highly
regarded butchers - see Athlone.

The Fish Market Castle Street **MULLINGAR**
(+353 (0)44 933 0610 www.seafoodcircle.ie). A former
chef, George Stevens decided to leave the catering
industry and go into the supply of quality food rather
than cooking it – now his fish shop attracts an
enthusiastic clientele, keen to enjoy the wide variety of
fresh fish and shellfish he stocks. Closed Sun & Mon.

Ireland Midlands: Food Markets

For further information on Farmers Markets throughout Ireland
www.bordbia.ie • www.irishfarmersmarkets.ie

CO CAVAN MARKETS

Belturbet Farmers Market McGowan's Garden (beside carpark) Belturbet. Fri 4-7 (May to Oct).

Cavan Farmers Market McCarren's Farnham Road Cavan. Sat 10-4.

CO LAOIS MARKETS

Portlaoise Market Market Square Portlaoise. Fri 10-3.

CO LONGFORD MARKETS

Longford Farmers' Market Market Square Longford. Fri 9.30-2.

CO MONAGHAN MARKETS

Ballybay Farmers' Market Ballybay Square & Riversdale carpark Ballybay. Fri 10-12.

Castleblayney Monaghan Farmers'/Country Market Castleblayney Livestock Salesyard. Last Sat 9-1.

Monaghan Farmers' Market In front of Monaghan Town Courthouse. Fri 10-2.

CO OFFALY MARKETS

The Full Moon Market The Chestnut Courtyard Birr. Every 3rd Sunday.

Tullamore Country Fair Millennium Square Tullamore. Sat 9- 4.

CO WESTMEATH MARKETS

Athlone Farmers Market Market Square. Sat 9-2.

Mullingar Farmers' Market Fairgreen. Sun 10.30-2.

The Olde Post Inn, Co Cavan

Eat & Stay

CO CAVAN

Blacklion

♣ MacNean House & Restaurant

Some of the best cooking in Ireland is to be found at Neven Maguire's family restaurant in this little border town, and the prospect of a meal here brings devotees from all over the country, and beyond. Despite his popularity as a TV chef, cookbook author and celebrity supporter of food events, Neven's commitment to the restaurant never waivers: his exact, perfectly judged food makes the most of meticulously sourced ingredients from the local and artisan producers he so strongly advocates, and is an experience to treasure. Lovely accommodation too, in thoughtfully furnished rooms.
Main Street, Blacklion, Co Cavan
+353 (0)71 985 3022 www.macneanrestaurant.com

Cloverhill

♣ The Olde Post Inn

Gearoid and Tara Lynch's charming restaurant was once a post office – now it makes a lovely setting for Gearoid's excellent classical cooking. A committed Euro-Toques chef, Gearoid sources ingredients with great care and shows due respect for regional and seasonal foods. His route to Cloverhill included time in some fine establishments – including a much-missed Dublin restaurant which lives on here, in a house speciality: 'Le Coq Hardi' chicken breast (stuffed with potato, apple, bacon & herbs, wrapped in bacon and served with an Irish whiskey sauce). Upstairs, seven comfortable bedrooms await.
Cloverhill, Co Cavan
+353 (0)47 55555 www.theoldepostinn.com

CO LAOIS

Abbeyleix

Café Odhran

Since completion of the M8 Dublin-Cork motorway, traffic is no longer forced through this pretty little town – but it's well worth a short detour. Just south of the entrance to the Sensory Gardens, Patricia Ward's café is a pleasant place to break a journey, with friendly and efficient service and lovely wholesome, locally sourced food. Expect a fresh and healthy breakfast, hand-cut doorstep sandwiches made to order, home-made soups, salads and quiches… Apple, rhubarb or blueberry tarts, scones and jams are delicious, and available to take away too.
Upper Main Street, Abbeyleix, Co Laois
+353 (0)57 875 7380

Durrow

♣ Castle Durrow

Peter and Shelley Stokes' impressive 18th century country house hotel is midway between Dublin and Cork; it offers comfort and relaxation with style – and good food, in both restaurant and bar. Head chef David Rouse's policy is for careful sourcing of all food, and the quality shows. Wild Irish venison is a speciality in season, fish cookery is always impressive, and a good cheese plate might include the delicious local Lavistown cheese - but best of all perhaps are the fresh vegetables, herbs and fruit from the beautiful walled gardens. A gorgeous place.
Durrow Co Laois
+353 (0)57 873 6555 www.castledurrow.com

Portlaoise

❧ Ivyleigh House

An exceptionally pleasing place to stay, and known especially for their delicious breakfasts, this lovely early Georgian house is a listed building and the present owners, Dinah and Jerry Campion, have restored it immaculately. Their commitment to using quality local produce is obvious from the extensive breakfast menu; speciality hot dishes include Cashel Blue cheesecakes - light and delicious, like fritters - served with mushrooms and tomatoes – all perfectly cooked and beautifully presented. No evening meals, but guests are directed to the best restaurants nearby.
Bank Place Church Street Portlaoise Co Laois
+353 (0)57 862 2081 www.ivyleigh.com

The Kitchen & Foodhall

Jim Tynan's informal restaurant, food shop and art gallery is definitely worth a little detour. Delicious home-made food, an open fire, relaxed atmosphere - a perfect place to break a journey, or for a special visit. The food hall stocks a wide range of Irish and imported speciality foods, also home-made terrines, ready meals, breads (including gluten-free breads), lovely home-bakes like Victoria sponges, crumbles and bread & butter pudding, and home-made chutneys and jams; Christmas baking and ingredients are an autumn speciality. Regular art exhibitions held; no corkage on wines bought in the shop.
Hynds Square Portlaoise Co Laois
+353 (0)57 866 2061

CO LONGFORD

Longford

Aubergine Gallery Café

Chef/proprietor Stephen Devlin and his sister Linda were the area's culinary pioneers by many a year yet their popular restaurant feels as fresh and committed as ever, and never fails to please. The style is lively and international but Stephen's delicious, fresh-flavoured dishes have their foundation in carefully sourced, mainly local, ingredients; a good steak is de rigeur in these parts, as well as delicious poultry, but seafood is well represented too – and there's an unusually strong emphasis on vegetarian dishes.
1st Floor, The White House, 17, Ballymahon Street, Longford, Co Longford +353 (0)43 334 8633

Torc Café & Foodhall

Chocoholics taking the N4 (Westport road) up to Mayo or Sligo will find not only healthy home-made food at Ruth McGarry-Quinn's relaxed modern café, but also the very good chocolate creations that are their speciality. Behind the smart white modern frontage, café and foodhall blend seamlessly into each other; appealing menus with strong emphasis on 'homemade' are offered throughout the day – alongside the servery, shelves laden with home-made and carefully sourced foods from Ireland and abroad beg to be browsed. An ideal place to find an unusual gift, including wines and hampers.
1 New Street Longford Co Longford
+353 (0)43 334 8277; www.torccafe.com
Also At: Dublingate Street Athlone Co Westmeath
+353 (0)90 647 0529

"VM" Restaurant at Viewmount House

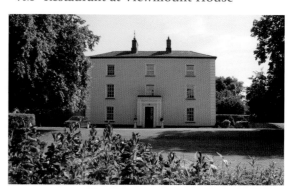

Set in beautiful gardens on the edge of town, James and Beryl Kearney run 'VM' Restaurant in the classic stone outbuildings of their lovely 1750s house. Overlooking a Japanese garden with water features, VM has transformed Longford into a dining destination; all the little niceties are observed and, although menus include the mandatory steak (28 day dry-aged from local butcher Donald Russell), the offering – which reads like a hymn to the best artisan suppliers - is both varied and sophisticated. Well worth a detour.
Dublin Road Longford Co Longford
+353 (0)43 334 1919 www.viewmounthouse.com

CO MONAGHAN

carrickmacross

♣ Nuremore Hotel & Country Club

Although golf may seem a more obvious attraction, what brings many people to this fine owner-managed country hotel is the cooking by head chef Raymond McArdle, who has been wowing guests since his arrival here in 2000 and has earned a national reputation for the hotel as a food destination. Raymond sources ingredients meticulously, using local produce as much as possible in top rank daily menus which read simply but are invariably impressive in the execution - and offer outstanding value for money.

Carrickmacross Co Monaghan
+353 (0)42 966 1438 www.nuremore.com

Clones

♣ Hilton Park

The Madden family's wonderful 18th century mansion is set amidst 200 acres of woodland and farmland, and staying here is a unique experience. Formal gardens have been restored and Lucy Madden, an enthusiastic organic gardener and excellent cook, supplies the kitchen with fresh produce from the walled gardens, while other ingredients are carefully sourced from trusted suppliers. Dinner for residents is served in a beautiful dining room overlooking the gardens and lake - and the next morning's memorable breakfasts are taken downstairs in the Green Room. Events hosted here include the annual Flat Lake Festival and Grow Your Own weekends

Clones, Co Monaghan
+353 (0)47 56007 www.hiltonpark.ie

Glaslough

♣ The Lodge at Castle Leslie

The Leslie family's fascinating history intrigues guests as much as anything they find here today. Guests now have the choice of staying in the Castle, or at the newer Lodge at Castle Leslie Estate (above), an attractive new hotel built around a stable courtyard - equestrian holidays are a speciality. Various food options are offered including bar meals, all good and with an emphasis on local artisan produce. In addition, Castle Leslie Cookery School, offers a choice of courses in the Castle's restored Victorian kitchens, and there's a range of Castle Leslie products on sale too.

Glaslough Co Monaghan
+353 (0)47 88100 www.castleleslie.com

CO OFFALY

Birr

Brambles Café & Deli

You won't find a better place in town to enjoy a really well made cup of coffee and some excellent home baked produce than Gillian Delahunt's inviting café in Birr. Gillian makes and sells her own soda bread, carrot cake, chocolate biscuit cake, scones and other sweet treats along with home made soup and deep filled pies which have regulars coming back for more every day. Seating in the café is cosy and comfortable, newspapers are available for customers and it is a very child friendly place too.

Mill Street Birr Co Offaly +353 (0)87 745 3359

Tullamore

♣ Annaharvey Farm

Although best known for equestrian holidays, good home cooking has always been at the heart of Henry and Lynda Deverell's farm. Rachael Deverell's "Annaharvey Farm Foods" www.annaharveyfarmfoods.ie) became so successful that it moved to production at Bunclody, Co Wexford and, here at the farm, Lynda now runs a cookery school, offering both day and residential courses, with the emphasis on 'showing people how to make good Irish food using seasonal fruit and vegetables, locally produced beef and lamb, organic cheeses, and amazing desserts.' Great fun!

Annaharvey Farm Tullamore Co Offaly
+353 (0)57 934 3544 www.annaharveyfarm.ie

CO WESTMEATH

Athlone

The Left Bank Bistro

Annie McNamara and Mary McCullagh's casually elegant contemporary restaurant near the Castle is first port of call for many when eating in Athlone. Short, keenly-priced menus – and blackboard specials - offer inviting dishes with a multi-cultural stamp which, together with carefully sourced ingredients and stylish cooking, make this a top choice for an informal meal. Fresh fish is a special strength (separate menu), also great salads and a farmhouse cheese plate. *Speciality products for sale too - salamis, pestos, house dressing, oils, olives, pastas, and coffee, for example - plus breads, dressings, chutneys and desserts from the restaurant.

Fry Place Athlone Co Westmeath
+353 (0)90 649 4446 www.leftbankbistro.com

Collinstown

♣ Lough Bishop House

In a beautifully scenic area awash with lakes, gentle hills and rich farmland, Helen and Christopher Kelly's organic farm comes complete with Irish Draught

horses, and offers a warm welcome in a genuine Irish family home - with excellent home-cooked food, showcasing the fine foods the area has to offer. Breakfast includes delicious home baked bread, fresh fruit and apple juice from the orchard and, if dining in, it's probably the only place in Ireland you'll get a chance to eat purebred traditional Irish Moiled beef as well as home produced lamb, free range eggs and fruit.

Derrynagarra Collinstown Co Westmeath
+353 (0)44 966 1313 www.loughbishophouse.com

Glasson

The Fatted Calf

This attractive village pub has parking, outdoor seating and space for children to run around – and good cooking by Euro-Toques chef Feargal O'Donnell. Well known for his commitment to seasonal and local foods, Feargal's enticing, frequently changed, menus promise innovative modern Irish food in both the bar and restaurant, with suppliers detailed on the menu. Cooking lives up to the promise, with tasty fare including simply delicious burgers enriched with bone marrow, and flavoursome mussels in a practical pot with a deep lid to invert for shell debris. Speciality cakes made to order.

Main Street Glasson Co Westmeath
+353 (0)90 648 5208

Glasson

♣ Wineport Lodge

Ray Byrne and Jane English's lovely lakeside lodge offers thirty luxurious rooms - all with private balconies overlooking the lake - a hot tub and treatment rooms. The overall effect is stunning, and it has earned its place as one of Ireland's more desirable destinations. But Wineport Lodge began life as a restaurant, and faithful fans continue to beat a path to the door at the slightest excuse, to be treated to Cathal Moran's fine cooking. Local ingredients including game in season, eels, home-grown herbs and wild mushrooms direct his strongly seasonal menus - a treat indeed.

Glasson Co Westmeath
+353 (0)90 643 9010 www.wineport.ie

Horseleap

♣ Temple Country Retreat & Spa

It may seem strange to dine in a spa, but you could travel a long way before finding anything to match the Garden Room Restaurant at Declan and Bernadette Fagan's wellbeing retreat in the unspoilt Westmeath countryside, which offers much more than healthy eating. Top quality ingredients - local and organic where possible, including lamb from their

own farm, garden vegetables, organic midland beef, cheese and yoghurts - are the sound foundation on which seriously tasty and beautifully presented meals are based. Special dining events are held, eg Traditional French Cuisine Menu, offered with or without accommodation. Organic wines.

Horseleap Moate Co Westmeath
+353 (0)57 933 5118 www.templespa.ie

Multyfarnham

Weirs Bar & Restaurant

In the gloriously unspoilt rolling countryside just north of Mullingar, and near Lough Derravaragh – where the mythical Children of Lir spent 300 years of their 900 year exile - this delightful village is well worth seeking out. Pat and Una Weir's handsome stone pub and restaurant is charming and friendly, with a well-earned a reputation for good home-cooked food, notably steaks (Angus sirloin, Hereford fillet); they take pride in using as much local and organic produce as possible, with daily specials focusing on seasonal availability - and everything is home made, including desserts. A lovely country pub.

Multyfarnham Mullingar Co Westmeath
+353(0)44 937 1111 www.weirsmultyfarnham.ie

WWW.IRELAND-GUIDE.COM FOR MORE OF THE BEST PLACES TO EAT, DRINK & STAY

Blueberry Crisp Rice Cobbler

For this appealing dessert the Sligo GP and seaweed expert, Prannie Rhatigan, and her family pick blueberries at Derryvilla Blueberry Farm, in Co Offaly. While you might not expect to find seaweed in a dessert, the secret ingredient here is ground nori (which is more familiar in sushi). Blueberries are best eaten uncooked, either fresh or in smoothies from frozen, but they're also delicious cooked. Prannie finds that this dish also works well using rice milk and spelt flour, and blackcurrants can replace the blueberries, too. Rice flakes are available from health stores and shops selling Asian foods, or you could use Irish oatflakes instead.

Serves 6

125g /4 ^{1}/$_2$oz rice flakes, or oat flakes

225ml/ 8fl oz rice milk, or milk

50g/2oz butter, softened

80g/3 ^{1}/$_2$ oz plain flour

50g/2oz walnuts, chopped roughly

40g /1 ^{1}/$_2$ oz ground almonds

25g /1oz flaked almonds

^{1}/$_2$ teaspoon arrowroot

75g/ 3oz brown sugar

2 teaspoons vanilla extract

^{1}/$_2$ teaspoon allspice

2 tablespoons nori, flaked or finely ground

1 tablespoon lemon juice

250g/9oz blueberries

Soak the rice flakes in a bowl in the milk or rice milk for about 30 minutes, until softened.

Meanwhile, preheat the oven to 190°C/375°F/Gas 5, and grease a 25-30cm (10"-12") flan dish.

Rub the butter into the flour until the mixture resembles coarse breadcrumbs. Stir in the walnuts, ground and flaked almonds, arrowroot and sugar; mix well. Stir in the soaked rice flakes, then add the vanilla extract, allspice, nori and lemon juice and mix gently together.

Spoon half of the mixture into the flan dish. Scatter the blueberries on top and spoon over the rest of the mixture, to keep the blueberries from drying out during baking.

Bake in the preheated oven for 20 minutes, or until golden.

Serve warm with natural yogurt, custard or cream, and some fresh blueberries.

Traditional Irish Breakfast & Potato Bread

Although no longer a daily meal, the traditional Irish breakfast is still a holiday treat, and is frequently just one choice offered to visitors from an elaborate menu, beginning with juices, fresh and poached fruits, yogurts and cereals or porridge. After that, alternatives to the fry may include scrambled eggs with smoked salmon, or cheese & bacon scramble; fresh or smoked fish dishes; vegetarian dishes; local farmhouse cheeses; traditional cured hams and other cured meats and salamis... Success with the "Full Irish" depends on using the best quality ingredients: crispy dry-cured bacon, black and white pudding, handmade sausages, tomatoes, flat mushrooms and fried eggs are the basics, plus optional extras like lambs' kidneys (baked or fried with knobs of butter and seasoned with mustard and black pepper), all accompanied by freshly baked soda bread and scones.

Potato bread or boxty are a popular part of the fry, especially in northern areas, and there are many versions of both. Potato bread (also called potato cakes) is best made with freshly cooked potatoes - some versions are baked in the oven rather like a scone, others are griddle-baked (in a pan) as below; also known as 'fadge' in Northern Ireland, it is an indispensable ingredient of the Ulster Fry. Commercial versions of potato bread are available throughout Ireland as thin, pre-cooked potato cakes, and can be frozen. Boxty is related to potato cakes but a fundamental difference is that raw potato is used. There are three basic groups: boxty bread or cakes ("boxty on the griddle"); boxty pancakes, ("boxty on the pan"); and boxty dumplings, which are less well known - it's said that "there are as many recipes for Boxty as there are parishes in Leitrim".

Serves 4

For the Potato Bread:

1 lb/450g freshly cooked potatoes in their jackets, preferably still warm

A good pinch of salt

1 oz/25g butter, melted

About 4 oz/100g flour

To make the Potato Bread: Peel the cooked potatoes and mash them until very smooth. Season with a sprinkling of salt and drizzle the melted butter over. Knead in as much flour as is needed to make a pliable dough - soapy potatoes will need more than naturally floury ones. The dough should be elastic enough to roll out, but avoid over-kneading as this toughens the dough.

Roll out to make a large fairly thin circle, cut into farls (quarters) and bake on a hot griddle or heavy frying pan, until brown on both sides. Any surplus potato bread can be kept in the fridge or frozen until required.

8 rashers best quality dry-cured Irish bacon, back or streaky

8 best quality breakfast sausages

8 slices each of black & white pudding (or 8 slices 'combination' pudding)

4 flat 'field' mushrooms, or 100g/4 oz button mushrooms

2-4 tomatoes, as required

4-8 free range eggs, as required

Potato bread or boxty, see below (optional)

Freshly ground black pepper to taste

Fresh parsley sprigs to garnish

To cook the fry: Grill the bacon, sausages and pudding slices, or cook them in a dry non-stick pan until crispy; to avoid crowding the pan, use a very large one or cook in batches and keep warm until everything is ready. Cook the mushrooms and tomatoes with a little butter, in a separate pan, or under the grill. When everything else is ready, take the pan that the bacon was cooked in (or drain off any remaining fat from the grill pan, for flavour) and, adding extra oil or butter if necessary, fry one or two eggs per person in it, also the potato bread, if required.

To serve: Arrange everything on heated plates, add a grinding of black pepper and a sprig of parsley and serve with freshly baked soda bread or toast and lashings of tea or coffee.

Abbey Feta Cheese Quiche with Tomato, Basil & Aubergine

This summery tart originated from Sarah Webb of the Gallic Kitchen, Abbeyleix, and it would make a nice lunch or supper dish. The feta cheese suggested is made by Paddy Jack Hyland, nearby at Ballacolla and, unusually for a quiche, it uses puff pastry so the dish is easy to make, and a lighter option than traditional shortcrust. Courgettes might be more easily available than aubergine, and would do equally well.

Serves 4

300g/11oz puff pastry

400g/14 oz beef tomatoes, sliced

15g/^{1}/$_2$ oz approx fresh basil

325g/12oz aubergine, sliced
& sprinkled with salt

125g/4^1/$_2$ oz Abbey St Canice feta cheese

250 ml/9fl oz cream

4 free range eggs

Pinch of salt and freshly ground
black pepper

Preheat the oven at 200°C/400°F/gas mark 6

Roll out the pastry and use to line a 23 cm/9 in. round quiche tin. Arrange a layer of sliced tomato in the base of the tin. Season the tomatoes and sprinkle with basil.

Rinse the salted aubergine slices, drain well and pat dry with kitchen paper.

Cover the tomatoes with a layer of aubergine slices. Arrange the remaining beef tomato and alternately with pieces of feta cheese in a circle around the edge of the tin. Place the remaining slices of aubergine in the centre, overlapping in a circle.

Whisk the cream and eggs together, season lightly and pour into the quiche tin. Place in the preheated oven and cook for 45 minutes. Serve warm or cold, with relish or chutney and a seasonal salad.

Braised Beef in Stout

There are many recipes for beef and stout, this one comes from a classical kitchen and is very special…
Braising is ideal for the tasty but tougher cuts of meat, as their connective tissue melts down and tenderises
to release flavour during the slow cooking. Home cooks might not wish to discard the 'pot vegetables' that
have been cooked with the meat for flavour - they are perfectly edible so you could skip that stage,
although the dish will be less refined.

Serves 4

*1 kg/2¹/₄lb stewing steak, trimmed and
cut fairly thinly into bite-sized pieces*

30ml/2 tbsp good quality oil

1 onion, chopped

2 leeks, washed, trimmed & chopped

2 carrots, peeled & chopped

2 celery sticks, trimmed & chopped

2 cloves garlic, finely chopped

250ml/9 fl oz well reduced beef bouillon

125ml/ 5 fl oz stout

Salt and freshly ground black pepper

50g/2oz butter

*75g/3oz streaky bacon, cut across the
grain into small slices*

100g/4 oz whole button mushrooms

50g/2 oz small pickling onions, peeled

25g/1 oz flour

Heat the oil in a large heavy-based pan, then add the meat in batches and brown it well; do not overcrowd. Transfer
the meat to a flameproof casserole as each batch is ready.

Next sauté the onion, leeks, carrots and celery in the same pan until softening slightly, adding more oil if necessary.
Add the vegetables to the meat, along with the garlic. Pour in the stock and stout, season and simmer gently over low
heat or in a cool oven, about 150°C/300°F/gas mark 2 for about 1¹/₂ hours, or until the meat is tender. Remove the
meat from the casserole and set aside. Strain the cooking liquid and discard the vegetables, then rinse the casserole
and replace the meat in it, with its liquid.

In a separate pan, melt some of the butter and sauté the bacon, mushrooms and small onions in it until just
tender. Add them to the casserole, stir to mix and reheat everything over moderate heat. To thicken the liquid,
blend the flour with the remaining butter and add it in pieces to the hot casserole, stirring well to make a rich
sauce. Taste for seasoning and serve in deep dishes, with buttery mash.

Ireland: West
Galway, Clare & Limerick

Farmland in The Burren, Co Clare

Ireland's rugged Atlantic seaboard is thought of as being the ultimate wilderness region of the country. And so it is in many ways, while also being an area of contrasts and contradictions. But despite the image of a sparsely populated storm-battered coastline on the outer edge of an island on the outer edge of Europe, the West region includes two lively yet very different cities - the vibrant culturally-inclined Galway, and the grittily energetic sports-mad manufacturing centre which is Limerick city.

These two cities in turn exemplify the west's contrasts. In historic Galway, they're into festivals. If they're not celebrating the theatre, then it's the cinema, or for a third week there's the arts.

Galway's Ancient Seaport at the Claddagh

About the Region

Maritime themed happenings abound around the harbour in the centre of town and, with a major racecourse nearby at Ballybrit, the Galway Races at the end of July provide a mind-bending national celebration of the horse. Then too, Galway Bay is famed for its oysters, so they've at least two festivals to celebrate the benevolent bivalve.

The location and layout of the city lends itself to the good life. The most maturely comfortable suburb is the long-established Taylor's Hill on the west side of town, a place where any affluent urban dweller would feel at home. Yet Taylor's Hill maintains its air of discreet and exclusive comfort only a short distance from the popular seaside holiday area of Salthill. And barely a dozen kilometres westward along the south-facing northern shore of Galway Bay, you are already getting into the Gaeltacht areas which soon become Connemara, the land of the sea, where the ocean winds its way among a myriad of rocky islands and peninsulas with the land rising slowly among fish-filled rivers and lakes until suddenly the terrain soars to become that most elegant mountain range, the Twelve Bens of Connemara.

In such highlands, the weather is often rapidly changeable and in the mountains they seldom suffer from drought. But in the lower coastal regions, and particularly in the offshore islands, it can frequently remain sunny all day while spectacular clouds of many hues build over the mountains where they eventually release their contents.

In addition to the inshore islands of south Connemara, Galway county has four offshore islands which are healthily populated - Inishbofin to the northwest of Clifden is a world unto itself, while the three Aran Islands - cast across the mouth of Galway Bay as an enormous breakwater against the Atlantic - have been celebrated in folklore and art for centuries.

Through Galway city, the salmon-rich Corrib river reaches the sea from the large expanse of Lough Corrib, an island-studded lake which its adherents simply know beyond all question to be the most

Adare, Co. Limerick

beautiful in Ireland. The Corrib waterway divides Galway county in two. The mountains and sea are to the west, while the east is flatter country, the farms marked by drystone walls. It's superb territory for hunting and home to the Galway Blazers, wild fox-hunting men and women who once held a joint hunt with the Ormonde in Offaly across the Shannon, and afterwards the party in Dooley's Hotel in Birr reached such a pitch that it seemed an excellent idea to torch the hotel to round out the evening, so they've been the Galway Blazers ever since.

South of Galway, County Clare is spectacularly varied coastlines and mysterious inland country. One of Ireland's top counties for Gaelic sport and traditional music, it has a much-indented northern coastline along Galway Bay, then the Atlantic seaboard soars to the Cliffs of Moher and oceanic waves which reach their peak in Aileens, the enormous breaker which is a magnet for surfers from all over the world. Where there's any beach at all, there are sand dunes in profusion, so the golf is mighty. The south coast is the northern shore of the Shannon Estuary, all 60km of a tidal waterway which becomes ever more rural as it nears Limerick city. Beyond the hydro-electric barrier just above Limerick at Ardnacrusha (built

1925-29, it is a World Engineering Heritage Site, still churning out clean electrical power) the Shannon is totally free of salt water as it comes down the pretty miles from the inland sea of Lough Derg, whose beautiful southern end provides Clare with an east coast in total contrast to its western Atlantic buttresses.

Clare's most renowned inland area is the Burren in the northern part of the county, a seemingly barren region of steep bare limestone hills which on close examination proves to be a natural wonderland, home to rare plant species and secret narrow valleys where it feels like a hundred miles from the nearest town. Yet a relatively short journey up narrow winding boreens soon returns you to the modern world of motorways and Shannon International Airport and the sharp-edged vitality of Limerick.

But for those journeying gently along the western seaboard and seeking to avoid urbanization, the

Ballynakill, North Connemara

opening in 2010 of the Shannon Tunnel under the estuary west of Limerick has transformed travel in the region. With it, you are immediately transposed from the Clare countryside into the rich farmlands of County Limerick, without the distraction of wall-to-wall Limerick city on the way. The estuary can also be crossed in urban-free style by using the car ferry near the estuary mouth from Killimer near Kilrush in Clare to Tarbert in Kerry, but the added option of the Shannon Tunnel means that combining Clare with County Limerick in the same region is now making much better sense.

Not that Limerick county, which extends from the Golden Vale shared with Tipperary in the east to the growing sense of the nearby Atlantic at Glin on the Shannon estuary to the west, feels it needs to share an area with anywhere, not even the city which shares its name, for all that Limerick city has unexpected gentler aspects such as some fine Georgian architecture and the impressive Hunt Museum.

But Limerick county - now here is somewhere else altogether. The pinnacle of the farming is its worship of the horse, both for racing and hunting. The essence of rural Limerick is the picture-postcard village of Adare, which avoids any of the pitfalls of being overly pretty by its location in the heart of working farmland. It has a manor house (now a hotel) in high Victorian architectural style at the centre of a leisure complex in which golf is prominent, while equestrian pursuits are always present.

Then too, Adare makes for the perfect stopover on the long journey from Dublin to Ireland's most westerly extremities in Kerry. You're by no means already in Kerry if you overnight in Adare, but next day's journey will be pleasantly manageable, and Adare in itself is an attractive venue. But it could be that you like the place and the people so much that you'll give in to temptation and cross under the Shannon by the tunnel and linger awhile in Clare and maybe even Galway before re-joining the road to the southwest via the Tarbert ferry.

Ireland: West
Food of the Region

Lough Corrib, Co Galway

Although, in many people's eyes, the rugged coastal landscape of the west *is* Ireland - captured in the haunting images of Connemara mountain and sky, and island life, by Paul Henry and his followers - the western counties are in fact very diverse, and include inland areas of lush farmland and productive rivers (notably the mighty Shannon and its hinterland) as well as the challenging beauty of the coastal areas.

The produce of this stunning land - and sea-scape is inevitably full of character, most obviously seen in the outstanding **FISH AND SEAFOOD** taken from the cold, clean Atlantic waters - and rightly given pride of place in the many excellent seafood restaurants along the long and fascinating coastline of Clare and Galway. A wide range of beautiful, fresh fish and seafood is always there be enjoyed, with seasonal variations, but a couple of specialities are reverentially respected: the best **smoked salmon** you'll eat anywhere is to be found in these parts - and, of

course, this is also the home of the wonderful native oyster *ostrea edulis*, also known as European flat oysters or, more usually, simply **Galway oysters.** This not-so-humble bi-valve mollusc is the inspiration for two major festivals each autumn, and in demand at top hotels and restaurants throughout Europe, but it's hard to beat the pleasure of eating them on their home patch, in a waterside pub like **Moran's Oyster Cottage** at Kilcolgan.

As for the king of fish, despite conservation restrictions on fishing wild salmon, the exposed west coast has come up trumps thanks to the exceptional fish produced by an offshore organic fishery off neighbouring Mayo (see North West Region). Although often enjoyed fresh – you will see it on many menus – this wonderful fish makes a superb **smoked salmon** of international standing and is the salmon of choice for many of Ireland's top smokers, including **The Burren Smokehouse**, **The Connemara Smokehouse** and **Kinvara Smoked Salmon**. At **Aran Gourmet Foods** (+353 (0)87 676 5335; Mill Lane, Galway), Michael Browne produces an unusual range of specialities, including peat-smoked organic salmon, gravadlax, smokes patés and terrines, which he sells at Galway and Farmleigh markets.

Off the coast of Galway and Clare, the **Aran Islands** not only top of the list of very special places that visitors most want to see for themselves when visiting Ireland, but they also make a particular contribution to the region's food culture. Fishing, in the familiar lightweight currachs, and foraging have been important all along the west coast for many generations and, although there have been changes – you don't see too many people foraging for sea birds' eggs on dangerous cliffs these days – foreshore foraging remains an everyday activity for many people, especially on the islands. Many varieties of seaweed grow abundantly all around the Irish coastline and have been important to traditional ways of life, for use on the land and also for culinary and medical use. Seaweed has long been essential as a soil conditioner and fertiliser, and foraged foods such as **EDIBLE SEAWEEDS** are especially relevant to the islands, where they are harvested commercially by Maírtín Concannon of the small company **Bláth na Mara** (+353 (0)99 61411), on Inis Mór; a variety of seaweeds - including dillisk (*Palmaria palmata*),

Seaweed School

kombu (*Laminaria digitata*) and carrageen (*Chondrus crispus*) - is harvested by hand and dried for use as sea vegetables. Prannie Rhatigan's inspiring book *Irish Seaweed Kitchen* lists suppliers of sustainable harvested seaweeds which, on Galway's mainland, includes Shane Forsythe's **Cleggan Seaweed Company** (www.clegganseaweed.com) producing a range of sea pickles as well smartly packaged dried seaweeds. Seaweeds are easily found in shops and **online**, and you will see them on menus in the region too – including restaurants on the islands, which also feature produce grown on small holdings and in gardens, wherever shelter can be found.

Away from the coast, the west of Ireland takes on a different character – the stone-walled landscape of East Galway is unique, for example, while County Limerick and parts of East Clare are much more pastoral and influenced by loughs and rivers, especially the Shannon and its vast estuary. And, important as fish and seafood is in the West of Ireland, it is not the only speciality food and the farmers of the region have

plenty of great produce to share as well. There is plentiful **lamb** throughout the region and, as elsewhere in Ireland, you will find excellent **beef and dairy products** – and also free-range **pork and poultry.** Names to keep an eye open for include Hegartys **Burren Free Range Pork**, which is raised happily at Kilfenora, Co Clare; traditional beef, saddleback pork and pasture-fed poultry from Ronan Byrne, aka **The Friendly Farmer,** (thefriendlyfarmer.blogspot.com) at Athenry, Co Galway; and, in Co Limerick, the rare breed pork from Rigney's Farm, which is sold under the acclaimed **Curraghchase** brand. And the jewel in the region's carnivorous crown is **Connemara Hill Lamb** (www.connemarahilllamb.ie), which has European Protected Geographical Indication (PGI) status.

Visitors with a particular interest in **biodiversity**, environmental matters and the nuts and bolts of organic farming will find plenty to please them in the West. An interesting initiative aimed an conserving the unique habitat of the Burren is the **Burren Farming for Conservation Programme** (www.burrenlife.com), which encourages farmers to practice sustainable agricultural methods and produce species-rich grassland. Places of environmental interest to investigate include the **Irish Seed Savers Association** (+353 (0)61 921866 wwwirishseedsavers.ie), which is

Dulse Seaweed

Inagh Goats

an organisation of international importance at Scarriff, Co Clare; **Beechlawn Organic Farm** (www.beechlawnfarm.org) at Ballinsaloe, which is one of the region's most notable organic growers and a Demonstration Farm that holds open days; and the **Drumcollogher Organic College & Garden** (www.organiccollege.com) which can be visited by appointment. On a smaller scale, **The Green Apron** (thegreenapron.ie) at Ballingarry, Co Limerick offers kitchen gardening courses in a beautiful location.

As elsewhere in this bountiful country, the West of Ireland has plenty of **ARTISAN CHEESES**, and these too tend to reflect the rugged nature of the landscape – many areas are ideal for goats, for example, resulting in an exceptional choice of goats' cheeses, especially in Co Clare where some of Ireland's best artisan producers make wonderful goats' cheeses - **Bluebell Falls Goat's Cheese** (www.bluebellfalls.ie) of Ballynacally, for example, and **Inagh Farmhouse Cheese** (www.st-tola.ie), producers of the organic St Tola range; in fact goats are so much a party of Co Clare life that there's a pub - **Cassidy's** (www.cassidyspub.com), at Carron, that makes a feature of goat (well, kid) and goat products when in season.

Some cheesemakers use the milk of both goats and cows; in east Galway, for example, Marion Roeleveld uses local cows' milk to make her gouda-style **Killeen**

Farmhouse Cheese (www.irishcheese.ie) which is available plain and flavoured, and also goats' milk from their own herd for a range of plain and flavoured goats' cheeses of varying stages of maturity; you'll see them at Sheridans and speciality shops in Galway and at On the Pig's Back in cork, also at farmers' markets. And at Glen O'Sheen near Kilmallock in Co Limerick, experienced cheesemakers Rose and Rochus van der Vaart use milk from their own goats and cows' milk from a neighbouring farm to produce their range of **Oisin Farmhouse Cheese** (+353 (0)63 91528; www.iofga.org), which includes an unusual blue goats' cheese.

Sheep are an integral part of the landscape here, of course (is there any part of Ireland where they are not a feature?), and a special cheese to seek out is **Cratloe Hills Sheep's Cheese** (www.cratloehillscheese.com) – a beautiful product that is full of character and has earned much praise. And, while **dairy** farming may be less prevalent than in some other parts of Ireland, it makes up in interest anything that may be lacking in scale – there is a special resonance to sharing quiet coastal areas with wading cattle while they enjoy the cooling waters, as they do near New Quay, in Co Clare, where the Fahy family make their beautiful **ICE CREAM Linnalla** (www.linnalla.com); it's well signed from the 'main' road, but don't give up as the road narrows; visitors are welcome and you can buy ice cream and maybe have a cup of tea at the little ice cream parlour/shop, where some of their remarkable range of seasonal flavours will be available. Cattle in the region tend to be less common, sturdy breeds, including shorthorns which are typical of The Burren; the excellent traditional cheddar style cheese, **Mount Callan** (www.irishcheese.ie), is made from the milk of unusual Montbéliarde cows, near Ennistymon in north Clare, and other cows' milk cheeses to look out for in the area include **Kilshanny** and, of course, **Burren Gold,** which is made by cheesemaker and apiarist, Ben Johnson at Aillwee Cave.

But, lest it seems that the west of Ireland is only for those with savoury tastes, you will find that there's plenty of indulgence to be had too: great **BAKERIES** such as **Griffin's, Goya's, Foods of Athenry**, and **Sweetie Pies** in Galway City, and **The Yew Tree** in Oughterard offer plenty of temptations, along with many others around the region, including a clutch of very good ones in West Clare. An interesting example is a small artisan food and catering company **Minihans** (www.minihans.com) in Kilrush, who specialise in making 'restaurant quality food, homemade'; they do dinner parties as well as events - and also fridge/freezer-filling, which could be useful for self-catering visitors. Some producers, such as **West Clare Artisan Bread** (www.westclareartisan.com) and **gingergirl**, in limerick, have partnered baking with the logical accompaniment – **PRESERVES** – others, such as the **Clare Jam Company** near Doolin, and **Nature's Bounty** of Kilcornan, Co Limerick simply concentrate on preserves; Nature's Bounty (+353 (0)61 393942; www.mychefathome.ie) is especially interesting as Colette O'Farrell is a forager and uses hedgerow fruits for her products. Other local names that might catch your eye include **The Green Apron** in Ballingarry (www.thegreenapron.ie), and **Wild Orchard** (www.wildorchard.ie), a small company producing fresh juices and smoothies at the village of Hospital in Co Limerick – not actually wild, but fresh, good and winning awards.

For serious indulgence you can't beat **CHOCOLATE** of course, and there's hardly a corner of Ireland these days without a really good artisan product – names to look for around here include the wickedly good **Wilde Irish Chocolates** (www.wildeirishchocolates.com) of Tuamgraney, Co Clare, a gorgeous range which includes Fairtrade bars; another chocolatier is quickly establishing a reputation nationwide is Nicole Dunphy of **Pandora Bell** (www.pandorabell.ie) in Co Limerick - yet the confectionery that has really caught the public imagination is not the chocolate (gorgeous as it is) but her big handmade lollipops, which are unique.

For a very different kind of indulgence, whiskey aficianados should plan a visit to Ballyvaughan to coincide with the mainly evening opening hours of the charming old world pub, O'Loclainn's **Irish Whiskey Bar,** (+353 (0)65 707 7006) where you will find an extraordinary range of 300+ whiskeys to taste. But not all indugences are either alcoholic or laden with calories - as a visit to the herb gardens at Sadie Chowan's beautiful, remote **Burren Perfumery & Tea Rooms** (www.burrenperfumery.com) will prove.

Burren Pefumery, Co Clare

Four of the Best...

McGeough's Connemara Fine Foods

Ever since Eamonn McGeough opened up shop here in 1971, McGeough's of Oughterard have been known as outstanding butchers - and, now under the management of Eamonn's son, James McGeough - a German-trained master butcher - this butchers shop and fine food retailers has achieved national renown. From September to December they sell the famed Connemara Hill Lamb, which is unique to the area - and something else that makes them very special indeed these days is what goes on the back of the shop. Here, in a purpose built production unit, James McGeough supervises the production of speciality meats that are unique to McGeough's: air-dried and smoked meats and salamis that take up to six months to cure, and are showcased at leading restaurants. Beginning always with top quality Irish meat - most famously Connemara lamb, but also beef, pork and bacon - the meat goes through a lengthy process of curing in a mix of local herbs and spices, hanging for many months in temperature controlled drying rooms and finally smoking for one day using beech chips, turf or oak for their distinctive flavours…Not surprisingly, these products are much sought after - they are simply superb.

Camp Street, Oughterard
+353 (0)91 552351 www.connemarafinefoods.ie

Connemara Hill Lamb

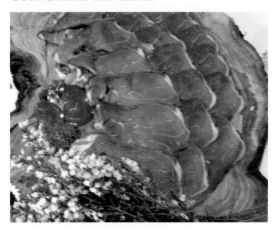

Born and bred on the beautiful hills of Connemara, Connemara Hill Lamb is a seasonal product. It has European Protected Geographical Indication (PGI) status and is one of only a handful of Irish products to have comparable recognition: the use of the name is reserved exclusively for hill lamb born and reared within the designated area by registered members of Connemara Hill Lamb Ltd., and is protected against imitation, exploitation or misuse. This seasonal product has a very special flavour, and is something to look out for especially if visiting the area in late summer and autumn. The seasonality of Connemara Hill Lamb is part of its charm but it can be extended, thanks to the skills of an exceptional local butcher, James McGeough, who has developed a wonderful range of smoked, air-dried and other speciality meats at his butchers shop in Oughterard, Connemara Fine Foods (see left); these products are now widely distributed and feature on top menus locally, including Ashford Castle. Hill lamb is also a speciality of other areas, including Donegal, the Comeragh Mountains in Co Waterford and the Ring of Kerry. In seaside locations, lightly-salted vegetation creates the special flavour of the delicacy *pré salé* lamb, which is in great demand on the continent.

www.connemarahilllamb.ie

Inagh Farmhouse Cheese

A familiar product on many of the country's best menus, and winners of more awards than most products ever enter - Great Taste Awards, British Cheese Awards, National Organics Awards, Irish Food Writers' Guild and many more - St Tola organic goat cheese has been made in the townland of Inagh, just south of the Burren, since the early 1980's - originally by Meg and Derrick Gordon then, since 1999, by their neighbour Siobhan Ni Ghairbhith. Organic since 2001, the 65 acre farm provides the herb-rich grass and hay which is the main diet for the 220 or so Saanen, Toggenburg and British Alpine goats in the St Tola herd, and gives the cheeses - soft, feta style and hard, plus a gorgeous new cream cheese aptly named Divine - their distinctive flavour. Available from speciality food shops and cheese counters - eg Sheridans, Burren Smokehouse, Superquinn - the cheeses can also be ordered for courier delivery from the farm (see website). Visitors, including school tours, are welcome to the farm by prior arrangement.

Inagh Co Clare
+353 (0)65 683 6633 www.st-tola.ie

Connemara Smokehouse

Founded in 1979 by John and Bridget Roberts, this famous and beautifully located smokehouse near Clifden is now run very successfully by their son Graham and his wife Saoirse. They offer an appealing range of products and have earned a reputation for excellence, as they explain it themselves, "by following a simple recipe: fresh fish, natural ingredients, and traditional smoking methods that have stood the test of time." Recognition has come from many quarters, including Rick Stein's Food Heroes and Good Food Ireland awards for specialities that include wild and organic salmon, line-caught Irish tuna, other traditional smoked fish such as kippers and mackerel, and also marinated fish products - including a gorgeous gravadlax. But one of the best things about the Connemara Smokehouse is the smokehouse tours which operate every Wednesday in season (at 3pm - booking advised), when the whole process is demonstrated and tastings are offered. There is a shop at the smokehouse and visitors are welcome on weekdays (except lunch hour, 1-2pm); group tours can be arranged at any time, all year.

Bunowen Pier, Ballyconneely
+353 (0)95 23739 www.smokehouse.ie

where to Buy

the Special Foods of the West...

A guide to food shops, markets, farm shops, local stores
and internet suppliers in counties Galway, Clare, Limerick

Galway City

The Fisherman Galway Shopping Centre Headford
Road **GALWAY** *(+353 (0)91 583827)*. Proprietor
Patrick O'Malley has been fishing since the age of 14
and now supplies much of the fish from his own
vessel to The Fisherman, which stocks a wide variety
of fresh fish and shellfish. Closed Sun.

Martin Divilly Westside Shopping Centre Seamus
Quirke Road **GALWAY** *(+353 (0)91 523947)*. Third
generation butcher Martin Divilly and his wife Audrey
offer an exceptionally wide range of ready-to-cook
dishes in their bright modern shop, as well as excellent
meats (including dry-aged beef) an organic range
(including Ballysax chicken) and less usual products
such as ox tongue and rabbit, also home cured bacon.

Duanes Fish Market Ballybane Industrial Estate
Ballybane **GALWAY**. The Duane family have been
involved in the seafood business in the Galway area
for many years; they wholesale to many West of
Ireland establishments and this recently relocated
shop stocks a wide variety of fresh fish and shellfish.
Closed Sun & Mon. Also at Henry Street, Galway
(+353 (0)91 586641).

Gourmet Tart Company 65 Henry Street **GALWAY**
(+353 (0)91 588384). French bakers work through
the night at Fintan and Michelle Hyland's bakery, to
provide fresh croissants when the shop opens at
7.30a.m. The Gourmet Tart Company has a
philosophy of celebrating good food at a fair price;
what started as a French-style bakery using artisan
techniques has become a foodie haven of bakery, deli,
and gourmet food shop. Expanded by popular
demand, the range offered now includes savoury
items (all available for take-away in biodegradable
boxes) and oustanding sandwiches. All products are
made from natural ingredients and are chemical-free.
Also at: 7 Abbeygate Street Lower, Galway; Upper
Salthill (opposite Seapoint); Galway Shopping Centre.
Times vary slightly. They attend Limerick Milk Market
(Sat), and there is now also a restaurant at Salthill.

Goyas Kirwans Lane **GALWAY** *(+353(0)91 567010
www.goyas.ie)*. Emer Murray's speciality bakery and
café is best known for its tempting range of pastries
and treats and now also has an equally appealing deli
and savoury takeaway. Specialities include wedding
cakes and Christmas baking.

Griffin's Bakery Shop Street **GALWAY**
(+353(0)91 563683 www.griffinsbakery.com). In
business since 1876, fourth generation baker Jimmy
Griffin is keeping up the family tradition in style and
has won many an accolade, notably for the Griffin's
Artisan range which includes allergy-specific, yeast-free
and a collection of 'Galway' breads (try the whiskey
brack!). Novelty cakes and all sorts of other good
things too; buy from the shop, order **online** – or
sample them in the charming traditional tea rooms.
Open 7 days (times vary).

Joyce's Supermarket Shangort Road, Knocknacarra,
Salthill area **GALWAY** *(+353 91 589300)*. One of a
small family-owned chain of supermarkets
committed to providing good service and locally
sourced food since 1951, Joyce's is now in a
partnership which has seen the opening of Horgan's
Delicatessen Suppliers' first Food Emporium, at the
Knocknacarra shop. Horgan's (www.horgans.com), of
Mitchelstown, Co Cork, is a long-established supplier
of speciality foods to retailers, with a range including
farmhouse and continental cheeses, speciality meats,
pâtés and salami.

Sean Loughnane (Loughnane's Food Hall) Foster Court **GALWAY** *(+353 (0)91 564437)*. A legend among butchers, Sean Loughnane established Galway's (and one of Ireland's) first 'super butchers' with a deli section; while based on tradition, with topnotch beef finished on the family farm and local specialities offered including old-fashioned cuts like salted beef brisket and the internationally acclaimed Connemara lamb, this forward-looking business also offers an outstanding range of prepared and freshly cooked foods – with quality and service unsurpassed.

Brendan Loughnane Unit 5 Ballinafoyle Headford Road **GALWAY** *(+353(0)91 380214)*. 'Master Butcher Est. 1984', Brendan Loughnane is a brother of Sean (above) and best known in Limerick; he has recently opened on the Headford Road in Galway, beside Tesco Express, and the same principles of quality and customer service apply. Closed Sun.

McCambridges of Galway Ltd. Shop Street **GALWAY** *(+353 (0)91 562259 www.mccambridges.com)*. The name is now synonymous with bread (their little loaves of pre-sliced brown soda bread are widely distributed), but there is much more than bread to this family owned deli and fine foods shop on Galway's main street. Established in 1925 and now run by siblings Eoin, Natalie and Norma, who take pride in continuing the family tradition, it's first port of call for many food lovers visiting Galway. You'll find an ever-changing range of carefully selected food and wines from Ireland and abroad, including artisan jams, preserves, chutneys, Irish cheeses, speciality meats, ice creams – and, especially, irresistible Irish and continental chocolates including the gorgeous Skelligs from the Ring of Kerry (see South-West Region). Customised gift hampers are a speciality; browse the website and call, or email (retail@mccambridges.com) to order.

Mortons of Galway Lower Salthill **GALWAY** *(+353 (0)91 522 237 www.mortonsofgalway.ie)*. A top-quality food store for the lucky people of Salthill. Eric Morton's long experience in premium retail shows in the selectivity of this fine shop: freshly baked breads, pies, crumbles and quiches; fresh salads, cooked meats and deli foods, all prepared from scratch; fresh fruit and vegetables; traditional in-house butchery; fresh fish and seafood ("if we can't get it fresh we won't stock it"). Definitely a one-stop shop.

The Seafood Centre New Docks **GALWAY** *(+353(0)91 563011 www.galwaybayseafoods.com)*. Shop attached to the fish processing plant of Galway Bay Seafoods, a family-owned business established in 1950 by John V. Holland and currently run by his two sons John Jnr and Noel. Recently completely revamped, the shop offers a wide range of whitefish and shellfish, with live lobster, crab and oysters available from a tank in-store; they also have their own salmon smokery, and a purpose-built fish and seafood cookery school above the shop. Closed Sun.

Sheridans Cheesemongers Churchyard Street **GALWAY** *(+353(0)91 564 829 / (0)91 564 832 www.sheridanscheesemongers.com)*. Synonymous with good cheese in Ireland, Sheridans' most famous shop is perhaps on South Anne Street in Dublin, but the business originated in Galway, where the current premises incorporate a wine bar as well as the shop selling their incomparable cheeses and other speciality foods. Also still selling from their original stall at the Saturday Galway Farmers' Market (held on the church square just outside the shop) and other markets in the Dublin area.

Solaris Botanicals Unit 3 Ballybane Enterprise Centre **GALWAY** *(+353(0)91 750020 / (0)91 442450 (SkypeIn) www.solarisbotanicals.com*. Medical herbalists Jorg Muller and Karin Wieland specialise in blending organic and herbal teas for discerning, health-conscious tea-lovers. Accolades include a Euro Toques award in 2009, for their organic whole leaf: "an innovative product, based on passion and expertise, with an environmental conscience and excellent business practices". Karin, daughter of Hans and Gaby Wieland who have been instrumental in the Organic movement in Ireland, grew up on an organic farm in

Sheridans Cheesemongers, Galway

rural Sligo, where growing herbs and using them on a daily basis was part of everyday living; Jörg started to blend herbal teas in the 1990s to supply a community of 90 people - both have a passion for growing and working with healing plants. Try the beautiful flowering teas, made in glass teapots. Available from specialist stores and **online**.

Sweetie Pies The Old Pro Cathedral Building Middle Street **GALWAY** *(+353 (0)87 256 6887 www.sweetiepiesofgalway.com)*. Sisters Maureen Foley and Jenny Griffin started their artisan bakery and tea shop in Athenry in 2005, specialising in high quality cakes – particularly cupcake wedding cakes – fruit pies, handmade mince pies at Christmas, and children's parties. They now have tea rooms and a shop in the atmospheric Pro Cathedral buildings in Galway city centre, where they offer the familiar cakes and home bakes, along with teas and coffees etc, and proper afternoon teas. Very family friendly, they "love to involve younger customers by giving them the choice to ice their own cupcake or gingerbread man when they visit for a treat." Sweetie Pies products are also stocked in good shops locally.

C R Tormey Unit 17 Galway Shopping Centre Headford Road **GALWAY** *+353(0)91 564067 www.crtormeys.ie)*. Third generation family butchers involved in farming and retailing for over 65 years, with shops in Mullingar, Tullamore and Galway. All offer a combination of high quality traditional butchery and innovative products, earning them many accolades through the years.

County Galway

The Foods of Athenry Oldcastle Kilconieron **ATHENRY** Co Galway *(+353 (0)91 848152; www.foodsofathenry.ie)*. Former dairy farmers Paul and Siobhan Lawless started their farmhouse bakery, "The Foods of Athenry", in a converted bicycle shed in 2000. When demand grew, the bakery moved into the old milking parlour, where they continued making the same healthily delicious home bakes with no additives (including salt and yeast). They have also planted native variety apple orchards, and these environmentally-aware Good Food Ireland members use innovative biodegradable packaging too. Widely available in the region, including McCambridges, Mortons and Joyce's of Knocknacarra, Galway.

The Friendly Farmer Knockbrack **ATHENRY** Co Galway *(+353 (0)87 6203765 www.thefriendlyfarmer.blogspot.com)*. Artisan farmer Ronan Byrne specialises in 'pasture rearing' of chickens, ducks, turkeys, geese, and saddleback pigs - with the aim, through sustainable farming, to produce good, wholesome food, sold locally under the *friendly farmer* brand. Not supplied to shops but you can buy directly (phone to arrange) or see him at Athenry Market on Fridays, Galway on Sat.

Beechlawn Organic Farm Beechlawn **BALLINASLOE** Co Galway. *(+353(0)90 9646713 www.beechlawnfarm.org)*. Husband-and-wife team Padraig Fahy and Úna Ní Bhroin run this National Organic Demonstration Farm in a very open, visitor –friendly way and hold courses and farm walks several times a year; although mainly geared towards other growers, group visits for about 25 people can be arranged at any time. They sell at markets (Loughrea Thu am, Moycullen Fri pm) and operate a box delivery scheme (home or business addresses); visitors welcome to buy vegetables at the farm on Tuesdays, while they pack the home delivery vegetable boxes.

Kylemore Acres Ltd. Kylemore Laurencetown **BALLINASLOE** Co. Galway *(+353 (0)90 968 5857 www.kylemoreacres.com)*. Richard and Diana Murray's unique taste-tested handmade food rubs and seasoning mixes are all-natural, based mainly on hand cut and naturally processed herbs; they include rubs for traditional joints like roast beef and chicken, seasoning mixes for stews and casseroles, spicy rubs and seasonings for fish; also mulling spices and – a recent addition – a herb and spice mixture for pork sausages (used in sausages at Tony Carroll's butchers, Ballinasloe). The carefully packed sachets are mainly available from selected butchers and seafood outlets; **online** shop.

Connemara Smokehouse Bunowen Pier **BALLYCONNEELY** Co Galway *(+353 (0)95 23739 www.smokehouse.ie)*. Specialises in wild and organic salmon, line-caught Irish tuna, other traditional smoked fish such as kippers and mackerel, and also marinated fish products. Open weekdays (except lunch hour, 1-2pm); smokehouse tours in season, Wednesday 3pm, booking advised); group tours all year by arrangement. Closed Sat & Sun. **Online shop**.

The Connemara Hamper Market Street **CLIFDEN** Co Galway *(+353 (0)95 21054 www.connemarahamper.com)*. Eileen and Leo Halliday's well-stocked little shop sells handmade Connemara baskets, and provides a showcase for many excellent artisan products, both local and from further afield, but mainly Irish: Connemara smoked salmon, Irish farmhouse cheeses, yummy cakes from Goyas of Galway, handmade local preserves and much more. Also local organic produce in season, a range of continental goodies including organic wines, and Illy coffee to go. Well worth a visit. Closed Sun. No **online sales**, but mail order service for delivery within Ireland/EU.

Kelly Galway Oysters Michael Kelly (Shellfish) Ltd. "Aisling" Tyrone **KILCOLGAN** *(+353 (0)91-796120 www.kellyoysters.com)*. Kilcolgan is synonymous with native oysters, the famed 'Galway Bay oysters'. Kellys are not only highly respected suppliers to hotels and restaurants in Ireland and abroad (including Rick Stein), but you can also buy them **online** (Oct-Apr) in smaller quantities – anything from 25 oysters, and very good value too.

Kinvara Smoked Salmon KINVARA Co. Galway *(+353 916 37489 www.kinvarasmokedsalmon.com)* Ireland can boast a good few high quality smoked salmon producers and here, on the south side of Galway Bay, Declan Droney's family business in the picturesque seaside village of Kinvara is among the most highly-praised. Personal endorsements abound and they have won many awards, including one from the Irish Food Writers' Guild. Using traditional smoking methods and the best organic Irish salmon (produced 6km off the coast of Co Mayo - see North-West Region, Clare Island Organic Salmon), the Kinvara products are known for their firm flesh and subtle smoking: delicious! Available in good stores, eg Superquinn, and from their **online** shop.

Kylemore Abbey LETTERFRACK Co Galway *(+353 95 41437 www.kylemoreabbey.com)*. Beautifully located Kylemore Abbey is a major tourist destination and, although you need to be able to tolerate crowds in high season, there is something for everyone. Restored Victorian walled gardens supply seasonal produce, including the ingredients for the many jams and preserves which are made by the Bendictine community and feature in their cafés, and also in the shop, alongside Irish crafts, clothing and giftware. An **online shop** offers a limited product range.

'Enjoy' at White Gables MOYCULLEN *(+353-(0)91 555 744 www.whitegables.com)*. Good Food Ireland members Kevin and Ann Dunne have been known for good traditional cooking at the charming White Gables restaurant for many years. They now have a lovely deli/bakery next door to the main restaurant, offering a welcome range of home-cooked foods, breads and cakes for sale – and, more recently, a café 'Enjoy More'.

McGeough's Butchers Camp Street **OUGHTERARD** Co Galway *(+353 (0)91 552351 www.connemarafinefoods.ie)*. Whether for a special joint of meat (local Connemara Hill Lamb, perhaps), or to top up with speciality foods, a visit to this wonderful shop is *de rigeur* for foodies when heading west from Galway.

McGeough's Butchers, Co Galway

The Yew Tree Bakery Main Street **OUGHTERARD**
Co Galway *(+353 (0)91 866986)*. It is well worth
factoring in a visit to this outstanding bakery when
travelling through Oughterard; known for their
breads – including 'the best brown soda ever' and a
lovely range of yeast breads, they also make
wonderful cakes which are highly professional yet
also 'real' looking... they also have an outlet at An
Fuaran In Moycullen and can be found at the
Moycullen Friday Market.

The Winehouse Bishop Street **TUAM** Co Galway
(+353 (0)93 42512). Although wine produced
elsewhere is not strictly within the remit of this book,
Cathal Reynolds' wine shop near the cathedral is a
worthy exception. Cathal, a Euro-Toques chef, was the
original owner of Cré na Cille restaurant (established
by him and his wife Sally in 1979), which earned
fame throughout Ireland for good cooking and an
outstanding and moderately priced wine cellar. Now
his focus is on wine, especially the wines of France; a
real wine enthusiast, he imports many wines directly -
and still offers good value too.

county clare

Bluebell Falls Goat Cheese BALLYNACALLY Ennis
Co Clare *(+353(0)86 813 4600 / (0)65 683 8024
www.bluebellfalls.ie)*. The Keane family's delicious
Bluebell Falls Goats Cheese is made daily, exclusively
from their own milk. As their goats' diet is mainly
grass, freshly cut for their delectation, the cheese takes
its flavour from their grassland in the hills
overlooking the Shannon Estuary. Their constantly
evolving range of beautiful cheeses includes plain and

flavoured soft cheeses, which all freeze well; two
white mould goats cheeses with stronger flavours; and
Orion, an interesting semi-hard cheese which is aged
for up to a year. Their excellent **online shop** "Cheese
to your Door" offers not only the Bluebell Falls
cheeses, but also a range of other outstanding artisan
products including other cheeses – Milleens,
Gubbeen, Crozier Blue, Knockanore, Bay Lough etc –
Gubbeen meats and oatcakes, Burren Smokehouse
fish, G's Gourmet Jams, Wilde's chocolates, and even
gift vouchers. Free delivery in Ireland on orders above
a set price.

Aillwee Cave BALLYVAUGHAN Co Clare
(+353 (0)65 707 7036 www.irishcheese.ie). A visit to
Ireland's premier showcave is a very worthwhile
experience when visiting the Burren, and full of
surprises - at the Farm Shop, for example, you can
watch the award winning Burren Gold Cheese being
made by cheesemaker and apiarist, Ben Johnson.
Made with milk from pedigree Friesian cows, this
unpasteurised Gouda style cheese takes its character
from the area's special herbs and grasses. available in
a range of flavours including smoked, you can taste
the cheeses in the shop, and also buy other speciality
foods including local jams, bread mixes (brown
bread; potato bread), speciality homemade fudge –
and, of course, honey. Cheesemaking courses are
occasionally offered.

An Fear Gorta Tea Rooms Pier Road
BALLYVAUGHAN Co Clare *(+353 (0)65 707 7157)*.
Dating back to 1790, when it was built as a residence
for 'coast security officers', Jane O'Donoghue's bakery
and tea room is full of character and makes the perfect
spot for a light meal, especially in fine weather when
the beautiful back garden or the conservatory can be
idyllic. A tempting display of home-baked fare is laid
out on an old cast-iron range to cheer and restore -
and there's home-made jam and marmalade on sale.

Burren Fine Wine & Food Corkscrew Hill Road
(N67) **BALLYVAUGHAN** Co Clare *(+353 (0)65 707
7046 www.burrenwine.ie)*. Although primarily a
charming spot for a daytime bite to eat (including
traditional Afternoon Tea), Cathleen Connole's
restaurant just off the Burren Waymarked Walk also
offers packed lunches for walkers and they sell
hampers, including artisan produce such as Burren
Smokehouse smoked salmon, Doolin Jams and
Burren Gold cheese - as well as wines, some with an

Irish connection; the house wine is the highly regarded additive-free Galway Bay Wine produced in the Languedoc area of France by Cathleen's brother, Noel O'Loughlen.

Burren Perfumery & Café CARRON Co Clare (*www.burrenperfumery.com*). Man of Aran, Ilaun, Frond, Fraoch and Burren Botanicals - the evocative names of fragrance ranges made and sold at Sadie Chowan's unique garden and perfumery. Visitors can see a free audio visual on the Burren, view the distillation and soap making areas, visit the herb garden and organic tea rooms and browse the shop, which offers a wide range of smartly presented natural products.

The Clare Jam Company Luogh North off Coast Road **DOOLIN** (*+353(0)65 707 4778*). In an idyllic location just a mile south of Doolin, you'll find David and Vera Muir's little cottage shop. Their small company packs quite a punch, with over two dozen homemade preserves on offer, and widely distributed in the west of Ireland; strawberry champagne jam and Connemara whiskey marmalade are keenly sought out, and you'll find delicious rendition of all the old favourites such as raspberry jam, orange marmalade and tomato chutney, too.

The Chocolate Shop Fisher Street **DOOLIN** (*www.wildeirishchocolates.com*). This seasonal outlet for Wilde's handmade chocolates is next door to Doolin's most famous pub, O'Connors.

Ennis Gourmet Store Barrack Street **ENNIS** (*+353(0)65 684 3314 www.ennisgourmet.com*). Founder Anne Leyden and wine expert David Lasbleye run this well known shop and café, which stocks a wide range of speciality foods from Ireland and the continent, with local artisan products taking pride of place. Hampers are a speciality and it's a good place to stock up for a picnic. Some products available **online**.

Chocolat Barrack Close **ENNIS** Co Clare (*+353 (0)65 686 8599*). Speciality chocolate shop focusing on the best of Irish and Belgian handmade chocolates.

Inagh Farmhouse Cheese INAGH Co Clare (*+353 (0)65 683 6633 www.st-tola.ie*). A familiar product on many of the country's best menus, and winners of more awards than most products ever enter, St Tola has been made in the townland of Inagh, just south of the Burren, since the early 1980's.

Available from speciality food shops and cheese counters - eg Sheridans, Burren Smokehouse, Superquinn - and can be ordered for courier delivery from the farm (see website). Visitors are welcome to the farm by prior arrangement.

The Pantry O'Curry Street **KILKEE** Co Clare (*+353(0)65 905 6576 www.thepantrykilkee.com*) This bustling bakery and restaurant is a first stop for many families coming to Kilkee for the holidays. Imelda Bourke and her husband, Pat, start baking at 5.30 each morning, and they produce an amazing selection of breads, cakes and desserts. They use butter in everything and only the best of ingredients, quoting Darina Allen saying that "if everyone on the street is making scones, you just make sure yours are the best"; that's what they have done for over 20 years, and every year it gets better.

Minihans KILRUSH Co Clare (*+353 (0)87 675 5574 www.minihans.com*). The familiar 'free from' phrase takes on a different meaning at Annette Minihan's West Clare artisan catering company, where it means no freezing and no long refrigeration as well as no colourings and no preservatives. Best local ingredients and traditional methods make for a home made taste – earning recognition from, for example, the Blas na hEireann (National Irish Food Awards). Freezer filling, party catering and cooking for special diets are all offered. Baking is a speciality and you'll find these goodies in independent stores and at Kilrush, Ennis and Limerick (Bedford Street) farmers' markets.

Burren Free Range Pork LAHINCH Co Clare (*+353 (0)86 881 597*). Whey from the Kilshanny cheese-making process nearby is one of the natural products used to feed the happy Burren pigs –

Saddlebacks and Saddleback/Tamworth cross - that Eva Harald and her husband Stephen Hegarty raise for the Burren Free Range Pork that she sells at local markets (Ennis, Ballyvaughan, Kilkee). You may also see her pork credited on menus, and it can be bought from the farm (by appointment).

Kilshanny Cheese Derry House Kilshanny **LAHINCH** Co Clare *(+353 (0)65 707 1228)*. Peter Nibbering's gouda style cheeses are made with the milk from neighbouring farms and quickly become familiar to visitors to Clare, as they feature on menus and in food shops in the area; Kilshanny is also listed by Trevor Irvine's company Cheese Etc (www.cheesesofireland.com) and sold at the Milk Market (Saturday) in Limerick - each of his six varieties has followers and all are offered every week. The Burren Smokehouse cheese is also made at Kilshanny.

Birgitta Curtin

The Burren Smokehouse LISDOONVARNA Co Clare *(+353 (0)65 707 4432 www.burrensmokehouse.ie)*. Established in 1989, Birgitta and Peter Curtin's Burren Smokehouse is most famous for their salmon; produced using the renowned Clare Island organic salmon, it is among Ireland's finest. You can taste it at their Burren Smokehouse Visitor Centre (going since 1995), where they have an excellent shop with some crafts as well as their own smoked fish range (trout, mackerel, possibly eel) and a selection of other speciality products such as the Clare Jam range, local cheeses (including their own smoked cheese made in Kilshanny, a lovely mild Gouda with a distinctive smoked flavour), Dittys oat biscuits, seaweed products, honeys and local fruit wine… They also have a good **online shop** – and, just up the road, the

Curtins run The Roadside Tavern, home to good food and music. Smokehouse Visitor Centre open all year, times vary.

Linnalla Ice Cream NEW QUAY The Burren Co Clare *(+353 (0)65 707 8167 / (0)87 785 7569; www.linnalla.com)*. Using the milk from their shorthorn cows, which are native to the Burren, Brid and Roger Fahy started making ice cream in 2006 - the name inspired by the farm's waterside location, Linn-éalla' meaning 'swan lake'. Made with fresh cream, and fruits and nuts sourced in the Burren, where possible, they also make ice cream cakes for special occasions - and even offer an unusual bespoke 'choose your own flavour combination' service! Distributed throughout the West of Ireland, and you'll see Linnalla on menus too, perhaps in signature flavours such as Moher Mist (with whiskey & schnapps), served at the Cliffs of Moher Visitor Centre. The farm is well signed from the coast road, although it may seem a long way; little shop/ice cream parlour.

Wilde Irish Chocolates TUAMGRANEY Co Clare *(+353 (0)61 922080 www.wildeirishchocolates.com)*. Inspired by Oscar Wilde's most famous quote 'I can resist anything but temptation', Patricia Farrell's business is well and truly artisan, as all the chocolates are made, decorated and packaged by hand on the shores of Lough Derg in East Clare. The range - which includes Fairtrade Organic Bars, artisan handmade and sugar free chocolate bars, chocolate spreads, fudge, gift boxes, and fun lollies - has attracted many accolades (try the Artisan Toasted Almond and Orange Dark Chocolate Bar …) Widely distributed and sold at markets; also available from the factory shop at Tuamgraney, and an excellent **online shop**.

Irish Seed Savers Association SCARRIFF Co Clare *(+353 (0)61 921866 www.irishseedsavers.ie)*. A registered charity, the Irish Seed Savers Association is a large environmental non-governmental organisation in Ireland. They research, locate, preserve and use traditional varieties, cultivars of fruit, vegetables, potatoes and grains. Visitors are welcome to this fascinating place (Mon-Sat 9.30-5, Sun 12.30-5; "wet weather gear and good walking shoes are advisable so that you can walk around the gardens and orchards in comfort") and guided tours are available for groups on request; workshops on various subjects around

Organic Gardening and Sustainable Living themes run throughout the year. Café and shop; also interesting **online** advice and sales - including starter packs for various situations (apartments, housing estates, polytunnels etc).

Limerick city

The Country Basket Thomas Street **LIMERICK** *(+353 61 319621)*. Louise and Simon Wilkinson's shop is a relatively recent arrival in Limerick city centre's fashionable Thomas Street and aims to provide 'Good Quality, Good Service and Great Great Food'. Quickly dubbed 'Limerick's Fallon & Byrne', their commitment to seasonality and local artisan foods has attracted a keen foodie following. Stocks include many Irish products featuring elsewhere in this book, eg Iseult Janssen's gorgeous patisserie from The Cake Stand (www.thecakestand.ie), Janet's Country Fayre (www.janetscountryfayre.com) chutneys, relishes and sauces, and the best local products such as Pónaire coffee. They hold frequent tastings.

René Cusack Fish St Alphonsus Street **LIMERICK** *(+353 (0)61 440054 www.renecusack.ie)*. This family business was founded by Rene Cusack and is now run by his son Paul. They offer a wide range of whitefish and shellfish with live lobster and oysters available from a tank in-store - the shop is supplied daily from the company's plant in Raheen Industrial Estate, Limerick. Also at: The Milk Market. Closed Sun & Mon.

Jim Flavin Butchers Dublin Road Castletroy **LIMERICK** *(+353 (0)61 331977)*. No stranger to awards, Associated Craft Butchers of Ireland (www.craftbutchers.ie) member and 'Limerick's sausage king' Jim Flavin raises his own animals and has earned a loyal following for his excellent meat and butcher products.

Gingergirl LIMERICK *(+353 (0)87 611 6360 www.gingergirl.ie)*. 'Local, seasonal, and simple' is the mantra for redhead Helen Keown's aptly named 'Gingergirl' products. Well known for the excellent handmade jams, chutneys and home baking she sells at markets and through carefully selected speciality food stores - such as Fallon & Byrne, Dublin; Kate's Kitchen Sligo; Castlemine Farm,

Roscommon; and Hennessey's Fine Food Store, Carlow Town - she also does tastings in speciality food stores (not exclusively in Limerick), and offers an **online** hamper service with delivery available within Ireland. More unusually, this former marketing executive offers marketing, branding and sales training programmes to a range of businesses within the retail, services and tourism sector.

Alchemist Earth Sarsfield Street **LIMERICK** *(+353 (0)61 404218)*. Dedicated to 'green glamour' and mainly known for its outstanding ranges of high-end organic skincare and haircare, this store also offers wholefoods (their motto is 'skin and within') and natural remedies; artisan food demonstrations and samplings are held, eg Gingergirl, Mossfield Organic Cheese.

Loaf Roches Street **LIMERICK** *(+353 (0)61 404460 www.loaf.ie)*. Recently opened artisan bakery, traditional foodstore and deli; also freshly prepared ready meals.

Limerick Milk Market Cornmarket Row **LIMERICK** *(www.milkmarketlimerick.ie)*. Following a major renovation, this famous old market re-opened as an all-weather, all-year covered market in summer 2010 and, in addition to the main Saturday food market, there is now all-week interest. Established in 1852, it is one of the oldest markets in Ireland but now has the most up to date facilities in the country – attracting new stallholders and some high profile speciality retailers, including **Country Choice** of Nenagh and the highly regarded artisan coffee roasters **Pónaire Coffee** (www.ponaire.ie) from Annacotty; Pónaire (Irish for bean) operate a Roastery and Coffee Bar (Fri-Sun), where they do small batch roasting and bag up their acclaimed custom-blended beans or freshly ground coffee while you wait. Other notable newcomers to the Milk Market inclcude Maria Mulcahy-Durrheim's **Knockara Patés** from Co Tipperary, **Quarrymount Free Range Meats** (www.freerangemeats.ie) and **Spanish Point Sea Vegetables** (www.spanishpointseaveg.ie), while longstanding traders **Sallymills Artisan Cakes & Desserts** (www.sallymillsbakery.com), now have a shop, open Wed-Sun; having built a reputation on using only the very best ingredients, it's well worth a visit.

The Hunt Museum, Limerick City

Loughnane's Butchers Upper William Street
LIMERICK *(+353 (0)61 414213).* A brother of Sean
Loughnane, of Forster Court in Galway City, master
butcher Brendan Loughnane has won many accolades
and has himself recently opened a shop in Galway
but is more closely associated with this busy butchers
in Limerick. They are known especially for Hereford
and Angus beef, which is finished on the family farm
near Loughrea, and minded carefully right up to the
point of sale.

Mortells Delicatessen & Seafood Restaurant
Roches Street **LIMERICK** *(+353 (0)61 415457).* On a
busy street just off O'Connell Street, Brian Mortell's
appealing deli and daytime restaurant/coffee shop is
well worth remembering. Open from an early hour,
they offer a full breakfast menu (unusually including
seafood, which also features at lunch time) and have a
tempting range of fresh-baked scones, pastries, cakes
and other light foods on display to go with their (very
good) coffees. Freshness, friendly service and an eagle-
eyed proprietor make this a place to return to – which
many of their customers clearly do. Closed Sun.

Micheal O'Loughlin Butchers Upper William Street
LIMERICK *(+353 (0)61 414 102).* A member of the
Associated Craft Butchers of Ireland and proudly
styled 'Old World Master Butchers', this is a reminder
of the way butchers used to be, with lots of character,
proper local supplies - lamb and beef from The
Burren, Co Clare, ham, organic chickens, free range
eggs, duck eggs, rabbit ...and an emphasis on service.

county Limerick

The Green Apron Derryclough **BALLINGARRY**
Co Limerick *(+353 (0)69 68524
www.thegreenapron.ie).* This small artisan preserves
company was started in the 1970s by Theresa Storey's
parents (who sold their products at the Limerick Milk
Market for many years) and is now run by Theresa
and her family. Many of the ingredients for her
preserves come from their own family garden, the
walled garden of her parents' 18th century castle
nearby, and also the hedgerows in the area - fruits like
wild crab apple, damsons, brambles, hawthorn,
elderberry and rosehip all make wonderful traditional
jellies. Made in small batches according to family
recipes, her extensive (seasonal) range of jams,
marmalades, chutneys, ketchups, sauces, herb mixes,
butters, mustards and pickles has earned a loyal
market following, of customers who appreciate the
variety and the authenticity of their natural goodness.
They also teach courses in kitchen gardening and
smallholding, and hold home preserving workshops.

Rigney's Farmhouse B&B **KILCORNAN** Co Limerick
(www.rigneysfarm.com). Good Food Ireland members
Caroline and Joe Rigney offer a traditional farm
experience for guests visiting their west Limerick farm,
and also have a Farm Shop, where their rare breeds
pork products, Curraghchase Meats, are the star of the
show. Made from the meat of free range rare breed
pigs such as Tamworth and Saddlebacks, their
products - notably dry cured bacon and ham, and
homemade sausages, puddings and burgers - have won
numerous awards, and you'll also find other artisan
products in the shop, too. Farm Shop: Sun, 10-6.

Pandora Bell **KILLONAN** Ballysimon Co Limerick
(+353 (0) 61 339300 www.pandorabell.ie). Nicole
Dunphy's artisan confectionery range is a relatively
recent addition to market for high quality treats in
Ireland, but the simple philosophy ('The secret to our
taste is using the best ingredients') and visual appeal
– of the big handmade lollipops in particular – made
a big impact. The beautifully presented range was an
immediate success, and is distributed to selected
outlets nationwide; also available on their pretty
website, to buy from the **online shop**.

For further information on Farmers Markets throughout Ireland
www.bordbia.ie • www.irishfarmersmarkets.ie

GALWAY CITY & COUNTY

Eyre Square Centre Market Level 1 Eyre Square Centre, GALWAY. Thu, Fri, Sat 9.30-6.30

Galway Saturday Farmers' Market St Nicholas's Church, GALWAY. Sat 8.30-4, Sun 2-6.

Gort Farmers' Market Fri 10-2

Athenry Farmers Market (100% Organic) Market Cross Friday. 9.30-4

Ballinasloe Farmers Market Croffy's Centre Main Street. Fri 9-2

Clanbridge Farmers Market Clanbridge Garden Centre. Last Sun 12-6.

Claregalway Market Cois Chlair Shopping Centre (between Arches and Spar). Sat 10-2

Headford Farmers Market Keady's Carpark The Square. 2nd and 4th Saturday.

Kinvara Farmers Market Johnstons Yard Kinvara. Fridays 10-2.

Loughrea Market Barrack Street. Thu 10-2

Mountbellew Local Food Market Mountbellew Ballinasloe. Wed 11-5.

Moycullen An Fuaran Moycullen. Fri 1-6.

Oranmore Market Behind Church. Thu 1-6.

Portumna Country Market Portumna Town Hall. Every Fri 8.30-12.30

Tuam Farmer's Market (100% Organic). Market Cross. Thu 9.30-4

COUNTY CLARE

Ballyvaughan Farmers Market Village Hall Car Park. Sat 10-2.

Ennis Farmers Market Upper Market Street. Fri 8-2.

Kilkee Farmers' Market O'Curry Street Kilkee. (May-Sept) Sun 10-2.

Killaloe Farmers Market Between the Waters. Sun 11-3

Kilrush Farmers Market The Square. Thu 9-2.

Miltown Malbay Market Community Hall. (May- Sept) Fri 4-6.30.

LIMERICK CITY & COUNTY

Crescent Farmers' Market The Crescent Shopping Centre, LIMERICK. Wed 9.30-2.30

Milk Market LIMERICK Sat 8-1.30

Riverside Market Bedford Row LIMERICK. (Apr-Dec) Sun 12-5

UL Farmers' Market Students Union Courtyard University of LIMERICK. Tue 12-5.30

Abbeyfeale Farmers Market Parish Hall. Fri 9-1.30

Kilmallock Farmers Market Kilmallock GAA Club. Fri 9-1.

Newcastlewest Farmers Market Market Yard. Thu & Sat 9-3

Of the twenty eight islands dotted around Ireland's coast, the ones with the strongest fascination for visitors are the three Aran Islands – Inis Mór, Inis Meáin and Inis Oirr –twelve miles off the Galway coast. There has always been good food to be found on all three islands but, of the many reasons for visiting the islands, food has not been a particular priority until recently. That all changed suddenly in 2007, with the opening of Ruairi and Marie-Thérèse de Blacam's stunning contemporary restaurant with rooms on Inis Meain, a destination that food lovers are happy to fly to for as little as a day just to see and sample it for themselves – and this new arrival also brought fresh appreciation of long-established businesses which had been offering more traditional hospitality over many years, as illustrated by the small but representative selection here.

♣ Inis Meáin Restaurant & Suites

Old traditions of farming, sport, and music are a large part of daily life on Inis Meáin. Ruairi de Blacam is a native of the island and a chef; he and his wife, Marie-Thérèse, who is from Cork and has a business and fashion background, decided to create a business on the island that would allow them live in this peaceful landscape of terraced limestone and traditional culture. Although very modern, their long, low cut-stone building blends into the surrounding limestone landscape and is true to the spirit of the island. Contemporary and spare, the dining space and kitchen are almost one, with an amazing panoramic view of the island, sea and sky. Ruairi's ingredients are mainly sourced on the island – it will be a simple meal but presented and cooked superbly. Lobster and crab are caught by fishermen who use the local currachs - and an increasing amount is produced by the couple themselves, who aim eventually to source everything on the island. Polytunnels enable them to grow a very wide range of crops, and they have their own pigs – also free-range chickens, as the island is a fox-free zone. There are plans to raise cattle on the island too, meanwhile other meats are sourced from the south Galway organic butcher, Justin Flannery,

The Aran Islands...

whose beef - hung for six weeks – is so tender that steak knives are not used in the restaurant. Guests love the simplicity of the accommodation, where fishing rods, bicycles and books of interest are provided instead of TV, to help guests discover the peace and quiet of the island In winter the couple turn to their other business, the de Blacam family's famous Inis Meáin Knitting Company.

Inis Meáin, Aran Islands, Co Galway
+353 (0)86 826 6026 www.inismeain.com

Potatoes, vegetables, fruit and herbs are home-grown on the restaurant site – an amazing range including spinach, broad beans, peas, scallions and onions, carrots, parsnips and radishes, fennel bulbs, rocket, lollo rosso, masses of herbs, rhubarb, pears and soft fruits like raspberries, strawberries gooseberries and blackberries – and even the elderflower cordial is handmade in Cork by Marie-Thérèse's mother, Breda Leahy.

♣ Man Of Aran Cottages

Despite its fame - this is where the film Man of Aran was made - Joe and Maura Wolfe make visiting their home on the largest of the islands a genuine and personal experience. A 6.5km/4 mile mini bus or cycle ride from Kilronan, the cottage is right beside the sea and Kilmurvey beach, surrounded by wild flowers. Joe has managed to make a productive garden in this exposed location, so their meals - for residents only - usually include his organically grown vegetables (even artichokes and asparagus), salads, nasturtium flowers and young nettle leaves as well as Maura's home-made soups, stews and freshly-baked bread and cakes. Dinner is served in the little dining room but there are benches in the garden, with stunning views across the sea towards the mountains, where you can enjoy an aperitif, or even eat outside on fine summer evenings. The three little bedrooms are basic but full of quaint, cottagey charm and they're very comfortable, although only one is en-suite.

Kilmurvey Inis Mor +353 (0)99 61301;
www.manofarancottage.com

♣ South Aran House & Fishermans Cottage Restaurant

Inis Oirr, the smallest and most easterly of the Aran Islands is a tranquil place, perfect for quiet contemplation, relaxed walks and swimming in crystal clear waters. At the south end of the island and a 5 minute walk along the sea from the pier, you arrive at Maria and Enda Conneely's Fisherman's Cottage, a lovely white and blue cottage with half door, set among interesting herb and flower gardens, and a conservatory with lovely views of the bay. As Slow Food members, Enda and Maria try to use organically produced foods as well as locally caught wild fish and other produce from the Island - the aim is to do what they can to provide tasty local food that is unique to the island. Enda, a native of South Aran, has studied widely, including medicinal cooking in Switzerland, and cooking at the Cordon Vert Vegetarian School in Manchester, and Maria has studied Shiatsu and Macrobiotics, so the food reflects their love for a natural healthy lifestyle. Nearby, the recently built cottage-style South Aran Centre offers accommodation for adult guests - and yoga, cookery and Irish/English language classes are sometimes held here.

Inishere Aran Islands
+353 (0)99 75073 www.southaran.com

Tig Congaile

Arriving on Inis Meain by boat, you will see Tig Congaile on the hill above the little port, just a 3-minute walk from the pier or beach. Vilma Conneely worked in banking in California, met and married Padraic, came back home with him and opened Tig Congaile in 1993. Freshly brewed Guatemalan coffee is served in a large dining room, which has a wonderful view and is hung with the work of local artists, displayed for sale. An all day/evening menu on the wall is ideal for the non-stop visitors coming on to the island on the various ferries. Vilma specialises in organic and sea vegetables, and uses as much seafood as she can get locally and from Galway - she is lauded quietly by many of the marine biologists in UCG for her interest in this, and her wonderful Sea Vegetable Soup is a speciality known well beyond the islands.

Moore Village Inis Mean +353 (0)99 73085

Foyles Hotel
Co Galway

Eat & Stay

CO GALWAY

Galway City

Ard Bia

Proprietor Aoibheann MacNamara is well known in Galway for her enthusiasm, energy and commitment to quality and this is a favourite destination for both Galwegian food lovers and visitors to the city - who happen on it very easily in this central spot. Everyone loves its character and atmosphere, the interest of both the food and exhibited artwork, and the long opening hours offered between the three operations: the daytime **Ard Bia; Café Nimmo's**, a lively evening restaurant on the ground floor; and **Ard Bia Restaurant**, offering a more sophisticated experience (priced accordingly), and very seasonal, broadly Mediterranean/Irish menu.

Spanish Arch Galway City
+353 (0)91 539897 www.ardbia.com

Goyas

Emer Murray is well known for her terrific baking and, if only for a cup of cappuccino or hot chocolate and a slice of quiche or lemon meringue pie, a restorative visit to her delightful contemporary bakery and café is a must when visiting Galway. There's something very promising about the cardboard cake boxes stacked up in preparation near the door, the staff are super, there's a great buzz and the food is gorgeous. If you're wondering where to start, why not give in gracefully and try a wedge of their speciality 3-layer chocolate gateau cake…

Kirwans Lane, Galway City
+353 (0)91 567010 www.goyas.ie

♣ The Heron's Rest B&B

Sorcha Molloy's delightful B&B enjoys the best location in Galway city – very close to Spanish Arch, yet quietly situated with views across the river and out to sea. And the name of this charming house is far from fanciful – you may well see Arthur the visiting heron sitting on a car roof at the door…Nothing is too much trouble for Sorcha when considering the comfort of her guests and helping them to get every ounce of enjoyment from their visit. Breakfast brings an extensive choice of delicious things, and both afternoon tea and gourmet picnic baskets are available on request.

Longwalk, Spanish Arch, Galway City
+353 (0)91 539574 www.theheronsrest.com

McDonaghs Seafood House

McDonaghs was serving fish and chips long before this part of town became a magnet for tourists in search of food and drink. Nationally renowned as one of the best of its kind, it is today a thriving multi-faceted business: takeaway fish bar, indoor restaurant and boulevard seafood café in summer. Their extensive listing of fish species in over a dozen different languages is confident confirmation of a cosmopolitan clientèle: everybody knows McDonaghs! The fare itself is predictable enough - what you get here is a definite local flavour of a bustling chipper, offering a pleasant experience at fairly reasonable prices.

Quay Street Galway City
+353 (0)91 565001 www.mcdonaghs.net

Oscars

For a truly one-off experience when in Galway, head for Oscars. You can't miss the cheerful frontage and, once inside, you'll find a darkly atmospheric interior – it's reminiscent of a theatre, with the ceiling draped like an Arabian tent and gentle background jazz creating a relaxed atmosphere. And it's home to Galway's most exciting, creative and technically skilled chef, Michael O'Meara, known for his passionate support of the best and freshest local produce – used to create a wide range of dishes that delight and amaze in equal measure.

Dominick Street Galway City

+353 (0)91 582180 oscarsbistrogalway.blogspot.com

Barna

O'Grady's on the Pier

In a stunning position, with views over the harbour and beach to distant mountains, Michael O'Grady's charming seafood restaurant is deservedly popular among Galway diners, who love its informality and nautical character - and share Michael's enthusiasm for seafood "simply prepared and very fresh as my father did it years ago". And, while the daily blackboard specials give a nod to world cuisine, the best dishes are indeed the simplest: a dozen Clarenbridge oysters; Galway Bay lobster served with lemon & salad; grilled whole black sole on the bone with lemon & parsley butter. Simply delicious.

Sea Point Barna Co Galway

+353 (0)91 592 223 www.ogradysonthepier.com

♣ The Twelve Hotel

Fergus O'Halloran's unique hotel is handy to both Connemara and Galway City and, since opening in 2006, has achieved national recognition for its fresh style, hands-on management and focused food and wine offering. Their motto "True to The Region, True to The Season" sums up a philosophy which can be seen at work in every aspect of the hotel. Good all day food in The Pins Bar includes excellent pizzas and breads, baked in their own bakery, while the wine-centred fine dining restaurant, West, showcases outstanding producers: try their 'Signature Braised Beef' - James McGeough beef, cooked for 12 hours.

Barna Village Co Galway

Tel:+353 (0)91 597 000

Clifden

♣ The Quay House

Long-time hoteliers Paddy and Julia Foyle offer wittily decorated and sumptuously furnished rooms at this 1820's former harbourmaster's house and the adjacent building, where newer studio rooms have small fitted kitchens and balconies overlooking the harbour. It's a fine house, with spacious rooms - including a stylishly homely drawing room with an open fire – and a charming conservatory, where breakfast is served. Good food is at the heart of everything this hospitable couple do, and breakfast is outstanding: treats include a tempting buffet, individual jugs of freshly squeezed orange juice and perfectly cooked hot dishes. Nearby, the traditional **Foyles Hotel** www.foyleshotel.com) is run by Paddy's twin brother, Eddie Foyle.

Beach Road Clifden Co Galway

+353 (0)95 21369 www.thequayhouse.com

Kilcolgan

Moran's Oyster Cottage

This is just the kind of Irish pub that people everywhere dream about - as pretty as a picture, with a neat thatched roof and a lovely waterside location. People from throughout the country beat a path here at every available opportunity for their wonderful local seafood, and especially for the native oysters (from their own oyster beds) which are in season from September to April (farmed Gigas oysters are on the menu all year). Then there's chowder and smoked salmon and seafood cocktail and the mussels, delicious crab salads - and lobster, with boiled potatoes & garlic butter…

The Weir, Kilcolgan Co Galway
+353 (0)91 796 113 www.moransoystercottage.com

Renvyle

♣ Renvyle House Hotel

Remote and romantic, the Lutyens-esque house at the heart of this hotel has a fascinating history. Snuggling down for shelter amidst the magnificently rugged scenery, it feels cosy with its dark beams and rug strewn floors – and a snug conservatory where guests can contemplate healthy outdoor activities while enjoying the scent of a turf fire and a comfortable armchair. All this, plus head chef Tim O'Sullivan's excellent food, can be magic. Menus (in both bar and restaurant) feature Connemara produce, including Renvyle rack of lamb, local lobster and vegetables in season.... And it's all in Tim's cookery book, too.

Renvyle Co Galway +353 (0)95 43511 www.renvyle.com

COUNTY CLARE

Ballyvaughan

♣ Gregans Castle Hotel

Surrounded by trees and gardens, Simon and Freddie Haden's uniquely serene late 18th century house is an oasis of warmth, comfort and hospitality, contrasting with the surrounding landscape of the Burren. Anyone is welcome to drop in for lunch or afternoon tea in the Corkscrew Bar, or book a table to savour gifted head chef, Mickael Viljanen's evening menus - a 9-course Tasting Menu offers outstanding value. This very environmentally responsible hotel is a member of the Burren Beef and Lamb Producers Group and has always been committed to using the best local and organic produce - a philosophy relished by Mickael, who sources his ingredients with meticulous care, many from small Burren producers.

Ballyvaughan The Burren Co Clare
+353 (0)65 707 7005 www.gregans.ie

Carron

Burren Perfumery Tea Rooms

When touring Clare you will be pleased to find this charming spot - the perfumery is beautifully laid out, with a herb garden (where many native plants are grown - and later used in the organic herbal teas), pleasing old buildings and lovely biodynamic scents. Although small and simple, the tea rooms are pretty, with floral waxed tablecloths, fresh flowers and cups and saucers all creating a happy mismatch of pastels - and what they do is made freshly on the premises, and uses local and organic produce. A summer minestrone & herbs soup with freshly baked brown bread, perhaps.

Carron Co Clare
+353 (0)65 708 9102 www.burrenperfumery.com

Lahinch

Barrtra Seafood Restaurant

Views of Liscannor Bay take centre stage from Paul and Theresa O'Brien's traditional, whitewashed cottage just outside Lahinch - but seafood is the real star. They are

known for quality and value and Theresa's excellent, unfussy cooking makes the most of a wide range of local seafood, all offered at customer-kindly prices; the richly flavoured Barrtra fisherman's broth is a signature dish, and lobster - when available - attracts only a moderate supplement on the dinner menu. Exact timing, perfectly judged seasoning and excellent saucing are the hallmarks, and fish is always allowed it to be "itself". Interesting and keenly priced drinks list too.
Lahinch, Co Clare
+353 (0)65 708 1280 www.barrtra.com

Liscannor

Vaughan's Anchor Inn

The Vaughan family's traditional bar has great character, with open fires and lots of memorabilia - and seriously good seafood at fair prices, in the bar and a newer restaurant area at the back. Although famed locally for their seafood platters (which are delicious - and great value), there's much more to the menu than that. Denis Vaughan is a creative chef who cooks everything to order. Patience may be needed, as it gets very busy and everything really is fresh: they offer about twenty varieties of fish - and the menu changes if there's something new coming up off the boats.
Main Street Liscannor Co Clare
+353 (0)65 708 1548 www.vaughans.ie

Lisdoonvarna

❧ Sheedys Country House Hotel & Restaurant
John and Martina Sheedy's much-loved small hotel offers some of the most luxurious accommodation and

the best food in the west of Ireland, yet it still has the warm ambience and friendly hands-on management which make a hotel special. John Sheedy's cooking offers pleasing combinations of classic and modern Irish styles, and menus reflect pride in carefully sourced local foods (including some extremely local, from the potager in front of the hotel). Fresh seafood features of course, also tender and uniquely flavoured lamb and beef, and local farmhouse cheeses from the Burren. And equal care is taken with breakfast.
Lisdoonvarna Co Clare
+353 (0)65 707 4026 www.sheedys.com

❧ Wild Honey Inn
Aidan McGrath and Kate Sweeney re-opened the former Kincora House Hotel in 2009 and, together with established forces in the town like the Sheedys and the Curtins of Burren Smokehouse, they're showing Lisdoonvarna in a new light - as a destination for food lovers. A respected chef, Aidan cooks with style and his menus demonstrate a commitment to locally sourced and organic ingredients, with valued suppliers acknowledged. There's a leaning towards seafood but everything is delicious – perfectly cooked and attractive, but not too fancy; details are good (lovely breads and coffees) and prices are reasonable. A great destination.
Doolin Road Lisdoonvarna Co Clare
+353 (0)65 707 4300 www.wildhoneyinn.com

Newmarket-on-Fergus

❧ Dromoland Castle

The ancestral home of the O'Briens, this is an enchanting place, where wide corridors lined with oak panelling are hung with ancient portraits and scented with wood smoke, and it has all the crystal chandeliers and massive antiques to be expected in a real Irish castle. Dining here is always a treat. Executive Head Chef David McCann's offering is predictably glamorous, with both wine list and service a match for the food. Although the style is basically classic French, the sourcing of ingredients is immaculate and some dishes highlight local ingredients and are more Irish in tone. The Fig Tree Restaurant at Dromoland Golf & Country Club is also excellent.

Newmarket-on-Fergus Co Clare
+353 (0)61 368 144 www.dromoland.ie

CO LIMERICK

Limerick City

* No. 1 Pery Square Hotel & Spa

The first choice for discerning visitors to Limerick, restoration of this fine property overlooking the city's most gracious Georgian square was a labour of love for proprietor Patricia Roberts. In public areas and rooms all is comfort and elegance, but food and wine are of equal importance too. Local suppliers are proudly listed on Scottish head chef Alan Burns' menus, which offer a combination of classic and rustic dishes in Brasserie One - at the fine dining end of the spectrum, yet not over-formal; similar pride is seen in informal meals like Afternoon Tea - and a very good breakfast.

Pery Square Limerick Co Limerick
+353 (0)61 402 402 www.oneperysquare.com

Ballingarry

* The Mustard Seed at Echo Lodge

Dan Mullane's famous restaurant The Mustard Seed started life in Adare in 1985, then moved just ten minutes drive away to Echo Lodge, a spacious Victorian residence set in lovely gardens, with mature trees, shrubberies, kitchen garden and orchard – and luxurious accommodation. The wonderful organic gardens supply the kitchen with much of the seasonal produce for the restaurant - do allow time to see them before dinner and, perhaps, hazard a guess as to what will be on the menu - while other ingredients are carefully sourced from organic farms and artisan food producers nearby. A treat by any standards.

Ballingarry Co Limerick
+353 (0)69 68508 www.mustardseed.ie

Kilmallock

* Flemingstown House

Imelda Sheedy King's welcoming farmhouse is on the family's dairy farm just near the medieval village of Kilmallock; it sits well back from the road up a long drive flanked by fields of grazing cattle. Aside from the many things to do and see nearby, Flemingstown House is well placed to break a journey to or from the south-west, and it is a lovely place to stay - the standards of housekeeping, service and breakfast are remarkable, and it is representative of the very best rural Irish welcome. Dinner by arrangement (BYO).
Kilmallock, Co Limerick
+353 (0)63 98093 www.flemingstown.com

Recipes

Roast Leg of Lamb

The west of Ireland is famous for its sheep, and the best cooking method - and number of servings - will depend on its age and where it comes from. Nimble animals from mountainous areas, including the acclaimed Connemara Hill Lamb (PGI), tend to be small and lean - and best suited to very simple cooking, eg roasting without extra flavourings, to allow full appreciation of the unique flavour. Early season spring lamb is small and delicate, but you can be more creative with older animals - hogget, perhaps, which is one year old - and those raised on lush lowland pastures, like parts of Co Limerick, which are naturally larger. This recipe makes a lovely Sunday roast and is easy to prepare.

Serves 6-8

1 leg of Irish lamb, about 2.7kg/ 6lb, trimmed

3 cloves garlic, slivered

Few sprigs of rosemary

2 onions, roughly chopped

1 head of garlic

2 cloves garlic, crushed to a paste with some salt

Grated rind of 1 orange

30ml/2 tbsp runny Irish honey

30ml/2 tbsp olive oil

Glass of dry white wine or natural cider

Port & Mint Dressing:

60ml/4 tbsp redcurrant jelly

Juice of 1 orange

Dash of port (or red wine)

Few sprigs of mint, chopped

To cook, set the oven 200°C (400°F) Gas Mark 6.

Make about 10 incisions in the lamb with a sharp knife. Push a sliver of garlic and a sprig of rosemary into each hole. Place the lamb in a roasting tin, with some chopped onions and a head of garlic cut in half horizontally.

Mix together the crushed garlic, orange rind, honey and olive oil. Spread the mixture over the lamb.

Place in the oven and roast for 30 minutes. Then add the glass of wine and a glass of water, this will prevent the honey from burning.

Reduce the oven temperature to 180°C (350°F) Gas Mark 4 and continue the cooking for another hour for pink lamb. Allow 15 minutes for the joint to rest before serving.

When the lamb is cooked, remove from the roasting tin, cover loosely with foil to keep it warm and set aside to rest. Keep the garlic to serve with the lamb. Strain the pan juices, if necessary, and return to the rinsed roasting tin; add another dash of wine and a tablespoon of redcurrant jelly, then boil it up to make a jus. Finish with a knob of butter and taste for seasoning.

To make the dressing: Gently heat the redcurrant jelly, orange juice, port and mint. Add a little lemon juice if you think it is too sweet. Serve warm with the sliced lamb and seasonal vegetables.

Boulangère Potatoes are very good with roast lamb and can be cooked in the oven at the same time. Simply layer some thinly sliced potatoes in a baking dish with thinly sliced onions which have first been sautéed in a knob of butter. Add seasoning and a few more knobs of butter as you do the layers. Finish off with some chicken stock and a sprinkling of grated hard cheese. Bake for 40-50 minutes until the potatoes are tender and the topping is golden and crispy.

Gerry Galvin's seafood coddle

Gerry Galvin, the acclaimed chef-patron of The Vintage in 1970's Kinsale and later of Drimcong House Restaurant at Moycullen, Co Galway, is now a food writer and Euro-Toques consultant chef. He edited The Galway Ingredient recipe booklet (limited availability from local tourist offices) and gave several of his own famously straightforward recipes, along with a selection from other chefs in the area including Michael O'Meara of Oscars (www.oscarsbistro.ie) in Galway, who also contributed some wonderful photography. "This dish is simplicity itself," Gerry says, "I have always liked broth/stock based, light fish soups and this one started in Drimcong many moons ago. I call it Coddle because of its comforting quality and it qualifies for the Coddle title because of its closeness to the traditional Dublin Coddle, albeit with fish/seafood rather than sausage and bacon. It is also very versatile - any fish will do."

Serves 4

900ml/1 ¹/₂ pints fish or vegetable stock

3 scallions (spring onions), trimmed & finely chopped

2 medium carrots, peeled & chopped small

1 stick celery,trimmed & chopped small

480g/generous 1lb mixed fish/seafood such as shelled prawns, salmon, white fish, crabmeat, cooked mussels, shucked oysters - all or any combination of these

Salt & freshly ground pepper

30 ml/2 tbsp fennel or parsley, finely chopped

Bring the stock to the boil in a large pan. Add the scallions, carrots and celery.

Cover, bring to the boil and simmer for 20 minutes.

Add fish and/or seafood of your choice and simmer for another five minutes.

Taste, and season if necessary.

Serve in deep plates or bowls, with generous sprinklings of fennel or parsley.

Tip: To give a richer flavour, grated cheese may be sprinkled over the finished dish.

Beetroot, Goats' Cheese & Walnut Salad

With its lovely delicate herbal flavours, St Tola goats' cheese from Co Clare contrasts well with sweet and deeply coloured beetroot to make a deliciously subtle starter or light lunch. Be careful to use fresh walnuts, as they spoil and take on a bitter flavour when stored for too long.

Serves 2-4

A selection of seasonal salad leaves

115g/4 oz St Tola or other soft goats' cheese

3 beetroots, cooked

10-15 fresh walnuts, coarsely chopped

Dressing:

15ml/1tbsp balsamic vinegar

45ml/3tbsp extra virgin olive oil

2.5ml/^{1}/$_2$ tsp Dijon mustard

Wash and dry the salad leaves.

Put a small handful of leaves onto each plate.

Slice the goats' cheese and beetroot into wedges and place 2-3 of each onto each plate. Sprinkle the walnuts over the salads.

Put all the ingredients for the dressing into a small bowl or screw-top jar and mix well to emulsify.

When ready to eat, sprinkle the dressing over the salads and served with freshly baked crusty bread.

Galway oysters

Irish oysters enjoy an enviable reputation internationally - indeed, some of the most famous restaurants in Europe feature them on their menus. It is a source of pride for Irish visitors to Rick Stein's celebrated Seafood Restaurant in Cornwall, for example, where two varieties of Irish oyster feature - both the seasonal native Galway oyster, and Carlingford oysters (the all-year Pacific oyster, *crassostrea gigas*), farmed in the beautiful lough at the foot of the Mountains of Mourne - and they sit easily alongside those from the River Fal in Cornwall, which are famously dredged only under sail, as a conservation measure.

Although the main species now produced in Ireland is the oval frilly-shelled Pacific oyster, Gigas (crassostrea gigas), which is cultivated in many coastal counties and available all year, it is widely acknowledged that the very best oysters are the native oysters (ostrea edulis) from the Galway area. Smaller, rounder and almost flat, the native oyster - which grows naturally on tidal sea beds and is also cultivated in managed plots - is easy to distinguish from its buxom foreign cousin. Strictly seasonal, native oysters are only harvested in months with an 'r' in them, i.e. September to April, and therein lies much of their charm.

Every September the start of the new season is celebrated with much fanfare, with festivals held in Galway and Clarenbridge; just south of the city at the mouth of the Claren River, the village of Clarenbridge is the heart of the Galway oyster industry, having 700 acres of beds in nearby Dunbulcan Bay, a place protected from Atlantic storms and with just the right mixture of fresh and seawater needed for oyster development.

One of the most popular of the Galway Oyster Festival's many events is the Guinness World Oyster Opening Championships, which is open to competitors from all over the world, all trying to out-do each other for the annual title - and also to beat the fastest time recorded, which was in 1977, when Ireland's Willie Moran, of Moran's on the Weir, opened 30 oysters in 1 minute 31 seconds, which is still an unbroken record at the time of going to press.

Although they were once plentiful enough to be the food of the poor, Galway oysters are now a highly prized (and highly priced) delicacy and, some say, aphrodisiac. Most connoisseurs believe that their delicate flavour and special texture are best appreciated raw and unadorned, when they just 'taste of the sea', but they are sometimes served in combination dishes - starters like Oysters Bloody Mary, for example, or the hot cocktail snack, Angels On Horseback. The larger Pacific oyster is also very good eaten raw of course and, being meatier, is more suitable for cooking.

To get the best from Galway oysters, buy them with their shells tightly clamped together, showing that they are still alive. Seaweed makes an appropriate garnish for oysters, and is often sold with them - simply wash it well, shake dry and arrange attractively on top of the crushed ice. Some people like dash of Tabasco or a grinding of black pepper - others prefer their native Irish oysters without so much as a squeeze of lemon, keeping such additions for the frilly Gigas instead.

oysters on the Half shell

This is the classic way to serve oysters. For many more suggestions, and a wealth of fascinating background information, see Máirín Ui Chomáin's book, *Irish Oyster Cuisine*, (A.&A. Farmar, www.farmarbooks.com).

Serves 2-4

24 Galway oysters, in the shell

4 lemon wedges

Use a blunt-ended oyster knife to shuck the oysters: insert the end of the knife between the shells near the hinge and work it until you cut through the muscle which holds the shells together. Catch the oyster liquid in a bowl.

When the oysters are all shucked, discard the flat shells and divide the oysters, in the deep halves, between four plates lined with crushed ice and fresh seaweed.

Strain the reserved liquid back over the oysters and serve with the lemon wedges, freshly baked brown soda bread and butter - and, if you like, a glass of stout.

Donegal, Leitrim, Mayo, Roscommon & Sligo

Roscommon – the castle may crumble but the pastures endure

It is typical of the northwest region that it should include Ireland's three most distinctive mountains. In Mayo, soaring elegantly above island-studded Clew Bay, is Croagh Patrick, the loveliest peak of all, in harmony with its surroundings. Known in more homely style as The Reek, it is Ireland's Holy Mountain, its sacred nature long pre-dating Christian times. But it was St Patrick who provided the modern name, and on the last Sunday of July - Reek Sunday - its peak becomes the setting for a rugged yet very crowded pilgrimage, a devotion which has left the scar of a well-worn track on the mountain's flank. In Sligo, it is Ben Bulben which has the high recognition factor.

"Bare Ben Bulben" has been commemorated by William Butler Yeats, and the poet is buried in Drumcliff churchyard beneath its steep slopes. But in any case, it has such a clearcut and stark shape that once seen, Ben Bulben is not forgotten.

Lough Swilly, Co Donegal

About the Region

Mount Errigal in northwest Donegal, the county's highest peak, is perhaps most distinctive of all. It is a massive quartzite cone, of decidedly raw appearance. Happily, though, Donegal has an abundance of beautiful hills and mountains, and as the sight of Errigal means you are nearing the enchanted region of The Rosses and Gweedore, it is a welcome milestone.

Of the other two northwestern counties, Leitrim and Roscommon, it is Leitrim which surprises. The perception is that it is a small county. Certainly it is small in agronomic terms, as generally it has poor soil, making its pockets of fertility into green oases. But Leitrim isn't small physically - it has many mountains, and the Shannon is becoming a lordly river as it flows through its first fine lake, the wide expanse of Lough Allen in north Leitrim. The county even has some Atlantic coast away to the northwest. But it's just four sea-swept kilometres, said to be a relic of the time when bishops of the ancient church had to be able to travel to Rome without traversing the lands of any neighbouring prelate. Whatever about the bishops, it was a useful state of affairs for any local ruler on bad terms with his or her neighbours.

Roscommon's eastern boundaries are set by the Shannon, although any towns along the river seem keen to be claimed by the counties along the east bank. To the southwest, Roscommon is bordered by the exuberance of Galway, and to the west the contrast is with the magnificence of Mayo. But Roscommon has some lovely scenery too, most notably in the north, in the area around Boyle and Lough Key.

There is a highly individual spirit to Roscommon which commands respect. And though it may lack any seacoast, in the distant past when any river was of strategic significance as a means of transport, the fact that all of Roscommon's eastern frontier is along the Shannon, its lakes, and the inland sea of Lough Ree, made Roscommon a centre of power. Thus at Rindun near Leecarrow on Lough Ree's west shore, there are the almost invisible remains of an important lakeside stronghold of once immense power. And Roscommon's gentle topography provided ideal grazing for the chieftains of old when the ability to move huge herds of cattle to fresh grassland was central to economic strength, with Roscommon being for a time the homeland of the

Boyle, Co Roscommon

Clonalis House, Co Roscommon

High Kings. It is still the home of The O'Conor Don, the chief of the clan, whose house of **Clonalis** (www.clonalis.com) at Castlerea lovingly preserves the harp of the blind musical genius Turlough Carolan (1670-1738).

To the west, Mayo is mighty. Majestic mountains, Ireland's largest island in Achill, multiple sea inlets, and numerous cliffs and beaches - Mayo has all that and more. Between the highlands, there are many fertile valleys, with a busy county hub in Castlebar towards the west, and beyond it the perfect little township of Westport at the head of Clew Bay augmenting the graceful presence of Croagh Patrick.

In the east of the county, the River Moy is one of the greatest salmon rivers in the world, so abundant that one of its finest fishing spots, the Ridge Pool, is right in the heart of the lively town of Ballina, where the Moy meets the sea in the wide expanse of Killala Bay.

The small county of Sligo has significant swathes of prosperous farmland, but this is ancient country too, with remarkable prehistoric sites in several upland locations. Myth lives with modernity, and the town itself is well accustomed to its celebrated links with the Yeats family, indeed it is wall-to-wall Yeats with

the poet's associations with Rosses Point and the great house of Lissadell on the coast to the north.

Beyond Sligo county is the vast and varied land of Donegal. Cross northward over the seamouth of the River Erne at Ballyshannon, and you're aware of a different mood, an unruly territory which lives in defiance of the wild weather of the North Atlantic at its most aggressive, and the demanding nature of the terrain, with its relative isolation through being distant from Dublin, and west of the political border with Northern Ireland.

And Donegal's much-indented shoreline means it has the longest sea coast of any Irish county. Yet all these factors of isolation and obstacles to convenient access mean that the many regions and pockets of hospitality in Donegal seem to glow with an added vitality. Donegal has everything which is quintessentially Irish, only more so, and it also has - particularly in its northern areas - a hint of the Scottish Hebrides which is well rooted in history. But the rugged terrain is far from being totally dominant. Any shelter and natural fertility is lovingly used, and in the extensive lowlands beside the southeast shore of Lough Swilly, Donegal's largest inlet, there is some of the finest farmland in all Ireland.

Ireland: North-West
Food of the Region

Temple House, Co Sligo

different!' as they say in Donegal. By a happy chance, you'll find some of the best places to stay in the whole of Ireland in the North-West - and also some extremely good food.

With important commercial fishing ports like Killybegs and Greencastle in the region, outstanding **FISH & SEAFOOD** are to be expected, especially in coastal areas, but the clean seas, lakes and rivers also make **sport fishing** one of the main attractions, so game fish – especially salmon – is a point of pride on many a table, and there are numerous businesses involved in one way or another. At one end of the spectrum, for example, you'll find everything you need to know about fisheries and angling at specialists like **Tiernan Brothers of Foxford** (www.themoy.com) where Michael & PJ Tiernan will do just about everything for you except catch your fish and cook it, they'll even arrange angling holidays – just visit their fantastic website (and online shop) first, and take it from there; once you've seen what they offer, and how they do it, visiting for real is almost inevitably the next step. At the other end of the spectrum – the finished product – companies like **Clarke's Salmon Smokery** (www.clarkes.ie), Ballina and Westport, have built their reputation on the quality of their traditional oak-smoked fish – and if you're lucky enough to land your own salmon or trout, they'll smoke your catch for you.

By contrast there are also some interesting fish farming enterprises in this region: **Clare Island Organic Salmon** (+353 (0)74 915 9805; www.marineharvest.com), for example, is produced in the wild Atlantic waters off the coast of Mayo and successfully provides an alternative to the wild fish (which are almost unavailable on a commercial scale at the time of going to press). Nearby, thanks to Michael Flanagan and Raymond Mairs' turbot farm, **Achill Island Turbot** (+ 353 (0)98 47023; www.achillislandturbot.ie), at Bunnacurry on Achill Island, a very different newcomer to the scene looks set to become an important player in Ireland and beyond, as top quality fresh turbot are now coming onto the market; a sedentary fish ideally suited to land-based farming in pristine sea water, turbot is

If wild and unspoilt is your thing, then head straight for the North-West of Ireland - this is big country, and the least inhabited part of Ireland: just the place for discerning people who don't like crowds. With Ireland's 'first genuine ecotourism destination', **The Green Box** (+353 (0)71 9856898; www.greenbox.ie), sited mainly in Leitrim and surrounding counties, it is in a sense the 'greenest' region, with an emphasis on sustainability before profit. And there's a real sense of community that seems to spring from the landscape and create a special brand of genuinely warm and relaxed hospitality – it's as if visitors are especially welcome once they've made the effort to get there. Not that it's really so isolated any more, with faster access roads and airports at Sligo, Knock (Ireland West), Carrickfinn (Donegal) and Derry City making it handy to reach all areas of the region, but the glorious thing about being up in the North-West is that it *feels* so away from it all - 'Up here it's already successfully farmed in Scotland and this new facility is expected to reduce pressure on wild stocks.

Another important coastal product is **SEAWEED** which, in addition to its traditional use on the land, is harvested commercially for culinary use, particularly in Co Sligo, by long-established experts such as Frank and Betty Melvin (+353 (0)96 49042) **of Carrig Fhada Seaweed**, at Easkey, who have earned a nationwide reputation for their work. The seaweed most widely used currently in cooking (throughout Ireland) are carrageen moss (*carraigín*) and dillisk (*duileasc*); these and many more are explored and explained by Sligo GP Prannie Rhatigan who is introducing these once familiar foods (now recognised as 'superfoods') to a new generation through talks and her book, *Irish Seaweed Kitchen*. Growing interest in the area – perhaps partly due to the increasing number of Japanese restaurants thriving in Ireland – has encouraged 'newcomers' like **Lotide Fine Foods** (www.lo-tide.com) of Westport, Co Mayo; the Moran family have been involved with the sea, shellfish and seaweeds on Clew Bay since the 1880s - Seamus and Carmel Moran, who represent the fourth generation, now produce a smartly presented range of sea vegetables and former chef, Seamus (who has some nice simple recipes on their website), has developed a unique range of Seafood Sausages, which are going down a treat. They also make a seaweed mix for breads, which not only adds texture, flavour and nutrition – but works as a natural flour improver and seasoning too. And, true to the area's tradition for therapeutic seaweed baths - **Kilcullen's Hot Seaweed Baths** (www.kilcullenseaweedbaths.com) at Enniscrone are famous worldwide - Lotide also produce a Seaweed Bath mix, made from the iodine rich seaweed *fucus serratus*.

And, not to be outdone, the land of this fascinating region produces **MEATS, GAME and DAIRY FOODS** which are every bit as special as those of the sea and river. Well known to sportsmen for its feathered game, notably snipe and woodcock, in season with winter shoots at great wooded estates such as Temple House Tubbercurry, Co Sligo, attracting sporting visitors - the region has more recently become known for the **venison** farmed at the superb **Coopershill**

House (www.coopershill.com), Riverstown, which features on many other distinguished menus as well as their own. In neighbouring Roscommon, excellent meats include **free range pork** produced at farms that have earned a national reputation such as **Tullywood Farm** (www.tullywoodfarm.com) Keadue, where the Delaney family raise rare breed animals, especially pigs, on their small holding - and hold pig-keeping courses too. And, just a few miles north of Roscommon Town, Derek and Brendan Allen run **Castlemine Farm** (www.castleminefarm.ie), a traditional mixed farm producing a range of products including rare breed pork, and known especially for the quality of the lamb and beef they sell at Moycullen Country Market, at their farm shop and online. Events, such as farm walks and cheese making demonstrations, are occasionally held at the farm. Also in Co Roscommon, **Kay and Ted Mole** (+353 (0)71 963 3775; www.organicguide.ie) have an interesting range of crops and livestock on their mixed organic farm near Strokestown, including geese as well as rare breed pigs, and they host farm walks and pig courses for the National Organic Training Skillnets (www.nots.ie).

Castlemine Farm, Co Roscommon

With top quality meats produced in the region, it follows naturally that the North-West should have more than its fair share of excellent BUTCHERS – several of whom have their own abattoirs. One in particular, Sean Kelly (www.kellybutchers.com) of Newport, Co Mayo, has gained international renown for his prize winning products, attracting a trail of very focused visitors to this small riverside town, and to Kelly's.

While this is not a major dairy farming area, it is home to some outstanding **DAIRY PRODUCTS** including the long-established **Carrowholly Cheese**, a delicious slightly crumbly gouda style cheese (plain and with nettles) made near Westport and sold at the weekly market there as well as featuring on local menus, and another Gouda style cheese, **Old Russet** which, as the names suggests, is aged; both will be seen in shops and restaurants in the area and are also listed by Cheese Etc (www.cheesesofireland.com). Look out also for **Tullynascreena Goat's Cheese**, which is made in Dromahair and, although not widely available, is highly respected by leading chefs in the area, including Brid Torrades, Euro-Toques owner-chef of Tobergal Lane, in Sligo Town, where it features on the menu. And, thanks to the Butler family, who farm near Castlebar, Co Mayo and run **Cuinneog Dairy Products** (www.cuinneog.com), the region is also home to some once familiar dairy products which are now almost unique – Irish farmhouse country butter and natural buttermilk; started by Tom and Sheila Butler in 1990 and originally known as 'Sheila's Country Butter', the business was re-launched recently as Cuinneog but

the product is unchanged and still made by traditional methods – and now, smartly re-packaged, this fuller-flavoured butter and natural buttermilk is distributed nationwide.

A great strength of cooking in the North-West - shared with their neighbours in Northern Ireland – is a love of **BAKING**, indeed it is so highly valued that there's even a dedicated **School of Home Baking** in Rathmullan, Co Donegal (Kathleen Loughrey; +353 (0)74 9158122). Enthusiasm for this wholesome and hospitable activity means that delicious just-out-of-the-oven bakes are to be found everywhere throughout the region, in shops, restaurants, B&Bs and cafés – down-to-earth, traditional tea time home baking at café/tea rooms like **The Beehive** and **The Cottage** on Achill Island, and **Mary's Bakery** at Ballycastle, for example, where you might stop for a cuppa and a scone or a slice of apple pie; or small artisan bakeries like **Jinny's** (www.jinnysbakery.com) at Drumshanbo, that supply local shops. A local speciality is the potato dish **boxty**, which may be found in some local shops and markets, and on menus (for breakfast, perhaps, in B&Bs).

By contrast to this rustic treat, there is also sophisticated work such as the special occasion cakes and confectionery made at Sharon Sweeney's **Cannaboe Bakery** (www.cacamilis.com) in Ballinamore, and also continental baking and patisserie by experts who have settled in the area such as Julien Vial at Tobergal Lane in Sligo Town.

Where there is good home baking, delicious handmade **PRESERVES** are unlikely to be far away – and this is certainly true of North West Ireland: since 1997, for example, **Filligan's** (www.filligans.com), one of Ireland's most respected ranges of traditionally handmade preserves, has been made by Sara and Philip Moss away up in the unlikely location of Glenties in north-west Donegal; they started making their small batches of jams and chutneys for one shop, and their growing range is now available from a network of carefully selected specialist outlets. More recently, at Furnace in the Newport area of Co Mayo, Patti Moss started her successful business, **A Taste of Days Gone By** (pattishomemadejam.com) when she decided to recreate the recipes found in her grandmother's cookbook. And the North-West has its share of seriously good speciality **CHOCOLATES** too, with notable local brands including **Helena Chocolates** (+353 (0)94 902 2755), of Castlebar and **Marlene's** (www.chocolatehaven.net) of Westport.

But, important (and beguiling) as they may be, the North-West of Ireland is not all about tradition and old-world treats. You'll find some less predictable specialities – such as the superb **Noodle House Pasta** (www.noodlehouseorganics.ie) which is made at Curry, Co Sligo, and the new **Galway Hooker pale ale** (www.galwayhooker.ie), made by cousins Aidan Murphy and Ronan Brennan at a small craft brewery in Roscommon; interest in real ale is growing fast in Ireland but craft breweries are still a rarity, so this is an especially welcome development. Other forward looking enterprises include **Donegal Rapeseed Oil Company** at Raphoe (www.donegalrapeseedoilco.com); a Good Food Ireland member, the company was set up by Austin Duignan and Stephen Allen in 2009 to make a home produced culinary oil, Donegal Virgin Rapeseed Oil. They work with a number of individual small farms in Donegal and Northern Ireland, and have selective distribution in place in much of the country – so, with strong market demand established, the enterprise looks set for success.

Others that are now well-established and capture the imaginative and determined character of the special people who have chosen to settle here and live out their philosophy include Thomas Becht's unusual **Organic Farm** (www.donegalorganic.ie) at Glenties, which offers eco workcamp experience and a Nature Trail in addition to more usual farm activities. Based at The Enterprise Centre in Drumshanbo, the **Leitrim Organic Farmers Co-Op Society** (www.leitrimorganic.com) assists small scale producers by wholesaling the meat of about 150 organic farmers to farmers' markets, supplying organic contracts in Britain and Ireland and providing low-cost support services to members; see them at farmers' markets. Then there is Rod Alston's legendary Co Leitrim herb nursery, **Eden Plants** at Rossinver (www.organic-trust.org); what must have looked like an impossible dream when he set up here in 1975 is now one of Ireland's most respected food-related operations and open every afternoon, when

generous advice is available to anyone who would like to tap into a lifetime's experience of successful organic production in an apparently inhospitable climate. And nearby, **The Organic Centre** (www.theorganiccentre.ie) has been operating since 1995 and it's a huge success story, a veritable hive of activity offering a multiplicity of day events and courses on everything from small scale amateur gardening to certificate courses for budding commercial producers, to advising on school gardens and community projects and so much more. Maybe you'd like to learn about dry stone wall construction, reedbed systems, or beekeeping, or basket making, or how to plan your allotment, or cooking with seaweeds, or cheese-making - this last course may be given by the Centre's administrator Hans Wieland and his wife Gaby, who were the original producers of Carrowholly Cheese; Gaby also offers cooking classes, including a course on grains, breads and sourdough which teaches you how to mill your own flour, and how to make grain sprouts. The range of events, courses and activities they offer throughout the year is astonishing (including some in outreach centres in Co Clare and Co Wicklow) but, alternatively, maybe you'd simply like to have a look around their demonstration gardens, and then visit the eco-shop; they offer organic seeds sales on site – and also have an online shop. A very special place.

Rathmullan Hens, Co Donegal

Four of the Best...

Clare Island Organic Salmon

The great challenge, when facing the ever-growing threat to fish stocks in the wild, is to find ways of producing sustainable, high quality alternatives that will ease demand on threatened species and themselves be environmentally friendly. No easy task, but Clare Island Organic Salmon - which is located in Clew Bay, six miles off the Mayo coast - is an encouraging success story. Produced at the world's most exposed salmon farm, in pure Atlantic waters where winter storms lasting for days can produce waves over ten metres, and the strength of the tidal exchange constantly provides strenuous exercise, Clare Island organic salmon is renowned for its superb flavour, lean flesh and firm muscle texture. Certified organic since 1997, the feed is made in Ireland, from natural organic and GMO-free ingredients, and the huge nets below the exposed cages hang in up to 30 metres of water and are big enough to allow the fish to shoal naturally and control proximity to each other. These conditions explain the consistently excellent quality that makes Clare Island salmon an ingredient of choice at leading restaurants (where you'll often see it named on menus), with discerning shoppers - and also top fish smokers like Kinvara, Belvelly Smokehouse, Ummera and the Burren Smokehouse.

Clare Island Co Mayo
+353 (0)74 915 9805 www.marineharvest.com

Dominick Kelly's Butchers

Speciality pork products have long been a strength in Ireland but some producers seem to have a unique magic ingredient, and Kelly's of Newport would certainly be up there among the chosen few. An excellent traditional butchers with a licensed abattoir where they slaughter all their own locally sourced lamb and beef, Kelly's history is one of brothers - Dominick and Michael, who founded the business in the 1930's, Dominick's sons Sean and Seamus, who took over from them, and Sean's sons Kenneth and Cormac who have now joined the business. It's a great team, headed up by Sean who is the very essence of the cheery traditional butcher - and, between them, they do an exceptional job. Although their products are now widely distributed, people love the shop and travel great distances to buy Kelly's black and white puddings and sausages - and, especially, their traditional 'putóg' black pudding, a unique product similar to haggis (but with a different recipe - a family secret of course); the name translates as 'gut', 'intestine' or 'belly', referring to the sheep's stomach traditionally used for the casing. Among many awards received down the years, a particular point of pride is successive honours in the international competition run in France by the Confrérie des Chevaliers du Goute-Boudin (The Brotherhood of the Knight of the Black Pudding) leading, in 2010, to a full ceremonial visit by the Chevaliers, when Sean was made an official member. An honour indeed.

Main Street Newport Co. Mayo
+353 (0) 98 41149 www.kellysbutchers.com

Enniscoe House

In converted outbuildings at the back of Susan Kellet's fine 17th century house on Lough Conn, The Mayo North Family Heritage Centre (+353 (0)96 31809) is one of the region's main attractions, and it includes an agricultural and social history museum, with a forge where Colin Highfield repairs implements donated to the museum, and also a craft training centre dedicated to developing skills in ancient and traditional crafts. Enniscoe is a very special place for anglers and visitors with a natural empathy for the untamed wildness of the area - and, with its unspoilt charm and the many activities going on around the estate, it is one of those truly great Irish country houses which have adapted gently to the times without losing any of their character. Thoughtful changes recently introduced include a lovely nature trail through woodlands, a working run of old bog railway and an interesting little shop offering unusual gifts both antique and contemporary. Tearooms overlook the walled gardens which are of particular interest for many visitors (open April-October, times vary); a pleasure garden has been restored in Victorian style, and there's a productive organic garden. It includes a number of allotments as well as supplying produce commercially for local customers, and also the house - where, if overnight guests are lucky, freshly caught brown trout or salmon may be on the menu for dinner.

Castlehill Crossmolina Ballina Co Mayo
+353 (0)96 3111 www.enniscoe.com

Irish Seaweed Kitchen

Seaweed has always been an important part of life for Ireland's coastal communities, for use on the land and in the home. Today, the shoreline is mysterious to many of us - but it's as familiar as the back garden to families living along the coast or on islands, who have grown up with the rhythm of the tides and the briney harvest that is revealed every twelve hours. People like Sligo GP and Slow Food member, Prannie Rhatigan, whose beautiful book Irish Seaweed Kitchen is the first comprehensive guide to harvesting, preparing and cooking Irish seaweeds, which she describes as "... a living treasure by the shore, more valuable by far than any golden coins that may lie buried beside it in the sand." While there have been many academic papers written on the subject, this accessible celebration of the beauty and riches of the Irish shoreline is for everybody. Fifteen varieties of red, brown and green seaweed feature, all with (considerable) health benefits as well as culinary uses. Some may already be familiar - carrageen (carraigín), for example, is still widely used as a setting agent, and dillisk (duileasc) has many current uses. Prannie recommends starting with easy to use seaweeds in simple recipes, and perhaps having the following in stock in your kitchen: a pack of alaria, a pack or jar of seaweed stock, ground nori, sheet nori, some sea spaghetti and kelp; a full list of Irish seaweed suppliers is in the book, also web addresses for buying online.

Prannie Rhatigan's Irish Seaweed Kitchen
www.prannie.com

the Special Foods of the North-West...

A guide to food shops, markets, farm shops, local stores
and internet suppliers in counties Donegal, Leitrim, Mayo, Roscommon, Sligo

County Donegal

McGettigan & Sons Main Street **DONEGAL TOWN**
(+353(0)74 972 1605). A member of the Associated
Craft Butchers of Ireland (ACBI), this family-run
butchers shop has won awards a-plenty (including
the All Ireland Award for speciality sausages) and is
first port of call for many visitors to the town.

The Green Man Main Street **DUNFANAGHY**
(+353 (0)74 9100800 www.greenmandunfanaghy.com).
Eileen Gallagher and Neil Hougardy provide a great
service for discerning residents and the many visitors
to this popular holiday area, by offering a range of
hard to find wines and carefully sourced foods, from
Ireland and beyond. Over a thousand product lines
are stocked, and as many as possible are sourced
locally, organic and/or fair trade. The many local
goodies offered include freshly baked breads and
croissants, organic milk, eggs and butter, local
Hornhead honey, Filligans preserves and chutneys,
fresh local crab and lobster in season, and sea

vegetables from Burtonport as well as locally grown
salad leaves. They offer a pre-order service, allowing
customers to phone in their orders from regular
stock – and to order speciality items such as game
and oysters. This little gem is understandably
popular with regular visitors – and it's open all year.

McGee's Butchers Letterkenny Shopping Centre
LETTERKENNY *(+353 (0)74 917 6567
www.mcgeesfood.com)*. This ACBI butchers shop is a
branch of the acclaimed family-run Belfast business of
the same name – and they share the benefit of
sourcing their meat from the fourth generation family
farm in Co Tyrone.

County Leitrim

Cannaboe Confectionery Willowfield Road
BALLINAMORE *(+353 (0)71 964 4778
www.cacamilis.com)*. Fans of the RTE TV Nationwide
programme may already be familiar with Sharon
Sweeney's impressive special occasion cakes and
handmade chocolate. There's an **online shop** for
chocolate, including wedding favours and lollipops.

The Market Yard Centre **CARRICK-ON-SHANNON**
(www.themarketyardcentre.com). This attractive old
courtyard is bounded by interesting businesses
ranging from an art and craft gallery to a healthfood
shop, and several eating places. On Thursdays (10-3)
it is transformed by the arrival of one of the country's
best the famers' markets, current recipient of a
Farmers' Market Good Practice Standard Certificate
and meeting place for some of the best producers and
purveyors of local, seasonal and organic foods. This is
the place to buy ultra fresh fish from 'The Donegal
Fisherman' or the local potato speciality, boxty, from
'Eileen's Boxty' (made near Mohill), home baking
from 'The Fluffy Meringue' - and you'll find as
interesting a bunch of foodie people here as you'd
meet anywhere, including many featuring elsewhere
in this book: Kearns Organic Growers; Monsieur

Lyons Café, Co Sligo

Frank Pasquier, 'The French baker'; Tattie Hoaker organics, Roscommon; Trevor Irvine of Cheese Etc; Declan McCarthy of Irish Organic Meats; Coopershill Venison… and many more

Cheese Etc Carrowerin DROMAHAIR *(+353 (0)71 916 4395 www.cheesesofireland.com).* Trevor and Myra Irvine's original Cheese Etc shop opened in Carrick-on-Shannon in 1999, and its cheery frontage was easily spotted beside the bridge. They made a lot of friends in that busy town, many of whom have followed them to their little shop in Dromahair, and to the markets that they now attend (Thursday in Carrick-on-Shannon, Friday and Saturday at St. George's Market, Belfast, Friday in Manorhamilton, and Saturday in Sligo) and also Tullywood Farm Shop, at Keadue in Co Roscommon, where they spend their Sundays. By visiting the cheesemakers and learning what gives each cheese its special character, they have built up a great knowledge of Ireland's cheese, and not only take care to sell them in prime condition but, in order to share their knowledge, they also ensure that one of them will always be there to serve customers personally. You'll also see them credited in some restaurants and shops, "but only when we see a similar awareness, knowledge and care that we have ourselves". Their love of Irish cheese is boundless, and easily explained: "Why look for Camembert when Cooleeney exists?"

The Co-Op Shop Main Street **MANORHAMILTON** *(+353 (0)71 55609).* This is just the place to go when you want to find locally grown produce at its best. Closed Sun.

The Organic Centre **ROSSINVER** *(+353 71 985 4338 www.theorganiccentre.ie).* The Eco-Shop at The Organic Centre (see Food of the Region) offers seasonal produce from their own gardens as well as a range of gardening and home items, books and organic herb tinctures, and there's a coffee shop too. Also a fascinating **online shop**.

County Mayo

Clarke's Salmon Smokery & Seafood Delicatessen O'Rahilly & Connolly Streets **BALLINA** *(+353 (0) 96 21022 www.clarkes.ie).* Renowned throughout the North-West and beyond, 'Clarke's Master Fishmongers & Salmon Smokers since1945' has recently been transformed into Clarke's Seafood

Clarke's Seafood, Co Mayo

Delicatessen, a bright modern shop offering wines, Irish farmhouse cheeses and other speciality foods as well as ultra fresh seafood and shellfish. They also sell an innovative range of prepared seafood - their own smoked salmon specialities include traditional oak-smoked salmon (made to the founder Jackie Clarke's original recipe), organic salmon and salmon flavoured with, for example, dill, or whiskey, and they sell (and explain the value and uses of) sea vegetables. Many of their products have won Great Taste Awards and they offer a fantastic range of services all round - anything from providing advice and recipes or lending a fish kettle, to smoking salmon and trout for anglers, who can have their catch smoked, sliced and packaged to order. Gift hampers are available, and there's an **online shop**. And the same wonderful selection of ultra fresh fish is also available at their newer Westport shop, beside the Octagon.

Heffernans Fine Foods Market Square **BALLINA** *(+353 (0)96 21218).* Anthony and Geraldine Heffernan's long-established family butchery underwent a 'total revamp' in 2007, emerging as a butchers with café, deli, and bakery. Butchery remains the core business - they have their own abattoir, and the range of fresh meats displayed on one side of the shop is impressive – but the other end is now given over to delicatessen fare and home bakes (made according to Ballymaloe recipes), which are also served in the café area alongside.

Helena Chocolates Cavendish Lane **CASTLEBAR** (*+353 (0)94 902 2755 www.helenachocolates.ie*). Having lived here for over a quarter of a century, Dirk Schonkeren is by now an honorary Mayo man – together with his wife Elaine, this Belgian chef and chocolatier was one of the pioneers in Irish chocolate making when they first set up business in 1980s Castlebar. Now not only do they continue to produce their beautiful handmade chocolates, cakes, desserts and one-off pieces, but also run their shop and café as 'a chocolate experience'. Dirk is Ireland's only World Chocolate Ambassador, an honour bestowed by the Swiss chocolate manufacturer Barry Callebaut, whose 70-strong 'chocolate ambassador club' is dedicated to passing on their skills to others. **Online sales** are planned; meanwhile a telephone mail order service is offered, with gift wrapping if required.

Dirk Schonkeren, Helena Chocolates

Rua Deli Spencer Street **CASTLEBAR** (*+353 (0)94 9286072 www.caferua.com*). The younger retail sister of the McMahon family's excellent Café Rua on New Antrim Street, this brilliant deli stocks a wide range of the delicious foods and ingredients that have been served in the café for over a decade. International speciality foods feature too, of course, but among the local goodies on sale you'll find Stephen Gould's finest mixed salad leaf selection, from Headford; Ingrid Basler's excellent Noodle House organic pasta and jams from Curry, Co Sligo; the unique Cuinneog country butter, from nearby Balla, Castlebar; Carrowholly raw milk cheese from Westport, and St Tola Organic Goat's Cheese from Inagh, Co Clare; Westport Grove jams and relishes (and an unusual quince paste); and Connemara Smokehouse smoked salmon and tuna from Ballyconneely, Co Galway. Most local of all, there are the foods they make themselves - including a range of chutneys, relishes and dressings – and they also sell non-food items like cookbooks and the gorgeous Bunbury chopping boards from Lisnavagh Estate, Co Carlow. And that's only the beginning. Closed Sun & bank hols.

Clare Island Organic Salmon **CLARE ISLAND** (*+353 (0)74 915 9805 www.marineharvest.com*). Fresh Clare Island Organic Salmon is available locally from good fishmongers, notably Clarke's in Ballina and Westport; elsewhere you will find it mainly in speciality shops, eg in the Dublin area: Cavistons, Dun Laoghaire; The Organic Supermarket, Blackrock: Beshoff's, Howth. A range of pre-packed products has also been developed for the retail market, and many of Ireland's top fish smokers use Clare Island Organic Salmon for their premium smoked and cured products.

Derrymore Farmhouse Derrymore Partry near **CLAREMORRIS** (*+353 (0)94 954 3173*). About a kilometre from Partry on the road to Westport, you'll see The Blue Teapot signposted on the left turnoff for Tourmakeady. This will lead you to Derrymore Farm farm (known locally as The Blue Teapot) where the Dutch owners, Vincent and Manita van Dulmen, serve wonderful homemade breads, scones, tarts and so on in their little daytime café and sell their own products such as cheese and honey. It's a gem for walkers, and fun for visitors to find.

The Food Store Ballyhaunis Road **CLAREMORRIS** (*+353 (0)94 936 2091*). Easily spotted by its smart façade, Good Food Ireland member Niall Heffernan's thriving store began as Heffernan Meats and is still known especially for quality meat – the beef is Mayo Aberdeen Angus, lamb comes mostly from their own farm nearby, they sell their own dry-cured bacon and an impressive range of home-prepared ready meals – but this surprising place is actually a latter day version of the traditional country shop that stocked everything. There's an in-house bakery, a deli section specialising in home cooked meats, fresh local organic produce and a carefully selected range of niche products including organic ranges like Noodle House pastas and sauces and Sowans bread mixes – and a second store at the town's Silverbridge Shopping Centre.

Tiernan Brothers Main Street **FOXFORD** *(+353 (0)94 925 6731 www.themoy.com / www.tiernanbrothers.8k.com).* For many, angling is the lifeblood of Co Mayo and the River Moy is its heart. A one stop shop of a very different kind is Michael and PJ Tiernan's 'Mayo Angling Advice Centre', an extraordinary place with a century and a half's experience of providing everything that could possibly be needed by anglers hoping to bag one of the noble river's wild Atlantic salmon or sea trout. They sell tackle and bait, offer a ghillie service – and even arrange angling holidays; steeped in history but very much of the present, they also have two websites which, between them, cover pretty much everything anyone could ever need to know about fishing the Moy, and have an **online shop**. And, once bagged, successful anglers can drop their catches into Clarke's of Ballina to avail of their bespoke smoking service. A real taste of Mayo.

A Taste of Days Gone By Furnace near **NEWPORT** *(+353 98 41717 www.pattishomemadejam.com).* Patti Moss's background is in marketing and – with recipes inspired by her Irish grandmother's cookery book and products all named after friends and relatives - her experience is being put to good use in this

relatively young company, which specialises in flavoursome handmade jams, marmalade, relishes, sauces, and salad dressings. You'll find her products at Sligo Farmers' Market every Saturday – and at her **Online shop**.

Dominick Kelly's Butchers Main Street **NEWPORT** *(+353 (0)98 41149 www.kellysbutchers.com).* A legend in the West of Ireland, this excellent family-run butchers shop operates its own licensed abattoir; especially famous for sausages and puddings, notably the traditional 'Putóg.

Clarke's Seafood Delicatessen Peter Street **WESTPORT** *(+353 (0)96 21022 www.clarkes.ie).* In the centre of town beside the Octagon, you'll find the Westport branch of the Clarke brothers' renowned Ballina business. Ultra fresh fish and seafood, of course, along with a great range of wines and deli fare headed up by their smoked salmon. Look out for the local Gouda-style cheese, Carrowholly, made just outside the town by Andrew Pelham-Byrne.

Kate McCormack & Sons Bridge Street **WESTPORT** *(+353 (0)98 25619).* John McCormack is currently the main man at Kate McCormack's sixth generation butcher's shop in Westport and not only is this Associated Craft Butchers of Ireland member continuing the tradition of supplying the people of Westport with excellent meats but, up the stairs (where you will also find an art gallery), Annette McCormack's daughters Katrina and Mary Claire, run a small, unpretentious restaurant. Locally reared meats go into specialities like bacon and cabbage, and a casserole of spring lamb – and many of the deli dishes from the shop are also on the menu, as well as farmhouse cheeses including the local Carrowholly cheese. It all makes for very neat and tasty interdependent package.

Marlene's Chocolate Haven James Street Car Park **WESTPORT** *(+353(0)98 24564 www.chocolatehaven.net).* Handmade with the best Belgian chocolate, Marlene's Chocolates offer a range of sweet indulgences, with no additives or preservatives added. Wedding favours, children's party novelties and corporate gifts are a speciality and there's a wide range to choose from in the shop, along with a café offering diabetic chocolates, a range of coffees and the speciality of the house – Marlene's Hot Chocolate. No online sales but informative website - call Marlene to place an order. Closed Sun.

County Roscommon

Castlemine Farm Fourmilehouse **KEADUE**
(+353 (0)90 662 9866 / (0)87 2231202
www.castleminefarm.ie). Sean Allen and his two sons,
Derek and Brendan, are the latest generations to run
this family farm near the exceptionally tidy town of
Keadue (several times a winner in the annual Tidy
Towns competition) and, as they say tellingly, to care
for the land. Viewers of the RTE TV series Higher
Ground may be familiar with this likeable and
innovative family, who produce pasture fed beef
(Aberdeen Angus, Limousin, Charolais and
Hereford), lamb, rare breed pork (Saddlebacks,
Gloucester Old Spots, Tamworths and crosses),
poultry and vegetables; while not organic, it is a
traditional farm run on extensive principles and with
animal welfare at its heart. The stock is all free range,
fed mainly on home grown fodder when grass on the
farm's limestone pastures is unavailable, and allowed
to grow at nature's slow pace – and they then hang
beef for at least 21 days and lamb for 7 to 10 days
before butchering. All this care is reflected in the
quality and flavour of the produce sold in their farm
shop (Friday and Saturday 10am to 6pm), and
online. Visitors are welcome – it's about 9km/6 miles
north of Roscommon town by the N61 - and there
are occasional farm walks and activities such as
cheese-making demonstrations; see website for news.
You'll also meet them at Galway and Moycullen
Farmers' Markets .

Tullywood Farm Tullytawen **KEADUE** near Boyle
(+353 (0)71 964 7905 / (0)87 9012975
www.tullywoodfarm.com). This part of the country is
generously endowed with interesting farms, and
Tullywood – which is surrounded by forests, on a
mountain overlooking Lough Meelagh, and has
been farmed for two centuries – is now in the
energetic ownership of Joseph and Julie Delaney,
who moved here with their daughter Tara in 2001
and decided to 'rekindle the past'. This has involved
a lot of (ongoing) restoration work, and they now
specialise in rare breed pigs (Tamworth, British
Saddleback and Gloucestershire Old Spots) and free
range hens and ducks. At weekends they sell the
meats, home made sausages, burgers and eggs at
their farm shop (where you may well meet other
characters of the artisan food world, including
Trevor Irvine of Cheese Etc on Sundays), along with
fruit juices, garden preserves, pickles – and art: Julie
is a painter specialising in landscapes and animal
portraits, especially past pets (from photos). They
also run pig keeping courses, which include a tour
of the farm and butchery, and have rare breed pigs
for sale. Farm shop: Fri 10.30-4.30; Sun 1.30-4.30.
Also **online shop**, with delivery to Belfast and
Dublin, as well as locally.

Kearns Organic Growers Druminardly **ROOSKEY**
(+353 (0)87 769 5268 / (0)1 240 2669
www.organicguide.ie). Operating here since 2005, this
small family-run horticultural enterprise grows a wide
range of vegetables, soft fruit and herbs. They sell

Castlemine Farm Shop

Castlemine Farm, Co Roscommon

their fresh fruit and vegetables, and the seasonal products they make with them - jams, chutneys, ratatouille - at the farm, and at Farmers' Markets in Carrick-on-Shannon, Longford, and Boyle.

Gleeson's Artisan Food & Wine Shop Market Square **ROSCOMMON** *(+353 (0)90 662 6954 www.gleesonstownhouse.com)*. Mary and Eamonn Gleeson have always placed great emphasis on food, buying local produce, organic when possible, for their guests - and the weekly Farmers' Market is held next door. They also have a specialist food and wine shop nearby; it includes international speciality products, of course, but the main focus is on local artisan produce and their own home-made foods, including baked goods like brown bread and scones, home-baked ham, freshly-made sandwiches, a home dinner range, hampers and picnic baskets… Well worth a look.

The Tattie Hoaker Goff Street **ROSCOMMON** *(+353 (0)86 157 5623 - Aidan Gillan www.organicguide.ie)*. This well known health food store sells organic wholefoods, as well as a wide range of health supplements and health and beauty products. They operate a weekly home delivery organic fruit and vegetable box scheme, and trade at

Farmers' Markets, including The Market Yard at Carrick-on-Shannon (Thursdays). Once a year, in late June, they hold an Open Day, when professional therapists and counsellors are on hand with free advice. Closed Sun.

county sligo

Coopershill House Irish Venison **RIVERSTOWN** *(+353 (0)71 916 5108 www.coopershill.com)*. Coopershill Venison is the tender meat of the O'Hara family's young grass-fed fallow deer; often served to guests at this beautiful place, it is also seen on some of the best restaurant menus in the area. Offered in a wide range of cuts – they are, quite rightly, especially proud of the recently launched smoked haunch of venison – you can buy anything up to a full carcass, freezer-ready. The price list is on the website and there's a recipe booklet to help home cooks get the best from this delicious and versatile meat. Animal welfare is a high priority and farm visits are welcome by arrangement – and the meat is available to purchase direct from the farm, from selected retailers and from Sligo famers' market.

Coopershill House, Co Sligo

Cosgrove's Market Street **SLIGO TOWN**
(+353 (0)71 914 2809). You could be forgiven for
thinking you have stepped back in time – and into
the local community - when visiting 3rd generation
grocer Michael Cosgrove's delightful traditional shop,
which has been trading since 1898 and not only sells
all manner of good things but also offers a level of
personal service that is becoming increasingly rare,
even in Ireland. It's a place where regular customers
are known by name, and you'll find more real choice
than in any of the big multiples.

The French Market Tobergal Lane **SLIGO TOWN**
(+353 (0)87 683 4397). French chef Franck Pasquier's
classic continental baking includes superb sourdough
loaves made with specially sourced hard flour, and he
also stocks speciality patés and terrines and other
treats not easily sourced in Ireland. Attends local
markets (eg Dromohair and Carrick-on-Shannon).

The Gourmet Parlour Bridge Street **SLIGO TOWN**
(+353 (0)71 914 4617 www.gourmetparlour.com). Self
catering visitors to the area will be particularly glad to
find that Sligo is well supplied with quality food
stores, including Catherine Farrell and Annette
Burke's shop and deli, where the Ballymaloe trained
chefs turn out some very tasty fare using carefully
sourced, mainly local, ingredients. As well as offering
an extensive menu, including wholesome ready
meals, soups, salads and sandwiches (and some
seriously tempting cakes and desserts), they do
catering and wedding cakes.

Kate's Kitchen Castle Street **SLIGO TOWN**
(+353 (0)71 914 3022 www.kateskitchen.ie). This well
known shop was established in 1982 by Kate Pettit
and Frank Hopper and is now run by local girl Kate
O'Hara who, with her younger sisters Beth and Jane,
has taken on the challenge of sourcing and selling a
wide range of the finest foods available. Along with
fine wines and European specialities, Irish artisan
producers are extremely well represented, including
many from the immediate area such as Bluebell
Organic Farm eggs and vegetarian quiches, Noodle
House pasta from nearby at Curry, baked goods
(including excellent breads as well as treats for the
sweet-toothed) from several regular local bakers and

also Declan Ryan's Arbutus Breads in Cork – and local
butcher Keith Clarke supplies his own Knocknarea
honey. Speciality meats come from around Ireland –
Coopershill Venison from nearby Riverstown, Brady
Family's whole hams from Co Kildare, O'Doherty's
black bacon from Enniskillen and Gubbeen smoked
fish and salami from West Cork, for example – and
you'll find Murphy's of Dingle and Tickety Moo ice
creams here too.

Tir na Nog Grattan Street **SLIGO TOWN**
(+353 (0)71 916 2752). Sligo is a great town for good
old-fashioned shop-keeping, and this excellent
wholefood store is one of its best-loved institutions,
having supplied the town with a great range of health
foods, organic vegetables and homeopathic remedies
for many years. Also advice a-plenty, and plenty of
goodies to tempt you too - there's even vegan ice
cream in the freezer.

Lyons Café, Sligo

For further information on Farmers Markets throughout Ireland
www.bordbia.ie • www.irishfarmersmarkets.ie

COUNTY DONEGAL

Ballybofey GAA grounds. Fri 12-4.

Donegal Town Diamond. 3rd Sat of Month 10-2.

COUNTY LEITRIM

Carrick-on-Shannon Farmers' Market The Market
Yard Centre. Thur 10-3.

Origin Farmers Market Beepark Resource Centre
Manorhamilton. Fri 9-2.

COUNTY MAYO

Ballinrobe Food & Craft Market Cornmarket. Sat 10-1.

Ballina Farmers Market Market Square. Sat 9-2.

Castlebar Farmers Market Market Square. Fri 9-6.

Charlestown Farmers Markets Murphy's Londis Car
Park. Thu 9-2.

Claremorris Country Market Town Hall Claremorris.
Fri- 10-2.

Foxford Woollen Mills Market Woollen Mills
Foxford. Sat 10-2.

Killala Farmers Market Pastoral Centre (beside
Catholic church). Sun 10.30-1.

Kiltimagh Farmers Market Market Square Kiltimagh.
Sat 10-1.

Louisburgh Market Louisburgh. Fri 9-3.

Westport Country Markets Ltd Pete Callaghan Centre
off James Street. Car Park, Thur 8.30-1.

Westport Food & Craft Market The Mall Westport.
Sat 9-5 (from March).

COUNTY ROSCOMMON

Origin Farmers Market Grounds of King House
Boyle. Sat 10-2.

Roscommon Farmers' Market Market Square
Roscommon Town. Fri 10-2.

COUNTY SLIGO

Origin Farmers Market Sligo IT Sports Field Sligo.
Car Park Sat 9-1.

Cromleach Lodge, Co Sligo

Eat & Stay

County Donegal

Danny Minnie's Restaurant

This atmospheric restaurant has been run by the O'Donnell family since 1962. Hidden behind a frontage of overgrown creepers comes a surprise: once through the door you are in a world of antiques and elegantly appointed candle-lit tables - there may even be a harpist playing. Brian O'Donnell's menus are in both Irish and English, with seafood starring - lobster and other shellfish, availability permitting – while local meats include both Donegal beef and delicious Donegal mountain lamb, typically with a honey, garlic and rosemary gravy, and lovely flavoursome local vegetables. And the staff are lovely too - there's nowhere quite like Danny Minnie's.

Annagry Co Donegal
+353 (0)74 954 8201   www.dannyminnies.com

Harry's Bar & Restaurant

Donal and Kevin Doherty and chef Raymond Moran operate this well-run bar and restaurant with a real passion for the food of the area – a philosophy shared by their well-informed staff. "Local Food From Local People" is their mantra and equal prominence is given to 'The Greencastle Fishbox' and the 'Famous Well Hung Donegal Steaks' that make this a serious destination for beef eaters. A seasonal 'Best of Local Produce' selection may include wild Donegal venison; Inch Island pheasant; an Inishowen Lamb Plate; and – a special source of pride – Inishowen organic saddleback pork. Or try the "Taste of Inishowen" menu, with the main elements all sourced in Inishowen.

Bridgend Inishowen Co Donegal
+353 (0)74 936 8444   www.harrys.ie

♣ The Mill Restaurant

Susan and Derek Alcorn's lovely restaurant with rooms is beautifully located on the shore of the New Lake, which is a special area of conservation. Derek's classically based menus are inspired by the best seasonal local ingredients, and the cooking style is his own - ingredients are sometimes unusual or under-used, but the originality is less in the choice of ingredients than how they are combined. House specialities include an unusual upside down fish pie, which is filled with all manner of good things - lobster, crab claws and john dory in a brandy cream sauce.

Figart, Dunfanaghy, Letterkenny, Co Donegal
+353 (0)74 913 6985   www.themillrestaurant.com

Kealys Seafood Bar

Handily located for the ferry between the fishing port of Greencastle and Magilligan Point in Northern Ireland, this excellent seafood restaurant is a low-key little place where simplicity is valued – well worth a visit, if only for a daytime bowl of Tricia Kealy's Greencastle chowder and some delicious home-baked brown bread. Cooking combines classic dishes and others which are modern in tone yet also echo traditional Irish themes - baked salmon with a wholegrain mustard crust served on Irish spring cabbage and bacon, perhaps - and delicious local organic vegetables are used with fish to make the most of both precious resources.

The Harbour Greencastle Co Donegal
+353 (0)74 938 1010

♣ Rathmullan House

Set in lovely gardens on the shores of Lough Swilly just outside Rathmullan village, the Wheeler family's gracious nineteenth century house is fairly grand, but

has a laid-back charm. Renowned for their food –
including tremendous breakfasts - cooking here is
upbeat traditional and meticulously-sourced menus
are based on the very best of local and artisan foods.
Working closely with organic gardener, Dennis
Hawke, chef Kelan McMichael transforms fresh
produce from their own beautiful walled garden into
delicious dishes, and they offer a proper little person's
version of the adult menu for children too.
Accommodation includes some especially desirable
newer rooms.
Rathmullan Co Donegal
+353 (0)74 915 8188 www.rathmullanhouse.com

County Leitrim

The Oarsman Bar & Café

Brothers Conor and Ronan Maher inherited "the
hotelier's gene" from their parents, Tom and
Rosaleen (of lovely Hollywell country house,
nearby), and everything at this characterful pub is
invariably spick-and-span, welcoming and efficiently
run, even at the busiest times. Very much a food
lovers' destination, they take pride in sourcing
produce locally and crediting suppliers; a strong
kitchen team produces consistently excellent modern
food, offered on appealing lunchtime bar menus and
more extensive evening menus (reservations
recommended for both, no food Sun or Mon). Cosy
fires in winter, and a sheltered beer garden for
summer too; a place to savour.
Bridge Street Carrick-on-Shannon Co Leitrim
+353 (0)71 962 1733 www.theoarsman.com

County Mayo

♣ Enniscoe House

With crackling log fires, warm hospitality and good
home cooking, Susan Kellett's 17th century house on
the shores of Lough Conn has great charm. Beautiful
big bedrooms furnished with antiques have lough and
woodland views and the main rooms include a very
fine drawing room, and a more intimate dining room,
where Susan's delightfully simple dinners are served.
Strongly seasonal menus make good use of home-
grown and local produce in dishes like poached
salmon, fresh from one of the neighbouring loughs or
rivers, and there are homely desserts such as rhubarb
and orange crumble, or farmhouse cheeses - which are
also offered as part of an excellent breakfast.
Castlehill Ballina Co Mayo +353 (0)96 31112
www.enniscoe.com

Mary's Bakery & Tea Rooms

Ballycastle is a brilliant village. Remote, beautifully
located and cultured, it even has the perfect pub in
Polke's immaculate old world shop and bar, just up
the road from Mary Munnelly's homely restaurant.
This is the perfect place to stop for some tasty home
cooking. Baking is the speciality, but Mary does "real
meals" as well - home-made soups like smoked bacon
& potato, and free range chicken dishes. Walkers love
the full Irish breakfast and, depending on the
weather, you can tuck in beside a real fire or enjoy sea
views from the garden. Home-made chutneys and
jams on sale too.
Main Street Ballycastle Co Mayo
+353 (0)96 43361

♣ Stella Maris Country House Hotel

Once you find Ballycastle, you will want to stay – and Terence McSweeney and Frances Kelly have just the place for you. This mid 19th century coastguard regional headquarters makes a very special small hotel, restored by proprietors who have created a warm and stylish home from home with magnificent sea views. Admirably simple, seasonal cooking is by Frances, or under her direct supervision: organic produce from nearby Enniscoe and the hotel's own gardens, also Ballycastle lamb, and the local organic salmon, from Clare Island, then refreshing desserts using seasonal fruits. A very enjoyable experience – and delicious breakfasts too.

Ballycastle Co Mayo
+353 (0)96 43322 www.stellamarisireland.com

Café Rua

Wholesome, home-made fresh food is the order of the day at the McMahon family's highly-esteemed café, and careful sourcing of ingredients is a point of pride - thus pasta dishes are based on the excellent Noodle House pastas from Sligo, Irish farmhouse cheeses are supplied by Sheridans cheesemongers, fish comes from Clarkes of Ballina - and ingredients for 'the full Irish' (sausages, puddings) come from renowned butchers, Kelly's of Newport. Although very serious about the food they serve, the tone is light-hearted, with cheerful oilcloths and a large blackboard menu listing good things. Also at: Rua, café, deli and bakery on Spencer Street.

New Antrim Street Castlebar Co Mayo
+353 (0)94 902 3376 www.caferua.com

♣ Newport House

Former home of the O'Donnells, Earls of Tir Connell, this fine creeper-clad house has been close to the hearts of fisherfolk for many years – oenophile owner, Kieran Thompson, is himself a former fishing guest - but all enjoy the warmth of this gracious place. John Galvin (chef since 1983) displays no interest in fashion, instead producing meals of magnificent relevance. "Cooking which reflects the hospitable nature of the house" showcases home-produced and local foods, notably superb home-smoked salmon (only wild salmon is used) and ultra-fresh produce from a walled kitchen garden that has been worked since 1720, established before the house was completed.

Newport, Co Mayo
+353 (0)98 41222 www.newporthouse.ie

An Port Mór

With his interest in freshness and quality, and sound, no nonsense cooking, the friendly and talented Euro-Toques chef Frankie Mallon delights everyone lucky enough to find his atmospheric restaurant. The food is Irish and local with an emphasis on fish; suppliers are credited – and local staff share a knowledge of the foods featured on the menu: treats like Inishturk lobster, Clew Bay king scallops, and delicious fresh mackerel, sit alongside rump of Mayo lamb and less usual dishes like roasted pig's cheeks with Kelly's (of Newport) black pudding…it's delicious fare and, once hooked, the people keep on going back for more.

Brewery Place Bridge Street Westport Co Mayo
+353 (0)98 26730 www.anportmor.com

♣ Knockranny House Hotel & Spa

This spacious and well-appointed privately owned hotel has earned a reputation for genuine hospitality – and outstanding food, served in a restaurant blessed with views over handsome Westport town towards Croagh Patrick. Acclaimed head chef, Seamus Commons – a local man, returned to delight visitors with his sophisticated yet playful cooking - takes local ingredients (lobster, Clew Bay prawns, sweet Mayo lamb, samphire, oyster cress…) and classic French technique as his starting point and develops its own individualism, taking a particular delight in contrasts of flavour, texture and colour. An 8-course Tasting Menu sees this gifted chef at his best.

Knockranny, Westport, Co Mayo
+353 (0)98 28600 www.khh.ie

County Roscommon

♣ Gleesons Townhouse and Restaurant

Mary and Eamonn Gleeson's 19th century home overlooking the town square has seen big changes in the 15-odd years since they opened, with just four rooms and a coffee shop. Today, although much larger, they steadfastly continue to provide what every visitor wants: a warm welcome, comfortable rooms and first-class food. Committed Good Food Ireland members, they're the very model of what that organisation is all about, and they've turned this town into a destination sought out by food lovers. Avid supporters of local produce, they have an Artisan Food & Wine shop, and the weekly Farmers' Market is held next door.

Market Square Roscommon Co Roscommon
+353 (0)90 662 6954 www.gleesonstownhouse.com

County Sligo

♣ Temple House

If you love really old houses, this is the place for you. Roderick and Helena Perceval's 1665 mansion is a 'modern' build overlooking the original lakeside castle (1200 A.D); redesigned and refurbished in 1864, some of the furnishings date back to that last big revamp…It's set in 1,000 acres of farm and woodland, source of Temple House lamb and other produce of field and garden for the table, and providing woodcock and snipe shooting in winter. And then there's the *craic*: Temple House is a venue for occasional one-off events, and traditional Irish music and dancing sessions are often held nearby. 'Quirky Cooks' cookery demos too.

Ballinacarrow Ballymote Co Sligo
+353 (0)71 918 3329 www.templehouse.ie

♣ Cromleach Lodge Hotel & Ciúnas Spa

Christy and Moira Tighe's very special hotel enjoys one of the finest views in Ireland, overlooking Lough Arrow. It has earned a reputation as a luxurious retreat for discerning guests, and for exceptional food – and, although it has grown larger of late to accommodate weddings, it remains a wonderful place to stay and the refurbished older rooms are especially desirable. Moira Tighe (a former GCGuides Chef of the Year) remains very involved with the kitchen; her menus are based on meticulously sourced, mainly local, ingredients - and specialities created over the years feature, as ever, along with new dishes.

Lough Arrow Castlebaldwin via Boyle Co Sligo
+353 (0)71 916 5155 www.cromleach.com

♣ Coopershill House

One of Ireland's most delightful and superbly comfortable Georgian houses, the O'Hara family's sturdy granite mansion was built in 1774 to withstand the rigours of a Sligo winter and it's a warm and friendly place. Immaculately maintained and luxurious, it retains some fascinating features - notably a Victorian rolltop bath with integrated cast-iron shower 'cubicle', all in working order – and a reputation for wholesome countryhouse cooking. Coopershill Venison is produced here (and available to purchase) so you may well find delicious speciality on the dinner menu – roast loin with red wine sauce is a favourite - along with other seasonal fare including produce from their neatly maintained vegetable garden.

Riverstown Co Sligo
+353 (0)71 916 5108 www.coopershill.com

Hargadon's

This famous and much-loved traditional bar is a listed building c.1860 and, much to the delight of its many fans, recently re-opened following a lengthy closure.

Now it's back in all its glory, restored and renovated with its snugs and fires and grocery shelves intact (and the marble counter cleaned and back in place) – and still offering the same warm welcome. And then there's the food. Chef Joe Grogan sources ingredients carefully for his enticing menus and, with stylish cooking, an old-world ambience, and lovely service, it all makes for a great experience – and you might get some traditional music too. Home bakes offered in the afternoon.
O'Connell Street Sligo Co Sligo
+353 (0)71 915 3709 www.hargadons.com

Lyons Café

In business since 1878 and still with its original shopfront, a visit to the magnificently traditional Lyons Department Store is must when visiting Sligo; it's a joy to find a quirky owner-run store these days and, on the first floor, you'll find fresh and wholesome locally-sourced food: 'Possibly the oldest café in Sligo town', Lyons Café opened in 1923 and has changed little since. However, while retaining the best of older ways – especially the good scones and treats for those of sweet tooth, served with lashings of cream - the food also appeals to the more contemporary palate. Sligo's best kept secret, perhaps.
Quay Street Sligo Co Sligo
+353 (0)71 914 2969 www.garystafford.com

Tobergal Lane Café and Osta Café & Wine Bar

Brid Torrades is a leading figure in Irish food, active in the Euro-Toques and Slow Food campaigns for better food, and well-known for her ardent support of local organic food and small producers. The freshness of local ingredients gives immediacy to the food at her two cafés in Sligo Town, and even modestly described dishes (notably the soups) have real depth of flavour; breads and pastries are a speciality, baked by in-house patissier Julien Vial, also Irish cheeses – including the rarely seen local Tullynascreen herb goats' cheese - and charcuterie. Local beers at Tobergal Lane too, plus Friday night jazz.
Tobergal Lane Café Off O'Connell Street
+353 (0)71 9146 599 www.tobergallanecafe.ie
Osta Café Garavogue Weir View (near Hyde Bridge)
Stephen Street Sligo +353 (0)71 914 4639 www.osta.ie

WWW.IRELAND-GUIDE.COM FOR MORE OF THE BEST PLACES TO EAT, DRINK & STAY

Recipes

carrot & sea spaghetti salad

Ralph Waldo Emerson's definition of a weed as 'a plant whose virtues have not yet been discovered' is particularly true of seaweeds... They can be used whole as a vegetable, ground or flaked as a herb in cooking, or to sprinkle over food as a replacement salt and/or pepper. In this colourful dish, willowy sea spaghetti and delicate carrot strips combine with a sweet garlicky dressing, to create a salad that seaweed expert Prannie Rhatigan (www.prannie.com) makes regularly for demonstrations - it never fails to delight even first time seaweed tasters. The seaweed used is sea spaghetti, which is very easy to recognise - the name says it all.

Serves 4-6

15g/¹/₂ oz sea spaghetti, dried, or a handful of fresh sea spaghetti

30ml/2 tbsp lemon juice

15ml/1 tbsp wine vinegar

4-5 carrots, unpeeled

Dressing:

45ml/3 tbsp good quality olive oil

20ml/1¹/₂ tbsp lemon juice

5 ml/1 tsp coarse whole grain mustard and honey

15ml/1 tbsp mixed seaweed

2 cloves garlic, crushed

A pinch of cayenne pepper

A pinch of grey (unrefined) sea salt

To prepare the sea spaghetti: Rinse dried sea spaghetti and soak in warm water for 1 hour, or steam briefly until al dente. If using fresh sea spaghetti, rinse well and steam for 10 minutes until al dente.

Rinse the seaweed again and then marinate in lemon juice and wine vinegar for a few hours, or overnight.

Set aside some full length strands to decorate, then chop the remainder into 2.5-5cm (1-2 inch) pieces.

Wash the unpeeled carrots well, and slice into long, fine lengths with a vegetable peeler.

To prepare the salad: Combine the dressing ingredients in a small jug or bowl. Pour the dressing over the carrots and sea spaghetti and leave for at least an hour allow to marinate before serving.

smoked salmon
& cream cheese omelette

As long as there are a few free range eggs in the kitchen, it's easy to rustle up a quick and tasty meal. While it has plenty of fancier relatives (tortilla, frittata, and many more…), in our family 'flat egg' was the down-to-earth name for this open omelette, and it's the most versatile dish imaginable. It can be made with whatever other ingredients are to hand and, while speed and simplicity are the bottom line - my father often made it after coming in, hungry, from the garden - this version is also special, thanks to the inclusion of delicious smoked salmon.

Serves 4

8 eggs, preferably free range

2 tbsp chives, chopped

1 tbsp basil, chopped

Salt and freshly ground black pepper

1 tbsp/15 ml olive oil or rapeseed oil

50g/2oz soft feta style cheese, diced

75g/3oz smoked salmon, preferably Irish organic, thinly sliced and chopped

Red onion slices to garnish

Salad leaves and brown bread to serve

Preheat the grill on high.

Whisk the eggs with the chives, basil and seasoning.

Heat a non-stick pan over moderate heat, with the olive oil.

Pour in the egg mixture and stir for a moment or two, allowing the liquid egg to flow on to the base of the pan.

Scatter on the diced cheese and continue cooking until the egg is almost set but still moist on top.

Add the smoked salmon pieces, pressing the salmon lightly into the egg.

Place the pan under the hot grill for 1-2 minutes, to finish cooking.

Cool for 2 or 3 minutes, and then loosen the edge with spatula and slide onto a large plate.

Cut into wedges, garnish with red onion slices and serve warm with a leaf salad or a seasonal green vegetable, and some freshly baked brown soda bread.

Roast Loin of Pork with Apple & Spinach Stuffing

The three main ingredients in this recipe have been in common use in Irish kitchens for centuries and it still makes a delicious meal. Free range Irish pork production is increasing but it is slow to filter through to mainstream retail sales; a few specialist butchers stock it, but it's more likely to be found through farm shops, farmers' markets and online farm sales.

Serves 6-8

2kg/4^1/$_2$ lb loin of free range pork
Salt and freshly ground black pepper
1 onion, peeled and sliced
60ml/4 tbsp water
Juice of 1 orange

Stuffing:

50g/2oz dried apricots, chopped
*50g/2oz spinach, blanched and chopped
(or use 2-3 tbsp chopped parsley)*
50g/2oz hard Irish farmhouse cheese, grated
*1 cooking apple, eg Bramley's Seedling,
peeled and grated, or finely chopped*
Grated rind of ^{1}/$_2$ of the orange

Topping:

*15ml/1 tbsp mild wholegrain Irish mustard,
eg Lakeshore or Dalkey*
30ml/2 tbsp Demerara sugar

Preheat the oven at 350°F, 180°C, gas mark 4.

Prepare the stuffing, by putting all the ingredients into a bowl and mixing well together.

If the joint has the skin on, remove it to cook separately for crackling. Place the meat, fat side down, on a chopping board and spread the stuffing over it. Roll up and tie neatly with cotton string; season. Put the joint in a roasting tin with the peeled and sliced onion and the water. Cook uncovered for about 35 minutes per 450g/1 lb.

If making crackling, score the pork skin, rub in a little salt and roast in a separate tin until brown and crunchy. The drippings are perfect for cooking roast potatoes in. 40 minutes before the end of the cooking time, pour off the liquid into a small saucepan and discard the onion. Add the orange juice to the liquid. Spread the joint with mustard and sprinkle with the Demerara sugar. Return the joint to the oven and turn the heat up to get a crisp finish. Boil up the juices, thicken if you like and serve with the sliced meat, roast potatoes and fresh vegetables.

carrageen Moss with a compôte of Garden Berries

This recipe comes from Rathmullan House on the Fanad Peninsula in Co Donegal, where carrageen moss is a very plentiful seaweed. This lovely, simple dish (often known as 'carrageen pudding') is a traditional Irish way of using carrageen as a setting agent, and it is equally at home among the desserts at dinner, or on the renowned breakfast buffet served at Rathmullan each morning. Poached seasonal fruits make the perfect partner - this compôte is made with soft fruit from the organic walled garden at Rathmullan House.

Serves 4

10g/¹/₂oz dried carrageen moss

30ml/2 tbsp sugar

1 egg, preferably free range

1.8 litres/3 pints milk

Compôte:

100g/4 oz (total weight) seasonal mixture of berries, eg strawberries, raspberries, blackberries, blackcurrants, blueberries, or loganberries

100ml/4 fl oz cold water

20ml/2 dsp caster sugar

To make the carrageen pudding: Soften the carrageen in cold water; this also helps to wash it. Strain. Mix the sugar and egg together and set aside. In a saucepan, bring the milk to boiling point then, after shaking off all the excess water, add the carrageen. Stir gently, then turn down the heat to a simmer, and cook, stirring occasionally, for 15 minutes. Whisk in the egg and sugar mixture. Remove from the stove and strain into a clean bowl. Pour into a serving bowl (or into individual dishes) and place in the fridge to set for at least 30-45 minutes.

To prepare the compôte: Put the sugar and water into a saucepan; heat to dissolve the sugar, and bring to the boil. Add the berries and reduce the heat to very low, then cook for about 10 minutes. Pour into a serving dish and allow to cool.

To serve: Arrange the compôte and carrageen moss to complement each other, and serve.

Northern Ireland:
Belfast, Antrim, Armagh, Down, Fermanagh, Londonderry & Tyrone

Northern Ireland is a world unto itself. It is everything from lakelands and forests through handsome mountains to a varied seacoast with sheltered inlets, tide-riven channels, unspoilt beaches, imposing headlands, open ocean, towering cliffs, and Rathlin, one of Ireland's most interesting inhabited offshore islands. Amidst the ruggedness, there are large tracts of immaculate farmland with pretty villages, busy towns and lively cities. Despite being only half the area of Belgium, there are distinctive regions which closely match the old counties. In the north, as in the rest of Ireland, people are comfortable with the concept of the county. It's a size of terrain with which they can identify, and for the visitor the six northern counties each provide the minimum of a day-size touring area, while the more attractive regions comfortably provide interest, entertainment, and hospitality for as long as you might wish.

Rathlin Island, Co Antrim

About the Region

Belfast is Ireland's newest major city. The others were originally monastic establishments or river crossings which became Viking trading bases which in turn were expanded by the Normans. But in the Belfast region, the main monastic centre was fifteen miles east at Bangor where the Vikings later settled nearby, while the Normans fortified Carrickfergus across in County Antrim in 1180. Until the late 16th Century, Belfast wasn't marked on maps. But once it got going, this prime site at the head of the lough rapidly outstripped everywhere else, such that by 1900 it was the largest city in Ireland, and a global force in heavy industry developed around the enormous shipyards.

Although some relics of the industrial greatness survive, there are also buildings of a gentler style from earlier times. The great era of expansion from 1850 to 1910 is exuberantly expressed in the heavily-domed neo-classical City Hall (1906), though the City Hall pales in comparison with Government Building (1932) dominating the hill at Stormont east of the city. However, Queen's University (1845) suggests a more thoughtful approach, and despite the powerful architectural images, Belfast today is a vibrant, friendly and very human place which revels in its capacity for reinvention and zest for life.

Out of town, County Antrim's boundaries are clearly set by the sea to the north, east and southeast, by river and lake to the west and southwest, and by Belfast to the south. Only towards the southwest is there landward interface between Antrim and Down. From low ground in the west along the Bann and Lough Neagh, the county rises steadily through the Antrim plateau to the commanding heights of a coastline at its most spectacular. There is the unique attraction on the north coast of the Giant's Causeway - a World Heritage site - and Rathlin off Ballycastle. There's the quiet charms of the seaside villages clustered at the foot of the lovely Antrim Glens along the east coast, and along the north coast, there are handsome cliffs and sand-dunes, the latter providing some of Ireland's finest golf links around the resort town of Portrush.

At the other end of Northern Ireland, Fermanagh contrasts vividly with Antrim. In a country of many lakes, rivers and canals, it's quite an achievement to be the most watery county of all. Fermanagh is the only county in all Ireland within which you can travel between the furthest extremities entirely by boat, using the many lakes and channels of the River Erne.

Southeast of the historic county town of Enniskillen, Upper Lough Erne is a maze of small waterways which have meandered their way into Fermanagh from the Erne'e source in County Cavan. To the northwest, the river channels open out into Lower Lough Erne, an inland sea set off against the spectacular heights of the Cliffs of Magho.

County Armagh is apples and archbishops. In the more fertile northern part of the county, orchards are important in the local economy, while the cathedral city of Armagh itself is the ecclesiastical capital of Ireland, and many a mitre is seen about it. Its significance long pre-dates Christian times. Emhain Macha - Navan Fort- to the west of the town, was a royal stronghold and centre of civilisation more than 4,000 years ago. The county's northern boundary, the inland freshwater sea of Lough Neagh, provides sand for the construction industry, eels for gourmets, and recreational boating of all sorts.

East of Armagh, County Down rings the changes in elegant style, from its affluent shoreline along Belfast Lough - the "Gold Coast" - through the rolling drumlin country which provides Strangford Lough's many islands, with the view southward to the purple slopes of the Mountains of Mourne soaring to the highest peak of Slieve Donard (850m). Seen across Down's patchwork of prosperous farmland, they have a beauty which is in keeping with the well-groomed style, set off by a much-indented coast which is the longest of any county in Northern Ireland.

When its boundaries were first defined for "modern" times, County Londonderry was known as the County of Coleraine, named for the busy little port on the River Bann a few miles inland from the Atlantic coast. It was an area long favoured by settlers, for Mountsandel nearby is where the 9,000 year old traces of some of the oldest-known habitations in Ireland have been found.

Today, Coleraine is the main campus of the University of Ulster, with the vitality of student life spreading to the nearby coastal resorts of Portstewart and Portrush in the area known as the "Golden Triangle", appropriately fringed to the north by the two golden miles of Portstewart Strand. Southwestward from Coleraine, the county - which was re-named after the City of Derry became Londonderry in 1613 - offers a fascinating variety of places and scenery, with large areas of fine farmland being punctuated by ranges of hills, while the rising slopes of the Sperrin Mountains dominate the southern boundary.

The road from Belfast to Derry city sweeps through the Sperrins by the Glenshane Pass, and from its heights there's the first glimpses westward of the Donegal highlands. It's a hint of the new atmosphere in the City of Derry itself. This lively place, with Ireland's best-preserved walls, could claim to be the most senior of all Ireland's cities, as it can trace its origins directly back to a monastery of St Colmcille, otherwise Columba, founded in 546AD.

Tyrone is Northern Ireland's largest county, yet its geography appears to be dominated by a range of mountains of modest height, and nearly half of these peaks seem to be in the neighbouring county of Londonderry. That's how it is with Tyrone and the Sperrins, with broad upland territory and moorland giving the impression that the Sperrins are even more extensive than is really the case.

It's a character-forming sort of place, the ancestral homeland of a remarkable number of early American Presidents, and this connection is commemorated in the Ulster American Folk Park a few miles north of the county town of Omagh. In such a land, the lower country and the fertile valleys gleam like jewels, and there's an abiding impression of a reasonable living - and indeed prosperity - being wrested from a demanding environment.

The Mountains of Mourne at Newcastle, Co Down

Northern Ireland:
Food of the Region

Largely rural and still staunchly traditional in most areas – something now recognised as a plus, as traditions long lost elsewhere remain a vibrant part of everyday life in Northern Ireland, making for a distinctively different culture - the region shares many traditions with Scotland, which is just 12 miles away at its closest point, between Torr Head and the Mull of Kintyre. The influence is seen especially in the **BAKING** which is a great strength of Scottish cooking and, quite rightly, Northern Ireland's pride and joy; and, of the region's wide range of excellent baked goods, the Ulster Scots tradition of using oats and potatoes in bread and cakes is of special interest, with POTATO CAKES, POTATO BREAD, FADGE and BOXTY among the many speciality dishes that are unique to, or originated in, Northern Ireland. As elsewhere in Ireland, bicarbonate of soda ('bread soda') is the traditional raising agent, used together with buttermilk, which is a by-product of butter production – and traditionally enjoyed as a drink as well as to mix the soda breads (white, wheaten and fruit), potato bread and pancakes (drop scones) and contribute to their distinctive flavour and texture. A combination of convection (oven) and griddle (over heat) baking is used to make, for example, the round loaves with their distinctive crosses (for even cooking), which divide into farls (quarters). Like scones, soda breads are best served just-cooled from the oven and thickly spread with salty butter – and must be eaten on the day of baking; but this is no hardship, as they are quick to prepare – and leftovers can be fried in bacon fat for breakfast, as an addition to the Ulster Fry.

Small **BAKERIES** thrive in almost every town and village, sometimes in the same family for several generations, and the baking tradition is unique. Although their local customers would probably be surprised to find that their everyday purchases are regarded as unusual, visitors enjoy the distinctive range of baked goods offered – especially visitors from Britain, where craft bakeries are almost a thing of the past - are also charmed by the bakeries themselves. They all make a familiar range of soda bread (white), wheaten bread and batch loaves, potato breads and drop scones, together with various

With a dramatically varied landscape and coastline, Northern Ireland is remarkably diverse for its size and this is reflected in its food: although the region shares many products with the rest of Ireland, the character of the food is unique. Whether you visit the beautiful Glens of Antrim, the dramatic Causeway Coast and its fertile hinterland, the upland areas of the scenic Sperrins Mountains in the west, the Fermanagh lakelands, or the amazing world within a county that is Down – which takes in not only world-famous beauty spots like the Mountains of Mourne and Strangford Lough, but also some of the region's most fertile farmland, and its major sea fishing ports – you will find outstanding produce, much of which finds its way to Belfast and other towns and cities for visitors, shoppers, cooks and chefs to enjoy.

savouries, fruit tarts, tea bracks, cakes and biscuits – and each will have its own variations of scones, 'wee buns' and 'tray bakes'.

'Good plain food' is the backbone of traditional fare in Northern Ireland and the outstanding fresh food products are mainly basic, everyday ingredients of the highest quality that can transform simple cooking into memorable meals: **POTATOES**, of course, of varying types are grown throughout the region, with early Comber Potatoes from County Down a special point of pride, and other areas such as Glens of Antrim Potatoes putting their stamp on later varieties. The region can claim a number of outstanding **MEATS** with easily recognised names – Sperrin Lamb and Fermanagh Black Bacon, for example – and, with rare breed **BEEF**, **PORK** and **LAMB** increasingly appreciated, a growing number of producers are opting to specialise in organic and/or free range production; these speciality meats are becoming more easily available each year and they will be seen on restaurant menus as well as in the butchers that continue to thrive in every community, farmers' markets and **FARM SHOPS**. Top quality **VENISON** (branded Finnebrogue or Oisin) has become synonymous with Northern Ireland in recent years too.

Small **family FARMS** are the norm here and, needing to diversify and often keen to educate, some of the most interesting and unusual farms welcome visitors to experience rural life first hand, as well as to buy their produce. The best farmers are passionately dedicated people, committed to protecting the environment and encouraging bio-diversity; some offer accommodation, with or without meals, some allow people to walk on their farms, or they may organise courses and events. The farms listed here are all outstanding for their produce and perhaps other reasons too, so a visit to their websites is recommended to keep up with their news and see what's on offer.

Rural communities have a tendency to turn their backs on the sea, and that has certainly been a factor in the culinary history of this region. With a long and varied coastline, abundant lakes and rivers - including Lough Neagh, renowned for its Silver Eel Fishery – there has been no shortage of top quality fish and seafood, but much of it has been exported, to find its way onto top restaurant menus in Britain and Europe. But now, with seafood restaurants enjoying unprecedented popularity, there's great emphasis on local **FISH and SEAFOOD** throughout

Donaghadee, Co Down

Northern Ireland, and also a revival of the traditions associated with collecting and using **SEAWEEDS**. Wild and cultivated **SHELLFISH**, mainly from Strangford Lough, Dundrum Bay and Carlingford Lough, are highly prized and feature on the best restaurant menus. Salmon is the most popular fish; although wild salmon is now a treat reserved mainly for anglers, excellent Glenarm farmed salmon is produced off the Antrim coast and it is available both fresh and smoked. More unusual specialities include Ardglass potted herrings, which were commonplace when herrings were abundant and are still sold as snacks in some butcher's shops and coastal fish stalls; not to be confused with rollmops, the rolled fillets are marinated and baked with vinegar, spices and breadcrumbs. Another unusual snack is dulse, a chewy seaweed sold in pubs, and now also used as a flavouring in cheese and savoury biscuits; like **Yellow Man**, a yellow honeycomb-like confectionery that is unique to Northern Ireland, dulse is traditionally associated with Auld Lammas Fair at Ballycastle. **FRESHWATER FISH** abundant in the inland lakes and rivers of the region include pike and brown trout; also Pollan, a freshwater herring, and Dollaghan, a type of trout found in Lough Neagh – which is Britain and Ireland's largest freshwater lake, and one of the most productive eel fisheries in Europe. Although **EEL FISHING** is currently banned elsewhere in Ireland for conservation purposes, restrictions have not been imposed in Northern Ireland to date and eel is a unique feature on menus here; traditionally they may be dipped in flour, fried in butter and served with white onion sauce and creamy mashed potato, but creative chefs are now giving both fresh and smoked eels starring roles in more contemporary dishes.

With one of the world's oldest licensed distilleries attracting record numbers of visitors to the little town of Bushmills (www.bushmills.com) in Co Antrim, the **DRINK** especially associated with the region is, of course, **WHISKEY** – which is used widely in cooking as well - but **CRAFT BEERS** are also beginning to make their mark; there are only four micro breweries in Northern Ireland but, with their products earning high praise from critics and pleasing a growing

number of discerning drinkers, they punch way above their weight. A growing number of pubs stock craft brewed beers and some - the John Hewitt (www.thejohnhewitt.com) in Belfast is an outstanding example – specialise in stocking a wide range, with guest beers and events spreading the message. Some microbreweries own their own pub or restaurant – The White Horse Inn (www.whitehorsesaintfield.com) at Saintfield is part of the largest of the micro-breweries, the Whitewater Brewing Company, which is based near Kilkeel, Co Down; and Northern Ireland's oldest independent brewery, Hilden Brewery, owns Mollys Yard (www.mollysyard.co.uk) in Belfast.

Traditional Fish & Chips

Northern Ireland's **SPECIALITY DISHES** tend to be traditional, beginning with the Ulster Fry, which is a variation on the Traditional Irish Breakfast (bacon, sausages, fried egg, mushrooms and tomato, served with tea or coffee, toast and marmalade) plus the magic local ingredient of fried potato bread and/or soda bread. Once the routine start to the day for farming families, a fry is now more likely to be a treat reserved for weekends and holidays - which is the reason visitors will find it on every breakfast menu, often alongside other hot dishes such as porridge (made with pinhead or rolled oats, and sometimes served with cream, honey and perhaps a splash of Bushmills whiskey) and other lighter choices, possibly including fish. Variations on the Ulster Fry are also sometimes served in the early evening for high tea (the 'meat tea'), together with bread and jam, tea and cakes. Still to be found on some menus, this was once common in country areas throughout the country and is now unique to Northern Ireland, where it may also include (or be replaced by) another local speciality known as 'vegetable roll', a mixture of minced meat and vegetables which is sold by butchers and served sliced.

County Antrim

There are many ways to experience the food culture of **BELFAST,** and a fun idea to get know the city through its food and drink might be to sign up for one of the **Belfast Bred** (www.belfastcity.gov.uk/lovefood)

summer walking tours in which "you'll sample the delights of Belfast food and discover the city's fascinating culinary history in the company of Barney, a chef from RMS Titanic. Restored to life following the melting of the iceberg in which he had been frozen, Barney has two and a half hours to complete an ingredient hunt in contemporary Belfast and recreate the famous ship's launch menu. If successful, Barney will cook the Titanic Centenary Dinner in 2012." Well it's certainly different and on the tour, which begins at Sawers Deli on College Street and ends in St George's Market, you'll encounter many of the foodie treats, producers and chefs highlighted in this book.

Seafood, potatoes, cheese and chutney – and good whiskey to wash them down with, these are among the good things to look for in Antrim… After a long period with very little cheese making activity in the area,

Belfast Bred Culinary Tour

Damian and Susan McCloskey's **Causeway Cheese Company** at Loughgiel (+44 (0)28 2764 1241; www.causewaycheese.com) caused quite a stir with their distinctive hexagonal Causeway Cheeses, which are both a commercial success and a source of pride throughout the region. And what better accompaniment for these fine cheeses than Virginia Maxwell's range of unusual chutneys and relishes, made with locally sourced fresh products? You'll see her **Causeway Chutneys** (19, Semicock Road, Ballymoney, Co Antrim BT53 6PX +44 (0)28 2766 6394; www.vmaxwell@tinyworld.co.uk) in local butchers and craft shops and they offer something a little different - the range includes apple & Bushmills whiskey, plum & cardamom, tomato relish, and apple and clove jelly.

For many people, the small town of Bushmills is a key destination when visiting Northern Ireland, and the historic **Old Bushmills Distillery** (2 Distillery Road Bushmills BT57 8XH +44 (0) 28 2073 3218; www.bushmills.com) is certainly well worth a visit. The original licence to distil whiskey was granted to

the Bushmills area in 1608 – for the 400th anniversary a special limited edition 'Bushmills 1608' whiskey was created. Bushmills is the only distillery in Ireland currently making a triple-distilled malt whiskey, the secret of the unique combination of smoothness and richness that genuinely sets Bushmills apart – the portfolio includes five award-winning whiskeys: Bushmills, Black Bush, Bushmills 10 year Malt, 16 year Malt and 21 year Malt. Visitors can see whiskey production – and taste the results, and it's advisable to phone ahead to book a time.

The Glens of Antrim are renowned for the quality of their potatoes and, since 1972, a relatively small organisation, **Glens of Antrim Potatoes** Ltd (118 Middlepark Road Cushendall Co Antrim BT44 0SH +44 (0)28 2177 1396; www.goapotatoes.co.uk), has been supplying a range of potato varieties from the Cushendall area to leading Irish retailers. They work closely with acclaimed Belfast chef Paul Rankin, an avid supporter of high quality local produce, in developing production of new varieties to suit changing market demands, such as reintroducing the traditional Fianna and Arran Victory varieties.

Fishing for wild salmon off the Antrim coast was a way of life for many small communities until recently, but conservation measures have made that a thing of the past. Many would say that farmed salmon is no substitute, and high quality farmed salmon is certainly rare - but it is to be found here, and is the salmon of choice for many top chefs. Based near the castle in the charming village of Glenarm, **Glenarm Organic Salmon** (8 Castle Demesne Glenarm Co Antrim BT44 0BD +44 (0)28 2884 1691 www.glenarmorganicsalmon.com) has had organic status since 2001 and is renowned for its excellent flavour and texture, due to sustainable organic aquaculture practices and the clean, fast moving coastal waters of the Irish Sea which give it muscle tone. The company - which saw its stock wiped out by a jellyfish invasion in November 2007, but is now back in full production - produces up to 500 tonnes of organic salmon each year, which is distributed to discerning customers throughout the UK and overseas markets.

SEAWEED harvesting also has a long history in Northern Ireland, having been appreciated for many generations as a food and a natural medicine. Like many traditional crafts, it fell by the wayside in recent years but a revival of interest has opened up new markets for entrepreneurs like Robert McColm, of **Atlantic Ocean Delights** (60 Mill Road Larne Co Antrim BT40 3BX +44 (0)28 9338 2743), who harvests a range of edible seaweeds from the Antrim coast, including dulse and carrageen moss as well as lesser known varieties, for supply to speciality shops in Belfast. He also offers a vast range of seaweeds for sale from his stall at St George's Market on Saturdays - where Nick Price of Nick's Warehouse is a regular customer, buying mixed seaweeds for his breads.

Craft brewing is enjoying a gradual renaissance in Ireland, and it began in 1981, with the opening of Seamus and Ann Scullion's **Hilden Brewing Company** (Hilden, Lisburn, Co. Antrim BT27 4TY +44 (0)28 9266 0800; www.hildenbrewery.co.uk); it is now managed by their son Owen, while their daughter Frances manages the Tap Room Restaurant in the Georgian Courtyard of Hilden House, adjacent to the brewery. You can sample the beers here, also at Mollys Yard, Belfast, and a growing number of pubs, restaurants and off licences.

county Armagh

Synonymous with apples, 'The Orchard County' has a history of apple growing that goes back 'forever'; St Patrick, the early monasteries, William of Orange are among the many with historical references linking apples – and cider – to the area, and there are many folk customs associated with apples, especially at Hallowe'en. Of today's 4,500 acre production the main variety grown is Bramley's Seedling, a relatively modern apple dating from the 19th century, with most of the crop prepared for apple sauce and bakery, and the rest retailed whole or juiced. In recent springs a **Bramley Apple Blossom Fair** has been held at **Loughgall Manor Estate and Country Park** (Main Street, Loughgall, Armagh BT61 8HZ; +44(0) 28 3889 2900; between Portadown and Armagh via the B77), which is in the heart of the apple growing area. It has a walled garden containing a fascinating **Heritage Orchard** with a collection of 130 native Irish apple varieties established by The Armagh Orchard Trust (+44 (0)28 3889 2312); and the research centre, Agrifood & Biosciences Institute (AFBI) is also on the property (+44 (0)28 3889 2344; www.afbini.gov.uk). Aside from their historical importance, old varieties are of interest because they flourished before chemical treatment for pests and diseases was commonplace, so they tend to have natural resistance to diseases such as scab – and their flowering habits made them less vulnerable to late frosts, providing quality fruit over longer harvesting periods. Armagh Bramley Apples are among a very small number of Northern Irish products to have applied to the European Commission for PGI (Protected Geographical Indication) status. Others include Northern Ireland Beef, Lough Neagh Eels and New Season Comber Potatoes.

Although most of the area's Bramley apples are processed for commercial use, some growers have more diverse orchards and use their crops for artisan production of speciality products such as **PRESSED JUICE** and **CIDER.** For example, Kenneth and Faith Redmond, the current generation of a long-established fruit growing family, make pure **Barnhill Apple Juice** (Barnhill Farm, 23 Drumanphy Road, Portadown, Co. Armagh BT62 1QX; +44 (0)28 3885 1190). They grow traditional varieties to produce their pure, naturally cloudy pressed juices, made directly from whole fruit, with no additives; they now also make flavoured blends by including berry juices, elderflower or cinnamon ('liquid apple pie'!), for example. You'll

find it in local restaurants and it's on sale from selected retailers at St George's Saturday Market, Belfast, and from the farm. Not far away, the Troughton family's **Armagh Cider Company** is based at Ballinteggart House (73 Drumnasoo Road, Portadown, Armagh BT62 4EX; +44(0)28 3833 4268; www.armaghcider.com Contact Kelly Troughton, Mon-Fri 9-6).They also sell apples on to other commercial operators, and make a pure pressed juice, AJ Apple Juice, but their USP is real cider produced exclusively from additive-free fresh pressed apple juice; look out for the original Carsons Crisp Cider and a new slightly sweeter version, Maddens Mellow Cider, launched in 2010. Although there is a history of cider making in the area, these products are unique – the background information on their website is interesting, and you'll also find details of some appealing niche products including mulled cider and natural cider vinegar.

Where there are apple orchards can **PIGS** be far away – well, in Armagh there's no need to look further than Tandragee, where Kenny and Jennifer Gracey rear free-range Glouchestershire Old Spot and Saddleback pigs, at **Forthill Farm**

Forthill Farm, Co Armagh

Forthill Farm, Co Armagh

the retail sector, an Irish Food Writers' Guild Award winner Wilson's Country has earned a reputation for reliable quality and it is a brand to know and trust when shopping – look for the ones packed in paper bags. They also supply peeled potatoes to the food service sector and a lesser known fact is that they're the largest fresh cut fruit processors in Ireland, supplying the retail and food service sector.

County Down

On the eastern flank of Northern Ireland – in fact the island of Ireland's most easterly point is near Ballyhalbert, on the Ards Pensinsula – Down is varied and blessed with great beauty, especially in the Strangford Lough and Kingdom of Mourne areas. The region's main fishing ports are all in Co Down - at Ardglass, Kilkeel and Portavogie - and the land is also extremely productive, with the area known especially for beef, lamb and potatoes.

If travelling with children, make a note to consider visiting Stewart and Lorraine Donaldson's **Ark Open Farm** (296 Bangor Road, Newtownards, BT23 7PH; +44 (02)8 9182 0445; www.thearkopenfarm.co.uk). Its main aim is the preservation of rare and endangered species of domestic animals; set in forty acres of unspoiled countryside, it is home to about two hundred animals, of all kinds - cattle, sheep, pigs, poultry, goats, donkeys, llamas, alpacas, ponies - all tame and friendly. Open all year.

As well as the wide range of top quality **FISH AND SEAFOOD** supplied by the three main ports on the Down coast, **Strangford Lough** is renowned for certain species, notably mussels, scallops and Dublin Bay prawns (langoustine). Fishing is limited, as a conservation measure - there is no fishing by mobile gear (ie trawling, scallop dredging etc) anywhere in the Lough, although pot fishing is permitted. No fishing for shellfish is permitted by mechanically propelled vehicle unless with a Fish Culture Licence - but a certain amount of non-intrusive fishing still takes place; hand diving for scallops, for example, is permitted in season, November to April. Mussels are

(80 Ballymore Road, Tandragee, Armagh, BT62 2JY; +44 (0)28 3884 0818/ +44 (0)771 0804 819; www.forthillfarm.co.uk). Excellent for flavour, succulence and good, crisp crackling when roasted fresh, the bacon and gammon are dry cured and sausages (available in a choice of flavourings, including apple and cider) have a very high meat content. The Graceys also rear rare breed **BEEF** - Longhorn and Belted Galloway, selected for their flavour, cooking quality and healthy benefits – and the cattle are naturally raised to the same high standards, as the pigs. Visitors are welcome and they have a Farm Shop.

And to complete the meal: **POTATOES**. Craigavon is the base for one of Ireland's leading potato packing and distribution companies **Wilson's Country Ltd** (25 Carn Road, Carn Industrial Estate, Craigavon, Armagh BT63 5WG; +44 (0)28 3839 1029; www.wilsonscountry.com). Known to public mainly for the range of pre-packed potatoes they supply to

*Oyster and Mussel Farming,
Carlingford Lough, Co Down*

usually fished from farmed beds (but only with a Fish Culture Licence) and, as elsewhere in Northern Ireland, there are restrictions on the numbers of crabs and lobsters which can be landed in any day if you are not a licensed fisherman.

Portavogie is synonymous with big fresh prawns (the magnificent Dublin Bay prawn/ langoustine) and further south, there are not only busy fishing ports but also specialised fisheries: **Dundrum Bay Oyster Fishery** (5 The Quay Dundrum, Newcastle, BT33 0LS; +44 (0)28 4375 1810), for example, has farmed mussels and oysters in Dundrum Bay on the northern edge of the Mountains of Mourne since 1984, whilst **Mourne Seafood** (www.mourneseafood.com) has shellfish beds in Carlingford Lough to the south of the mountains which – along with fresh fish from Kilkeel and Annalong - supply their three restaurants in Belfast, Dundrum and Newcastle. Mourne Seafood also retail fresh fish, and run **The Mourne Seafood Cookery School** at the Nautilus Centre in Kilkeel.

Some of the best – and most interesting – **MEATS** in the region are produced in Co Down, and it is well worth seeking them out. Perhaps the most famous is the renowned **Finnebrogue Venison** (23 Finnebrogue Rd, Downpatrick BT30 9AB; +44 (0)28 4461 7525; www.finnebrogue.com) which is produced on Finnebrogue Estate by Denis and Christine Lynn, who have farmed free-range pure-bred red deer here since 1997. A key factor in their success is that only deer under 24 months old are used, providing the consistently tender and delicately flavoured meat that has earned it an unrivalled reputation with chefs and food lovers in Ireland and beyond – not too many products can count Heston Blumenthal, Rick Stein and Jimmy Doherty among their fans. Finnebrogue also produce exceptional sausages and for these they include organic and free range pork from selected farmers. You'll see Finnebrogue venison (also branded Oisin) on restaurant menus and at good retailers, including Marks & Spencer.

Just down the road between Downpatrick and Killyleagh, at **Pheasants' Hill Farm** (+44 28 4461 7246; www.pheasantshill.com), Janis and Alan Bailey specialise in rare breed animals, and their achievements are truly astonishing. They breed **traditional farm animals** - Tamworth, Berkshire, Saddleback and Gloucester Old Spot pigs, and also Southdown sheep and Eriskay ponies – and hens, too, of several traditional breeds (Dorkings Welsummers, Light Sussex and Alconas), to produce both eggs and table birds. Naturally reared for flavour by traditional farming methods (free range and organically fed), their meats – which include dry-cured ham and bacon and excellent homemade sausages – are sold at their farm shops here and in Comber and, along with home grown fruits, feature on the breakfast menu at the farm guesthouse.

And not far away, at **Churchtown Farm** (Churchtown Road Strangford BT30 7AT; +44 (0)28 44881128; www.churchtownfarmorganicproduce.com), Dale and John Orr produce a range of **organic meats** which

includes not only several breeds of beef (Aberdeen Angus, Shorthorn and South Devon) and pure bred Lleyn lamb, known for its tenderness and flavour – but also **MUTTON**, which is available from October to March. The Orrs are very hands-on farmers, personally managing every aspect of production right through to delivery – to their own shop (where they also sell rare breed pork from other organic farms), the farmers' market, and their own meat delivery service.

There are many other great farmers in the area too, of course – including other breeders of Lleyn sheep – but those mentioned illustrate very well the exceptional quality of meats produced in Co Down.

But you certainly don't have to be a meat or fish eater to appreciate the great basic foods produced in this area, as one particular crop – **EARLY COMBER POTATOES** – is famous throughout the length and breadth of Ireland. The shelter of the Mournes and the Ards peninsula, together with the frost protection afforded by nearby Strangford Lough, create a mild microclimate around Comber that allows exceptionally advanced potato crops, coming in as early as May or June - and the arrival of the first new potatoes is greeted with as much acclaim as Dubliners welcome the season's first salmon from the River Liffey. The McKee family, who run the **Comber Potato Company** (3 Moat Road Comber Newtownards BT23 5QX; +44 (0) 79 0069 3668) from their farm overlooking Strangford Lough, are important growers in the area and keenly value the special reputation their crops have earned for quality and unique 'earthy, sweet and nutty flavour' as well as their earliness. A group of Northern Ireland potato farmers including the McKees were responsible for submitting an application to register 'New Season Comber Potatoes' as Protected Geographical Indicator (PGI Status). This would match Comber potatoes with the famous Channel Island early potatoes, Jersey Royals, which have protected status.

When driving in Co Down, you're bound to spot one or two delivery vans sporting the smart livery of fifth generation farmers Martin and Tracy Hamilton's innovative company **Mash Direct** (81 Ballyrainey

Clandeboye Yoghurt, Co Down

Road Comber BT23 5JU; +44 (0) 28 918 78316; www.mashdirect.com). It all started with a dream to have a production facility on their own farm for making champ (mashed potato with fresh chopped scallions); today they are market leaders in mashed potato and ready-to-serve vegetable and cabbage products, serving the growing market for healthy convenience foods. What sets them apart is firstly that they choose vegetable varieties for their taste above all, and then everything is grown, steam-cooked and packaged on the farm – and, with a commitment to get their products 'from field to fork in 24 hours', freshness is of the essence too. They're no slouches when it comes to sales and distribution either, so you'll find them on the shelves of the multiples as well as more local stores like Superquinn, SuperValu and Spar. A great Co Down success story – no wonder David Cameron chose to call in here on his first visit to Northern Ireland after becoming Prime Minister.

Other excellent growers in Co Down include John McCormick of **Helens Bay Organic Gardens** (Seaview Terrace, Holywood, BT18 9DT; +44 (0)28 9185 3122; www.helensbayorganicgardens.com), who operates a great system of vegetable bag deliveries based on **online orders** – you just fill in a form and there's free delivery within 15 miles of Helens Bay. Another source of fresh

organic produce in the same area is the **Camphill Community** (Shore Road Holywood BT18 9HX; +44 (0)28 9042 3203; www.camphillholywood.co.uk), who have an Organic Farm Shop as well as a Bakery and Café.

Diversification and innovation is the name of the game in farming these days, and on the Clandeboye Estate near Bangor, the flavour of the milk from Lady Dufferin's small award-winning **DAIRY** herd of pedigree Holstein and Jersey cows is the secret behind their **Clandeboye Estate Yoghurt** (Bangor Co Down BT19 1RN; +44 02891815194; www.candeboye.co.uk).

There are some very good artisan ice creams made in Co Down too. **Glastry Farm Luxury Ice Cream** (Glastry Farm 43 Manse Road Kircubbin Newtownards County Down BT22 1DR; +44 (0)7802 207838; www.**glastryfarm**.com) for example, is made by the Taylor family, who are Good Food Ireland members and have had a dairy farm here since 1856. Their milk produces a beautifully rich and creamy ice cream, which is made freshly each day in their own creamery – the fact that it is offered in National Trust and Taste of Ulster restaurants speaks for itself, and it's also on sale in good farm shops and selected stores, such as SuperValu. And a small south Down

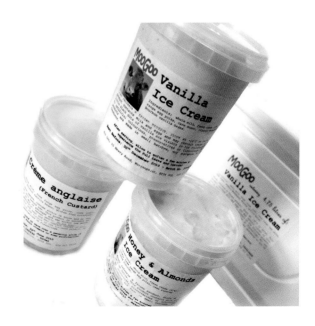

producer that deserves to be more widely known is **MooGoo** (5 Killowen Old Road Rostrevor Newry Co Down BT34 3AD; +44 (0)28 417 39704; www.moogoo.co.uk). They make a superb vanilla ice cream (always the acid test), custard and moreish chocolate sauces – and have been winning Gold at the Great Taste Awards. They're only made in small batches and taste very 'homemade' – look out for them at shows, fairs, farmers' markets, various select shops and direct from their kitchen (contact for details) and on the menu in some local restaurants, including the excellent Copper in Warrenpoint.

The great Northen Ireland **BAKING** tradition is very much alive and well in Co Down. Some outstanding examples include the organic bakery and shop at the **Camphill Community Holywood** (8 Shore Road Holywood BT18 9HX; +44 (0)28 9042 3203; www.camphillholywood.co.uk); **Heatherlea Bakery** in Bangor; **The Bay Tree** in Holywood (ww.baytreeholywood.co.uk), **Knott's Craft Bakery & Coffee Shop** (www.knottsbakery.co.uk; +44 (0) 28 9182 6365) in Newtownards and Holywood; **The Cookie Jar** in Newcastle; and **The Corn Dolly** in Newry/Warrenpoint. Bakeries generally have coffee shops/cafes attached.

Where good bakers thrive, artisan **PRESERVES** are usually to be found too - and the brand to look out for here is **The Offbeat Bottling Company** (Unit 73, Enterprise House, 2-4 Balloo Ave, Bangor, BT19 7QT; +44 (0) 28 9147 7555); they have a long track record (the Irish Food Writers' Guild singled them out for praise as early as 1999) and specialise in unusual flavour combinations, but they make excellent classics too – a thick cut orange marmalade has been a recent Great Taste Awards Gold winner, for example. Their range also includes chutneys, mustards, oils and vinegars; find them at good delis and St George's Saturday Market in Belfast.

CRAFT BREWING may have been slow to catch on in Ireland and the number of microbreweries is still small throughout the country, but there is growing enthusiasm for drinks with real flavour and individuality. Of Northern Ireland's five microbreweries (including Strangford Lough Brewing Co, which is a contract brewery, and the fledgling Inishmacsaint Brewing Company in Co Fermanagh), the oldest is **Hilden Brewing Company** (www.hildenbrewery.co.uk) and the largest is the **Whitewater Brewery** (Tullyframe Road Kilkeel BT34 4RZ; +44 (0)28 4176 9449; www.whitewaterbrewery.com) which was established in

1996 by Bernard Sloan and his wife Kerry, near the fishing village of Kilkeel. Pre-booked tours of the Whitewater brewery are available, and they have a pub, **The White Horse Inn** (+44 28 9751 1143) in Saintfield, where you will find their full range of beers on tap, and which has won CAMRA (Campaign for Real Ale) NI pub of the year several times. They produce a range of beers, of which the three leading bottled brands are Belfast Ale, Belfast Lager and Clotworthy Dobbin (all available online within the UK); several have won international acclaim, including their bestseller, the Belfast Ale (an aromatic russet ale), which is a Great Taste Awards Gold award winner. A number of pubs and restaurants offer their beers from the cask, including The John Hewitt and several others in Belfast; the Mourne Seafood Bar serves a special Oyster Stout developed by Whitewater and their bottled ales are offered in restaurants such as Nick's Warehouse and Made in Belfast, and in off licences throughout Northern Ireland.

A more recent arrival is **Clanconnel Brewing Company** (PO Box 316 Craigavon N. Ireland BT65 9AZ; (+44 (0) 7711 626770; www.clanconnelbrewing.com). Northern Ireland's fourth craft brewery, it was founded in 2008 by Mark Pearson, a craft brewer based in Waringstown, Co Down. The beer is handcrafted in small batches, using traditional artisan methods, and free from artificial colours and preservatives; the first − Weavers Gold blonde ale, a 'refreshing easy drinking beer to enjoy on its own or with food' − has earned admiration, and a second product McGrath's Irish Red, was launched at the 2010 John Hewitt Beer Festival, Belfast.

County Fermanagh

Mention Fermanagh and the chances are that the response will be 'Fermanagh black bacon' − in a county famous for its pork, this special product made (and trade-marked) by Enniskillen butcher Pat O'Doherty (www.blackbacon.com) has earned its place in the foodie hall of fame. The O'Dohertys keep

their own herd of free range Saddleback pigs on Inishcorkish Island on Upper Lough Erne, and the product is a great credit to both the standard of meat and the artisans who make it into unique dry-cured Fermanagh black bacon. Visits to the island can be arranged by appointment, and the shop in Enniskillen is a must-visit too - a model Northern Ireland butchers.

Also linked to an island, and possibly a local monastery, Gordon Fallis's **Inishmacsaint Brewing Company** is a new micro brewery that is working with the Food Technology Centre at Loughry College to produce Northern Ireland's first wheat beer; initial production is small and they supply exclusively to Russell & Donnelly in Enniskillen.

Nearby, on the shores of Lough MacNean, Slow Food members Gavin and Fidelma Goodman's small family run **MacNean Farm** (141a Lattone Road, Belcoo, BT93 5DZ; +44 (0)28 6638 6642; www.macneanfarm.com)

Fermanagh Black Bacon

is dedicated to the preservation of rare breed Tamworth, Oxford Sandy and Black Pigs. There's also a small flock of Soay and Hebridean Sheep, three Saanen-cross goats, two Exmoor Ponies, and a collection of geese, turkeys, ducks and hens. Tours of the farm are available for groups by arrangement and, not only can you buy Tamworth pork products (succulent meat with great flavour) but also free range chicken and duck eggs – and books from their 'piggy bookshop'! Mail order/ **online shop** too.

For other **MEATS** - mainly **beef, lamb and chicken** - a company that has been saying it for Fermanagh very effectively recently is **Kettyle Irish Foods** (Manderwood Business Park, Lisnaskea, BT92 OFS; +44 (0)28 6772 3777; www.kettyleirishfoods.com). This family-run business takes great pride in the standard of its meats, and has not only earned recognition through awards (including an Irish Food Writers' Guild Award) but top chefs are proud to credit Kettyle products on their menus.

Kettyle Fermanagh Chicken

An outstanding **DAIRY** product to keep an eye open for is Steve Giles and Gareth Grey's handmade **Tickety Moo** ice cream (Oghill Farm Killadeas, BT94 1RG; +44 (0)28 6862 8779; www.tickety-moo.com), which is made with the extra creamy milk of their Jersey cows. The range of flavours includes gorgeous 'Just Jersey', Rhubarb & Custard Crumble and Valrhona Chocolate... Tickety-moo ice cream shop is open afternoons, mid April – late September and you can see the cows being milked at 4.30pm daily in summer.

As elsewhere in Northern Ireland, excellent **BAKING** is a great strength of the local food culture in Fermanagh - good examples include the Charles family's **Cherry Tree Home Bakery** (Main Street, Lisnaskea, BT92 0JD; +44 (0)28 67721571; www.wheresmywheaten.com) where traditional breads like wheaten, fruit soda, plain soda and treacle are always on the shelves alongside scones, pancakes, potato bread and soda farls - but you'll also find continental breads, gluten free products, and cakes ranging from the familiar boiled fruit cake to more contemporary treats. Sandwiches and ready meals are offered, too. In Enniskillen, head for **Leslie's Bakery** (10 Church Street, Enniskillen; +44 (028) 6632 4902), where artisan baker Leslie Wilkin specialises in making the great traditional bakes of the area, in the traditional way.

With so much water around, Fermanagh is naturally green – and if you want to see a *really* **green** farm, take a trip to Teresa and Hugh O'Hare's **Orchard Acre Farm** (Moynaghan North Road, Lisnarick, Irvinestown, BT94 1LQ; +44 (0)28 6862 1066; www.orchardacrefarm.com), the eco-tourism centre of the Lakelands. These Good Food Ireland members say 'we don't grow food...we nurture it!', and they use only their own produce at the events they cater for, plus organic and fair trade products. Fancy a green wedding, an event in an eco-barn, a garden –themed gourmet evening or cookery class, or a tepee holiday? Then this is the place for you.

County Londonderry

Great baking and outstanding meats, especially free range and organic meats – these are the key foods to look out for in Co Derry, and they aren't hard to find.

Ditty's of Castledawson

Take the **BAKING** for a start – there are many great examples to choose from in Co Derry, which is home to one of the most famous bakeries in the island of Ireland, **Ditty's of Castledawson**, and its sister operation in Magherfelt. Another highly respected business, **Hunter's Bakery** (5-11 Market Street, Limavady, Londonderry, BT49 0AB; +44 (0)28 7772 2411), is based in Limavady (where there is also a café and gift shop) and has shops in Ballykelly and Coleraine. This fourth generation family run bakery specialises in traditional Northern Irish products and has been "making and baking" since 1920; now run by master baker Brian Hunter with his sons David and Sean, it's at the heart of the local community and sources everything possible locally - organic milk, eggs and flour - and constantly reinvests in the bakery itself and in training, so it should be around and thriving for a long time yet.

Some outstanding **MEATS** are produced in this area. The happy Landrace pigs that Trevor Barclay raises like

babies on **Mossbrook Farm** (Durnascallon Lane Desertmartin, BT45 5LZ; +(0)28 7963 3454) on the edge of the Sperrins are the secret behind the wonderful **sausages and dry-cured bacon products** that have earned him a reputation throughout the region – and a fan base that includes Rick Stein. The famously meaty sausages contain no unwelcome additives and, as well as producing delicious bacon (which cooks to make perfect crispy bacon every time), Trevor Barclay hand-cures the legs on the bone to produce an outstanding mild-cured gammon. Nearby, in the foothills of Keady Mountain just outside Limavady, **Mullan's Organic Farm** (84 Ringsend Road, Limavady, BT49 0QJ (+44 (0)28 777 64940; www.mullansorganicfarm.com) is in a lovely location overlooking Lough Foyle to the mountains of Donegal. In this beautiful place, Michael Mullan produces a diverse range of products – **Aberdeen Angus beef and hill lamb, poultry and eggs** - with the admirable aim of selling "good quality, locally produced organic food to local people", and this friendly farm also has self-catering accommodation available.

County Tyrone

The lush pastures of Tyrone make for excellent grazing and, of the county's many good things to eat, specialities they have made their own include sweet-flavoured **beef** and **dairy products.**

Traditionally, butchers had their own family farms and, although not as common as it once was, it remains a point of pride for many either to raise their own cattle or have close longterm relationships with the local farmers who supply them. Belfast butchers McGee's (www.mcgeesfoods.com), for example, produce their own mainly Angus and Hereford **BEEF** on their fourth generation traditional farm at Gortnagarn in the highlands of Co. Tyrone; the cattle are moved around between different parts of the farm and mature slowly, thriving on the hill pastures and spending most of the winter outside, and finally ending their lives humanely at an abattoir nearby.

A number of **DAIRY** products are unique to the county, including the **organic milk** supplied by the innovative

Castlederg company **Organic Doorstep** (125 Strabane Road Castlederg, BT81 7JD; 028 816 79989; www.organicdoorstep.net), both from their own herd and other small organic farmers in the area. On a much bigger scale, **Fivemiletown Creamery** (14 Ballylurgan Road Fivemiletown BT75 0RX; +44 (0)28 8952 1209; www.fivemiletown) is a remarkable co-operative, dating back to 1898. Cheesemaking is the speciality, using cows' and goats' milk from about 60 farmers in Fivemiletown and the Clogher Valley. Although producing on a much larger scale than artisan cheese-makers do, the creamery shares a similar commitment to the quality of the raw ingredient and the skills of the cheesemaker – and their products have achieved widespread recognition, including a number of Great Taste Awards. Their range includes speciality cheese such as the well known Boilie (balls of fresh fresh cheese in sunflower oil, with garlic, herbs and peppercorns), and O'Reilly's goat cheese with mustard and chives. Most of the production goes for export but there is still plenty to go round – the names that may be seen in shops or on restaurant menus are Ballyoak, Oakwood, Cooneen (goat), Ballyblue, Ballybrie, Boilie, and O'Reillys (goat), plus a range of everyday cheddar style block cheeses in several strengths.

Some interesting speciality cheeses are made in Co Tyrone, at **Erganagh Dairy** (29, Erganagh Road, Castlederg, BT81 7JQ; +44 (0)28 8167 062). These include **Springwell Sheep's Cheese**, which is made using the milk from Linda Gourley's flock of 150 milking ewes and is Northern Ireland's only sheep's cheese. There is also a **Springwell Speciality Goat's Cheese** and, although both are niche products, they are finding a ready market with cheese lovers who are allergic to cows' milk.

The health benefits of **SPROUTING SEEDS** are fast gaining recognition (an organic farmer in Co Cork is even investigating the practicalities of feeding them to cattle) so it is no surprise to find that **Good4U** (Loughry College 45 Tullywiggan Road BT80 8SG www.good4u.co.uk, +353 (0)71 914 5408) of Cookstown and Sligo is flying. Their informative website gives up to date information on the health benefits of eating sprouting seeds and shoots, and the range of products and retail outlets is growing all the time. They offer seeds, a sprouter and a special low speed juicer as well as a great range of sprouted seeds and shoots; awards are mounting up, and include an Irish Food Writers' Guild award for their BroccoShoots.

Northern hill farms

Four of the Best...

Fermanagh Free Range Chicken

Chicken with a texture and well-developed flavour
that attracts the attention of leading chefs and
speciality food retail outlets is a rare bird these days.
But, since 2004, producing really good chickens
been one of Maurice Kettyle's main aims at Kettyle
Irish Foods. This innovative food company
developed out of their 500 acre family farm in Co
Fermanagh, and now produces a variety of speciality
food products, such as dry-aged beef, Lough Erne
lamb, naturally reared Irish rose veal - and chickens
raised for flavour. The beef, in particular, is now well
known and is proudly credited on some of the best
restaurant menus in Ireland and Britain. The
chicken, however, has been a well-kept secret until
recently. No ordinary chickens, they follow a
carefully planned programme of good husbandry,
welfare and feeding - and they are genuinely free to
roam and scratch around outside in paddocks. Like
all animals, a stress-free end also has a beneficial
effect on the eating quality; add skilled butchery, a
processing system that does not use water and the
end result is tender, fully-flavoured, succulent flesh -
chicken like it used to be.

Kettyle Irish Foods Manderwood Business Park
Lisnaskea Co Fermanagh BT92 OFS
+44 (0)28 6772 3777 www.kettyleirishfoods.com

Clandeboye Estate Yoghurt

The folk at Clandeboye Estate are inordinately
proud of their cows. And so they should be, as
their small herd of 80 pedigree Holstein and
Jersey cows has won an outrageous amount of
rosettes - and it's the rich milk they make from the
lush grass on this 2,000 acre estate that makes
Northern Ireland's first artisan cows' milk yoghurt
so special. And then there is the personality of
their colourful owner, Lady Dufferin, the talented
artist who created the oil painting of those very
cows that is used on the packaging - and brands it
so effectively. It all came about because they, like
so many other farmers, needed to diversify. So
they did their homework, got expert advice - and
now make a product they are rightly proud of,
that contains no additives or preservatives and is
blended by hand, using the traditional techniques
that produce a rich creamy texture without high
fat content. Available in natural and Greek styles,
it tastes wonderful on its own or with fresh berries
(or with Clandeboye's own granola, perhaps) and
can be used as a recipe ingredient. You can also
call to the Estate Dairy, beside the Clandeboye
Lodge Hotel, to buy the product and perhaps see
the cows for yourself.

Crawfordsburn Road Bangor Co Down BT19 1RN
+44 (0)28 9181 5194 www.candeboye.co.uk.

Ditty's Home Bakery & Coffee Shop

Robert Ditty - second generation artisan baker, inspirational campaigner for real food and keen beekeeper - is the friendly shopkeeper at Ditty's of Castledawson while his wife, Helen, runs their second shop in Magherafelt. Robert is an avid supporter of his fellow artisan producers - just check out 'Ditty's Friends' on the website and you'll see what goes into their foods. A by-word for all that's best about the Northern Irish baking tradition, their bakery is a-buzz with life from the small hours, when work begins on the soda farls, potato and wheaten breads to be sold in local stores that day - and early shoppers popping in for a brown soda or coffee and a chat are greeted by the aroma of freshly baked loaves and trays of 'wee buns' warm from the oven. The most famous products are those with a longer shelf life - the delicious Ditty's Irish Oat Biscuits and Shortbread are distributed to speciality stores in Ireland and abroad; variations include thick triangular oat biscuits, celery & pepper, and dulse & sesame - all ideal companions for farmhouse cheeses - and several kinds of shortbread. And he'd like you to become a beekeeper too! (www.inibeekeepers.com)

44 Main Street Castledawson Co Derry BT45 8AB
+44 (0) 28 7946 8243 www.dittysbakery.com
Also at: 3 Rainey Street Magherafelt Co Derry BT45 5AA.

The Causeway Cheese Company

Although once common practice on farms everywhere, artisan cheesemaking was a craft lost to Northern Ireland for many years, until Damian and Susan McCloskey established The Causeway Cheese Company in 2001. Now, in the village of Loughgiel, near the Giants Causeway and the Glens of Antrim, they make a range of five cows' milk cheeses, using locally produced pasteurised milk. Easily recognisable by their distinctive hexagonal shape (reflecting the rock formations of the Giants Causeway) they are named after nearby townlands, emphasising their individuality: the original cheese, Drumkeel, is seasonal (mild and crumbly, made only in summer) and Castlequarter is a mature cheddar style cheese. There are also three flavoured cheeses - Ballyknock (black pepper); Ballybradden (herbs and garlic); and Coolkeeran - this is an interesting cheese, flavoured with the seaweed, dulse, which is a traditional food and abundantly available along this coast. They also make a clean-flavoured hard goat's milk cheese, Ballyveely. Online sales are planned, meanwhile Causeway cheeses are showcased in restaurants and sold in speciality food shops throughout the region. Visitors are welcome by arrangement and cheeses can be tasted on site; cheese making takes place several times each week in season (April-September).

Unit 1 Millennium Centre Lough Road Loughgiel
Ballymena Antrim BT44 9JN
+44 (0)28 2764 1241 www.causewaycheese.com

Yellow Man at Auld Lammas Fair, Ballycastle, Co Antrim

Where to Buy

the Special Foods of Northern Ireland

A guide to food shops, markets, farm shops, local stores and internet suppliers in Belfast, Antrim, Armagh, Down, Fermanagh, Londonderry & Tyrone

Shopping for good food in Northern Ireland should be a rewarding activity, and there is no shortage of information to introduce the visitor to the foods of the region and the places where they are to be found. Browsing the web will bring up a wide range of information - too much perhaps, as some sites can be confusing; the best place to start is the official tourism website **www.discovernorthernireland.com** which has a lot of food-related material including features, chef profiles, speciality foods, lists of food markets, shops, artisans, even a 'seasonal larder'… Dip in and have a look, you should find plenty of interest.

Belfast

Arcadia Delicatessen 378 Lisburn Road BT9 6GL *(+44 (0)28 9038 1779 info@arcadiadeli.co.uk www.arcadiadeli.co.uk)*. Long-established speciality food shop, with wines and some of the best local artisan foods – Clandeboye Estate Yoghurt, Causeway Cheeses, Bay Tree Relishes, Ditty's Oatcakes – alongside comparable products from abroad… Christmas hampers are a speciality. Closed Sun.

Avoca Belfast 41 Arthur Street Belfast BT1 4GB *(Shop +44 (0)28 9027 9950 Café reservations +44 (0)28 9027 9955 www.avoca.ie)*. Belfast sister to the famous craftshop, foodhall and café with its flagship store in Kilmacanogue, Co Wicklow; meticulously sourced ingredients sit happily alongside the home baking for which they are famous - much of which can be bought in the delicatessen.

SD Bell & Co Ltd 516 Upper Newtownards Road Knock Belfast BT4 3HL *(+44 (0)28 9047 1774 www.sdbellsteacoffee.com)*. This legendary tea and coffee emporium dates back to 1887 and was an institution in Belfast city centre until moving out to these suburban premises in the 1970s. Headquarters, retail sales and 'Leaf & Berry' coffee bar/restaurant are now all located at Knock, where the tradition continues; their premium quality teas and coffees are sold here, at St George's Market and quality outlets throughout Northern Ireland. An excellent **online shop** also offers tea and coffee accessories.

Cargoes 613 Lisburn Road BT9 7GT *(+44 (0)28 9066 5451 www.cargoescafe.com)*. Over more than a decade in business, Radha Patterson's very special little delicatessen and café has maintained a great reputation - fine delicatessen products are meticulously sourced, and the same philosophy applies to the food served in the café.

Clydesdale & Morrow 581 Lisburn Road BT9 7GS *(+44 (0)28 9066 2790 www.clydesdaleandmorrow.com)*. Owners Anne and Antoinette gave their respective family names to this unique cheese shop on the Lisburn Road, and with it a certain gravitas. The classy classical frontage is easy to spot and cheese lovers will be captivated, not only by the great range of cheeses offered in perfect condition and the informed, helpful staff, but also the choice of accessories, hampers and giftware. Irish cheeses stocked include well-established names from the South (Ardrahan, Durrus, Gubbeen, Cashel Blue) and newer cheeses from local Northern Irish producers such as Causeway Cheese Company, Fivemiletown Creamery and Springwell – and Ditty's oatcakes to accompany.

Chef Shop 29 Bruce Street BT2 7JD *(+44 (0)28 9032 9200 www.thechefshop.net)*. Specialist kitchenware shop, offering unusual lines; **online sales** (delivery in Ireland & UK); monthly cookery demos.

Deane's Deli Bistro 44 Bedford Street BT2 7FF *(+44 (0)28 9024 8800 www.michaeldeane.co.uk)*. Deli store with casual all day dining – at night it becomes 'Vin Café'.

Equinox 32 Howard Street BT1 6PF *(+44 (0)28 9023 0089 www.equinoxshop.com)*. The place to shop for the city's most desirable kitchen/house wares and gifts. Top international brands (Alessi etc); café (seasonal menus). **Online shop.**

Ewing's Fishmongers 124 Shankill Road BT13 2BD *(+44 (0)28 9032 5534)*. In business since 1911 and currently in the stewardship of one of Northern Ireland's most respected food suppliers, Walter Ewing, and his sons Crawford and Warren. Ewing's is the fish supplier of choice for many of the region's top chefs, who appreciate the quality and freshness of their prime fish and shellfish – also excellent cured and smoked fish, including Glenarm smoked salmon.

Foodie Folk Portview Trade Centre 310 Newtownards Road Belfast BT4 1HE *(+44 (0)28 9045 5279 www.foodiefolk.co.uk)*. Forward-looking mainly **online shop**, for delivery or collection; also open to personal shoppers on Thu & Fri. The range includes some more ordinary items (ie not necessarily all free range or organic) but also superior products, eg Dexter beef, good choice of poultry including Silverhill duck and the excellent free range chicken and duck from Lissara Farm at Crossgar in Co Down, a very good fresh fish range. Mainly sourced within Ireland – exceptions include Shetlands salmon.

High Class Family Butchers 3 Atlantic Ave BT15 2HN *(+44 (0)28 9074 3535 www.owenmcmahon.com)*. Owen McMahon's north city shop is the only Elite Butchers Association (www.elitebutchers.com) member in Belfast; sells not only meats but, like many Northern Ireland butchers, also fish, poultry and fresh fruit and vegetables. But the specialities they are best known for are pork butchery (once a particular point of pride in Belfast, indeed throughout Ireland) and award-winning products, such as their sausages - steak & Guinness, steak & cracked pepper, and regular pork sausages are all excellent.

Hilden Brewing Company & Tap Room Restaurant Hilden Brewery Hilden LISBURN BT27 4TY *(+44 (0)28 9266 0800 www.hildenbrewery.co.uk)*. Ireland's longest-established craft brewery is run by the Scullion family, in the former stables of historic

Hilden House; they produce five ales including a porter, a blonde, a premium red and two amber ales; also two bottled beers. Craft brews can be sampled both in and with food served at the adjacent Tap Room Restaurant (www.taproomhilden.com), and off-sales are available in working hours – see website for details. Try them also in Molly's Yard, The John Hewitt and other selected pubs – and at the increasingly popular beer festivals, which Hilden Brewery introduced to Ireland.

June's Cake Shop 376 Lisburn Road BT9 6GL *(+44 (0)28 9066 8886)*. Long-established traditional bakery - the place to go for Ulster classics, including Belfast Baps, scones (plain, wheaten, fruit, cherry and date), chocolate fudge cake and fresh cream pastries. Open from 7.30am, Mon-Sat.

McGee's Butchers Forestside Shopping Centre Upper Galwally Belfast BT8 6FX 028 *(+44 (0)28 9064 8885 www.mcgeesfood.com)*. This is a big business, with a number of branches throughout Northern Ireland, but Joe McGee takes great pride in the fact that his meats come from the fourth generation family farm at Gortnagarn in Co Tyrone. "People complain about the weather in Tyrone, but it's the soft mizzly rain that gives the grass and our meat their sweetness. There is no need for chemical fertilisers which force growth in the pasture and the beef. This slow easy pace is absolutely crucial to the distinctive taste and texture of our meat." Unsurprisingly, McGee's have won a string of awards over more than a decade. See website for details of other locations.

Molly's Yard 1 College Green Mews Botanic Avenue BT7 1LW *(+44 (0)28 9032 2600 www.mollysyard.co.uk)*. Owned by the Hilden Brewery (www.hildenbrewery.co.uk), this atmospheric former stables has a brewhouse on site (although beers are currently made at Hilden) and is home to a restaurant, where chef Siobhan Scullion's menus are based mainly on seasonal and artisan foods and craft beers like Belfast Blonde, Headless Dog and Molly's Chocolate Stout may be used in the cooking as well as being sold to accompany the food.

Sawer's Deli College Street Unit 7 Fountain Centre BT1 1HF *(+44 28 9032 2021)*. Belfast's 'oldest and best' deli - purveyors of the finest local produce and speciality foods from around the world since the 1890s - this is a place to relish. Current owner, Kieran

St. George's Market, Belfast

Sloan, continues the tradition of combining support for local artisan producers with exotic and novelty items – a heady mix that makes this an exciting place to visit. Especially renowned for cheeses (they stock over a hundred, including many Irish ones) and for fresh fish and shellfish, they also sell an extraordinary range of traditional (and some not so traditional) grocery products and deli items. Closed Sun.

St George's Market 12 East Bridge Street Belfast BT1 3NQ *(+44 (0)28 9043 5704 / (0)28 9032 0202 www.belfastcity.gov.uk)*. A must-visit for food lovers in Belfast at weekends, this classic Victorian covered market replaced an earlier open market that had traded since 1604. It was built between 1890 and 1896, and restored a century later with the help of Lotto funds; in recognition of the standard of both the restoration itself and the new Farmers' Market, it won the Irish Food Writers' Guild Supreme Award for Contribution to Food in Ireland in 2002, and this has since been followed by many other accolades. Markets are held at weekends (open to mid afternoon but mornings are best), with the City Food and Garden Market on Saturday and a Variety Market (which includes food, along with many other things) on Friday and Sunday; the Saturday market, especially,

attracts many of the country's best farmers' market stallholders and is one of the best markets in the UK and Ireland. St George's Market also makes a magnificent venue for a range of events hosted here throughout the year, including concerts.

Suki Tea 6 Twin Spires Belfast BT13 2JF *(+44 (0)28 9033 0938 www.suki-tea.com)*. This highly respected Northern Irish based tea company has an **online shop**. Ditty's of Castledawson are using their 'Belfast Brew' (a blend of the best leaves from the best Fairtrade tea gardens in Assam and Tanzania), for their special new Moist Irish Tea Cake. Suki Tea is described by Robert Ditty as 'smooth and bright yet strong and malty … a true ship builders' brew'.

Swantons Gourmet Foods 639 Lisburn Rd BT9 7GT *(+44 (0)28 9068 3388 www.swantonscom)*. Stewart and Gloria Swanton's speciality food store and café has a well-earned following amongst discerning Belfast people. Even in an area so well served with good places to shop and eat, it stands out for dedication to quality and value; both the carefully selected (and ever growing) range of deli fare, and the food freshly cooked on site are delicious. Baking - beautiful home baked desserts, tarts and tray bakes - is a speciality. Closed Sun.

Yellow Door Deli & Patisserie 427 Lisburn Road BT9 7EY *(+44(0)28 9038 1961 www.yellowdoordeli.co.uk)*. Simon Dougan is a key figure in the Northern Ireland food scene, known for his clear vision of simple, honest food and uncompromising standards - and the Belfast branch of his renowned Portadown business reflects this philosophy.

County Antrim

Ballylagan Organic Farm 12 Ballylagan Road Straid **BALLYCLARE** BT39 9NF (+44 *(0)28 9332 2867 www.ballylagan.com)*. No ordinary farm - Tom Gilbert's farm, near Carrickfergus, was the first in Co Antrim to achieve organic certification from the Soil Association in the early '90s, and then the first in Northern Ireland to have an organic farm outlet - and the shop was officially opened by H.R.H. the Prince of Wales, no less, on May 5th, 1999. It's a one-stop shop, open four days a week (Wed-Sat) and offering an unusually wide range of foods, including imported organic fruit, deli and store cupboard items and even organic toiletries. But the main aim is to sell their own carefully produced foods – Aberdeen Angus and Dexter beef, native British sheep, Tamworth pork, a variety of poultry and eggs, and home grown vegetables in season; no online sales, but the interesting and exceptionally informative website not only tells you about their own produce and philosophy but also lists products, with prices and special offers, so you can do the homework before shopping – and, while on the site, you'll enjoy reading Tom's 'Irregular Rant'.

Arkhill Farm 25 Drumcroone Road **GARVAGH** BT51 4EB *(+44 (0)28 2955 7920 www.arkhillfarm.co.uk)*. As well as sheep and pigs, Paul Craig has about 800 free range hens on this 10 acre organic family farm, and they also offer hostel type accommodation. The **Farm Shop** (Mon-Fri 9-5) offers organic produce including eggs; also preserves.

Country Kitchen Home Bakery Sloan Street **LISBURN** BT27 5AG *(+44 (0)28 9267 1730 www.countrykitchenlisburn.co.uk)*. Freshness is guaranteed at this home bakery, where the day starts at 3am for baker Chris Ferguson, who gets in first to start baking the breads and sodas, cakes, pastries and savouries needed for the day's orders as well as for their own bakery and restaurant. Bakery Mon-Sat 8.30-5.

County Armagh

Ballydougan Pottery Shop & Café Bloomvale House 171 Plantation Road **GILFORD** Craigavon BT63 5NN *(+44 (0)28 3834 2201 www.ballydouganpottery.co.uk)*. Originally a linen merchant's house, Bloomvale is now home to Ballydougan Pottery, where the potters can be seen at work making hand thrown stoneware kitchenware and gifts – all of which are oven, microwave and dishwasher safe. Shop; all day restaurant serving local produce and home baking; also offers self-catering cottages.

GlenTender 47a Ballymacanallen Road **GILFORD** BT63 6AE *(+44(0)75 9502 1245 www.glentender.co.uk)*. Run by three farmers - Andy Bryan from Co Down, Ivan McMullan from Co Antrim and Harry McGaffin from Co Armagh - this company specialises in premium 21-day matured Angus beef, all bred, processed and retailed 'using traditional and scrupulously ethical' methods. Outstanding tenderness, succulence and flavour have earned them multiple accolades at recent Great Taste Awards. Farm shop; home deliveries (phone-in orders). **Online shop.**

John R Dowey 20 High Street **LURGAN** BT66 8AW *(+44 (0)28 3832 2547 www.johnrdowey.co.uk)*. Established in 1936 this 3rd generation family butchers and deli offers a successful balance of tradition and innovation - and has plenty of accolades to prove it. Known especially for traditional cuts of beef and prize winning sausages, they make all their own butchery products and sell carefully selected deli products and speciality foods including Glastry Farm Ice Cream, made at Kircubbin on the Ards Peninsula (and sampled approvingly by H.R.H. Prince Charles on a visit to nearby Mount Stewart House & Gardens).

Derryhale Hampers 89 Derryhale Road **PORTADOWN** BT62 3SR *(+44 (0)28 3887 0008 / (0)79 6781 9237 www.derryhalehampers.com)*. Family run hamper company specialising in premium products including a well chosen range of artisan foods from producers throughout Ireland.

Armagh Cider Company Ballinteggart House 73 Drumnasoo Road **PORTADOWN** BT62 4EX *(+44 (0)28 3833 4268, Mon-Fri 9-6 www.armaghcider.com)*. A visitor centre is planned for the Troughton family's farm; meanwhile visitors are welcome to visit the orchards (just call ahead), and their stunning pure pressed 'AJ' Apple Juice (2 Star Gold at the Great Taste Awards), craft ciders and other unique products, including natural cider vinegar, can be purchased. Also available from Sainsbury's throughout Northern Ireland and selected outlets (see website for list).

Barnhill Apple Juice Barnhill Farm Drumanphy Road **PORTADOWN** BT62 1QX *(+44 (0)28 3885 1190)*. Ken Redmond's family have been growing fruit here for over a century and their naturally cloudy award-winning apple juice is made directly from whole fruit, with no additives except – in flavoured varieties - the juice of other whole fruit such as raspberries, blackcurrants or blackberries. Can be purchased direct from the farm and also at agricultural shows, craft fairs, farmers markets, and various select shops.

Yellow Door Deli & Patisserie 78 Woodhouse Street **PORTADOWN** Craigavon BT62 1JL *(+44 (0)28 3835 3528 www.yellowdoordeli.co.uk)*. Celebrated chef and entrepreneur Simon Dougan is particularly renowned for the speciality breads baked here every day and, while in no way restricted to Northern Ireland produce, the excellent deli/coffee shop showcases the best local foods. Outside catering and events are also a major part of the business and there's now an excellent book, 'The Yellow Door, our story, our recipes', (Blackstaff Press, 2010), in which he says, 'When I opened The Yellow Door Deli fifteen years ago, the whole idea was to provide customers

with the very food I eat every day; not stuffy, not overly lavish, just gutsy, flavoursome, honest food – proper pâtés, delicate desserts with buttery pastry and, of course, really good bread. This ethos has remained at the heart of The Yellow Door ever since.'

Forthill Farm Shop, Co. Armagh

Forthill Farm 80 Ballymore Road **TANDRAGEE** BT62 2JY *(+44 (0)28 3884 0818 www.forthillfarm.co.uk)*. Visitors are welcome to Kenny and Jennifer Gracey's farm (phone to make sure somebody is available to show you around). Their rare breed pork (Gloucester Old Spots and Saddleback) and beef (Longhorn and Belted Galloway) is on sale at the farm shop (Mon-Sat 9-5.30, late night Thu to 8pm). Orders can also be taken and delivery arranged, with discount on large orders.

County Down

Quails Fine Foods 13-15 Newry Street **BANBRIDGE** BT32 3EA *(+44(0)28 4066 2604 www.quailsfinefoods.co.uk)*. 'Purveyors of fine foods for over 100 years', this excellent family-run food hall and delicatessen evolved from a small butchers shop, and dry-aged 28 day matured Limousin heifer beef is among the many special foods available from the shop and **online**. As well as the butchery and deli there's a lovely café and art gallery.

Windsor Bakery & Café 36-38 Newry Street **BANBRIDGE** BT32 3HA *(+44 (0) 28 4062 3666 thewindsorbakery.com)*. Craft bakers since 1957, the current Master Baker, John Edwards, maintains the tradition of using the best of ingredients for the home

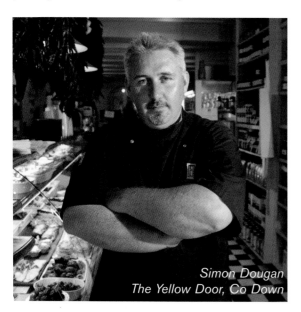

Simon Dougan The Yellow Door, Co Down

made breads, cakes buns and biscuits on sale in the shop and served in the café. Outside careering service also offered.

David Burns Butchers 112 Abbey Street **BANGOR** BT20 4JB *(+44 (0)28 9127 0073 burnsbutchers.co.uk)*. Now run by Brian, son of the late David Burns, these family butchers take pride in offering the best of local meats, including 4-5 week matured beef and 10 day matured lamb, along with prize sausages (they pioneered gluten free sausages), dry cured bacon and 'George's home cooked ham' among many other traditional and innovative prepared foods, also some other speciality products, eg Clandeoye Estate yoghurt. And this is a place to find that Northern Ireland speciality Vegetable Roll (it even featured in Rick Stein's Food Heroes series). No online sales but phone orders can be delivered.

Clandeboye Estate Crawfordsburn Road near **BANGOR** BT19 1RN *(+44 (0)28 9185 2966 www.clandeboye.co.uk)*. **Clandeboye Estate Yoghurt** Northern Ireland's only cows' milk yoghurt is made by hand daily in the estate dairy, beside the Clandeboye Lodge Hotel, where visitors are welcome (and may see the cows being milked; +44 (0)79 2979 6398, Bryan Boggs). Also widely available in local shops and throughout Northern Ireland (eg all Spar shops; St George's Saturday Farmers' Market in Belfast and speciality shops such as Swantons Gourmet Foods). The Estate gardens are also of interest, and botanical tours can be arranged (+44 (0)78 0194 9927, Fergus Thompson Firewood and Christmas trees also on sale in winter.).

Heatherlea Bakery 94-96 Main Street **BANGOR** BT20 4AG *(+44 (0)28 9145 3157)*. Traditional craft bakery (and Good Food Ireland member) selling a wide range of breads, cakes, buns, and speciality products including Ballyholme Irish oatmeal biscuits and a rich fruit loaf that has earned acclaim at the Great Taste Awards. Also well-stocked deli counter and busy café and restaurant, where local produce like Portavogie fish features in popular daily lunch specials.

Primacy Meats Food Village 26a Primacy Road (off Balloo Road) near **BANGOR** BT19 7PQ *(+44 (0)28 9127 0083 www.primacymeatsfoodvillage.co.uk)*. Originally a butchers providing a direct outlet for meats from the Bowman family's farm, this is now a busy one-stop

farm shop offering locally produced vegetables in season, home bakery and ready meals as well as the meats that made their name. Own-farm and in-store products are at the core of the business, augmented by carefully selected produce from other local farmers and artisan suppliers who are proudly credited; with a slogan like 'Meet our producers - good food begins with our suppliers' it's not surprising that they win accolades. Beef is matured for at least 30 days – it can be seen dry-ageing, through a viewing window in the farm shop – and other specialities include thick-cut bacon and slow-growing breeds of turkey, produced on the Bowman farm for Christmas. There's also an all day café, serving home-made soups, brown bread, carvery style lunches, desserts and freshly baked scone and tray bakes. Closed Sun.

Pheasants' Hill Hog Roast

Pheasants' Hill Farm Shop
3 Bridge Street Link **COMBER** BT23 5AT
(+44 (0)28 9187 8470 www.pheasantshillfarm.com).
This is the main outlet for the extraordinary range of rare breed pigs and cattle raised by Janis and Alan Bailey on their farm at Killyleagh, and the only Irish butchers selling only rare breed meat and poultry. Products offered include their highly-acclaimed sausages - a wide range, some of them named by breed rather than flavouring, eg the Tamworth butchers sausage. Also available from farmers' markets, and from **Pheasants Hill Farm** (see Downpatrick, below).

Crossgar Foodservice
Farranfad Road Seaforde **DOWNPATRICK** BT30 8NH;
(+44 (0)28 4481 1500). Wholesale suppliers well worth knowing about, and used by top chefs including Niall McKenna of James Street South. As well as offering plenty of 'ordinary' products in their vast range (over 10,000 products) there are gems,

especially in the 'Crossgar Provenance Collection', which includes dry aged Dexter and Irish Moiled cattle in its beef range, and local Lissara Farm free range duck among the poultry - one of a tiny number of Great Taste Awards entries to achieve 3 gold stars.

Pheasants Hill Farm 37 Killyleagh Road **DOWNPATRICK** BT30 9BL *(+44 (0)28 4461 7246 www.pheasantshill.com)*. Here Janis and Alan Bailey grow fruit using natural methods, and breed their rare breed animals. They also have a farm shop, as well as the main one at Comber (see above), and their delicious rare breed meat, old fashioned dry cured hams and bacon, and additive free sausages are served to B&B guests for breakfast. Outside catering is also offered, by Pheasant's Hill Farm Kitchen ('good food – fast'), using only their own and other local artisan foods; hog roasts and barbecues are specialities. Home delivery is available for meats (online sales planned).

Mourne Seafood Bar Main Street **DUNDRUM** BT33 0LU *(+44 (0)28 4375 1377 www.mourneseafood.com)*. Restaurant, with fresh fish also available to purchase.

Angus Farm Shop **GREYABBEY** *(+44 (0)28 4278 8695 www.angusfarmshop.com)*. Aberdeen Angus beef is the speciality here 'behind the yellow half door', but other meats, including their own lamb and homemade sausages and steakburgers, are also stocked, along with pork, poultry and a range of other local produce (dairy, baking, fresh fish).

Helen's Bay Organic Farm (Office: 13 Seaview Terrace **HOLYWOOD** BT18 9DT *(+44 (0)28 9185 3122 www.helensbayorganicgardens.com)*. Telephone or online orders accepted for seasonal organic vegetable and/or fruit bags.

Go! Bay Tree 118 High Street **HOLYWOOD** *(+44(0)28 9042 1419 www.baytreeholywood.co.uk)*. Every morning, owner Sue Farmer bakes dozens of her famous Cinnamon Scones for the **Bay Tree Coffee House** – now you can buy them (and many other good things, including her cookbooks) at her shop, Go!, beside the café.

Camphill Organic Farm Shop & Bakery Camphill Community 8 Shore Road **HOLYWOOD** BT18 9HX *(+44 (0)28 9042 3203 www.camphillholywood.co.uk)*. The shop stocks a wide range of organic products including locally sourced fresh vegetables and fruit,

dried foods and dairy produce and speciality chocolates. Breads on sale are all handmade and most are Soil Association certified; gluten-free, dairy-free and sugar-free options are offered, and bakery products are also available in the café, where lunch is served five days a week and 'cakes, pies and other sweet indulgences' are on offer all day, during shop opening hours.

Hannan Meats 9 Moira Industrial Estate Old Kilmore Road **MOIRA** BT67 0LZ. *(+44(0)28 9261 9790 www.hannanmeats.com)*. This quality Irish meat company now also produce under the Moyallon brand, with well known food pioneer and former owner of Moyallon Foods, Jilly Dougan, still actively involved. The company won no less than seven Great Taste Awards in 2010 for a range of meat products, including Glenarm Organic lamb rack; 21 day aged rib-eye (on the bone); Saddleback pork rack; and Dry-cured Bramley back bacon (sweet cure). The Moyallon range has also earled acclaim for products including Spiced Fruit chutney; Cool Pear and Lime Chutney; Hot Chilli Pickle. The quality products from Hannan Meats go to some of Ireland's best restaurants and hotels, and can be purchased locally at their own wholesale outlet, The Meat Merchant in Moira.

The Iona 27 Church Road **HOLYWOOD** BT18 9BU *(+44 (0)28 9042 8597)*. Small speciality wholefood shop; the range includes local produce from the Camphill Community.

Picnic 47 High Street **KILLYLEAGH** BT30 9QF *(+44 (0)28 4482 8525)*. Katherine and John Dougherty's well-named delicatessen and café near the gates of Killyleagh Castle offers simple, delicious food to eat in or out. A constantly changing range of local and

international stock is complemented by wholesome menus offering homemade soups, stews and casseroles, seasonal salads, charcuterie, artisan cheese boards and homebaked cakes. Closed Sun off season.

McCartney's Of Moira 56-58 Main Street **MOIRA** BT67 0LQ *(+44 (0)28 9261 1422 www.mccartneysofmoira.co.uk)*. Easy to spot by the queue forming out into the street, and still in the McCartney family after nearly one and a half centuries, this flower-decked shop in the pretty village of Moira is one of the oldest and best-loved butchery businesses in Northern Ireland. Renowned especially for their Award Winning Sausages in Northern Ireland (you'll see them on menus throughout the province), this impressive business is committed to supporting local farmers, and all meat is sourced within Northern Ireland.

Seasalt Deli & Bistro 51 Central Promenade **NEWCASTLE** BT33 0HH *(+44 (0)28 4372 5027)*. Aidan Small's café and deli is known for quality ingredients and an attention to flavour.

The Cookie Jar Bakery 121 Main Street **NEWCASTLE** BT34 1AE *(+44 (0)28 4372 2427)*. James Herron's craft bakery specialises in traditional breads and homemade cakes. Also at: The Market Square, Kilkeel.

The Corn Dolly Home Bakery Shop: 12 Marcus Square **NEWRY** BT34 1AE; *(+44 (0)28 3026 0524 www.corndollyfoods.com)*. Jim and Anthony O'Keeffe's traditional bakery is an institution in Newry and attracts shoppers from a wide area to purchase favourites from the tempting choice of quality breads, buns, cakes and savouries made here. Also at: Warrenpoint (with coffee shop).

Homegrown 66B East Street **NEWTOWNARDS** BT23 7DD *(+44 (0)28 9181 8318 www.homegrownni.com)*. Margaret White's greengrocery and deli is keen to promote tasty vegetables from the surrounding area, and local fruit such as Armagh apples, although imports are offered too. **Online shop.**

Knotts Cake And Coffee Shop 49 High Street **NEWTOWNARDS** BT23 7HS *(+44 (0) 28 9181 9098 www.knottsbakery.co.uk)*. Michael Knott's busy town centre bakery and restaurant is a hive of activity with customers eager to buy specialities such as fruit loaves and cakes from the bakery, or join the queue for tasty lunches in the restaurant and coffee shop at the back.

McKees Country Store, Co Down

McKees Country Store 28 Holywood Road near **NEWTOWNARDS** BT23 4TQ *(+44(0)28 9182 1304 www.mckeesproduce.co.uk)*. Third generation family farm in the Craigantlet hills, very successfully selling both their own farm produce – beef, pork and vegetables – and a range of other local produce. In addition to the butchery and fresh fruit and vegetables they started with, in the original farm shop, they now have a one-stop shop offering bakery, dairy, deli, groceries and frozen foods – and a coffee shop/restaurant. Open Mon-Sat. Also **online shop** (collection or delivery, free locally**).**

Rowallane Garden **SAINTFIELD** Ballynahinch BT24 7LH *(+44 (0)28 9751 0131 www.nationaltrust.org.uk)*. Gorgeous National Trust gardens, open 10-5 daily in summer, with a shop selling garden and gift items including some speciality foods (and there's also a secondhand bookshop, where some interesting food books might be found). Appealing food is served in the Kitchen Garden tea-room, including good home baking.

National Trust Tea Room

Churchtown Farm Organic Produce Churchtown Farm 30 Churchtown Road **STRANGFORD** BT30 7AT *(+44 (0)28 4488 1128 / (0)78 1614 1223 www.churchtownfarmorganicproduce.com)*. Organic farmers Dale and John Orr opened their farm shop (Thu-Sat 9-6) in April 2005, following a couple of years later with an **online service** (prices quoted in both sterling and euro, delivery anywhere in Britain and Ireland). Organic beef (Aberdeen Angus, Beef Shorthorns & South Devons), lamb and – unusually – mutton (Lleyn sheep) are all reared on the farm; rare breed organic pork (British Saddlebacks, Tamworth , Gloucester, Old Spot) is sourced from other organic farms within Northern Ireland and they use it to make traditional dry cured bacon and gammon, green or smoked. Meats are available fresh and (boxed) frozen. Also on sale at farmers' markets.

Corn Dolly Home Bakery 28 Church Street **WARRENPOINT** *(+44(0)28 4175 3596)*. Branch of the well known Newry craft bakery, with coffee shop.

County Fermanagh

MacNean Farm 141a Lattone Road **BELCOO** BT93 5DZ *(+44 (0)28 6638 6642 www.macneanfarm.com)*. The MacNean Farm Shop offers free range meats - rare breed pork products (bacon, gammon, sausages), pasture raised Belted Galloway beef (steaks, roasts, beefburgers) free range chicken and duck eggs – and a piggy bookshop. **Online shop**.

Leslie's Bakery 10 Church Street **ENNISKILLEN** BT74 7EJ *(+44 (0)28 6632 4902)*. Popular caft bakery specialising in traditional handmade breads, teabreads and buns.

O'Doherty's Butchers Belmore Street **ENNISKILLEN** BT74 6AA *(+44 (0)28 6632 2152 www.blackbacon.com)*. This is the first port of call for Pat O'Doherty's famed Fermanagh Black Bacon – an Irish Food Writers' Guild 'Best Irish Food Product', among many accolades; a unique local delicacy, it's dry cured and available in several versions - the oak smoked one tastes 'like the bacon that used to be left up the chimney of the farmhouse to smoke'; it can be ordered for postal delivery (see website for range of products) and there's even a Fermanagh Black Bacon Cookbook, which includes a lot of interesting information about pigs and pork. They also stock a wide range of speciality meats, and make many other products - the beef sausages, burgers and traditional black and white puddings, in particular, attract special praise.

Russell & Donnelly 28 Darling Street **ENNISKILLEN** BT74 7EW *(+44 (0)28 6632 0111)*. Run by the team who operate Merlot restaurant at the wonderful old pub **Blakes of the Hollow** nearby, this superb delicatessen, café and off licence specialises in artisan cheeses and cured meats – and stocks exclusive fine wines from small producers. They're also the first stockists of the wheat beer from Northern Ireland's newest micro-brewery, the local Inishmacsaint Brewing Company.

County Londonderry

Hunter's at the Oven Door 34 Main Street **BALLYKELLY** BT49 9HS. A favourite destination for traditional foods and home baking (see Limavady).

Ditty's of Castledawson Main Street **CASTLEDAWSON** BT45 8AB *(+44 (0)28 7946 8243 www.dittysbakery.com)*. This shop and café is the home base for Ditty's famous range of traditional breads, oatcakes and many other wonderful bakes that are Northern Ireland's pride and joy.

O'Kane Meats Main Street **CLAUDY** BT47 4HR *(+44 (0)28 7133 8944 www.okanemeats.com)*. These champion sausage makers have won multiple trade awards for butchery and retail - the shop has been a NI Butcher of the Year winner.

Belfry Deli Church Lane **COLERAINE** BT52 1AG *(+44 (0)28 7034 2906)*. Wide range of well selected Irish produce, artisan breads. Café adjacent.

Causeway Deli Unit 3, Loguestown Industrial Estate **COLERAINE** BT52 2NS *(+44 (0)87 0011 0673, Mon-Fri 9-1; www.causewaydeli.co.uk)*. **Online shop** offering a range of Irish and international speciality foods, with Causeway cheeses, Ditty's oatcakes, Kinvara salmon among the Irish products.

Kittys of Coleraine **COLERAINE** (see Hunters Bakery, Limavady).

McLaughlin's Home Bakery 3a Railway Road **COLERAINE** BT52 1PD *(+44 (0)28 7035 1387)*. Traditional home bakery, in business for over 30 years.

Moss Brook Farm 6 Durnascallon Lane **DESERTMARTIN** BT45 5LZ *(+44 (0)28 7963 3454)*. Trevor Barclay's fan base includes Robert Ditty, who uses the bacon produced at this scenically located farm on the edge of the Sperrins in both of his shops - and takes pride in explaining on his website how they are reared, slaughtered, butchered and cured. The Moss Brook Farm pigs are pedigree Landrace, born and bred on the farm, and the delicious meat - boiling bacon, dry-cured rashers, and mild-cured gammon - they provide is sold at the farm, and at St. George's Saturday Market in Belfast.

Arkhill Farm 25 Drumcroone Road **GARVAGH** BT51 4EB *(+44 (0)28 2955 7920 www.organicguide.ie)*. Visitors are welcome and hostel type accommodation is available at this 10 acre family farm, where Paul Craig has about 800 outdoor organic hens, as well as sheep and pigs. They sell arts and crafts at the farm shop along with their own organic produce - hen and duck eggs, lamb, Saddleback pork, chickens and vegetables – and operate a box delivery scheme.

Hunters Bakery & Cafe 5 -11 Market Street **LIMAVADY** BT49 0AB. *(+44 (0)28 7772 2411)*. This renowned 4th generation family run bakery and coffee shop specialises in traditional Northern Irish products, baked fresh on the premises every morning. Also at: 34 Main Street Ballykelly BT49 9HS; Kitty's of Coleraine, 3 Church Lane *(+44 (0)28 7034 2347*.

Hunter's 53-55 Main Street **LIMAVADY** BT49 0EP *(+44 (0)28 7776 2665)*. The late Norman Hunter was a household name in Northern Ireland, synonymous with quality meats, and his son Ian now runs this excellent butcher and deli with equal dedication.

Mullan's Organic Farm 84 Ringsend Road **LIMAVADY** BT49 0QJ *(+44 (0)28 7776 4940 www.mullansorganicfarm.com)*. Since gaining full organic status in 2000, Michael Mullan's traditional beef and sheep hill farm has diversified and now produces Aberdeen Angus beef and hill lamb (assorted breeds), poultry (chicken, ducks and geese) and eggs (hen and – unusually – quail). Their produce is available from several small retailers but main sales are at St. George's Saturday Market in Belfast and the farm shop (Fri & Sat 12-5). Self-catering accommodation also available.

North West Organic Co-Operative Ltd. 2 Foreglen Road Killaloo **LONDONDERRY** BT47 3TP *(+44 (0)28 7133 7950)*. Ireland's only cross-border, farmer owned organic co-operative. They sell produce wholesale and to the public via their home delivery service; organic breads are made to order for box scheme customers. They supply a range of vegetables and fruit, beef, lamb, pork, and chicken and attend Farmers' Markets in Derry, Donegal, Strabane and Coleraine every month. They also provide training, arrange educational visits and support **Derry City Guildhall Country Food Fairs**, which are hosted by the Rural Area Partnership in Derry (RAPID), Derry City Council, the Department of Agriculture and Rural Development. Events are held at Guildhall Square Derry/Londonderry, and the aim of the Guildhall Country Food Fairs is to provide an opportunity for local Organic and Speciality food producers to promote the sale and raise awareness of quality local produce. Further information from: Una Cooper Market Co-ordinator RAPID 2 Foreglen Road Killaloo Co. Derry/Londonderry BT47 3TP. *(+44 (0)28 7133 7149)* www.derrycity.gov.uk/market

McKee's Butchers 11 Fair Hill **MAGHERA** BT46 5AY *(+44 (0)28 7964 2559 www.mckeespies.com)*. Third generation family butchers, in business for over a century and – since the 1980's – especially renowned for their homemade pies.

Ditty's Home Bakery & Coffee Shop 3 Rainey Street **MAGHERAFELT** BT45 5AA. Helen, wife of Northern Ireland's most famous artisan baker, Robert Ditty, runs the Magherafelt bakery and shop, offering the

Ditty's Bakery, Co Londonderry

same excellent range of home baked local breads, pastries, cakes, oatcakes, biscuits, short breads, wee buns, scones and muffins – and the café is a popular place for a shopping break.

JC Stewarts I Union Road **MAGHERAFELT** BT45 5DF *(+44 (0)28 7930 2930 www.jcstewart.co.uk)*. "If it is a quality product, grown, reared or produced in Northern Ireland then JC Stewart Foodhall wants to stock it. That means local meat, local bacon, ham and dairy products, together with bread from a dozen local bakeries..." If only more supermarkets could match the JC Stewarts mission statement, we'd all be a lot better off. And 'local' also includes a range of homemade products, made fresh every day using local ingredients – queues form when the day's delivery of Rachel's soups and Irish stew arrive in the shop.

McLaughlins Bakery & Coffee Shop 91 The Promenade **PORTSTEWART** BT55 7AG *(+44 (0)28 7083 4460)*. Branch of the long-established Coleraine bakery, with a family-friendly coffee shop serving delicious Illy coffee to accompany their home made food.

County Tyrone

Organic Doorstep 125 Strabane Road **CASTLEDERG** BT81 7JD *(+44 (0)28 8167 9989 www.organicdoorstep.net)*. Orders: free phone 0800 783 56 56. The philosophy behind this innovative company is "that organic food should be accessible and affordable to everybody" thus Organic Doorstep delivers food – including organic milk at less than supermarket prices - produced 'as nature intended' by small farmers and growers, not multi national companies. Ditty's of Castledawson use their milk and cream right across their product range. The original products – milk, cheeses, yoghurt – have since been extended to include organic bread and bakery products, cereals, eggs, meat, vegetables, juices, nuts and fruits, even organic soaps and 'lotions and potions', all sourced locally where possible and delivered directly to addresses in Northern Ireland.

Erganagh Dairy 29 Erganagh Road **CASTLEDERG** BT81 7JQ *(+44 (0)28 8167 0626)*. Northern Ireland's first ewes' milk cheese, Springwell Sheeps Cheese, is made here using pasteurised milk from the sheep on Linda Gourley's family farm. Available plain and flavoured, it can be collected by arrangement and is sold at local markets.

Cloughbane Farm 160 Tanderagee Road Pomeroy **DUNGANNON** BT70 3HS *(+44 (0)28 8775 8246 www.cloughbanefarm.com)*. Fourth generation farmers, the Robinson family – Lorna and Sam, sons Robert and Richard, with occasional help from their nursing daughter, Clare - focus on beef (Aberdeen Angus/Limousin cross heifers), lamb (Texel cross) and free-range egg production on their185 acre farm. Now, in a beautiful and unspoilt environment, they also operate one of Northern Ireland's biggest and best organised farm shops, where they sell their own produce and that of hand picked local farmers who can live up to their telling slogan, 'Taste You Can Trust'. Selecting the best carcasses, beef is dry matured for 28 days, lamb for 10-14 days, for flavour and tenderness. They also sell locally produced chicken, pork, home cured bacon, prepared foods (including the famous Northern Ireland 'vegetable rolls') and cooked products including a range of pies. Shop: Mon-Sat (daily times vary slightly); **online shop** offers free delivery in Ireland & UK over a designated value.

Northern Ireland: Food Markets

For further information on Farmers' Markets in Northern Ireland
www.discovernorthernireland.com/Ulster-Farmers-Markets • www.bordbia.ie

BELFAST (County Antrim)

St George's Market *(+44 (0)28 9032 0202):*
Fri, Variety Market, 6am-2pm; Sat, Food & Garden
Market, 9am-3pm; Sun Market (inc local arts &
crafts), 10-4.

COUNTY ANTRIM

Lisburn Farmers' Market Last Sat 10-3.
Castle Gardens.

Coleman's Garden Centre Farmer's Market
Templepatrick. Last Sun 1-5.

Origin Farmers Market Ballymoney. Last Sat.

ARMAGH

Farmers' Market Stonebridge Restaurant Richill.

DOWN

Newry Dundalk Farmers Market Last Sat.

FERMANAGH

Enniskillen Farmers' Market Tesco carpark. 2nd Sat
9-1.30

LONDONDERRY

Coleraine Causeway Speciality Market Old Town
Hall. 2nd Sat 9-2.30

Londonderry Walled City Market City Walls. First Sat
10-4

Limavady Country Market Second Sat of the month.

TYRONE

Strabane Farmer's Market Last Sat.

Tyrone Farmers Market First Sat.

Northern Ireland:
Eat & Stay

Lough Erne Resort

Belfast

Cayenne

After over two decades as pioneers of Northern Ireland's food culture, Paul and Jeanne Rankin's large, funky restaurant is still doing what it has always done: cooking well sourced food skilfully, and presenting it with style at affordable prices. It opened as Roscoff in 1989 and was a sensation, becoming Northern Ireland's first restaurant to achieve a Michelin star and attracting foodie fans from all over Britain and Ireland. The Rankins reached the wider public and became culinary superstars through their cookbooks and the TV programme, Gourmet Ireland (1995), which visited producers and partnered artisan foods with smart cooking and ran to several series. At Cayenne, the cooking style is eclectic – but always underpinned by immaculately sourced ingredients.
7 Ascot House Shaftesbury Square Belfast BT2 7DB
+44 (0)28 9033 1532 www.rankingroup.co.uk

Deanes Restaurant

At this city centre hot spot, and currently Northern Ireland's only Michelin starred restaurant, Michael Deane continues to offer Northern Ireland's most exceptional dining experience – as he has done in a sequence of flagship restaurants that have borne his name since 1993. Uncompromising quality and impeccable attention to detail are the trademarks of this courageous and tireless pioneer of modern food: from the sourcing of raw materials to the presentation of the customer's meal everything has to be just so – qualities shared with an inner circle of talented chefs,

perhaps, but what marks Deane out is that he is also an exceptionally canny businessman. Always ahead of the game, anticipating the changing demands of his customers, he is ready for anything.
More casual sister restaurants at: **Deanes at Queens** 36-40 College Gardens Belfast +44 (0)28 9038 2111; **Deanes Deli** 44 Bedford Street Belfast BT2 7FF +44 (0)28 9024 8800; **Simply Deanes** Unit 1, The Outlet Bridgewater Park Banbridge Co Down BT32 4GJ +44 (0)28 4062 7220 www.michaeldeane.co.uk.
36-40 Howard Street Belfast BT1 6PF
+44(0)28 9033 1134 www.michaeldeane.co.uk

♣ The Fitzwilliam Hotel

A younger sister of the Fitzwilliam Hotel on St Stephen's Green in Dublin, this smart city centre boutique hotel enjoys a comparably covetable location, beside the Grand Opera House - and shares the kudos of association with Dublin's most creative chef in its restaurant, **Menu by Kevin Thornton**. The name correctly conveys a sense of honesty (Thornton does not cook here, although closely involved) and - taking a cue, perhaps, from the deceptively casual chic

that works so well for Michael Deane – the style of this affordable all-day restaurant is smart-casual, with the emphasis firmly on simple quality food, beginning with fresh local produce.
1-3 Great Victoria Street Belfast BT2 7BQ
+44 (0)28 9044 2080 www.fitzwilliamhotelbelfast.com

James Street South

Fine dining combines with Belfast warmth and value in Niall and Joanne McKenna's contemporary restaurant, housed in an old linen mill. Niall's network of valued suppliers provide his kitchen with wonderful produce: game (a speciality in season), superb meats (including rare breed Irish Moiled beef) from Crossgar Meats and Kettyle Irish Foods, while renowned Belfast fishmongers, Walter Ewing and Keenan Seafood supply fresh fish and seafood – and Belfast's only specialist cheese shop, Clydesdale and Morrow, carefully select cheeses in perfect condition. The result is, in a sense, simple food; having selected the best of fresh, local ingredients it is cooked with an assured elegance.
21 James Street South Belfast BT2 7GA
+44 (0)28 9043 4310 www.jamesstreetsouth.co.uk

The John Hewitt Bar & Restaurant

With its traditional interior, civilised conversational ambience, locally sourced food and artistic focus, this is a pub of choice for discerning Belfast people. It's owned by the Unemployment Resource Centre next door (opened by the poet and socialist John Hewitt in the 1980s and beneficiary of profits), and operates as a restaurant by day – daily menus are posted on their website – with music most nights. Another USP is an exceptional drinks menu, which includes a range of draught and bottled craft beers, both local and

international; the 'John Hewitt Great Northern Irish Beer Festival' is held here in July.
51 Donegall Street Belfast BT1 2FH
+44 (0)28 9023 3768 www.thejohnhewitt.com

Mourne Seafood Bar

There's an authentic Belfast atmosphere to this informal restaurant and fish shop owned by chef Andy Rae and business partner Bob McCoubrey, of the original Mourne Seafood Bar in Dundrum, Co Down, who have their own shellfish beds on Carlingford Lough. Andy's passion for seafood begins with the sourcing; menus change daily according to the catch and he favours underused local fish and, of course, mussels and oysters from Carlingford – try them with Mourne Oyster Stout, specially produced by Whitewater Brewery.
Also at: **Mourne Seafood Bar** 10 Main Street Dundrum Co Down BT33 0LU +44 (0)28 4375 1377 www.mourneseafood.com **Mourne Café** 107 Central Promenade Newcastle Co Down BT33 0EU +44 (0)28 4372 6401 www.mourneseafood.com.
34-36 Bank Street Belfast BT1 1HL
+44 (0)28 9024 8544 www.mourneseafood.com

Nick's Warehouse

Culinary pioneers of this now popular area of Belfast, Nick and Kathy Price transformed a derelict 19th century whiskey warehouse to create Belfast's first wine bar here in the early '80s – and there's a sense of fun about it, underpinned by serious commitment to wine as well as food. Nick – who recently published a delightful cookery book, The Accidental Chef – is a passionate advocate of local artisan food and a leading figure on the Northern Ireland food scene; he is Chairman of the Taste of Ulster group,

and generous with his time, supporting numerous food initiatives.

35-39 Hill Street Belfast BT1 2LB
+44 (0)28 9043 9690 www.nickswarehouse.co.uk

County Antrim

♣ Bushmills Inn

Bushmills is a key destination on many a visitor's itinerary and the lucky ones include a stay at this former coaching inn. Full of character, it's on just the right side of twee with a turf fire and country seating in the hall, and a traditional cottagey feeling throughout – a theme carried through to the wholesome traditional Ulster Scots cooking. Pride in Irish ingredients is seen in A Taste of Ulster menus that offer traditional dishes, often with Scottish influences, such as Dalriada cullen skink, a 'meal in a soup bowl' based on smoked haddock and topped with an (optional) poached egg - and, of course 'Bushmills coffee'…

9 Dunluce Road Bushmills Co Antrim BT57 8QG
+44 (0)28 2073 3000 www.bushmillsinn.com

County Armagh

♣ Newforge House

Although less than half an hour's drive from Belfast, John and Louise Mathers' lovely Georgian country house feels like worlds away, in a wonderful setting of mature trees, gardens and green fields on the edge of the quiet village of Magheralin. Built around 1785, and in the Mathers family for six generations, the property is substantial – and elegantly restored for guests. John is the chef, and he takes pride in presenting meals based mostly on home grown or local and organic produce – and his style of refined simplicity sits well in the fine dining room.

Newforge Rd Magheralin Craigavon Co Armagh BT67 0QL
+44 (0)28 9261 1255 www.newforgehouse.com

Yellow Door Deli, Bakery & Café

The energetic and talented Simon Dougan is one of the luminaries of the Northern Ireland food scene, and his in-house bakery produces some of the finest bread in Northern Ireland (a considerable achievement by any standards). They also retail a wide selection of the best speciality foods from Ireland and abroad, plus their own home-made specialities, including patés, terrines, chutneys, salads and ice cream, which are sold in the shop and served in the excellent café – where specialities include hot smoked Irish salmon with grilled soda bread, wild rocket and lemon dill cream. Their outside catering is another success story, as is The Yellow Door Cookbook. Also at: 427 Lisburn Road, Belfast BT9 7EY. (www.yellowdoordeli.co.uk; +44 (0)28 9038 1961).

74 Woodhouse Street Portadown Co Armagh BT62 1JL
+44 (0)28 3835 3528 www.yellowdoordeli.co.uk

County Down

Boyles of Dromore

Near the castle ruins in the historic town of Dromore, Darwin Martin and chef Raymond Murray now run this old pub more as a restaurant, with dining tables set up in a series of quaint rooms. There's clearly a genuine commitment to combining organic, artisan and local foods with informed, hospitable service – and value. Walter Ewing of Belfast's Shankill Road supplies the smoked salmon, fresh seafood is from nearby fishing ports Kilkeel and Portavogie, and meats include dry aged Angus beef. Simplicity is key, both on menus and in the excellent cooking, which allows quality ingredients to take centre stage.

8-10 Castle Street Dromore Co Down BT25 1AF
+44 (0)28 9269 9141 www.boylesofdromore.com

Balloo House

Ronan and Jennie Sweeney have transformed this famous old 19th century coaching inn into one of the finest country dining pubs in Northern Ireland. Acclaimed chef Danny Millar - a well known advocate of local seasonal produce - produces stunning food,

typically using ingredients like smoked Lough Neagh eel (with apple, beetroot, horseradish & micro salad); grilled Strangford Lough prawns (with garlic, parsley and lemon butter); rump of Finnebrogue venison (with spiced apple & sweet potato purée, watercress & wild mushrooms). **The Parson's Nose** (+44 (0)28 9268 3009; www.theparsonsnose.co.uk), is a very welcome younger sister, in Hillsborough.

1 Comber Road Killinchy Co Down BT23 6PA
+44 (0)28 9754 1210 www.balloohouse.com

Copper Restaurant

Everything served at Neil Bradley and Sarah Meaney's appealing restaurant is delicious. A strong advocate of local food, Neil's fish is bought straight off the boat at Kilkeel Harbour, herbs and vegetables are from Lurganconary Organic Farm at Kilkeel, and naturally reared beef and pork come from nearby Narrow Water Castle Farm. Just add seriously good cooking by a talented and dedicated chef, and you have a winning combination. And he'll even bend the 'all home made rule' a little, to showcase the gorgeous local MooGoo icecream. *Copper Café is at Newry & Mourne Museum (www.bagenalscastle.com), Newry.

4 Duke Street Warrenpoint Co Down BT34 3JY
+44 (0)28 4175 3047 www.copperrestaurant.co.uk

County Fermanagh

♣ Lough Erne Resort

Set in rolling lakelands, Jim and Eileen Treacy's property offers sweeping panoramic views of water and undulating greens from every room. The kitchen is currently under the leadership of Noel McMeel, a well known chef who has been actively involved in the development of Northern Ireland's food culture in recent years. Lough Erne Resort is a member of Good Food Ireland and, in keeping with their philosophy, the emphasis of the food is to showcase top quality local and artisan ingredients, in their natural season.
Belleek Road Enniskillen Co Fermanagh BT93 7ED
+44 (0)28 6632 3230 www.lougherne golfresort.com

The Sheelin Tea Shop

Bedecked with window boxes and hanging baskets, this picturesque thatched house houses the Sheelin Lace Shop and Museum - the latter displaying a unique collection of Irish lace - and ace baker Julie Snoddy's teashop. They do savoury foods too, but baking is the main magnet. Julie's speciality scones (blueberry & white chocolate, apple & cinnamon…) are popular with morning coffee, and there is always an array of baked goodies on display. It's just the kind of place that visitors hope to find when out and about; with the Lace Museum in the same premises, it makes an interesting destination for an outing.
178b, Derrylin Road Bellanaleck Enniskillen
Co Fermanagh BT92 2BA +44 (0)28 6634 8232

County Londonderry

Lime Tree Restaurant

Good cooking and good value go hand in hand with warm hospitality at Stanley and Maria Matthews' restaurant; loyal customers travel long distances for the pleasure of dining here - and no wonder. Stanley's cooking is refreshingly down-to-earth - new dishes are often introduced, but if it's on the menu it's because it works: there are no gimmicks. Many of the carefully sourced ingredients are local - Sperrin lamb (with classic onion white sauce; great steaks from renowned local butcher, Hunters - and specialities include home-made wheaten bread, the perfect match for a chowder of Atlantic fish & local potatoes.
60 Catherine Street Limavady Co Londonderry BT49 9DB
+44 (0)28 7776 4300 www.limetreerest.com

♣ Beech Hill Country House Hotel

Just south of Londonderry and beautifully set in 42 acres of peaceful woodland, waterfalls and gardens, Beech Hill dates back to 1729 and retains many original details. The hospitable proprietor, Patsy O'Kane, attaches a high value to the food of the region, and this has relevance to everything served in

the Ardmore Restaurant overlooking the gardens. Menus showcase quality ingredients, citing use of local seafood, dry-aged local meats, free-range pork and Thornhill duck, award-winning cheeses; similarly, the ingredients of the dishes themselves are described in detail, all of which is interesting and confidence-inspiring.

32 Ardmore Road Londonderry Co Londonderry BT47 3QP
+44 (0)28 7134 9279 www.beech-hill.com

Browns Restaurant & Champagne Lounge

Ian Orr, former head chef at nearby Rathmullan House Hotel in Co Donegal, now runs what has been the city's most highly-regarded restaurant over two decades. Ian is renowned for his dedication to fresh seasonal produce and support of local suppliers, and all menus showcase the best ingredients: fish from Greencastle, and Portavogie scallops and prawns from Co Down, Silverhill duck, from Emyvale, Co Monaghan, and the Kettyle Irish beef and chicken from Co Fermanagh all feature. Keen pricing in no way compromises quality and visitors keen to experience the best the area has to offer will not be disappointed.

1-2 Bonds Hill Londonderry Co Londonderry BT47 6DW
+44 (0)28 7134 5180 www.brownsrestaurant.com

Gardiners G2

Local man Sean Owens and his wife Helen run this impressive restaurant with the stated aim of bringing quality local food and service to the people of the area – a goal achieved through accessible ingredients-led menus that offer variations of many popular dishes. Sean is a committed supporter of local produce and suppliers, and you'll find some unusual specialities here too - Lough Neagh smoked eel, for example (a parfait, perhaps, on roasted soda bread), and dishes inspired by traditional rural products. And

it's not just good food that attracts people to Gardiners - it's a good night out.

7, Garden Street Magherafelt Co Londonderry BT45 5DD
+44 (0)28 7930 0333 www.gardiners.net

County Tyrone

♣ **Grange Lodge**

Ralph and Norah Brown MBE (awarded for her contribution to Food and Tourism) offer true family hospitality and good food at their renowned Georgian retreat just outside Dungannon. Norah is a key figure in the Northern Ireland food scene and well known for her support of local producers. She takes pride in traditional family recipes and, as well as offering good home cooking to residents (both dinner and a magnificent breakfast - porridge is a speciality, served with a tot of Bushmills whiskey, brown sugar and cream), they will cater for groups and offer "Cook with Norah" classes too.

7 Grange Road Dungannon Co Tyrone BT71 7EJ
+44 (0)28 8778 4212 www.grangelodgecountryhouse.com

Recipes

colcannon cakes with poached Eggs & Hollandaise

This modern dish is lovely on its own, or with a slice of baked ham or bacon if you have any leftover. (Alternatively, chop up the ham or bacon and add to the colcannon mixture before shaping into patties.) The hollandaise sauce is optional; traditionally the egg yolk (and a good nut of butter) would be enough to moisten the potato.

Serves 4

450g/ 1 lb potatoes, peeled

40g/11/2 oz butter

3 scallions, trimmed and finely chopped

50g/ 2oz Savoy cabbage leaves, shredded

A little salt and cracked or coarsely ground black pepper

A little plain flour, for dusting

Oil, for frying

1 tbps cider vinegar (optional)

4 large eggs

For the hollandaise sauce (optional):

2 tsp white wine or tarragon vinegar

2 large egg yolks

100g/4oz unsalted butter

To make the colcannon cakes: Cook the potatoes in a covered pan of boiling salted water for 15-20 minutes until tender.

Meanwhile, over high heat, heat a knob of the butter and one tablespoon of water in a heavy-based pan with a lid. When the butter has melted and formed an emulsion, add the scallions and cabbage with a pinch of salt. Cover, shake vigorously and cook over high heat for 1 minute. Shake the pan again and cook for another minute, then season with pepper.

Drain the potatoes and mash until smooth, then beat in the remaining butter. Fold in the cabbage mixture. Shape the mixture into four balls, dust with flour and press into neat patties.

Heat a thin film of oil in a heavy-based frying pan and add the patties, then cook for 3-4 minutes on each side until golden brown.

To poach the eggs: Bring a shallow pan of water to the boil. Add the vinegar, if using, and season with salt and keep at a very gentle simmer. Break the eggs into the water and simmer for 3-4 minutes until just cooked but still soft on the inside. Remove with a slotted spoon and drain well on kitchen paper, trimming away any ragged edges.

To make the hollandaise sauce: Place the vinegar and egg yolks in a food processor with a pinch of salt. Blend until just combined. Gently heat the butter in a heavy-based pan until melted and just beginning to foam. With the food processor running at medium speed, pour in the melted butter in a thin, steady stream through the feeder tube. Continue to blend for another 5 seconds, then pour back into the pan but do not return to the heat. Stir gently for another minute, allowing the heat from the pan to finish thickening the sauce. Season to taste with salt.

To serve: Place a colcannon cake on each warmed plate and place a poached egg on top of each one. Spoon over the hollandaise sauce and add a grinding of black pepper.

Bacon Chops with Apple & Cider Sauce

Pork, apples and cider are traditional companions and make an ideal partnership for some of the great products of the region, including Armagh apples. Pork chops could be used instead of the bacon chops suggested; either way it's the kind of meal you don't tire of - good simple comfort food.

Serves 4

1 tbsp oil

4 bacon or pork chops

Knob of butter

1-2 cooking apples, preferably Bramleys, sliced

1-2 cloves garlic, chopped

1 tsp sugar

125ml / ¼ pt dry cider

1 tsp cider vinegar

1 tbsp Irish wholegrain mustard

A few sprigs of thyme

Salt and freshly ground black pepper

Heat a frying pan with the oil.

Cook the chops for 10-15 minutes, browning well on both sides. Remove from the pan and keep warm.

Now add the butter and the apples to the pan Cook until the slices just being to brown.

Add the garlic and sugar. Cook for another minute.

Stir in the cider, vinegar, mustard and thyme, bring to the boil and then simmer for a few minutes to reduce the liquid.

Taste for seasoning. Serve the chops with the sauce - and lots of creamy mash.

chicken Breast with fennel & Rocket salad

Simple and special, this takes only 30 minutes to cook, and the salad can be prepared ahead. Its simplicity makes this an ideal dish for cooking free range chicken, allowing the flavour and texture to speak for itself.

Serves 4

4 free range part-boned chicken breasts, skin on

Juice of 1 lemon

1 tbsp rapeseed oil or olive oil

Salt and freshly ground black pepper

Fennel Salad:

2 fennel bulbs, trimmed and sliced as thinly as possible

2 tbsp rapeseed oil or olive oil

Juice of 1 lemon

1 tbsp good quality mustard

Handful of rocket leaves per person

To finish the dish:

Drizzle of oil (rapeseed or olive), mellow natural cider vinegar or balsamic vinegar and black pepper

An hour or two ahead, if possible, place the chicken breasts in a shallow dish. Pour over the lemon juice, olive oil and seasoning.

Meanwhile, prepare the salad: Put the sliced fennel into a large bowl. In a second smaller bowl or jug, mix the oil, lemon juice and mustard together; taste for seasoning. Mix the fennel and its dressing together and set aside.

When ready to cook, preheat a moderate oven, Gas Mark 4, 180°C, 350°F

Seal the chicken breasts on a hot pan until well browned. Then finish cooking in the oven for 10-15 minutes, until the juices run clear when tested in the thickest part.

To serve: Slice the cooked chicken, serve with a mound of the salad and the rocket leaves on top. Drizzle with a little olive oil and vinegar and add a grinding of black pepper.

Anna's House Wheaten Bread

Anna Johnson runs Anna's House (www.annashouse.com), a beautiful eco-friendly and organic B&B, set in the rolling countryside near Comber in County Down. This is the bread recipe for which she is so often asked.

Makes 2 cmall loaves

225g/8oz coarse wheatmeal

100g/4oz plain flour

25g/1 oz soft brown sugar

2 level teaspoons baking soda (bicarbonate of soda)

1 level teaspoon salt

100g/4oz butter, chilled

1 egg, lightly whisked

Buttermilk, made up to 275ml/10 fl oz with the egg.

Preheat a moderately hot oven, 200°C/400°F/gas 6 (fan oven about 195°/375°F - consult your instruction manual)

Grease two 900g/1 lb loaf tins and lay strip of greaseproof paper to run along base and two short sides.

Mix the flours, sugar, baking soda and salt in a bowl. Place a grater over the bowl and grate the butter into it, straight from the fridge.

Whisk the egg lightly and make up to 275ml/10 fl oz with buttermilk. Slowly pour the liquid into the mixture, mixing with a spoon. It should be soft dropping consistency - stop before the consistency becomes soggy, or add extra milk if it is too dry. (You can see Anna mixing the dough on the video on their website.)

Spoon the mixture evenly into the two loaf tins and, with the back of a tablespoon, make a dent in the dough along three quarters of the length of the tin. This will help it to rise evenly.

Bake for 25 minutes, then cover tins with foil and bake for another 10 minutes. When cooked, the bread will have shrunk slightly from the sides of the tin and an inserted skewer will come out clean.

Leave in the tin on a rack for 15 minutes, then invert, turn out onto the rack and cover with a clean cloth. It is best to leave this bread for an hour before slicing. This bread freezes successfully: when cold, wrap in tin foil, label, date and freeze.

Griddle Soda Bread Farls

"The great plus of this recipe is its ease and speed", says Anna, "Only seconds to mix!" A 'farl' is a quarter of the traditional round 'cake' of dough, which is cut deeply with a cross; this helps loaves to bake evenly and they can then be divided easily. Using the right flour is essential. Strong flours used for yeast baking are unsuitable; the flour should be soft and light - in Northern Ireland 'soda flour' is available, with the soda included, and it is ideal. If buttermilk is unavailable, plain yoghurt carefully thinned with water to single cream consistency will work well. Griddle baking is a skill like making pancakes and may need some practice: if the pan is too hot, the outside burns before the centre is cooked.

Serves 4

250g/9oz Neills Self-Raising Soda Bread Flour

OR use plain flour plus ¹/₂ teaspoon bicarbonate of soda

Half teaspoon salt

175ml/6 fl oz buttermilk

Heat a griddle or a large heavy frying pan over medium heat for 10 minutes.

Sift the flour and salt in a bowl then, when the hot pan is ready, spread one hand in starfish shape into the flour and rotate while slowly pouring in the buttermilk. Stop as soon as the mixture leaves the sides of the bowl. The dough should look soft and pliable. If you see some dryness in the centre, dribble in a tiny drop of milk.

Turn out onto a floured board and knead just once or twice, turn over and shape into a round approximately 17 cm/ scant 7″ in diameter and almost 2.5 cm/1″ thick. Cut through twice in a cross shape, to make four farls.

Sprinkle a little flour into the hot pan and place the farls into it. Time for 5 minutes. Carefully turn over with a spatula and time for further 5 minutes, reducing the heat by one notch. Now cook each of the three edges of the farls for 3 minutes each, again reducing the heat by one notch. To test if the farls are cooked, open up at the edge - when ready, the dough will be dry inside.

Place on a wire rack and cover with a clean tea towel, or serve straight to the breakfast table, cut into halves.

cookery schools & classes

For further information on classes throughout Ireland
www.discoverireland.ie • www.discovernorthernireland.com

Ballymaloe Cookery School

COUNTY CARLOW:

Tasteworks Cookery School LEIGHLINBRIDGE
www.tasteworks.ie; +353 (0)59 972 2786
Variety of informal but informative classes. Suitable for everyone.

Ballyderrin Cookery School TULLOW
www.ballyderrin.com; +353 (0)59 915 2742
Pamela Holligan offers a range of courses to suit all interests and abilities. Also produces baked goods and preserves.

COUNTY CAVAN:

Corleggy Farm BELTURBET
www.corleggy.com; +353 (0)49 952 2930
Spend a day with Silke Cropp making your own cheese on Corleggy Farm.

COUNTY CLARE:

Bunratty Cookery School BUNRATTY
www.bunrattycookeryschool.ie; +353 (0)61 713500
Offers a wide variety of courses catering for every level.

Berry Lodge MILTOWN MALBAY
www.berrylodge.com; +353 (0)65 7087022
Rita Meade gives classes at her renovated Victorian family home; with restaurant and accommodation.

COUNTY CORK:

Rory O'Connell Cookery School BALLYCOTTON
www.rgoconnell.com; +353 (0)86 851 6917
Chef and teacher Rory O'Connell trained at Ballymaloe House with Myrtle Allen, the grand-dame of Irish country house cooking.

Inish Beg House Cookery School BALTIMORE
www.inishbeg.com; +353 (0)28 21745
The Inish Beg Estate makes a lovely setting for interesting cookery classes.

The Good Things Café Cookery School DURRUS
www.thegoodthingscafe.com; +353 (0)27 61426
Small classes, fantastic ingredients, personal tuition, a great location and competitive prices.

Island Cottage Cookery School **HEIR ISLAND**
www.islandcottage.com; +353 (0)28 38102
Probably the smallest cookery school in the world. Two day cookery courses for two people, with an overnight stay on the island.

Ballymaloe Cookery School **SHANAGARRY**
www.cookingisfun.ie; +353 (0)21 464 6785
The world renowned Ballymaloe Cookery School is situated in the picturesque East Cork countryside in the middle of a 100 acre organic farm.

COUNTY DONEGAL:

Donegal Cookery School **DONEGAL**
www.donegalmanor.com; +353 (0)74 972 5222
Weekly demonstrations and masterclasses to help families plan their weekly meals.

Castle Murray Hotel & Restaurant **DUNKINEELY**
www.castlemurray.com; +353 (0)74 973 7022
Five week block courses run throughout the year.

The Crest Cookery School **LETTERKENNY**
www.hillcrestbedandbreakfast.ie; +353 (0)87 245 7497
Chef Martin Anderson gives classes in the homely surroundings of his B&B.

Kathleen Loughrey School Of Home Baking
RATHMULLAN
kathleenloughrey@eircom.net; +353 (0)74 915 8122
Learn how to bake cakes and scones for all occasions whilst enjoying a leisurely break.

COUNTY DUBLIN:

Alix Gardner's Cookery School **DUBLIN 4**
www.dublincookery.com; +353 (0)1 668 1553
Practical, fun, and informal cookery classes in Ballsbridge, in central Dublin.

The Cookery School@Donnybrook Fair **DUBLIN 4**
www.donnybrookfair.ie/thecookeryschool.asp;
+353 (0)1 668 9674
Popular cookery school above Donnybrook Fair food store.

Dublin Cookery School **BLACKROCK**
www.dublincookeryschool.ie; +353 (0)1 210 0555
Full range of cookery classes offered, including a one-month full-time certificate course.

Cooks Academy Cookery School **DUN LAOGHAIRE**
www.CooksAcademy.com; +353 (0)1 214 5002

*Offers a range of cookery and wine lessons for both the amateur enthusiast and the professional cook. *At time of going to press, move is planned to 18-19 South William Street, Dublin 2.*

The Kitchen in the Castle **HOWTH**
www.thekitcheninthecastle.com; +353 (0)1 839 6182
This cookery school is based in the beautifully restored Georgian kitchens in historic Howth Castle.

COUNTY KERRY:

Just Cooking **FIRIES**
www.justcooking.ie; +353 (0)66 979 3660
Well known chef Mark Doe runs this cookery school with his wife Berni.

COUNTY KILDARE:

The Village at Lyons Cookery School **CELBRIDGE**
www.villageatlyonscookeryschool.com;
+353 (0)1 627 9510
TV cook and author, Clodagh McKenna, runs this cookery school, also the adjacent shop and café.

COUNTY KILKENNY:

Ryeland House Cookery School **CUFFES GRANGE**
www.ryelandhousecookery.com; +353 (0)56 772 9073
Mrs. Anne Neary provides cooking classes at her home.

COUNTY LEITRIM:

The Organic Centre **ROSSINVER**
www.theorganiccentre.com; +353 (0)71 985 4338
Cookery courses with the emphasis on the use of organic produce.

COUNTY LOUTH:

Ghan House Cookery School CARLINGFORD
www.ghanhouse.com; +353 (0)42 937 3772
Cookery classes given in period guesthouse in this medieval village beside Carlingford Lough.

An Grianan TERMONFECKIN
www.an-grianan.ie; +353 (0)41 982 2119
An Grianan is a unique centre combining a mid-week break with courses in cookery.

COUNTY MAYO:

Marjorie's Cookery School BALLINA
www.marjorieskitchen.net; +353 (0)96 22609
Situated in Marjorie's home. (Check webpage for upcoming courses.)

Lisloughrey Lodge Cookery School CONG
www.lisloughrey.ie; +353 (0)94 954 5400
Courses at the beautifully located hotel teach the secrets of producing fine food using the best of quality Irish ingredients.

Pontoon Bridge Hotel Cookery School PONTOON
www.pontoonbridge.com; +353 (0)94 9256120
Two day cookery course on "how to become a skilled, creative and organised master of your own kitchen".

COUNTY MEATH:

Fairyhouse Food & Wine School RATOATH
www.fairyhousecookeryschool.com;
+353 (0)1 689 6476
Billie O'Shea owns and runs this purpose built cookery school in County Meath.

Bespoke Cookery School STAMULLEN
www.bespokecuisine.ie; +353 (0)1 835 5822
Aims to teach the basics and give students the confidence to cook for themselves, friends and families.

COUNTY MONAGHAN:

Castle Leslie Cookery School GLASLOUGH
www.castleleslie.com; +353 (0)47 88100
Offers a diverse range of evening demonstrations, one-day and two-day cookery courses for up to twelve people.

COUNTY OFFALY:

Annaharvey Farm Cookery School TULLAMORE
www.annaharveyfarm.ie; +353 (0)57 9343544
Cookery classes add an extra dimension to this appealing equestrian centre and farm B&B.

COUNTY SLIGO:

Quirky Cooks BALLYMOTE
www.templehouse.ie; +353 (0)87 9257066
Held in the 'big kitchen' of Temple House, the Quirky Cooks provide evening cookery demonstrations and entertainment.

COUNTY TIPPERARY:

Sarah Baker Cookery School CLOUGHJORDAN
www.sarahbaker.ie; +353 (0)87 969 0824
This cookery school has its own kitchen garden where you can learn how to grow your own vegetables combined with a cookery demonstration and lunch in a day.

Fiacri House ROSCREA
www.fiacrihouse.com; +353 (0)505 43017
Aims to teach cooking skills in an atmosphere in which students will also make new friends.

COUNTY WATERFORD:

Powersfield House Cookery Courses DUNGARVAN
www.powersfield.com; +353 (0)58 45594
Well known cook and caterer Eunice Power gives classes at her lovely B&B.

Tannery Cookery School DUNGARVAN
www.tannery.ie; +353 (0)58 45420
*Renowned chef Paul Flynn offers an exciting range of
courses to suit all tastes and abilities from evening demos
to a five day hands on course.*

COUNTY WEXFORD:

**Dunbrody Country House Cookery School
ARTHURSTOWN**
www.dunbrodyhouse.com; +353 (0)51 389600
*Kevin Dundon's chic cookery school has been designed to
cater for all levels of cooks, from budding enthusiasts to the
experienced gourmet.*

Phelim Byrne Cookery Academy WEXFORD TOWN
www.phelimbyrne.ie; +353 (0)53 9184995
*Chef Phelim Byrne offers professional catering services and
a cookery academy at Wexford Enterprise Centre.*

COUNTY WICKLOW:

Ballyknocken Cookery School ASHFORD
www.thecookeryschool.ie; +353 (0)404 44627
*Run by TV chef / proprietor Catherine Fulvio,
Ballyknocken Cookery School offers a selection of day,
weekend and resedential courses.*

NORTHERN IRELAND –

COUNTY DOWN:

Mourne Seafood Cookery School KILKEEL
www.mourneseafoodcookeryschool.com;
+44 (0)28 4176 2525
*This state of the art cookery school offers a range of
cookery courses and demonstrations on local seafood.*

COUNTY LONDONDERRY:

My Little Kitchen Cookery School GREYSTEEL
www.mylk.co.uk; +44 (0)28 7181 3712
*Philip and Nuala Ford offer classes at their beautifully
located farm overlooking Lough Foyle.*

Food Festivals

For the most recent listings and further information, throughout Ireland
www.discoverireland.ie • www.discovernorthernireland.com

COUNTY CARLOW:

Ducketts Grove Easter Craft & Food Fair
Food and craft market showcasing the best of Carlow with musical entertainment. Easter.

COUNTY CAVAN:

Virginia Pumpkin Festival
Artisan food and crafts fair on the church grounds features a wide variety of home-made foods. October.

COUNTY CLARE:

Burren Slow Food
The Burren makes a unique setting to showcase all that is good about food from County Clare. May.

COUNTY CORK:

A Taste of West Cork Festival
Offers a mix of food markets and demos, competitions, special dinners, banquets & food tastings. September.

Ballydehob International Jazz Festival & Food Fair
A festival of international jazz music with Irish and European speciality food producers. April.

Baltimore Seafood & Wooden Boat Festival
Harbour racing, food fair & more at this celebration of West Cork's seafood heritage. May.

Eat Cork
An independent festival celebrating Cork city's culinary heritage. September.

Kinsale Good Food Circle Gourmet Festival
A celebration of Kinsale's fine food tradition. October.

Mallow Food Festival
Showcases some of Munster's finest food producers. August.

Midleton Food and Drink Festival
A celebration of this area's outstanding food in a fun setting. September.

Mitchelstown Food Festival
A celebration of locally produced food. August.

COUNTY DONEGAL:

Dunfanaghy Seafood Festival
Three day event - local fresh seafood, contemporary music, street performances and participatory arts events. May.

The Food Coast Harvest Feast
Donegal's best ingredients make a four-course communal lunch at Rathmullan featuring some of Donegal's best chefs. September.

Rosbeg/Portnoo Seafood Festival
Fun weekend, free seafood, oyster opening competition, music go leor. June.

DUBLIN CITY & COUNTY:

Bloom, Phoenix Park
Garden show with artisan foods. June.

Taste of Dublin
Dublin's most prestigious restaurants and chefs celebrate the capital's finest food and drink at the Iveagh Gardens. June.

Temple Bar Chocolate Festival
Celebrates and explores chocolate through taste and sensory appreciation. December.

COUNTY GALWAY:

Clarenbridge Oyster Festival
September.

East Galway Food Festival
This festival at Loughrea introduces visitors to East Galway through a celebration of locally-produced food. June.

Galway International Oyster Festival
A weekend of non-stop entertainment. September.

COUNTY KERRY:

Dingle Food & Wine Festival
Cookery demonstrations, special menus in restaurants, a food market, culinary trails etc. October.

Listowel Food Fair
Food lovers from around the country gather to enjoy this celebration of local food. November.

COUNTY KILDARE:

Taste Kildare
Charitable food & craft festival at Straffan - sample the best local produce and craft in a family atmosphere. August.

COUNTY KILKENNY:

Savour Kilkenny
Irelands medieval capital provides the setting for the Kilkenny Food Festival. October.

COUNTY LEITRIM:

Harvest Feast Food Festival
Drumshanbo's Harvest Feast celebrates the food culture of the North West of Ireland. August.

COUNTY LOUTH:

Carlingford Oyster Festival
Since the early 80's this festival has showcased the world famous Carlingford Oyster. July.

Drogheda Food Festival
Promoting the best of local fare from the Boyne Valley. August.

Easter Craft and Food Fair
Charity craft & food fair held in Drogheda. Easter.

Taste of Carlingford
A taste of the range of cuisine on offer in all the restaurants, bars and cafés in the village. May.

COUNTY MAYO:

Feile Bia na Mara - Achill Seafood Festival
This weekend of fun and feasting is a celebration of Achill's rich maritime heritage. July.

COUNTY SLIGO:

So Sligo Food and Culture Festival
Entertainment, films, parades and street parties for all ages. March.

COUNTY WATERFORD:

Dunmore East Festival of Food, Fish & Fun
Food and the sustainable lifestyle concept are celebrated at this Festival. June.

Waterford Festival of Food
This weekend event celebrates all that is good about gastronomy in Co Waterford. April.

Waterford Harvest Food Festival
Event run by Slow Food Ireland and Waterford City Council celebrating the city's food heritage and culture. September.

COUNTY ANTRIM:

Auld Lammas Fair
Ireland's oldest traditional market fair is held in Ballycastle. August.

Belfast Food & Drink Festival
A month long celebration of all things gastronomic across the city of Belfast. September.

Continental Market at Belfast City Hall
Market offering continental and speciality foods as well as local specialities. November & December.

Garden Gourmet
Combines Northern Ireland's largest flower show with an entertaining food and drink festival in Belfast. September.

St George's Christmas Fair and Market
Seasonal food, tastes and smells brought by local producers at this Belfast food market. December.

Hilden Beer Festival
This weekend event in Lisburn offers more than 30 international beers. August.

COUNTY ARMAGH:

Apple Blossom Festival
Annual event in Armagh celebrating the local apple orchards. May.

COUNTY DOWN:

The Festival of Fish
Seafood tasting, competitions and festive menus, the four fishing villages of Kilkeel, Annalong, Ardglass, Portavogie celebrate seafood. September.

Hillsborough International Oyster Festival
This celebration of local food includes events such as the World Oyster Eating Championships. September.

COUNTY TYRONE:

Apple Day
Dungannon invites the public to come and enjoy the park, see apple crafts, apple cooking, apple products for sale and a variety of apple trees. October.

INTERNATIONAL:

Terra Madre Ireland
Slow Food event celebrating a different theme each year - part of global event. December.

Useful References

Informational bodies / associations / websites etc

Failte Ireland
www.discoverireland.ie
www.failteireland.ie
www.tourismireland.com

**Northern Ireland Tourist Board (NITB)
& other NI sites:**
www.discovernorthernireland.com
www.nigoodfood.com
www.greatbelfastfood.com

*First ports of call for information on tourism and
hospitality throughout Ireland.*

Associated Craft Butchers of Ireland (ACBI)
(www.craftbutchers.ie)

Bord Bia (www.bordbia.ie) *The Irish Food Board is the
central source of information on many aspects of Irish food
including Farmers' Markets, Country Markets, Organic
Suppliers, Food Awards, Drinks etc.*

Bord Iascaigh Mhara (www.bim.ie) *Irish Sea Fisheries
Board. BIM is the Irish State agency with responsibility for
developing the Irish Sea Fishing and Aquaculture
industries.*

Bridgestone Guides (www.bestofbridgestone.com)
*John and Sally McKennas' long established independent
and critical guides to the best places to eat, shop and stay,
have a strong emphasis on local artisan produce.
Recommendation is on merit (no charge).*

B&B Ireland (www.bandbireland.com) *Formerly Town
& Country Homes and Irish Farmhouse Holidays, this
marketing association represents families offering Irish bed
& breakfast accommodation.*

CAIS (www.irishcheese.ie) *Irish Cheesemakers
Association. Member group representing artisan
cheesemakers in Ireland since 1983.*

Celtic Orchards (www.theapplefarm.com/celtic)
*Group of Irish apple growers committed to grouping
resources, abilities and enthusiasm, and selling the very
best apples we could grow.*

Celtic Orchards (www.theapplefarm.com/celtic)
*Group of Irish apple growers committed to grouping
resources, abilities and enthusiasm, and selling the very
best apples we could grow.*

Easy Entertaining (www.easyentertaining.ie) *Innovative
bespoke catering service by Joe and Hazel Bourke,
committed supported of the best local, seasonal and artisan
produce with a reputation for simple excellence.*

Elite Butchers Association (EBA)
(www.elitebutchers.com) *Group representing a cross-
section of quality butchers, large and small, in Northern
Ireland.*

Euro-Toques (www.euro-toques.ie) *Irish branch of the
European Community of Chefs & Cooks, committed to
supporting local producers through quality local and
seasonal food sourcing.*

Game & Fishing
*Information on (licensed) game hunting (www.nargc.ie)
and fishing (www.irishfisheries.com).*

Georgina Campbell's Ireland
(www.ireland-guide.com) *Ireland's most comprehensive
independent guides to the best places to eat, drink and stay
plus related areas of interest including golf, gardens, events
etc. The Guide's annual awards are Ireland's longest
established hospitality awards. Recommendation is on
merit (no charge).*

Good Food Ireland (www.goodfoodireland.ie)
*Industry driven all-Ireland food tourism marketing
organisation committed to promoting Irish, local and
artisan food produce.*

greatfood.ie (www.greatfood.ie) *Irish food, recipe and
wine website with cooking tips, easy meals, traditional
Irish recipes and wine and ingredients.*

Grow It Yourself (www.giyireland.com) *Waterford
based Registered Charity encouraging productive gardening
in the community; established in 2009, over 70 GIY
groups involving approx 5,000 people sprang up all over
Ireland in the first year.*

Hidden Ireland (www.hidden-ireland.com) *Marketing
Group. Represents a collection of private country houses
throughout Ireland that are open to guests, some also with
self catering accommodation.*

Ireland's Blue Book (www.irelands-blue-book.ie)
*Marketing Group. Represents an association of country
houses, and selected hotels and restaurants throughout
Ireland.*

Irish Food Writers' Guild (IFWG)
(www.irishfoodwritersguild.ie) *Independent group
promoting high professional standards of knowledge and
practice among writers about food, nutrition, food history
and allied matters. The Guild's Annual Food Awards,
established in 1994, are widely acknowledged as the
country's most prestigious food awards.*

Irish Hotels Federation
(www.ihf.ie; www.irelandhotels.com) *Founded in 1937, IHF is the main representative and marketing organisation for Irish hotels and guesthouses.*

Irish Landmark Trust (www.irishlandmark.com) *A charity aiming to save smaller historic buildings at risk by restoration and conversion into self-catering holiday homes. Offers uniquely interesting accommodation.*

LocalMarkets (www.localmarkets.ie) *New online service offering home delivery of the local artisan produce otherwise found at farmers' markets and local producers' shops. Initially operating in Cork, with plans to cover other regions.*

Restaurants Association of Ireland (www.rai.ie) *Marketing group, representing the Irish restaurant industry; the RAI has over 500 members.*

Slow Food Ireland Members Group
(www.slowfoodireland.com) *Slow Food is a non-profit, eco-gastronomic member-supported organisation promoting local food traditions and interest in food - where it comes from, how it tastes and how our food choices affect the rest of the world.*

Taste of Kilkenny Food Trail (www.trailkilkenny.ie) *Food trail highlighting the variety of delicacies available within County Kilkenny and county and aiming to break the perception that good food has to be expensive food.*

A Taste of Ulster (www.nigoodfood.com) *Marketing group promoting restaurants committed to serving locally sourced foods, and supporting local suppliers.*

Tipperary Food (www.TipperaryFood.ie) *Umbrella group representing the wide range of quality foods produced within County Tipperary.*

US Conversions – Guidelines

TABLESPOONS
1 tablespoon = $1\frac{1}{4}$ US tablespoons
2 tablespoons = $2\frac{1}{2}$ US tablespoons
3 tablespoons = $3\frac{3}{4}$ US tablespoons
4 tablespoons = 5 US tablespoons

BUTTER
25g = 2 tbsp = $\frac{1}{4}$ stick
100g = 8 tbsp = 1 stick

CHEESE
Grated 115g = 1 cup
Cream cheese 225g = 1 cup

DRIED FRUIT
Raisins, sultanas 150g = 1 cup
Glacé cherries, etc 125g = 1 cup

FISH
Prawns, peeled 175g = 1 cup
Cooked and flaked 225g = 1 cup

FLOUR
Firmly packed 115g = 1 cup

LIQUIDS
Water, etc 225ml = 1 cup
150ml = $\frac{3}{4}$ cup
300ml = $1\frac{1}{3}$ cups
500ml = $2\frac{1}{4}$ cups
600ml = $2\frac{3}{4}$ cups
900ml = $1\frac{1}{2}$ pints/4 cups
Syrup, honey 350g = 1 cup

NUTS
Almonds, whole/shelled 150g = 1 cup
Almonds, flaked 115g = 1 cup
Ground nuts 115g = 1 cup

OATS
Rolled oats 100g = 1 cup
Oatmeal 175g = 1 cup

PULSES
Lentils 225g = 1 cup

RICE
Uncooked 200g = 1 cup
Cooked and drained 165g = 1 cup

SUGAR
Caster and granulated 225g = 1 cup
Moist brown 200g = 1 cup
Icing sugar 125g = 1 cup

VEGETABLES
Onions, chopped 115g = 1 cup
Cabbage, shredded 75g = 1 cup
Peas, shelled 150g = 1 cup
Beansprouts 50g = 1 cup
Potatoes, peeled & diced 170g = 1 cup
Potatoes, mashed 225g = 1 cup
Tomatoes 225g = 1 cup

Index

Terenure Branch Tel: 4907030